HELLENISTIC PALACES

STUDIES IN
HELLENISTIC CIVILIZATION

Edited by Per Bilde,
Troels Engberg-Pedersen, Lise Hannestad,
and Jan Zahle

V

HELLENISTIC PALACES
TRADITION AND RENEWAL

By Inge Nielsen

AARHUS UNIVERSITY PRESS

Printed on permanent paper conforming to ANSI Z39-48.1984
by Rosendahls Bogtrykkeri, Esbjerg
ISBN 87 7288 645 5

AARHUS UNIVERSITY PRESS
University of Aarhus, DK-8000 Aarhus C

79 Lime Walk
Headington, Oxford OX3 7AD

Box 511
Oakville, Connecticut 06779

PREFACE TO THE SECOND EDITION

This book was made possible by a grant from the Danish Research Council for the Humanities and constitutes one result of the Danish Interdisciplinary research Initiative on Hellenism, in the pertinent series of which it was accepted for publication. I should like to renew my thanks to the following colleagues for help and encouragement during the work with the book: Carl Nylander, Ehud Netzer, Lise Hannestad, Jan Zahle, Annette Rathje and Pia Guldager Bilde, and to the following Institutions for making the book possible: The Danish Research Council, Julie von Müllens Fond, and Aarhus University Press.

Since the first edition of this book on Hellenistic Palaces was published in 1994, much has happened in this field. One of the most spectacular events has been, and still is, the current under-water investigations of the submerged parts of the palace of Alexandria. Since, unfortunately, these finds have until now been presented only very sketchily and have not yet been published in scientific form, I can only here draw attention to these investigations, which will undoubtedly enlarge and revise our knowledge of this important palace in the future.

Several books of importance for this subject have been published in the last years. A very important addition to our knowledge is the publication of the conference on Hellenistic palaces held in Berlin in 1992 in the fine volume: *Basileia. Die Paläste der hellenistischen Könige*, Mainz 1996, edited by W. Hoepfner and G. Brands. This volume illustrates the very different notions among scholars of the role played by these Hellenistic palaces, and of their architectural placement in a Greek and Oriental context. I have already referred to some of the papers held at this conference in the first edition, and have taken the opportunity to add more articles in this volume.

Of importance, especially for the function of the palaces and the role of the Hellenistic kings, is also the publication from 1996 of the conference on *Aspects of Hellenistic Kingship* held in Fuglsang, Denmark, yet another result of the activities of the Danish research project on the Hellenistic period. You will find some of the articles referred to in the notes.

Finally, the long due publication in 1996 of the conference held in 1988 in Jerusalem on *Judaea and the Graeco-Roman World at the time of Herod the Great* reveals the widely differing views on the role played by Herodian architecture, and especially his palaces, in the development of Hellenistic and Roman architecture. Again, references to some of these articles have been included in the book.

In later years, a subject, which is of great importance also for the study of Hellenistic palaces, has attracted great attention, namely the role played by gardens and parks in Antiquity, although unfortunately the Hellenistic gardens have received only little of this attention. I had the great pleasure of participating in the conference on Roman Gardens, arranged by the "mother" of garden research in Antiquity, Wilhelmina Jashemsky, and by one of the new capacities in the field, Katherine Gleason. The discussions in that forum have drawn my attention to new literature on gardens, which has been added to the notes.

Finally, my participation in a conference on the Acheaemenid and post-Achaemenid World of Caucasian Iberia, held in Tbilisi, Georgia in 1997 and arranged by O. Lordkipanidse and A. Furtwängler, opened up a new world to me, and revealed the existence of a thriving palatial architecture in the kingdom of Iberia and in Armenia in the Hellenistic period, as well as before that time. As it has not been possible to add significantly to the main text, I have chosen to include literature on these palaces in the notes.

In this edition, the main changes are, for economical and practical reasons, thus to be found in the notes and constitute, beside a few new discussions, primarily an addition of new literature on various subjects; the same is the case in the catalogue, in which more "Modern Literature" has frequently been added. It is my hope that these additions, albeit of a rather limited scale, may help the reader to find further areas of research on palaces, and inspire to still more activity in this important field, which so badly needs the attention of scholars.

Copenhagen, February 1998   *Inge Nielsen*

CONTENTS

The Early Roman Palaces

INTRODUCTION

The importance of the Hellenistic palaces in the history of architecture has often been underestimated, one reason being their poor state of preservation. Pierre Grimal is one of the few who early understood the central role played by these palaces that in his time were almost entirely unknown, and in his book on Roman gardens posed the crucial question: "Entre le Palais de Palatitza et la Maison d'Or, quelles fûrent les intermédiaires?"[1] In recent years, several scholars have tried to fill this gap in our knowledge, which has hampered our understanding of the late Republican houses and villas of Italy as well.[2] The growing interest is largely due to the recent excavation of several royal palaces, both those of the Macedonian kings, in Vergina, Pella, and Demetrias, and those of the Hasmonean kings and Herod the Great, in Palestine. Moreover, Vera Heermann's important research on the Macedonian palaces,[3] several recent works on the palaces of Dura Europos, Aï Khanoum, and Araq el Emir in the Seleucid kingdom,[4] and the German interdisciplinary project on "Wohnen in der klassischen Polis"[5] have led to a renewed focus on the problems attending the study of Hellenistic palaces and of private architecture in general. This new awareness has also resulted in two seminars, one, on the palace institution in general — "Le système palatial en Orient, en Grèce et à Rome" — was held in Leiden in 1985, another, specifically on Hellenistic palaces, took place in Berlin in 1992.[6] Finally, the growing interest in the Hellenistic period in the 1980s has of course also included Hellenistic architecture in general: the main work on this topic is Hans Lauter's book of 1986.

Although much work has thus already been done in this field, research has focused mainly on single palaces or areas. Other issues have been the palaces as a source of inspiration for private architecture in the Hellenistic kingdoms, and, in the case of Italy, the relations between public and religious architecture on the one hand, and private architecture, including both palaces and houses and villas, on the other. Also the discussions on inspirational sources have been centred more on developments in Italy than in the Hellenistic kingdoms themselves.[7] Finally, it is my impression that in general the focus has been very much on the Greek side of the picture rather than the Oriental one, with the "panhellenic" or "hellenocentric" viewpoint dominating research.[7a] For these reasons, now seems to be a good time to attempt a re-evaluation of Hellenistic palaces. The last overall treatment of the subject was presented by G. Tosi in 1959, and in view of the many new finds, her article certainly needs revision. Increasing interest in the role of the Persian and other Oriental cultures in the creation of Hellenistic culture, i.e. the "Orientalistic" viewpoint, also makes a new treatment of the royal palaces, in particular, imperative.[8]

That I have chosen to include early Roman palaces as well, and thus treat these in a larger evolutionary context than is normally the case, is partly due to the belief that by revealing their inherent similarities and differences they will assist in throwing into relief the Hellenistic palaces and those who dwelt in them, and partly in the hope that they will help to elucidate the elusive transitional phase between the Hellenistic and the Roman period.

When writing on the Hellenistic period, a designation coined by J.G. Droysen in the middle of the last century, one inevitably runs into major terminological problems.[9] The key terms are: "Hellenistic", "hellenized", and "Hellenism", and they are used very differently in the literature. This is not the place to enter into a detailed semantic discussion, so I shall limit myself to a brief summary of the way in which they are used in this work: chronologically, the Hellenistic period, as it is normally understood by historians and archaeologists, covers the interval between Alexander and Actium, after which the culture of the former Hellenistic area is termed Roman.[10] Although Rome began to encroach politically upon the Hellenistic kingdoms as early as the 2nd century BC (effecting the inclusion in the Roman empire of Macedonia after Pydna in 168 BC, of Pergamon with its bequest to Rome in 133 BC, and of the Seleucid kingdom, or what was left of it, in 63 BC, with Pompey's conquest), it was not until the demise of the Ptolemaic kingdom after the Battle of Actium in 31 BC that Roman influence became manifest in the former Hellenistic kingdoms, expressing itself especially in architecture. As far as Italy is concerned, Augustus' assumption of power marks the point when the city of Rome also began to dominate culturally, as it had long done politically. From this time at least, the culture(s) of Italy too ought to be designated Roman rather than Italic.

Geographically and culturally, the term "Hellenistic" is used of the areas and cultures covered at one time or another by the Hellenistic kingdoms, whether or not the leading social stratum of the area was characterized by any Greek or Macedonian features. This definition is thus broader than the one which is normally used and which implies that Greek elements must be present before a monument may be termed Hellenistic.[11] The term "hellenized", on the other hand, almost invariably indicates the presence of Greek features; it is used about areas and cultures that were not politically a part of the Hellenistic kingdoms, but which nevertheless voluntarily adopted elements of Hellenistic culture. "Helle-nism", being an ambiguous term, has generally been avoided, but when it is used, it is as a general term covering both the Hellenistic and the hellenized areas and cultures.

As its title indicates the main emphasis of the book will be on the palaces of the Hellenistic period. To understand the types of palaces inhabited by the new dynasts, however, it is also important to study the models on which they may have drawn and which may well have determined the appearance of the new structures, at the same time taking into account any differences according to location, whether in Pella, Antiochia, Alexandria, or elsewhere. These precursors are to be found almost exclusively in the East, and the upper chronological limit is formed by the Neo-Babylonian and the Late Pharaonic palaces, since they were the earliest ones known to Alexander and his immediate successors. As the lower chronological limit I have chosen the end of Augustus' reign, and thus the palatial houses and villas of the late Republic as well as the early Roman royal palaces in Italy and elsewhere are included in the survey.

A work of this kind requires a fixed palatial terminology. The term "palace" indicates that both an official and a residential function are present, and I thus follow A. Giuliano's definition of the term: "...con palazzo si indicó qualsiasi residenza, anche non necessariamente dinastica, perché investita di una precisa funzione di interesse pubblico."[12] Three designations for palaces are used: "royal palaces", i.e. the palaces from which the dynasties wielded their power, in Greek sources normally called *basileion/basileia* or *aule* (which may also mean courtyard and the royal court),[13] in Latin *regia*; secondly, "governors' palaces", also sometimes called *aulai*, which served as bases for the king's provincial administrators, including satraps, *strategoi*, vassal kings, etc.; and finally "private palaces/palatial houses", *oikoi/ domus/villae*, i.e. the luxurious houses and villas of the élite. The third group will be only marginally used to illustrate elements otherwise missing, or to support an interpretation of certain elements in the royal and governors' palaces.

As far as typology is concerned, it has not proved feasible to create one which would facilitate the treatment of the subject. Although there are definitely differences between royal palaces, governors' palaces, and private palaces, with respect both to function and architecture, the last two groups are merely pale reflections of the royal palaces, which are our main concern here. It is also difficult to distinguish any definite subtypes. A division of at least the royal palaces into "compact palaces" (consisting of one large building) and "palace complexes" (with many buildings spread over a large area) may be meaningful in   some cases, although these two types seem, in fact, to overlap. I have, therefore, avoided a "type" rubric in the catalogue, but the distinction does sometimes crop up, both there and in the main text.

The book is structured in the following way: after a chapter on Life at the Hellenistic court, the nearest precursors, or models, are dealt with. This chapter is followed by an examination of the Hellenistic palaces, beginning with the place of origin, Macedonia (the palaces of which will be treated in detail), and gradually moving towards the east and south, to the periphery of the Hellenistic world. The royal palaces of Judaea deserve special attention, owing to their excellent state of preservation and their location in an area with a strong local, Jewish, culture. A chapter on the early Roman palaces of Italy and Palestine will conclude the book. All relevant palaces, as defined above, including the pre-Hellenistic ones closest in time, will be dealt with, so that hopefully the book may at the same time serve as a kind of general history of palaces within the chronological limits set. To facilitate reading and to avoid too many descriptions, I have collected much of the information on the most important palaces, including references to ancient and modern literature, in a Catalogue based on functional categories. This is placed at the end of the book, where a table summarizing the results is also to bc found (Fig. 115).

I. LIFE AT THE HELLENISTIC COURT: THE PALATIAL FUNCTIONS

Introduction

In dealing with palaces, it is important to remember that "form follows function", not the other way round. While the functions enumerated below (see Fig. 1) were normally present in a court society and should therefore be reflected in the architecture of the royal palaces, only some of them would be present in a governor's palace, and even fewer in a private palace. They did not change perceptibly in the course of time, either earlier or later. I shall here confine myself to a description of life in the Hellenistic royal palaces, since these buildings constitute the backbone of this investigation. The main emphasis will be on the written sources, and the few surviving pictorial sources will also be dealt with, though any treatment of the preserved palaces will be kept to a minimum, since it is the main subject of the following chapters.

Unfortunately we have only scanty information on court life in the Hellenistic period, in contrast to the well-documented reign of Alexander the Great. Most of what we know stems, as usual, from the court of the Ptolemies, while the courts of the Seleucids, the Attalids, and the Antigonids are only dimly illuminated. Our main sources are: from the Hellenistic period, Polybius' *Histories* and the *Letter of "Aristeas"*, the latter covering only the Ptolemaic court; from the Roman period, Plutarch, primarily his *Lives*, and Athenaeus' *The Learned Banquet*, which cites various Hellenistic authors, including Callixenus and Posidonius; but of course, limited information may be drawn from a great variety of sources.[14]

The pictorial sources are of even less help. Since, in Oriental as well as Roman royal iconography, the king holding audience, hunting, or in battle was a favourite theme, one would expect the same to be the case in the Hellenistic period. But excepting depictions of Alexander, such as the famous Alexander Mosaic in the Casa del Fauno,[15] renderings of such scenes are virtually non-existent. If we consider a change in taste unlikely, one explanation might be, as H. Gabelmann has suggested in connection with his study of audience scenes,[16] that the wall-paintings of the palaces have been lost. At all events, the motifs in the Macedonian tombs, as well as the second-style paintings of Italy and the above-

official and ceremonial	audience hall
	council hall
	court room
	reception hall/area
social	banqueting hall(s)
religious	temple for the tutelary deity
	dynastic sanctuary
	mausoleum
defensive	precinct walls
	citadel/akra
	barracks and arsenal
administrative	offices
	archives
	treasury
service	storerooms/magazines
	kitchens, etc.
	servants' quarters
A. residential: for the king/ governor and his family	bedrooms
	bathrooms
	private dining room(s)
	harem
B. residential: court/guests	apartments
"public"	gymnasium/palaestra
	library
	theatre
	hippodrome
recreational	gardens
	parks
	pavilions
	(swimming) pools

Fig. 1. Diagram showing the palatial functions and their architectural expressions.

mentioned Alexander Mosaic may indicate that such subjects were, in fact, much more common than is generally believed.

There can be no doubt that at least the direct heirs of the Achaemenid kingdom, i.e. the Seleucids and the Ptolemies, inherited a part of their court ceremonial from their predecessors, as already had Alexander, and since the sources describing

Persian court life are much richer than those concerned with the Hellenistic courts, we may use them, with due circumspection, in this connection also. Since the authors of these sources were Greek, our information is primarily concerned with the visits of famous Greeks, not least Themistocles, to the court of the Great King in Susa.[17] In general, what impressed the Greeks most were two things: the great luxury *(tryphe)* inherent in the Persian court ceremonial, including huge receptions and lavish banquets, and the custom of *proskynesis* to the Great King.[18] It was, in fact, Alexander's adoption of these two elements during his campaign which touched off the anger of his fellow Macedonians.[19]

Another way to discover Hellenistic court ceremonial is to study the customs of the Roman emperors, which are much better documented.[20] In particular, those of Caesar and the early autocrats, Caligula, Nero, and Domitian, may be of help; but the first *princeps*, Augustus, also had monarchical inclinations, albeit well camouflaged (see pp. 173f). As A. Alföldi puts it: "Die Vorstellungen der Römer von der Alleinherrschaft waren auf die Kenntnis der hellenistischen Könige und ihrer staatlichen Repräsentation gegründet. Je fester die Monarchie sich verwurzelt hatte, desto offensichtlicher traten auch im Insignienwesen die hellenistischen Elemente zu tage."[21]

The position which the king held in society determined the way of life at the Hellenistic court.[22] There has been much discussion as to whether or not the nature of the different Hellenistic monarchies varied. Although there has been a tendency to minimize the differences between them, all being the direct heirs of Alexander, I think we must at least distinguish between the basically "national" monarchy of Macedonia, and the "personal" and absolute monarchies of the Ptolemies, the Seleucids, and, to a certain degree, the Attalids, which all owed much of their inspiration to the realm of the Great King.[23]

Macedonia had for generations been ruled by a single dynasty, the Argeads, who, like the new, Hellenistic dynasty, the Antigonids, had the same ethnic background as the subject people and moreover governed a fixed, nuclear area. The Macedonian kings were probably not absolute monarchs, although the *primus inter pares* or constitutional model has not been demonstrated, nor is it even probable for Macedonia.[24] At least one must imagine that the native nobility had some say in state affairs, especially when a new king was to be installed.[25] But, as F.W. Walbank observes: "for practical purposes the Antigonids were the state", and Macedonia came increasingly to resemble the other Hellenistic kingdoms.[26]

The new kingdoms in the East, on the other hand, were based on conquest, and the local inhabitants did not have the same rights as the Greek and Macedonian population, who lived mainly in the newly founded Greek cities, or were attached to the army or the court. The kings of Macedonian stock were foreign to the area and the peoples they ruled, and were legitimized in the first place only with the aid of the army and of their "Friends" (*philoi, hetairoi*) and then by gradually creating a new dynasty with a fixed order of succession and/or setting themselves up as the heirs of a former dynasty. Among other things this process involved the creation of appropriate settings for the new court, and the setting up of an elaborate, ritualized court ceremonial dedicated to raising the king above his entourage and the world at large. The development was greatly assisted by the king's adoption of a tutelary deity and his institution of a dynastic cult that involved obeisance to the king, especially from the court and the army, and at the same time stressed the heritability of the kingdom within this dynasty. Moreover, the ruler cult, cropping up everywhere as it did, was an important tool in legitimizing the king's power, but in contrast to the sanctuaries for the cult of the tutelary deity and the dynastic cult, those for the ruler cult were placed outside the palace area, and in the cities themselves.[27] All these religious institutions promoted the image of the Hellenistic monarchy as a "divine kingship", a notion deeply rooted in the old Oriental monarchies.[28]

The king's position was necessarily reflected in his appearance and conduct, i.e. his charisma, his majesty (*semnotes*), his life-style, etc. His dignity was supported partly through the display of ceremonial luxury (tryphe), embracing the palaces in which he lived, the state he kept up, the religious feasts he arranged, and so on,[29] and partly through the display of regal qualities such as piety, philanthropy, and hospitality. These different aspects of the king's role are reflected in his titles: *soter, epiphanes, euergetes*, mirroring his semi-divine status, and thus used particularly often by kings of the Seleucid and Ptolemaic dynasties. Finally, his role as patron of the arts and sciences was of great importance. The same characteristics were gradually transferred to the powerful queens, in particular those of the Ptolemaic dynasty, who began to acquire royal power alongside their husbands and even alone, especially from the beginning of the 2nd century BC. Only a few Seleucid queens, and none of the Antigonid or Attalid ones, had a similar career.[30]

Also the king's insignia and royal effects made an important contribution to his prestige. While the tryphe surrounding the Achaemenid kings' ceremonial appearance is well documented from depictions on reliefs (Pl. 1), the material is, as already mentioned, unusually meagre as far as the Hellenistic kings are concerned.[31] In Macedonia, the rich grave goods found in the royal tombs of Vergina, especially in the so-called Tomb of Philip, may give an impression of the tryphe of the early Hellenistic court,[32] but our main sources are the ancient authors. Their interest in Alexander's growing tryphe has already been touched upon (see n. 19). Thus we know from Diodorus, describing the scene of the empty throne after Alexander's death, that diadem, sceptre and crown, as well as other insignia, undoubtedly including a baldaquin over the throne, were among the king's regalia, and some of the same elements are seen on the coins.[33] In connection with the death of Antiochus IV, the diadem, mantle, and signet ring are mentioned as symbols of the royal power.[34]

As far as the king's attire is concerned, the main dress was the Macedonian uniform of *chlamys*, boots, and broad-brimmed hat, worm for both hunting and campaigning.[35] But for official and ceremonial purposes, such as audiences, sacrifices, and processions, the royal dress was used. This consisted of a fine purple robe or mantle, perhaps not unlike the ones known from the Persian court reliefs and described in the sources, as well as a white diadem and a signet ring.[36] For example, a mantle is mentioned in connection with Demetrius Poliorchetes; like the Persian regal robe, it was blue and studded with stars, a sign of the cosmic quality of the kingship. Athenaeus, citing Duris, says that the wearing of gold-embroidered robes with precious stones was a sign of tyrannical inclinations, and gives as examples Pausanias, Dionysius, Alexander, and Demetrius Poliorchetes.[37] As for the queens, we hear that Cleopatra VII was dressed like Isis for public occasions, another sign of the divine aspect of monarchy.[38]

The king exercised political, religious, military, judicial, executive, and legislative powers; from these, the pseudo-Pythagorean "Diotogenes" gives a priority: "The duties of the king are threefold: military leadership, the dispensation of justice, and the cult of the gods". He, like many others, equates the king with "Animate Law" (*nomos empsychos*).[39] C. Préaux, in her definition of these royal duties, operates with three headings: (1) warrior and protector; (2) provider and guarantor of fertility; and (3) magician and judge.[40]

All these powers gave the king a full diary: his everyday duties thus crystallized themselves into the conduct of business through correspondence, receptions and audiences, councils, the holding of law courts, the worship of the gods, and royal banquets. It was to him that the bureaucracy was ultimately responsible. In turbulent times, he had to lead the army and defend his kingdom.

To help the king to manage all these duties, there was a large contingent of people at his disposal. The composition of the royal court seems to have been more or less the same, no matter which Hellenistic monarchy is concerned, although the number of members might differ considerably. In part the court consisted of a group with specialized functions related to the king's official duties and to ceremonial; this group of course included the royal guard. Important also was the group of Friends (philoi, hetairoi) who acted as the king's confidants and counsellors, participated in audiences, banquets and drinking-parties, and had various other functions as well (for example ambassadorial duties). In Macedonia, the nomination of a "King's Friend" was, as mentioned above, a prerogative of the local aristocracy, initially at least (see n. 26), while in the personal kingdoms, these people were chosen by the king himself. Finally "intellectuals", including scholars, artists, writers, philosophers, and doctors, were also present at court.[41] The only fixed requirement was that these courtiers be of Greek or Macedonian stock.

By and by, when the legitimacy of the dynasties had become universally recognized, this originally rather flexible system hardened, forming a hierarchic administrative class with fixed honorary titles that were more or less identical in all the kingdoms, e.g. secretary of state, head of treasury, chief scribe, grand vizier, prime minister, chamberlain, and captain of the guard. Of course a large contingent of slaves and special servants, including eunuchs, was an integral part of the court as well. As mentioned above, the size of the court, as well as the bureaucracy employed to rule the kingdom, varied enormously from place to place, with Ptolemaic Egypt topping the list.

The Functions

The powers and duties of the Hellenistic king of course affected the appearance and organization of the royal palace. The primary function of the royal palaces, namely the official and ceremonial function, was centred on the *chrematismos*, the audience, where business was concluded, embassies received, judgement pronounced, petitions considered, and council with the Friends held. Such audiences are well documented for the Achaemenid court (see n. 17, Pl. 1) and are mentioned also in the context of Alexander's reign, when, during campaigns, they were frequently held in a tent.[42] Sitting on a golden chair or throne (the words *thronos* and *diphros* are used) placed in the middle of the tent, Alexander held court surrounded by his hetairoi and his guard, on one occasion at least numbering more than 2,000 men.

In the case of the Hellenistic court, however, such audiences, though an established custom, have only seldom been described or depicted. But in the *Letter of "Aristeas"*, we find much information on this subject.[43] The main theme of this is the reception and entertainment of the seventy-two scholars from Jerusalem, who were to translate the Torah, at the court of Ptolemy II in Alexandria. The normal procedure was apparently that audience was granted after a certain number of days, depending on the supplicant's status and errand; periods of five days and thirty days are mentioned.[44] In another passage (81), we hear of a public audience (below), but in general only important persons had access to the king, although one gets the impression that many people were present, i.e. the Friends and the guards (cf. Alexander, above). It was the *archedeatros*, the chamberlain, who saw that all was conducted according to precedent (182, 298-9).

While this main audience took place during the day, usually in the afternoon, another kind of audience apparently took place in the early morning. Thus the seventy-two translators went to the palace every morning at the first hour to greet the king before they began work (304); and we hear of the same practice at the Seleucid court, where Friends, courtiers and the grand vizier assembled at this early hour.[45] One is reminded of the old Roman *salutatio*, which was continued, albeit in a restricted form, during the Roman empire, and of the morning ceremonial at the court of the Roi Soleil. This early audience was followed by a working-day, primarily taken up in dealing with the royal correspondence, before the main audience.[46]

The appearance and situation of the main audience hall, which was undoubtedly the largest and most impressive in the Hellenistic palace,[47] is known from a great variety of sources. As was the case with the Persian audience halls, it was frequently directly connected with the main entrance of the palace and was reached by ascending a staircase and passing through a large portal. A portico, sometimes included in a forecourt, was sometimes placed in front of the hall. The impressive façade that faced the supplicant certainly inspired the *scaenae frons* of the theatre and also the wall-paintings depicting such (theatrical) façades. In fact, there are indications that the *skene* of the theatre was originally inspired by such palace façades (see p. 49). For example, Vitruvius tells us that "the middle doors are figured like a royal palace" (*uti mediae valvae ornatus habeant aulae regiae*), and that the tragic style of scenery was "designed with columns, pediments, and statues and other royal surroundings" (*tragicae deformantur columnis et fastigiis et signis reliquisque regalibus rebus*).[48] The central door, called *porta regia*, might imitate the entrance to the audience hall, or to the palace, which might, sometimes, have been the same thing. Direct access to this hall from the outside is also indicated in Alexandria, where the designation *chrematistikon pylon* is used for the large audience hall, emphasizing the immense importance of the portal, as was also typical of the Roman palaces. The portal often symbolized the hall as well as the palace. One may adduce the façade of the Lefkadhia Tomb, the Moustapha Pasha Tomb I in Alexandria, and the Khasneh Tomb at Petra as possible reflections of of such façades, and also the reconstructed façades of the governors' palaces of Tyrus and Ptolemais (Cats. 21-22) (see Figs. 49, 75, 79, 81; Pl. 22).

We have, in fact, a description of such a façade consisting of a vestibule (*prostas*) with portals and columns, although its belonging to the famous Nile-boat of Ptolemy IV makes it rather atypical. One is reminded of the passage in Vitruvius, where in connection with the houses of the Roman élite, he mentions *vestibula regalia alta*, which could have had the same origin, although the function in the Roman context may have been different.[49] Taking into account that Lucan says of the dining-hall of Cleopatra VII (perhaps identical with the audience hall (below)),... *ipse locus templi..instar erat*, one may imagine that the entrance to this hall was furnished with a pediment (*fastigium*), flanked by columns, and looked like a temple front, a resemblance which would have been anything but accidental, for as a result of the semi-divinity of the monarch a royal palace was in fact also a kind of temple.[50]

Of course, lavish embellishment of the hall itself must be envisaged as well. Columns, whether attached to the wall or placed as in a basilica, were an integral element, and Vitruvius' description of the Egyptian *oecus*, which was, in fact, as he says, a *basilica*, may quite properly be taken as an illustration of such an audience hall.[51] As his choise of words indicate, such a hall would be expected in the royal palaces of Egypt. In general, one is reminded of the use of the basilica both by the Roman emperors and by the Christian Church, and an origin for these in a royal reception hall from the Hellenistic period seems, in fact, to be indicated (see n. 293).

For large receptions, even the audience hall was probably too small, and the "public audiences" that "Aristeas" mentions (81) could be held in the open, in the large forecourts of the palaces, by making use of portable thrones and a tribune (*bema*). In Alexandria, they could be held, for example, in the *aule* (i.e. courtyard) of the *megiston peristylon*, where a *bema* was raised in connection with a reception for the army in 203 BC. Perhaps this peristylar courtyard did, in fact, constitute the forecourt to the palatial façade and thus to the audience hall

(Chrematistikon Pylon). Such receptions could also, however, be arranged outside the palace proper. Thus during Mark Antony's stay in Egypt a large reception was held in the courtyard of the city's gymnasium, where he, Cleopatra, and their two sons sat on golden thrones on a tribune built specially for the purpose.[52] Outside the Hellenistic kingdoms, in the kingdom of Syracuse, we hear of audiences being held by Hieron II in a garden near the city.[53]

Another important royal function was the social one, represented by the royal banquet, variously called *deipnon* and *symposion*, which took place in the evening.[54] It was used for the entertainment of important guests, the court, and selected subjects, e.g. the intellectuals connected with the court. On special occasions very large banquets could be held, for example for the army. We know that banquets were already very popular in the pre-Hellenistic Macedonian kingdom, although they were completely overshadowed by the magnificent banquets held by the Great King of Persia, where they constituted an important part of court life.[55] But in contrast to the Greek/Macedonian dinner parties where the king banqueted together with his guests, the Great King was normally isolated from the other banqueters by a curtain, although he could, on special occasions, dine in their company. Both the Macedonian and the Persian kings might drink with their friends after dinner in small *symposia*.[56] That the Hellenistic kings participated in these formal banquets themselves is clear from the *Letter of "Aristeas"* (below), as well as from other sources.[57]

While depictions of royal banquets are non-existent for the Hellenistic period, we have a considerable amount of written testimony. Again, the reign of Alexander is well documented. We hear of the famous banquet following the mass wedding of the Macedonians and Greeks with the Persian women. A tent was used, with 100 *klinai*, and outside in the courtyard (*aule*) the army, foreign embassies, and Greek visitors were served. We are told that the formal *symposion* began with sacrifices, then came the dinner (*deipnon*), and finally the drinking-party, and that entertainment formed an integral part of the proceedings. The notorious banquet held in Persepolis, which according to tradition led to the destruction of this famous palace, undoubtedly took place in the banqueting hall of the Achaemenids (see p. 43). A banquet of heroic proportions, held by Alexander for 6,000 officers, took place outside, and the diners were sitting, not reclining, on the couches. Also smaller dinner parties, with sixty to seventy *hetairoi*, are sometimes mentioned and were undoubtedly very frequent.[58]

Shortly after Alexander's death, we hear of the *deipna* of Demetrius of Phaleron (or Poliorchetes); these overshadowed the Macedonian ones and could rival those held in Cyprus and Phoenicia, which were probably in Oriental style.[59] At about the same time in Alexandria, Ptolemy II held a great banquet in connection with a sumptuous procession in honour of his tutelary deity Dionysus, and for this occasion he had a lavish tent-like pavilion built especially for dining, again with 100 *klinai* (Fig. 70).[60] A century later in Daphne a banquet with 1,000-1,500 *triclinia* (i.e. for 6,000-9,000 guests), was given by Antiochus IV during the great feast for Apollo, likewise his tutelary deity. The king participated and even walked round entertaining his guests, conduct which, along with apparently even more unusual behaviour, invited censure from his contemporaries. According to Plutarch, the feast was designed to rival that held in Macedonia by Aemilius Paullus.[61]

As far as the halls, *symposia*, *androns*, and practical arrangements for such banquets are concerned, we are again well informed by the ancient authors: the *Letter of "Aristeas"* (180-300) tells us that since a banquet often followed upon the audience, movable *klinai* could be placed in the audience hall, thus transforming this, the largest and most sumptuous hall in the palace, into a banqueting hall (183). In the banquet in question, many people participated, besides the seventy-two translators and the king himself. They were served among others by the king's pages (*basilikoi paides*).[62] Because of the many different types of banquets and symposia, there must have been many forms and sizes of halls reserved for this purpose in the palaces. We have a description of the hall in the palace of Alexandria, in which Cleopatra held a banquet in Caesar's honour during his visit to the Alexandrian court; perhaps this, in fact, took place in the audience hall (above): it had marble walls, a wooden ceiling overlaid with goldleaf, a floor of alabaster, and decorations executed in precious stones and ivory. Also opulent, according to Josephus, was the embellishment of the banqueting halls called *androns megistoi* in Herod the Great's palace in Jerusalem.[63] A similar impression of great luxury is gained from the descriptions of special structures such as the dining-pavilion of Ptolemy II, and the dining-rooms aboard Ptolemy IV's Nilebarge (the Thalamegos (Fig. 71)), and on the Syracusia, the enormous ship built by Hieron II.[64]

All these sources help us to imagine, in a way in which the poorly preserved remains cannot, the lavishness of the decoration of the palaces, especially in the official part. (Among what does survive, dining-halls are, in fact, some of the easiest rooms to trace on account of their special arrangements for klinai (see e.g. Pl. 15)). It is important always to keep in mind the existence of such lavish decoration, since the tryphe displayed thereby constituted one of the means employed by the king to impress those around him.

As we know, the king had a religious function, besides actually being a sacred symbol or even a quasi-god in the eyes of the locals, and the performance of religious duties formed an integral part of palace life as well. We need only mention the great processions held in the honour of their tutelary gods by Ptolemy II (for Dionysus) in Alexandria and by Antiochus IV (for Apollo) in Daphne (above). Although we are not that well informed about the detailed procedures for sacrifice to and worship of these and other gods, we do know that temples and sanctuaries were placed in the palaces themselves or in close proximity to them.[65] Such sanctuaries for tutelary deities are mentioned for Egypt in connection with the Thalamegos. On the upper deck of this resplendent state-barge, there was both a *tholos* with a statue of Aphrodite, the favourite goddess of the Ptolemaic queens, and a dining-hall dedicated to Dionysus, the so-called *bakchikos oikos*.[66] Other shrines are actually preserved, e.g. in Pergamon (see p. 106).

On the other hand, the king played only a passive part, as the object of worship, in the sanctuaries for the ruler cult that were located outside the palace; and this was also partly the case in the dynastic sanctuaries connected to the palace, the first being created around the tomb of Alexander, the *sema*, in the *basileia* of Alexandria.[67] Again, the Nile-barge furnishes us with an example of such a sanctuary, since the above-mentioned "Bacchic Oecus" as well as being dedicated to Dionysus and used for dining, was furnished with an artificial grotto that was decorated with gold and jewels, and housed the statues of the royal family. In the Seleucid kingdom there were dynastic cults not only in the capitals, but also in the satrapies.[68] In the Attalid and Macedonian kingdoms, on the other hand, there was never an institutionalized dynastic cult, although one may, in fact, have been included in the royal palace of Pella from the time of Philip V (see p. 92).[69]

Seldom mentioned in the sources, probably because it was so obvious, is the residential function of the palace: i.e. the provision of living-quarters for the king, his family, and often the court. Again, the Thalamegos furnishes us with some information, since not only an *andronitis* but also a *gynaikonitis*, both with bedrooms and dining-rooms, are mentioned (see p. 136). From the *Letter of "Aristeas"* we learn that there were also guest-apartments in the grounds of the palace in Alexandria — at least it was no problem to house the seventy-two translators from Jerusalem for some days, until they could be transported to Pharos (181). We are told that these guest-rooms (*katalumata*), which were the best in the palace, were sited near the citadel (*akra*); perhaps it was here that Caesar stayed when he was in Alexandria, for his *domus* was also situated near the citadel and the harbour.[70] Archaeologically, the main residential part of the palaces can be rather difficult to trace, for bedrooms were often placed on the first floor, and private dining-rooms can be confused with official ones. But at least in the later palaces, the residential and the official functions were normally strictly separated, as the enhanced role of the king demanded. Bathrooms are one of the few elements which definitely indicate private use, unless related to the audience hall (see n. 234).

Primarily for private use also were the recreational elements of the palaces, whether consisting of gardens (*kepoi*) inside the palace, often in peristyle courts, or a park (*alsos, paradeisos*) around the palace. Elements connected with these areas of the palace are pavilions, pools, *nymphaea*, promenades, etc. We know them archaeologically from Palestine (see pp. 155ff, 181ff), and in addition, we derive a great deal of information on this important subject from the many descriptions of the Alexandrian Basileia,[71] with its various buildings spread over a regularly laid-out park that filled a quarter of the city area. From Josephus' description of Herod's palace in Jerusalem we learn that it included both peristyles with gardens and parks with trees in straight rows, as well as walks, water-channels, pools, and statues.[72] For hunting, which was a favourite and historic pastime of kings both in the Orient and Macedonia, the Hellenistic kings had game reserves.[73] The Seleucid kings were able to take over the great parks, or *paradeisoi*, for this purpose directly from the Achaemenids (see p. 49).

The royal palaces may or may not have had a defensive aspect, depending, of course, on the stability of the situation when the palace was built and used. The palaces located in the cities were mostly protected only by the city walls, although they may be connected with a citadel, too.[74] Associated with the palaces, there were always barracks for the guards as well as arsenals, although they are seldom mentioned by ancient authorities. In Alexandria, they were placed just outside the wall surrounding the Basileia, and are called *skenai* in the sources, which may mean both tents and barracks.[75] In Pergamon, both barracks and an arsenal were found in close proximity to the palace (see p. 110).

The administrative function, represented by treasuries, archives, and offices, was not a feature of all royal palaces. In the Ptolemaic kingdom, buildings for this purpose, including the treasury, were placed in the Basileia of Alexandria,[76] while in the Seleucid kingdom, it seems that the administration followed the king and was included in all his and his governors' palaces.[77] In Macedonia, the royal administration was undoubtedly permanently located in Pella, the capital, since the kingdom was rather small. Again, these administrative offices are difficult to trace, but at least in Aï Khanoum we have evidence for a treasury and archives in the palace,[78] while in Pergamon the archives were placed in the *temenos* of Athena, and were closely connected with the library, as was often the case too in the Oriental palaces, including that of Aï Khanoum.

One of the least conspicuous functions in the palaces was fulfilled by the service sector, without which, of course, life in the palace would have collapsed. Service quarters and the people working in them are naturally seldom mentioned, although we do hear, for example, of treasury guards (*riskophylakes*) ("Aristeas" 33), artisans (80), and the above-mentioned *basilikoi paides* (186). Moreover, one gets some impression of the enormous number of servants and slaves in the royal palaces from the throng recorded as participating in the processions of Ptolemy II and Antiochus IV (see notes 60-61). The storerooms, kitchens, and living-quarters for the servants are sometimes traced archaeologically, the two first elements being easily recognized.

The final function of the Hellenistic royal palaces is quite unique, not being present in the Oriental or Macedonian precursors. It is seen in the "public" elements that reflect both the hellenophile attitude of the Hellenistic kings and their eagerness to be patrons of the (Greek) arts and sciences. This attitude is shown up partly by the presence of Greek "intellectuals" and artists at the Hellenistic court, and partly by the inclusion of theatres, libraries, palaestrae, musea, and hippodromes, in the palaces. The hippodrome, one must admit, relates more to entertainment than to culture, but, like most of the other features, it is nonetheless a public building that had its origin in the Greek *polis*. These elements are not only mentioned in the written sources, but are actually preserved in many royal palaces.[79]

Summary

On the basis of the sources, nine main groups of functions may thus be distinguished, which, however, need not all be present even in a royal palace, and still less in other kinds of palaces (Fig. 1). These functions were served and supported by a considerable number of halls, rooms, and buildings:

1. Official and ceremonial functions required reception and audience halls, as well as council halls and courtrooms; these all needed to contain a throne and had to be spacious, since the king's Friends, as well as his guard, were normally present on such occasions. All these official activities probably

often took place in the same hall, which at the same time served as a throne-room, although it might be expected that receptions demanded more space, and thus frequently took place in the open.

2. Social functions were primarily served by banqueting halls. Here, the king could meet his guests and subjects and display his munificence. These banquets frequently followed audiences, and undoubtedly the same hall was often used, at least for large dinner-parties, since movable klinai and tables were common items of furniture. For minor parties, including drinking-parties, smaller halls were called for, while very large banquets could be held in the open or in temporary buildings.

3. Religious functions demanded the construction of dynastic sanctuaries, temples for tutelary deities, and often mausolea.

4. Defensive purposes were primarily served by city walls and citadels, but also, for example, by barracks for the all-important royal guards.

5. For administration, the provision of archives, offices, and treasury was a requirement. In the Hellenistic period, the archives were separate from the library, in contrast to the Assyrian palaces, for example.

6. Service functions were represented by kitchens, storerooms, living-quarters for the servants, etc.

7. Residential buildings for the king, his family, his guests, and often his court always formed part of the palace.

8. "Public" institutions such as theatres, libraries, palaestrae, hippodromes, etc., were frequently, but not always, present in the royal palaces.

9. Basically recreational elements, including gardens and parks, pavilions, (swimming-)pools, and game reserves, played an important role in royal architecture. Such parks could also be used for official purposes: for example for large receptions and banquets.

The diagram in Fig. 115 (pp. 214-15) shows the distribution of the various functions and their architectural expression in the different palaces and palace groups. The same division forms the basis of the Catalogue of palaces.

This functional pattern will also underlie the following treatment of the preserved palaces, including the models for the Hellenistic palaces with which the next chapter deals.

II. THE MODELS

As mentioned in the Introduction, only the models which Alexander the Great and the earliest Diadochi had a chance to become acquainted with and which thus might have inspired them when building their own palaces, are relevant. Therefore neither the Minoan and Mycenaean, nor the Mesopotamian and Assyrian palaces will be covered in detail, although they will be referred to where appropriate. The same applies to most of the Pharaonic palaces of Egypt, e.g. the Malkata Palace built by Amenhotep III in Thebes, and Ankhaten's palaces in Amarna. The relevant monuments are to be found in Egypt, Babylonia, the Achaemenid empire, Hellas, and Sicily.

Egypt

Probably only the palace that Apries (Cat. 1), pharaoh from 588 to 563 BC, built in Memphis still existed when Alexander arrived in Egypt, since it was used both by the Persians, and by the last pharaoh. This must thus be the palace in which Alexander stayed during his visit to Memphis in 332 BC, when he courted Egyptian recognition by sacrificing to the Apis bull.[80] It was here, also, that his satrap established his base, and undoubtedly Ptolemy, son of Lagos, stayed here as well, since he made Memphis his first capital.[81] Later, the Ptolemies probably built a new palace in the same area, for there are very few finds from the Ptolemaic period in the old palace. This new palace included the Temple of Arsinoe, Ptolemy II's queen, mentioned above (n. 67). The *akra* was nearby, and a large park (*alsos*) to the north, combined with a lake, was connected with the palace. This, and not the Palace of Apries, must be the one described by Strabo, although his description could also suit the Palace of Apries very well (Fig. 2).[82]

The Palace of Apries (Fig. 3), which is unfortunately only partly preserved and very badly at that, was situated in the northern section of a large and high terrace in the "palace area" in the northern part of Memphis; and north of this again, even at this period, there already extended the royal park refered to above. The palace proper was reached via a wide avenue, which gradually rose from the south, to create an impressive approach. An entrance portico gave access to a large forecourt surrounded by a wall; this would have been used for large receptions, etc.

The Models

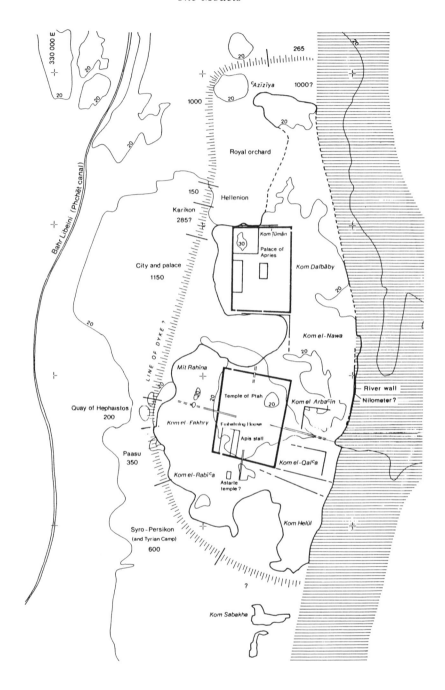

Fig. 2. Memphis. Plan of the city. (Thompson 1988, fig. 3.)

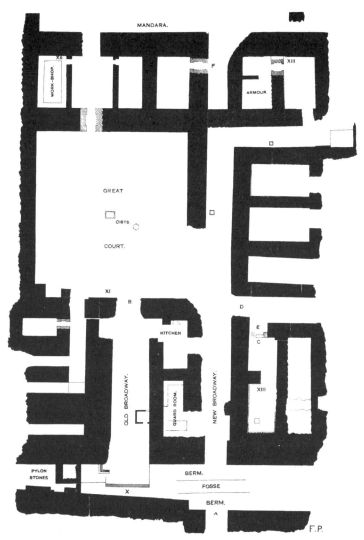

Fig. 3. Memphis. Plan of the Palace of Apries (Cat.1). 1:850 (Petrie 1909, pl. I.)

Also for official purposes, the palace had two large halls. The one reached first, by means of a broad corridor, was the large central throne-room/audience hall, probably a hypostyle hall, which was surrounded by rooms with other functions; none of these rooms could, however, be reached from the hall. Since there is a kitchen close by, one may imagine that the hall was also used for banquets. From here, there was access to another large hypostyle hall (*mandara*), as revealed by very solid foundations and fragments of large columns — perhaps another

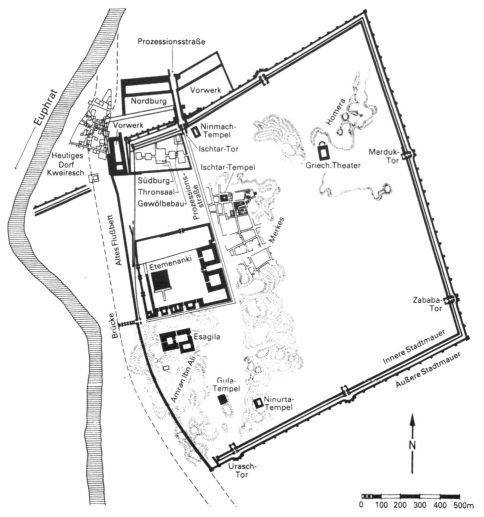

*Fig. 4. Babylon, plan of the inner city with the "Südburg" and the "Nordburg".
(Das Vorderasiatische Museum, Staatliche Museen zu Berlin, Mainz 1992, Abb. 17.)*

audience hall. The residential part of the palace was probably located to the east
of the central audience hall, and separated from the official section by a corridor,
towards which the residential rooms turned their back. The service area, on the
other hand, flanked the central hall to the north and south.

According to the excavator, W.M. Flinders Petrie, the building type represented
by this palace is also known from private palaces from as far back as the 12th
dynasty; there is a general relationship too with the old royal palaces, but they

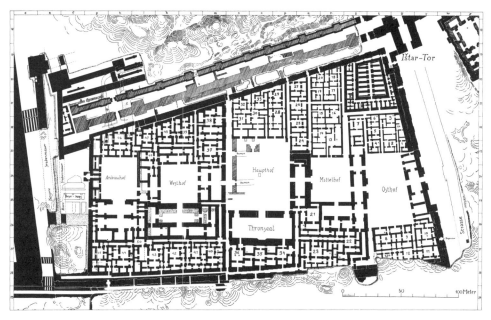

Fig. 5. Babylon. Plan of the "Südburg" (Cat. 2). (Koldewey 1931, Taf. 2.)

are rather "palace complexes" and not situated on terraces. Both in Thebes, Amarna, and Tell el-Dab'a, parks and gardens with lakes and pavilions were also associated with the palaces, and the appearance of such gardens may be gleaned from wall-paintings in the tombs, where they are depicted as formally laid out with pools in the middle and surrounded by walls.[83] In these royal palaces, there is a close connection with the most important temples, indicating the pharaoh's prominent religious role in society.

Since, as mentioned above, Alexander and the first Ptolemy undoubtedly lived in this palace, and the later Ptolemies resided in its immediate vicinity when visiting Memphis, it is possible that at least the park and the lake, which were undoubtedly incorporated in the new palace, could have inspired them when building their new main palace in Alexandria. Also, the monumental forecourt, the impressive avenue, and the official hypostyle halls, all characteristic elements of ancient Egyptian architecture, may well have had some impact on the palace architecture of the Ptolemies.

Babylonia

As was probably the case with the Palace of Apries, Alexander and his generals stayed for some time in the palaces of Babylon. The three royal palaces in

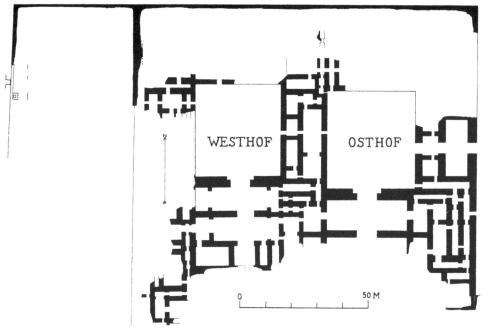

WESTHOF   OSTHOF

0   50 M

Fig. 6. Babylon. Reconstruction of the "Nordburg". (Koldewey 1932, Taf. 8.)

question were all built during the reign of Nebuchadnezzar (605-562 BC). Shortly after his death, in 538 BC, his kingdom was conquered by the Persian king, Cyrus the Great, and the Achaemenid dynasty took over the palaces. The largest of Nebuchadnezzar's three palaces, the Southern Palace or "Südburg" (Kasr) (Cat. 2; Fig. 5), was situated on a fortified hill above the eastern bank of the river on the northern outskirts of the inner city, and impinged upon the city wall near the Ishtar Gate (Fig. 4). The similarly fortified Northern Palace ("Nordburg") (Fig. 6) was located just to the north of the Southern Palace, and separated from it only by the city wall, while the Summer Palace was situated some 2 km north of the Kasr, on the Babil Hill, adjacent to the outer wall of the city and, again, not far from the river (Fig. 7).

Neither the layout of the Northern Palace nor that of the Summer Palace is wholly preserved, and therefore neither of them is found in the Catalogue. In both cases, however, two internal courtyards can be identified. The Southern Palace, on the other hand, is well preserved as far as the basic layout is concerned. It could be approached from the main street just before the Ishtar Gate, through a gate flanked by ornamental towers, and there was direct access to one of the five large internal courtyards without columns, which dominated the palace. The

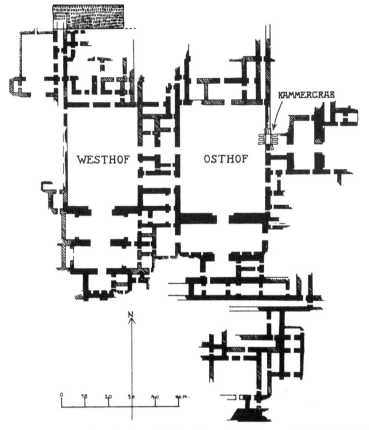

Fig. 7. Babylon. Plan of the Babil Palace. (Koldewey 1932, Taf. 32.)

courtyards were surrounded by rooms and linked with one another by means of gates of varying degrees of monumentality, those belonging to the official section being furnished with ornamental towers. The large courtyards had different functions: there were those intended for official purposes, with the large finely decorated audience hall, a "broad room" (= Breitraum), as the most prominent feature (Pl. 2); those intended for administration and service (stores, etc.); and finally, strictly segregated from the part open to the public, the area intended for the residence of the king, his harem, and the court. This section included private reception- and dining-rooms forming a "three-room suite in depth" (three rooms, two of them "broad rooms", connected and placed parallel to each other) another typical element in these palaces.[84] Behind the large halls were smaller apartments, consisting of small courtyards surrounded by rooms and separated from each other by the typical corridors and passages. The general impression is labyrinthine, with only a few large rooms and many small ones, and a host of corridors. The Southern Palace had gardens including the famous Hanging Gardens, currently mostly identified with the large western garden, in the vicinity of the king's residence. They were probably terraced down towards the river (Fig. 8).

These Neo-Babylonian palaces have many affinities with their precursors in these areas, not least the large Neo-Assyrian palaces, of which Sargon II's palace at Khorsabad is particularly well known. Indigenous features are the strictly linear architecture, the compact plan, and the use of internal courtyards for various functions, although they seem more institutionalized and systematizised in Babylonian than in earlier examples.[85] That parks and gardens formed an important part of the Neo-Assyrian palaces as well is demonstrated by the relief in Room 7 in the Palace of Sargon II in Khorsabad: here are shown an artificial hill and a pavilion with columns that is surrounded by water, either a river or a lake. Two reliefs from Ashurbanipal's North Palace of Nineveh, one with a pavilion in a hilly, wooded landscape, a royal stele, an aqueduct, and canals,[86] the other the famous frieze with a banqueting scene, tell the same story. In the latter the king and his queen are dining in a garden pavilion that is surrounded by trees and bushes, rather regularly planted; the park is enclosed by a fence, outside which are marshes by the river.[87] The banqueting scene reminds us that in both the Assyrian and the Neo-Babylonian court, banquets were an integral part of court life both as social events, to which the king could invite his subjects, and as a form of personal indulgence. In the vicinity of both the Assyrian palace of Khorsabad and the Southern Palace of Babylon there were religious sanctuaries, for the kings acted as intermediaries between the gods and the people, as did their predecessors.

The Neo-Babylonian palaces, which one might call "compact palaces", greatly influenced the Achaemenid and later the Hellenistic palaces, and might even ultimately have inspired the old Macedonian palaces as well (see p. 99). We know from the written sources that they were reused both by the Persian kings and by Alexander and his generals, as well as by the early Seleucid kings or their officials. The various occupants have all left their mark in minor restorations and additions. Thus in the Summer Palace on the Babil Hill, used by Alexander, peristyles were probably introduced into the courts, since roof-tiles have been found; the lack of column fragments is due to the fact that they were undoubtedly made of wood. Stuccoed decoration from the time of Alexander has also been

Fig. 8. Babylon. Reconstruction of the Hanging Gardens. (Wiseman 1985, pl. II.)

found in this palace. In the Southern Palace, which was used as a citadel by the Persians, the so-called "Persian Building", a kind of pavilion, was added to the western garden (Fig. 9). Finds of roof-tiles from the reign of the Seleucids indicate an addition of peristyles in the courts here, too.

Thus the early Hellenistic kings were very much of a presence in Babylon (although Seleucus Nicator built another royal residence in Seleucia on the Tigris[88]), and the role they played there was probably not very different from that of their predecessors, since they used the same palaces and inherited the attitude to monarchy that went with them. The Greek/Macedonian element is further visible in the presence of a theatre, probably built by Alexander, which might have had some connection with the Southern Palace, and which was restored several times in both Seleucid and Parthian times.[89]

The Achaemenid Empire

Royal palaces
While Alexander and the Seleucids reused all the Neo-Babylonian palaces of Babylon, this applied to only two of the preserved royal palaces of the Achaemenids, namely those of Susa, built by Darius I and Artaxerxes II respectively (Cats. 4 and 6; Fig. 20). But although the Palace of Cyrus the Great in Pasargadae (Cat. 3; Fig. 10) and the Persepolis Palace begun by Darius I (Cat. 5; Figs. 15, 17, Pl. 3) were abandoned after the fall of the Persian empire, their appearance was well known to Alexander and his court, including the future Diadochi.[90] The latter might even have used some of the skilled Persian-based architects when building their own palaces.[91] Also some of the palaces built by the satraps and governors, e.g. the preserved Palace of Lachish (Cat. 7), as well

The Models

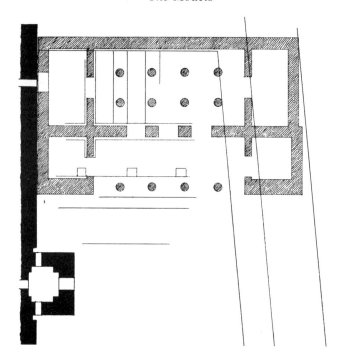

Fig. 9. Babylon. Reconstruction of the Persian Building. (Koldewey 1931, Taf. 28.)

as some of those known only from the written sources, were reused by the
Hellenistic kings.

With the Persians' great influence on Greek and Macedonian history in mind,
and taking into account the great fascination always exerted by the Great King
and his court, as well as the very closeness of the Persian dominions of Asia
Minor, there can be no doubt that the Persian palaces must have had a significant
effect on the development of both old Macedonian and Hellenistic palaces.
Although the Persian palaces thus constitute the immediate forerunners of the
Hellenistic ones, their role in the development of these has, nonetheless, been very
much underestimated on account of the "panhellenic" attitude which has dominated
research into Persian, and not least Hellenistic, palaces. Persian culture has
suffered from a bad press, and only in recent years have scholars begun to focus
on its great importance for the development of Hellenistic culture.[92]

The palaces of the Achaemenid kings, at all events that of Susa, were, according
to Darius I's famous building inscription, constructed by architects, artists,
craftsmen, and artisans from all over the Persian empire, including some from
Egypt, old experts in palace building, and others from the Ionian and Lydian

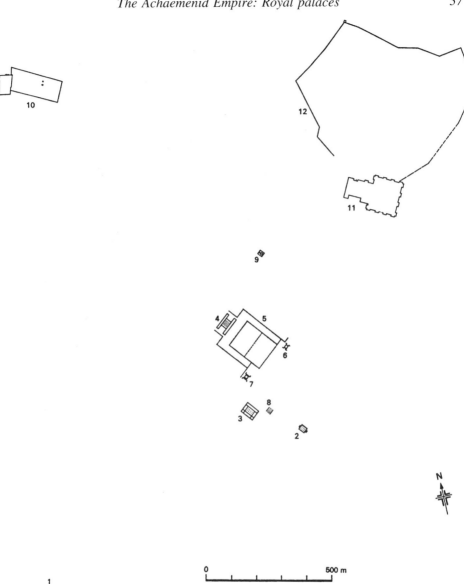

Fig. 10. Pasargadae. General plan of the palace and its surroundings (Cat.3): 1. Tomb; 2. Gate R; 3. Palace S; 4. Palace P; 5. Stone water-channels; 6. Pavilion A; 7. Pavilion B; 8. Bridge; 9. The Zendan; 10. Sacred precinct; 11. Tell-i Takht; 12. The outer fortifications of Tell-i Takht. (Stronach 1978, fig. 4.)

provinces in the far west, whence stone-cutters were in special demand.[93] This is, perhaps, one of the reasons why the four known royal palaces are so very dissimilar. Pasargadae, the palace of the first Achaemenid king, must be con-

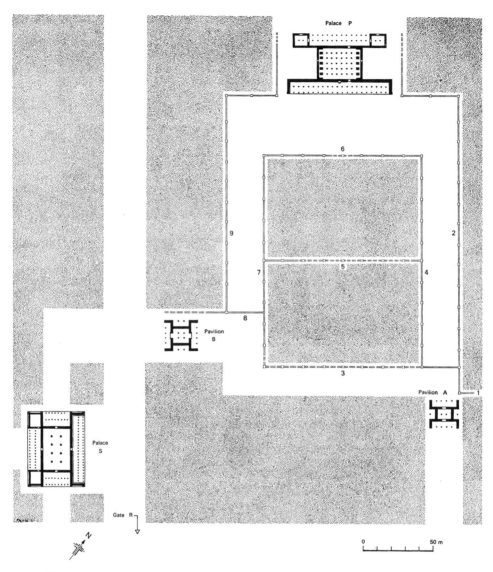

Fig. 11. Pasargadae. Sketch plan of the royal garden (Cat. 3). (Stronach 1978, fig. 48.)

sidered an experiment, and the various independent buildings scattered about the huge park that also contained a great platform (Tell-i Takht) (Fig. 10) were the precursors of the systematized architectural expressions we are familiar with from Persepolis. In Pasargadae, moreover, we know only a part, probably the official

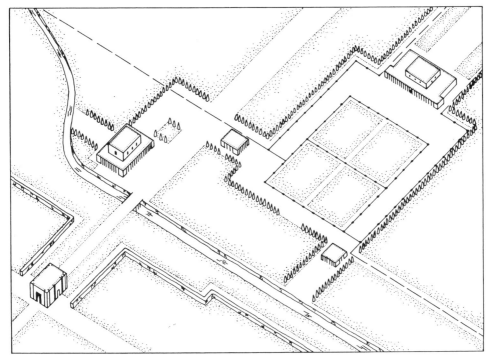

Fig. 12. Pasargadae. Schematic reconstruction of the palace and its gardens. (Stronach 1989, fig. 3.)

part, of the palace, and in Persepolis, the entire function of which has been much disputed, there are particular problems in respect of residential architecture.

The Palace of Darius I in Susa, on the other hand, was, as we know, the main palace of the dynasty, and incorporated all the functions needed in a palace of that kind. It was this palace which the Greek embassies, refugees, and captives visited, and about which stories were being told in Greece already from the early Classical period onwards (see p. 15). But it was situated outside Fars, and influenced by local, Elamite or Babylonian architecture as well, as is clearly shown by the presence of four large internal courtyards without columns, all with different functions (Fig. 19). The palace that Artaxerxes II built on the other side of the Shaour Stream has some of the same mixed features. It had only some of the palatial functions, since it lay so close to Darius' great palace (Fig. 21).

In spite of the differences, these palaces had many features in common. One of them is the large, partly artificial, platform, which raises (part of) the palace above its surroundings, and is probably an old Iranian feature. It was reached by

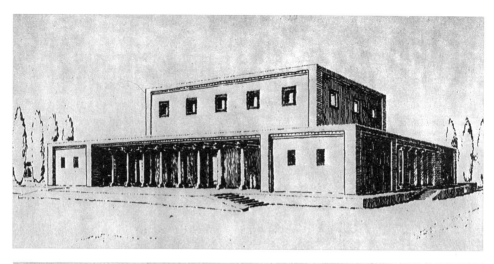

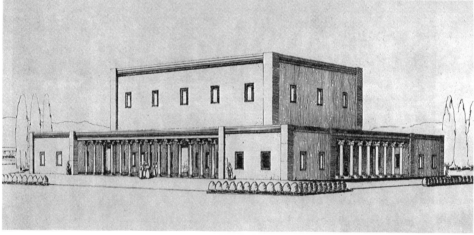

Fig. 13. Pasargadae. Two reconstructions of Palace S: Above by H. Herzfeld and F. Krefter (1941), below by F. Krefter (1973). (Stronach 1978, pl. 53.)

monumental staircases and furnished with large portals, to create an impressive approach.[94]

Another common feature is the presence of the most characteristic building in Achaemenid royal architecture, the airy, independent hypostyle hall surrounded on one to four sides by porticoes. This was primarily an official building, although it could have had other functions as well. The origins of this structure, which have been much disputed, will be discussed below. The earliest examples, from Pasargadae (Fig. 13), were oblong and constituted a kind of experimental phase on the way to the fully developed square form, the main representative of which

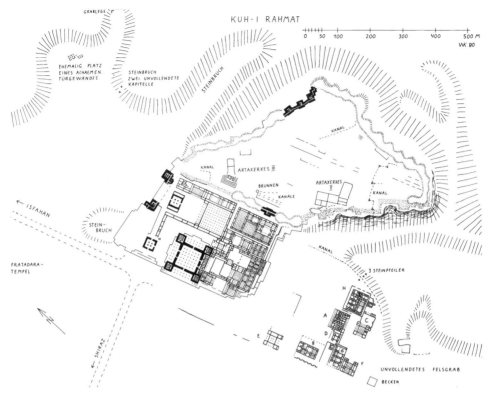

Fig. 14. Persepolis. General plan of the palaces on the terrace and its surroundings (Cat. 4). (Kleiss 1980, Abb. 9.)

was the *apadana* (the name is known from written sources): it was probably "invented" in Susa by Darius I and used also in Persepolis (Figs. 17, 19).[95] The apadana was an enormous building (c. 100 x 100 m), centred on a hypostyle hall and surrounded on three sides by porticoes, all the same height (18-20 m) as the interior columns, while on the fourth side were rooms. The roof was probably pyramidal and made of wood, while the columns were of stone. The reliefs on the staircases leading up to the Apadana in Persepolis show people carrying gifts to the Great King, and the function was undoubtedly that of a reception hall as well as an audience hall. The same functions must be attributed to its models, palaces S and P in Pasargadae, and probably to the smaller, apadana-like structure in the Palace of Artaxerxes II as well.

Another expression of this building type is the "Hall of 100 Columns" in Persepolis, with shorter columns and only one portico facing a forecourt (Figs.

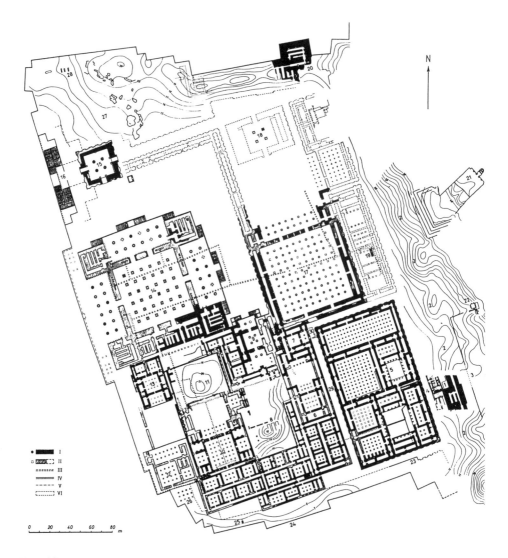

Fig. 15. Persepolis. Plan of the palaces on the terrace: 14. Apadana; 17. Hall of 100 Columns; 10. palace of Xerxes; 13. Palace of Darius. (EAA, s.v. Persepolis, fig. 79.)

15, 17). It has been variously interpreted as a throne-room, a huge office building, and a reception hall for the army. The last suggestion is supported by the reliefs that decorate the building, but it may well have served several functions; perhaps it was also a banqueting hall, although there is no sign of servants carrying food on the reliefs here.

Banqueting halls must indeed have formed part of all royal palaces, since

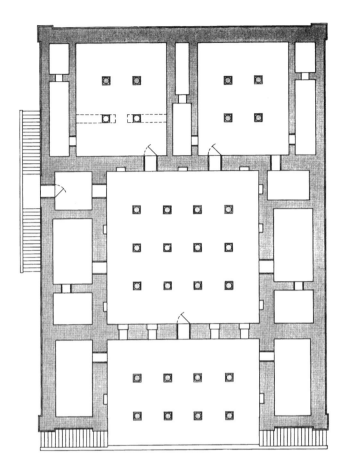

Fig. 16. Persepolis. Plan of the Palace of Darius. 1:375. (Schmidt 1953, fig. 92.)

banquets were a deeply rooted element in Persian court life. Thus Heracleides mentions that the Great King, who normally, as mentioned above, dined on his own, could sometimes dine with his guests in the great hall: *megalos oikos.*[96] In Persepolis, a banqueting hall was used by Alexander and his court before the destruction of the palace.[97] According to the reliefs, such a hall was, in fact, to be found in the Palace of Xerxes, and this represents another development of the hypostyle hall, since it was surrounded by rooms opening onto it (cf. Fig. 16). In Susa, the large audience hall, a "broad room" in Babylonian style, was probably also used for banqueting. Perhaps this was the hall in which the Greek ambassadors dined when visiting the Achaemenid court (which they did in

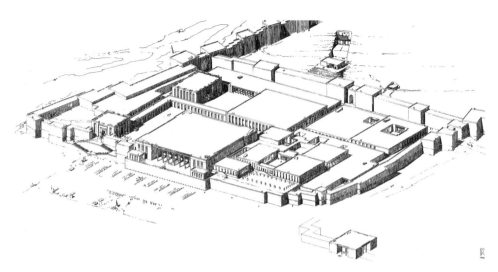

Fig. 17. Persepolis. Reconstruction of the terrace. (Krefter 1971, Beil. 34.)

increasing numbers during its last hundred years), and where Alexander placed himself on the throne.[98]

Apart from its official function, the hypostyle hall could apparently be used for a wide range of other functions, including residential purposes, and could belong to different kinds of complexes. This is to be seen in Persepolis, where, although some buildings on the terrace have tentatively been deemed residential,[99] the main residential quarter was undoubtedly to be found below the terrace, where a group of structures, among them two apadana-like buildings, perhaps for private banquets, were excavated in the 1970s (Fig. 14).[100] One of them faced a sunken courtyard, probably an enclosed garden. It could well be that the "Persian Building" added to the gardens of the Southern Palace of Babylon had the same function (Fig. 9) (see p. 35).[101] Although the Achaemenids thus had a canonical residential architecture, which was also represented in far off Dahan-i Ghulaman,[102] in Darius' Palace in Susa two of the four Babylonian-style courtyards were in fact used for residence, just as in the Southern Palace of Babylon. As far as Artaxerxes' Palace in Susa is concerned, it has often been called primarily residential, but at least the apadana-like building, facing away from the courtyard and towards the Palace of Darius, was certainly for official use. The function of the other buildings is uncertain, but since they face the garden, they were probably mostly residential and for service (Fig. 22).

As for the much-discussed origins of these airy, independent hypostyle halls,

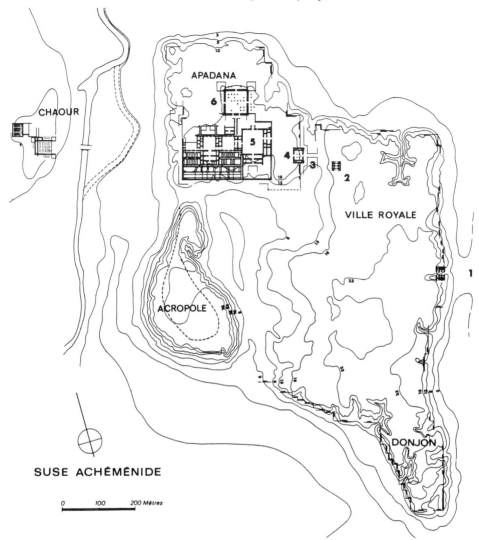

*Fig. 18. Susa. General plan of both palaces: 1. City gate; 2. "Propylée de Darius";
3. Road of sun-dried brick; 4. "Porte de Darius"; 5. Darius' Palace; 6. Apadana.
(Perrot 1981, tf. 34.)*

they undoubtedly had their beginnings in well-timbered areas, and apparently
existed in Urartaean, proto-Iranian, and Median architecture. As H. von Gall
stresses, however, these early halls were smaller than the Persian ones and
normally had only one entrance, at the end, and no porticoes. Taking the buildings
of Pasargadae as his point of departure, C. Nylander considers these Persian
buildings to be the result of combining a local building form, namely the hypostyle

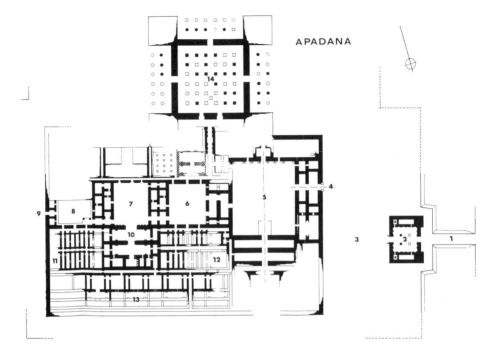

Fig. 19. Susa. Plan of the Palace of Darius (Cat. 5): 4. Entrance; 5. East court; 6. Central court; 7. Inner court; 8. West court; 9. Postern; 10. The king's apartment; 11-12. Magazines; 13. The apartments of the royal family; 14. Apadana. (Perrot 1981, pl. 2.)

hall, based on a "broad room", with Ionic porticoes or stoas known from the great Ionian sanctuaries. The inspiration from Ionic porticoes is argued from one of the types used being *in antis* in Pasargadae.[103] Nylander, however, concludes (in my view rightly) that the building type seems basically un-Greek, and that though its technique and aesthetics were Ionian, its essence and meaning were Oriental.[104] As we have seen, hypostyle halls were far from unknown in Egypt too, where the columns were of stone; but since these halls were very solid in appearance and also formed an integral part of the buildings they belonged to, and were never an independent building type, a direct inspiration from Egyptian architecture seems unlikely.

Even if we cannot rule out that the great Ionic temples and stoas had some influence on these Persian buildings, although in fact they developed only shortly before them, I find another theory concerning their origin (one which is especially propagated by von Gall) to be convincing: according to this, the Persian luxury tent, which was undoubtedly used for official purposes in the nomadic past of the

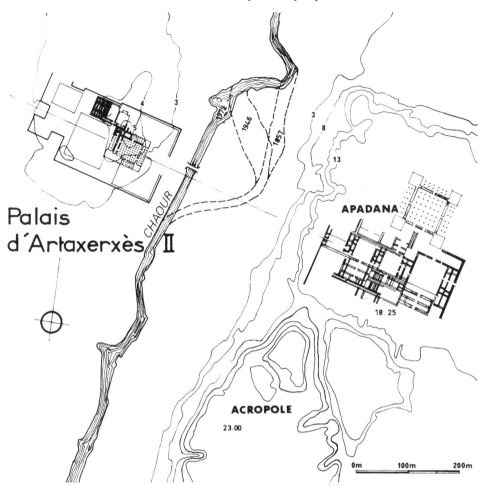

Fig. 20. Susa. General plan showing the relations between the two palaces. (Boucharlat & Labrousse 1979, fig. 10.)

Persians, should be the prime model, and the very tall and light columns of the hypostyle halls and the impost capitals would suggest wooden tent-poles, while the porticoes would indicate the tent walls, which could be raised by means of poles to form a covered walkway on one or more sides. Information on these tents, which may be gleaned primarily from the written sources, seems to support this notion. As mentioned above (p. 18), such tents later had official functions too, not only during campaigns, but also at home, e.g. for open-air banquets, in the parks (below).[105]

With the eclecticism which characterizes Achaemenid architecture in mind, it does not seem too rash to say that the inspiration to build independent hypostyle

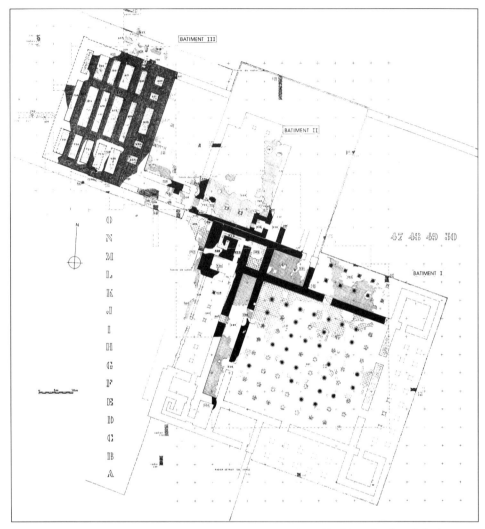

Fig. 21. Susa. Plan of the Palace of Artaxerxes II (Cat. 6). (Boucharlat & Labrousse 1979, fig. 37.)

halls may, in fact, have emanated from all these models, thus illustrating the truth of Darius' insciption (above).

That tent architecture could indeed be transmuted into stone can probably also be seen in Greece, in an example that shows a probable Persian influence on Greek architecture and at the same time warns us that the flow of inspiration is by no means always from West to East. Basing himself on the descriptions of Xerxes' war tent, abandoned at Plataea,[106] O. Broneer proposes that this was later taken to Athens and used as a skene building (= tent) in the temporary theatre of Dionysus. It would, for instance, have been very appropriate when Aeschylus' *Persae* was performed, since the tragedy took place in the palace of the Persian king.[107] In fact, the projecting corners of the *paraskenia* might reflect the corner rooms flanking the entrance to the hypostyle halls (above). Thus the stage building of the Classical Greek theatre may well ultimately have been inspired by the Persian palaces, of which several Greeks had first-hand knowledge from their visits to Susa. From Aeschylus' time on, tragedies often had palaces as the scene of action (see p. 19).

Broneer has moreover argued convincingly that Pericles' Odeion of 443 BC was in fact a direct copy in stone of the tent which still existed, for this Odeion had the shape of a hypostyle hall, with an entrance portico and a pyramidal, pavilion-like roof supported by a central pole. Excavations have revealed that it had 9 x 10 columns, measured 62.4 x 68.6 m, and had a portico in front.[108] Even the size is more or less the same as that of the Persian halls; particularly marked is the similarity to the Hall of 100 Columns at Persepolis (Fig. 23). This reception and audience hall may have had a pyramidal roof as well, since a thick layer of burnt cedarwood was found in the excavations. According to von Gall,[109] the same model was probably used in the second Telesterion in Eleusis and the Thersilion of Megalopolis.[110] That the Persian tent type was, indeed, well known among the Greeks is also indicated by the richly ornamented luxury tent of Persian type, which Alcibiades was given by the Ephesians, for use during his travels.[111]

Besides the hypostyle buildings and the platforms, the third main feature characterizing Persian palaces is the parks, or paradeisoi, for recreational purposes.[112] They have their background in the nomadic origins of the Persians and perhaps had an original function as hunting-grounds, but they were also planted with many trees and a large variety of useful plants, and often furnished with pavilions. Thus Xenophon uses the term in both senses.[113] This park was at its most extensive in Pasargadae, where several buildings were laid out on a regular plan in a huge fenced park, which was divided up by means of paths and by an extensive network of stone water-channels and basins, which irrigated the gardens (Fig. 11).[114] At Persepolis, the previously mentioned residential buildings below the terrace were probably situated in a large park with an artificial lake (Fig. 14), while in Susa, a large park was probably laid out to the south of Darius I's Palace on its huge terrace; and one can well imagine that Artaxerxes' Palace, which was laid out on the plain near the river, was set in a paradeisos, too (Fig. 18).

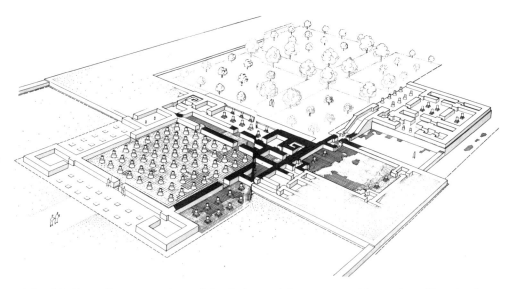

*Fig. 22. Susa. Reconstruction of the Palace of Artaxerxes with garden. (Boucharlat
& Labrousse 1979, fig. 25.)*

Besides those paradeisoi there was another kind of garden, enclosed and of
limited size, and directly related to and integrated with the palace. One is found
in Artaxerxes' Palace (Fig. 22), and another, a sunken garden, in one of the
palaces below the terrace of Persepolis. Gardens and water, it will be noted, are
elements always in great demand in dry climates.

Although the parks primarily served a recreational purpose, which includes their
original use as hunting-grounds, one should not overlook their use for ceremonies
taking place in the open. At Pasargadae a throne is actually preserved in one of
the porticoes of Palace P, and, what is more, it faces the garden (Fig. 12), which
indicates an audience and reception function in the open air — not inappropriate
for a nomadic people like the Persians. Undoubtedly, the large forecourt and the
courtyards of Persepolis and Susa, respectively, were used in that way too. Also,
one may well imagine large banquets taking place in the park, probably in tents.
At any rate the huge number of guests mentioned in the sources precludes the use
of permanent buildings for the largest banquets (see n. 17 and p. 15).

The Persian gardens were thus, in contrast to their Assyrian and Babylonian
predecessors, an integral part of Achaemenid palace architecture (as had been the
case in Egypt, albeit on a more limited scale), and were not merely an annexe

to the main scheme. These gardens and parks had a great future, not only, as has long been recognized, in the East, in the later Persian and Islamic gardens, but also, as we shall see, in the West, in connection with the Hellenistic and Roman palaces. As Stronach so aptly puts it: "... from the second half of the sixth century B.C. onwards, one of the more enduring of all Achaemenid contributions lay in the area of monumental garden design".[115]

Governors' palaces

Besides the royal palaces of the Persian empire, there also existed other types of palace from which the Hellenistic kings may have gained inspiration, namely those built by the Persian satraps and minor governors. It would be interesting to know which model the satraps used when building their palaces in the various satrapies, i.e. whether they brought with them the Persian royal architecture, or whether they used the local royal or princely style, as did, for example, the Persian kings themselves in Babylon and Susa. And again, did the vassal kings in the different localities follow the models set by the Persian governors in palace building, or was the flow of ideas in fact in the other direction?[116] Unfortunately, only a few of these governors' palaces are preserved, but we know of many from the written sources.

Information on such palaces, whether archaeological or literary, comes mostly from Anatolia, but Cyprus and Syria/Palestine also furnish us with much material. Taking as our point of departure the area closest to the Persian heartland, we have information on three palaces from Syria/Palestine. In connection with Cyrus the Younger's campaigns Xenophon mentions the palace belonging to Belyses, the satrap of Northern Syria. The only feature he finds worthy of attention, however, is its large *paradeisos*, with its many fruit trees. Cyrus burned down the palace and cut down the trees.[117] Of this palace, nothing has been found, and even the exact location is unknown.

Nearby Sidon, although it was ruled by its own king (but was probably also a seat for the satrap), had a *paradeisos* for the Persian king as well. Even though the palace itself has not been found, columns in the Persian style probably belonging to it have been preserved, and may well indicate the existence of Persian-style hypostyle halls.[118]

Fortunately, one of the governors' palaces in this area is actually preserved, namely that of Lachish (Cat. 7). This structure was built on a fortified hill, on a terrace incorporating an earlier palace from the 8th century BC (Fig. 24). Near

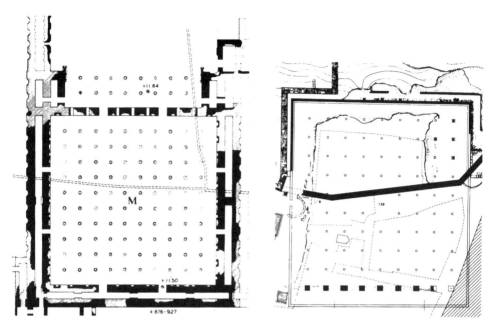

Fig. 23. Comparative plans of the Hall of 100 Columns in Persepolis (to the left), and Pericles' Odeion in Athens. (von Gall 1977, fig. 4 a-b.)

the palace was a temple. The date of this palace has been the subject of much debate. The latest investigations seem to favour a Persian date for the first phase and an early Hellenistic date for the second.[119] The palace consisted of a large square courtyard flanked on the east and north by small rooms that opened onto it (Fig. 25). On the south and west sides were the official rooms, consisting of two ante-rooms, both with two columns in antis, and each giving access to a "broad room". The southern wing is the more important, the columns being higher and the "broad room" larger; it was, moreover, reached by a wide staircase from the yard, creating an impressive approach to the ruler. In addition, a private apartment behind the official rooms could be reached from this "broad room"; it included bathrooms paved with stone slabs. This combination of official rooms with residential rooms placed behind them, or flanking them, usually called an "andron complex", is known also from Neo-Babylonian private houses (Fig. 27), and, on a more lavish scale, from the palaces. But in all these instances, columnar fronts are lacking. In Lachish, there were thus rooms on all sides of the yard, which was probably not provided with a monumental entrance, but only an angular, or "bent" one, probably in the north-east corner (Fig. 26). The main impression is that of a "compact palace".

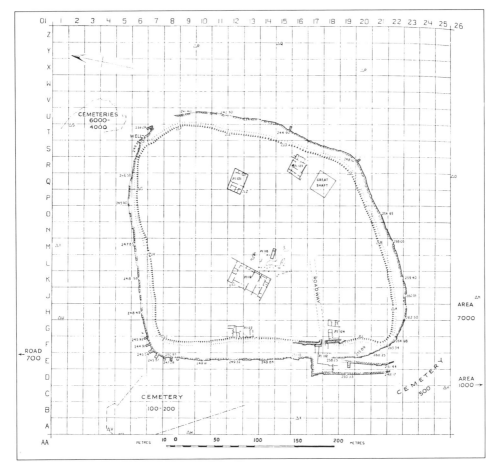

Fig. 24. Lachish. General plan of the fortified acropolis. (Tufnell 1953, pl. 108.)

As Y. Aharoni has emphasized (see n. 119), there is also a close resemblance between this palace and the North Syrian palaces of the 9th-7th centuries BC. The main element in these palaces is the *Bit-Hilani*, an independent building defined by H. Frankfort as "a palace with two long narrow rooms, both with their main axis parallel to the façade with from one to three columns often placed at the top of a low flight of steps. Stairs to the upper storey are set to one side of the portico." From the official "broad room" behind the portico a private apartment with bed- and bathrooms could often be reached. One might, again, call it an "andron complex" (above).[120] Such Bit-Hilani units are found in Lachish, here flanking a courtyard. Thus, in Lachish we see a Babylonian courtyard house (Fig. 27) combined with North Syrian Bit-Hilani units to form an integrated whole. In

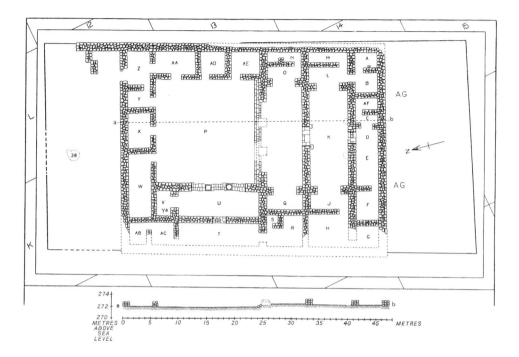

Fig. 25. Lachish. Plan and section of the palace (Cat. 7). (Tufnell 1953, pl. 119.)

general there is very little affinity to Achaemenid architecture. All the same, one might say that the Palace of Lachish is a typical building of the Persian period, adapting itself as it does to the local architectural forms, while at the same time adding some modern elements.

Moving to nearby Cyprus, the same may be said of the contemporary Palace of Vouni (Cat. 8), and the two palaces have a general resemblance to each other;[121] this is also true in respect of their sites, each being on an acropolis together with the principal sanctuary, which at Vouni towers above the palace (Fig. 28). This palace, which belonged either to a local prince of Soloi or to the Persian governor, was the subject of many changes (Fig. 29). There has been much discussion of the inspirational sources for this palace, not least between the excavator, E. Gjerstad, and V. Müller. Both agree, however, and rightly, in my opinion, that the palace is Oriental in style rather than Greek, at least in its first phase (Pl. 4).

There is no need to go into detail concerning the arguments, which are largely out of date. I shall merely record Gjerstad's outline of the development of the palace. There are two main phases. The first palace, built around 500 BC, had

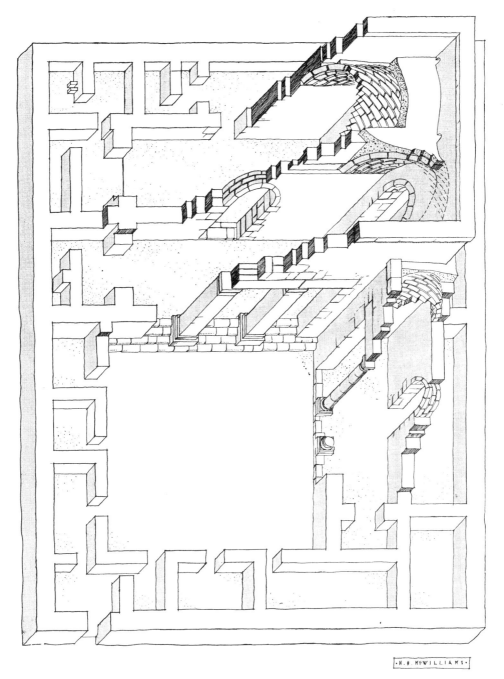

Fig. 26. Lachish. Isometric reconstruction of the palace. (Tufnell 1953, pl. 120.)

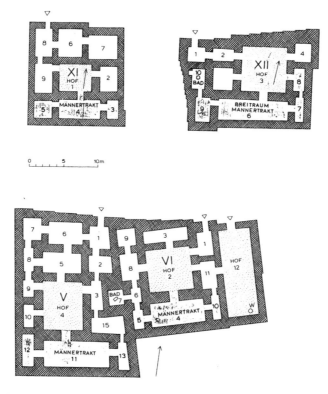

Fig. 27. Babylon. Houses from the city quarter "Merkes", belonging to the 6th to 3rd centuries BC. (Hoepfner & Schwandner 1986, Abb. 243.)

a monumental entrance and vestibule ("propylon") to the south, whence a large staircase led down to a central courtyard with rooms on all sides and porticoes on three sides (Fig. 30). On the west side was a large "broad room" that opened, like most of the other rooms, onto the courtyard. Finally there was a large bathroom without bath-tubs, and two service wings. In this phase, Gjerstad sees the influence of Syria and Anatolia. In the second phase, starting c. 450 BC, the entrance was moved to the north-west corner of the building and became "bent", although still monumental, with a broad staircase leading up to it (Fig. 31). The vestibule was made into a main hall with side rooms, while the former "broad room" to the west was partitioned into three smaller rooms. Another, larger, service courtyard was added at this time. Gjerstad sees in this rebuilding a Greek influence, and he regards the new main wing, the former "propylon", as a megaron-like complex. He relates the introduction of this Greek element to Cimon's conquest of several cities in Cyprus. Müller, on the other hand, considers

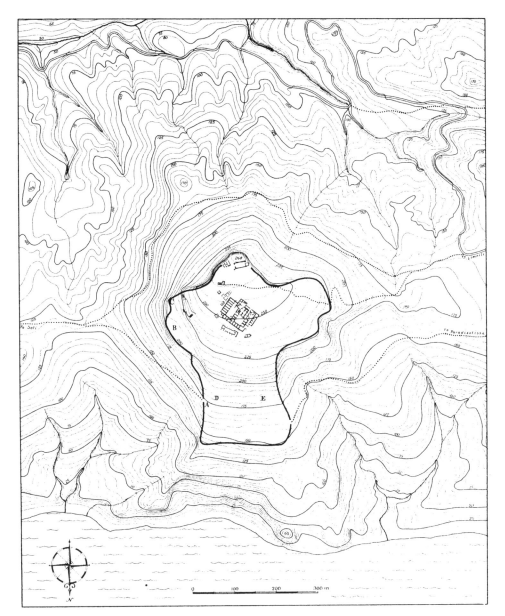

Fig. 28. Vouni. General plan of the fortified area. (Gjerstad et al. 1937, pl. VII.)

the building Babylonian rather than Greek in the second phase as well as the first (characteristic features being the central courtyard with rooms on all sides, the

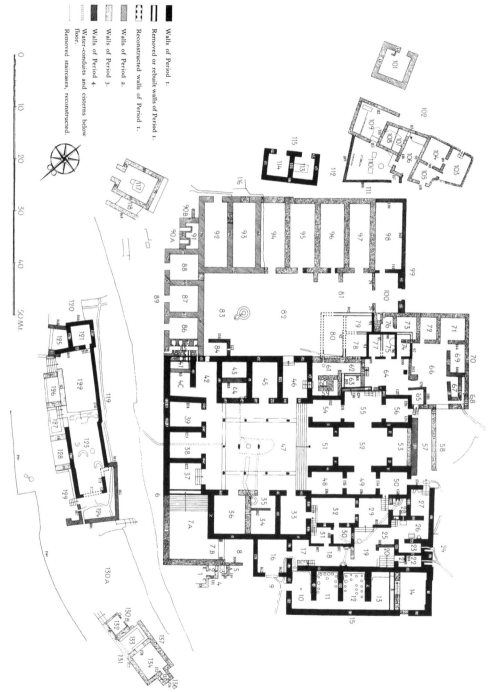

Fig. 29. Vouni. Plan of the palace with the different periods indicated (Cat. 8). (Gjer-stad 1932, Fig. 119.)

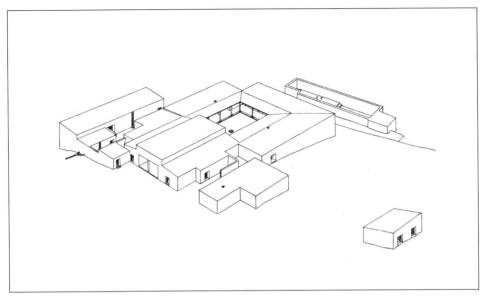

Fig. 30. Vouni. Reconstruction of the first main phase of the palace. (Gjerstad et al. *1937, pl. XXVI.)*

"broad room", and the "bent" entrance), while the peristyle is in his view an Egyptian feature. Neither of them mentions a possible Persian inspiration.

As far as the first phase is concerned, I question, like others before me, the identification of the south wing as a propylon. Rather this monumental group of rooms, at the top of a wide staircase and placed symmetrically about the main axis, must be identified as the official part of the palace from the outset, and the "megaron" theory must be rejected. Thus the smaller rooms surrounding the main hall, and connected to it by wide doorways, dispel the impression of an isolated main room, which is essential for the megaron. Rather, there is a certain similarity to the ceremonial rooms in the innermost courtyard of the Palace of Darius at Susa, the so-called "three-room suite in depth", although there "broad rooms" are used. While columns are lacking in the hall in Vouni, there are also some affinities with the main rooms of Darius' and Xerxes' palaces at Persepolis, which in fact look like de luxe editions of this wing (Fig. 16). An audience-hall function seems to be indicated, and this wing would thus house the main official function. The entrance to the palace should then be sought elsewhere in the first phase, probably in the vicinity of the second-phase entrance, which was much more accessible than one to the south would have been.[122] The use of a broad staircase to enhance the approach to the main hall is known from Lachish, the North Syrian

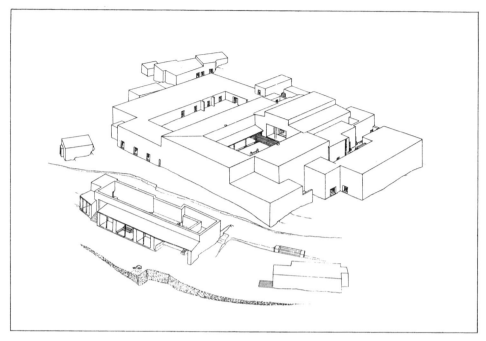

Fig. 31. Vouni. Reconstruction of the second main phase of the palace. (Gjerstad et al. *1937, pl. XXVII.)*

palaces, and the Persian palaces, the closest parallel being the "Persian Building" (Fig. 9) in the Southern Palace of Babylon (see p. 35).[123] An official function should probably be accorded to the large "broad room" in the west wing as well; perhaps it was a banqueting hall, while the private apartments of the prince or governor should be expected to lie principally in the northern and eastern wings, and to include the large bathroom.

One of the most interesting elements in the Palace of Vouni, and one which distinguishes it from the parallels mentioned above, is the three-sided peristyle in the courtyard. Several scholars have, in my opinion, underestimated the significance of this peristyle and seen a resemblance between this palace and the palaces of Larisa, when this town was still under Persian rule (below); but this similarity is superficial.[124] In Larisa there are many megara and rooms with two columns in antis, but no peristyle. The three-sided peristyle of Vouni is original and is surely not a development from columns in antis; in fact, it is entirely independent of the rooms behind it. Besides, peristyles in courtyards were not unknown in the Orient, as proved most recently by the finds in the Achaemenid town of Dahan-I Ghulaman in eastern Iran.[125] The Egyptian-type Hathor capitals used in Vouni also indicate an Oriental origin for this phenomenon, although peristyles were normally used only in forecourts in ancient Egypt. The Vouni Palace, however, presents one of the first instances of a peristyle in a courtyard house in the eastern Mediterranean, a motif which later became one of the most typical elements of Greek architecture (see p. 77).

Another early example is found in the Archaic building at Murlo (Poggio Civitate) in Etruria, put up around 590 BC, i.e. still in the Orientalizing phase, and deliberately destroyed around 550-530 BC. This structure has been variously interpreted as a meeting house for a religious league, and a princely palace (Fig. 32).[126] Whatever its function, there is certainly a palatial feeling about the large square building measuring c. 62 x 62 m (= 3,844 m^2), with its fine terracotta revetments. It is centred around a large peristyle courtyard with columns on three sides and rooms on all sides. On the north side there are two large halls, undoubtedly for official purposes, very likely including banquets, as depicted in the terracotta frieze. On the west side, the only one without columns, a small sanctuary in the middle was flanked by two almost symmetrical wings. The function of the rooms is not clear, since there are no finds to help us.

Since the two earliest examples of peristyles in internal courtyards in historical times in the Mediterranean are found in palatial buildings, I find it probable that this monumentalizing element was, in fact, developed in connection with palace architecture, where it remained an important feature.[127]

Other palaces existed in Cyprus in this period; a very badly preserved one was found in Palaipaphos.[128] It looks Babylonian/Persian, and consists of a compact building with very thick, fine ashlar walls and axially laid out small rooms and corridors. The building is dated to the Persian period, the beginning of the 5th century BC. Also, we know of a palace in Salamis belonging to the local prince Evagoras (411-374 BC), but the only remains are a unique Persian capital and some elements in Greek style.[129]

Finally, let us move to Anatolia where, as I have said, most information on governors' palaces is to be found.[130] Xenophon is one of our main sources here, and he refers to such palaces in Kelainai, Daskyleion, and Sardis. Common to them all is the fact that Xenophon stresses their recreational elements, *paradeisoi*, but says nothing of the buildings themselves.

In the case of Kelainai in Phrygia, Xenophon mentions that there were two palaces: one, which was abandoned in his time, was apparently built by Xerxes when he returned from Greece, and thus belonged to the Great King. It was situated below the fortified acropolis by the source of the River Marsyas. The other, which

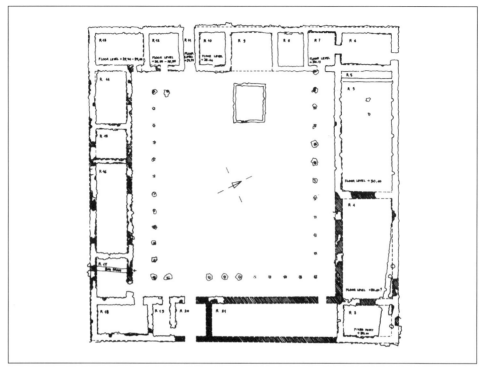

Fig. 32. Murlo (Poggio Civitate). Plan of the palatial building. (Nielsen & Philips 1985, fig. 3.5.)

belonged to Cyrus the Younger, had a *paradeisos* with game. Through it ran the River Maeander, which had its source near the palace.[131]

Of Pharnabazus the satrap's palace in Daskyleion we are informed only that a *paradeisos* with wild animals was associated with it, and that a river passed close by.[132] Before the new excavations only some walls in ashlar and some architectural fragments in the Ionic style of the 4th century BC had been traced, but recently the foundations of two palaces have been found, one from the Archaic period, belonging first to the Lydian governor and later to the first Persian satrap Megabetes, and the other the above-mentioned palace of Pharnabazus. The oldest palace was built above the town, on terraces sloping steeply from west to east. The second palace was built at the beginning of the 5th century BC for the Persian satrap Artabazus I. It was destroyed in 395 BC by the Spartan general Agesilaus, together with its paradeisos and the satrap's capital itself. Later, it was rebuilt by Pharnabazus, but in 334 BC the satrapy fell to Alexander, and the palace was burned, never to be rebuilt. Foundations of this palace and walls of sun-dried bricks have been found, and on top of it the Diadochi built palatial buildings.[133]

In Sardis, the old capital of the Lydian kingdom, the satrap simply took over King Croesus' Palace. Seemingly nothing is preserved of the palace proper, but there are indications that it was situated on the northern slopes of the acropolis, for monumental terrace walls of good quality as well as architectural terracottas belonging to the Lydian period have been found here, the latter suggesting a megaron form. In recent years the excavation of a second terrace, further down the slope, has revealed more Lydian terrace walls, making G.M.A. Hanfmann's suggestion of a palace here even more probable.[134] As already mentioned, the oldest palace of Daskyleion, put up, in fact, by the Lydian governor, was also built on steep terraces. Terraces and platforms were a typical element in Persian palace architecture, but they were also an old local feature in Anatolia.[135] Vitruvius, citing a Hellenistic author, relates that this palace was reused by the *gerousia* as a meeting place, and that the walls, built in sun-dried brick, were then still in good shape. Xenophon tells us, moreover, that Cyrus the Younger laid out a royal park, a *paradeisos*, in Sardis, undoubtedly below the terraces of the acropolis; he emphasizes the symmetrical arrangement of the trees in long rows, with a uniform distance between them.[136]

Thus from both Sardis and Daskyleion one gets the impression that, in Lydia, terrace architecture was frequently used when palaces were built, being calculated to create impressive approaches and give a fine view of the surroundings, including the royal paradeisos placed below the palace. Both palaces were taken over by the Persians and housed their satraps.

It is a great pity that Mausolus' Palace in Halicarnassus is not preserved, for he was both a Persian satrap and a local dynast. All we have is a reference in Vitruvius, which tells us that it was Mausolus himself who drew up the plan, that the palace was built in sun-dried brick like Croesus' palace at Sardis, and that it was still well preserved in Hellenistic times. It was clad in marble from the Proconessus and had stuccoed decoration which was so polished that it gleamed like glass.[137] Most scholars believe this palace to have been on the peninsula, where the Crusaders' Castle now stands (probably adjecent to the early Classical Temple of Apollo, Mausolus' tutelary deity), this position being best in accordance with Vitruvius' topographical description of the city (Fig. 33, Pl. 5).[138] Also, a large and well-preserved terrace wall of ashlars of the same type as those of the Mausoleum was found earlier in the castle, and in the new excavations not only a continuation of this wall but other walls also have been found, at right

Fig. 33. Halicarnassus. General plan of the city: a. Mausoleion; b. Presumed Palace of Mausolus and Temple of Apollo; Ze. The Zephyrion Peninsula and Crusaders' castle (drawing by O.A. Hansen).

angles to the preserved one, although at a higher level. These finds indicate the presence of a large platform carrying various structures (Pl. 6).[139]

One may compare the defensive position on a peninsula to that of the Palace of Dionysius I sited on Ortygia in Syracuse (see p. 80), and to that of the, later,

Ptolemaic Palace of Alexandria (Cat. 20), where the citadel (Akra), was built on the peninsula called Lochias (see p. 131). It is quite likely that the main builder of this palace, Ptolemy I, who participated in both sieges of Halicarnassus, in 334 and 309 BC, was inspired by the splendid position of Mausolus' Palace. In all three cases the palaces were connected with a secret harbour which housed the king's fleet, and they all had a defensive character. Probably they were also all built on terraces, somewhat above sea level.

We do not know which layout Mausolus chose for his palace, but from the appearance of his Mausoleum we can see that he had several different sources to chose from, including the Persian, the local Anatolian, and the Greek. As for the palace proper, we should probably envisage a building with a central court, perhaps with a large megaron as the main hall for official purposes. We may even imagine a *tetrapyrgion* model: this was at least known to him, and used in Theangala.[140] An East Greek rather than an Oriental plan would probably be expected from this hellenophile king's hand, although his status as a Persian satrap could have meant the inclusion of elements from Achaemenid royal architecture as well. I find, however, the arguments for a megaron as the main hall rather persuasive, both because it was an integral part of the house type chosen in Priene (i.e. the *prostas*), which was founded in Mausolus' time,[141] and because this building type dominated his main sanctuary at Labraunda.

This Sanctuary of Zeus Labraundus is, in fact, the best-preserved complex from Mausolus' reign. It was built mostly in local and Greek style, and dominated by buildings of the megaron type, here called *androns*, that were indigenous to western Anatolia (Fig. 34, Pl. 7) (below). These androns were axial and very large, with large windows and a large recess in the back wall; and in one of them, Andron A, measuring c. 20 x 10 m (= 200 m^2), remains of a podium for klinai have been found (Pl. 8).[142] Andron A and Andron B were dedicated by Mausolus and his brother Idreus, respectively. It is possible that a palace has, in fact, been found in the new excavations just above the propylon of Labraunda. A large courtyard with a stoa and six square dining-rooms of Greek type along the east side has been ascertained. Along the south side may have been another stoa, sitting on the terrace below. Another possibility is that the structure was used for ritual meals, like the ones which probably took place in the androns.[143]

A third possibility, which I have discussed with the director of the excavations, P. Hellström, is that the Labraunda complex served both as a palace and a sanctuary at the same time, since all the elements and functions constituting a palace were, in fact, present here: thus there was an impressive approach through

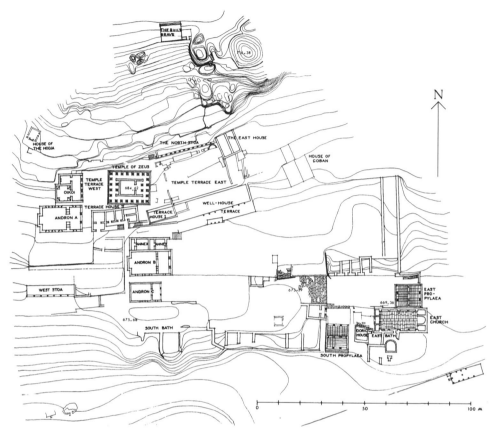

Fig. 34. Labraunda. General plan of the sanctuary. (Hellström 1989, fig. 1.)

the elaborate propylon and up a monumental staircase to the andrones, which had an official and ceremonial function (Pl. 9). The *oikos* behind the temple probably had an administrative function, while the banqueting house might also have been used for residential purposes. The Temple of Zeus, which was not actually the first structure to be built on a monumental scale, would thus constitute the temple of the tutelary deity, while the large recesses at the back of the andrones might have served as dynastic sanctuaries, for members of the dynasty enjoyed the status of cult kings. Finally, the monumental tomb above the sanctuary might have belonged to a member of the dynasty.

Moving north along the coast of western Anatolia, we reach the Palace of Larisa (Cat. 9). This was not a satrap's palace, and may not even have housed a Persian governor. Rather, a local dynast was installed here as vassal king by the Persians, or perhaps kept on from an earlier period, for the palace goes back a long way. There are remains of palaces from the Archaic period and up to the beginning of the 3rd century BC, when the city was destroyed by the Gauls, never to be rebuilt (Fig. 35). These palaces were all situated on a fortified acropolis in close proximity to the main temple of the city, a position typical of the area (compare, for example, Troy, Sardis, Pergamon).

In all periods, the main room-type for official purposes was the megaron, which in the Archaic phases was isolated, forming an independent unit facing a courtyard (below). The popularity of this building type in western Anatolia is documented from Bronze Age Troy, and also from 8th-7th century Phrygian Gordion, where several large megara have been found, and it is known also in this period from nearby Chios (below). In Gordion, the interior of the main rooms had inner wooden supports and galleries, and there were always large hearths.[144] Perhaps there was a megaron in the Palace of Croesus in Sardis, too, at least terracottas seemingly belonging to such a building have been found on the acropolis (above). One might well imagine that the Palace of Larisa was inspired by this palace. The importance of the megaron element in Larisa has been further increased by the proposal of H. Lauter to dismiss the current reconstruction of the late Archaic palace as a Bit-Hilani (Fig. 36) in favour of a traditional megaron. Moreover, he promotes an interpretation of the even earlier palace as an isolated megaron as well.[145] Since the state of preservation of the building is very poor, it is impossible to decide which reconstruction is the true one. An argument in favour of the Schefoldian Bit-Hilani is the close resemblance both to the *tetrapyrgia* or *dipyrgia*, known in Asia Minor, and to the *paraskenion* building of the Greek theatre, probably directly adopted from the palace façade of the period (above).[146]

In the later phases at Larisa, the megaron came to be included in the courtyard buildings. This applies to the palace as it appeared in the middle of the 5th century BC, when the city was still under Persian rule, and to the new palace added in the middle of the 4th century BC (Fig. 37). Opening onto the court of this palace there were *i.a.* four rooms furnished with ante-rooms with two columns in antis; of these rooms, the ones in the north wing, which was probably the main, official wing, were typical megara, or perhaps the designation prostas would be more appropriate, since they formed part of a larger building and were connected with other rooms. One may compare them with the contemporary houses of Priene. In this period the palace consisted of several courtyards with different functions, none of them including a peristyle.

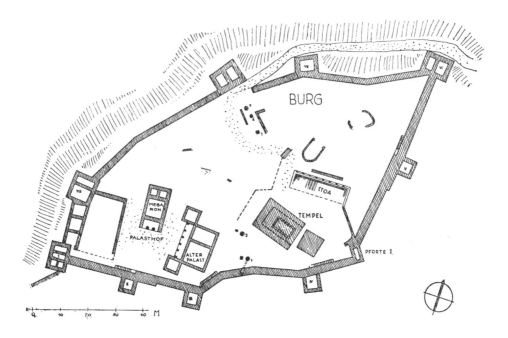

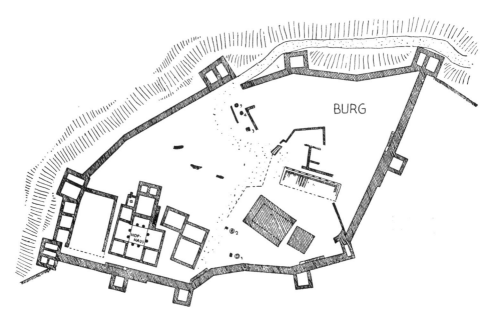

Fig. 35. Larisa. The four main phases of the palace: Above (A), around 500 BC;
below (B), mid-5th century BC.

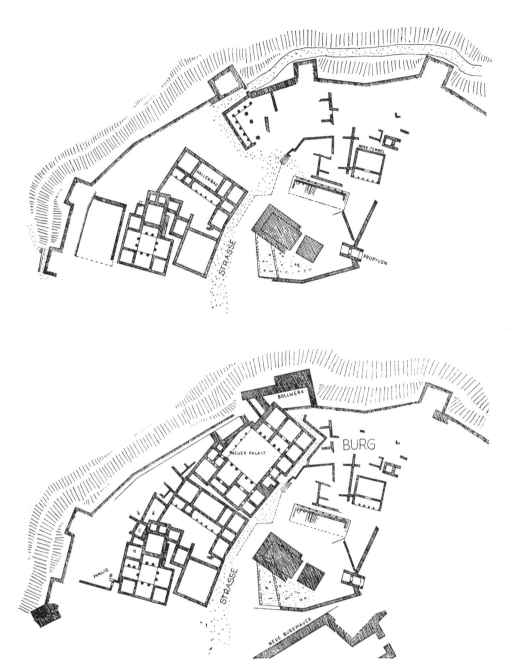

Fig. 35, continued: above (C), c. 430/20 BC; below (D), mid-4th century BC (Cat. 9). (Boehlau & Schefold 1940, Abb. 4-7.)

Fig. 36. Larisa. Reconstruction of the late Archaic palace as a Bit-Hilani. (Boehlau & Schefold 1940, Taf. 30.)

These megara probably served several purposes. In addition to their traditional use as audience halls, they were undoubtedly also used for banquets, a function which has been convincingly proved for the two andrones of megaron type in the Carian sanctuary of Labraunda, founded by Mausolus (Pl. 8) (above).[147] Unfortunately, the megara of the palaces of the various periods in Larisa are too poorly preserved to establish whether any of the characteristics of banqueting rooms, i.e. drains, raised "*kline* bands" (i.e. marked areas along the walls for couches), large windows, etc., were present. But a drain seems to have existed in connection with the megaron of the late Archaic palace,[148] and in the 4th-century palace a drain in the eastern megaron of the northern wing has been ascertained, which may, however, belong to an earlier period. It is difficult to identify the rooms serving the other functions, for instance the residence of the ruler.

Finally, one may mention the "residences" of the Archaic period found on the Lycian acropolis of Xanthus.[149] Two residences were excavated, built in the south-eastern part of the acropolis, one above the other. The oldest one, from the first half of the 7th century BC, measuring c. 14.70 x 16 m (= 232 m^2), must have belonged to a local dynast. It consisted of one compact building rather closely related to the Bit-Hilani type, with "broad rooms" as the dominating room-form.[150] The second "palace" (c. 310 m^2), built after the first had been

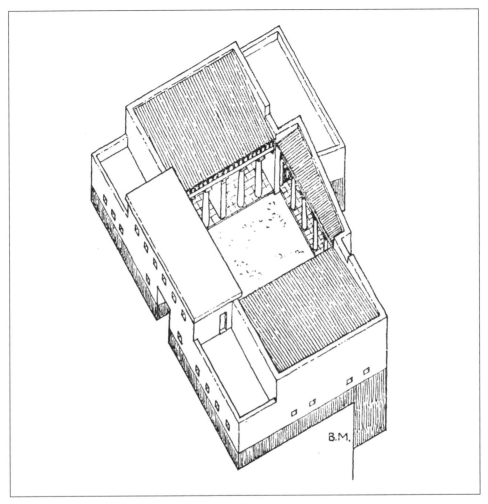

Fig. 37. Larisa. Reconstruction of the 4th century palace (phase D, Fig. 35). (Boehlau & Schefold 1940, Abb. 41.)

destroyed, probably by the Persians in 540 BC, was of another type; it consisted of a closed and compact ground floor for storage, etc., and a first floor, mainly in wood, for residential and probably also for official purposes, a typical Anatolian house type. This palace had a large forecourt, and storerooms associated with it, and was situated close to the main temple. As at Larisa, we do not know whether it was the Persian governor who resided in Xanthus, or rather a local vassal king; the latter seems the more probable. The complex was destroyed in c. 470 BC. While the inspiration for the first building came primarily from Northern

Syria, the one built during the Persian domination was of a local, Anatolian type.

To judge from the preserved examples of governors' palaces, Persian influence on the architecture in the three areas in question seems rather limited.[151] This would then be another instance of Persian tolerance with respect to the selection of building types by their subjects along with their acceptance, and even adoption, of local building types such as the Bit-Hilani, the megaron, and the Lycian house type. However, typical Persian architectural elements were, in fact, found both in Cyprus and in Sidon, and from the written sources we frequently hear of *paradeisoi* both in Syria/Palestine and Anatolia, so that at least that feature of the Persian palace was taken over by the satraps in these areas also. The recurrent mention of the *paradeisos*, in which the palace lay or above which it was raised, is an indication of the great importance these parks had in palace architecture, even outside the area of the Achaemenid kingdom, where the concept originated.

Hellas

Although this area was never ruled by the Persians, the poleis of which it consisted had close contact with the great empire in the East (above). This contact was primarily diplomatic, although the Persian Wars of course made a great impact on Greek society as well. The relationship did not, however, result in the creation of palatial buildings, for which there was no need in a polis society, although, as we have seen, the hypostyle hall did become popular in Greece as a result of this contact, albeit for other purposes (see p. 49).[152]

Thus there were no direct models for Hellenistic palaces on the Greek mainland, always excepting Macedonia, which will be dealt with in the next chapter. Genuine monarchies belonged to the mythical past, the only exception being the magisterial monarchy of Sparta. To use Homer as a source for these early royal or princely palaces, i.e. from the 9th-8th centuries BC, may seem risky. However, if we combine Homer's information on palaces with details of the few for which we have archaeological evidence, some common aspects may be discerned. In very general terms, Homer's palaces consisted basically of a courtyard, often with columns, reached from a porch (*propylon*), and surrounded by rooms, probably partly on two storeys. The main hall (*megaron*), had a hearth and was multifunctional, being used for all official purposes including the banquet; as an example of decoration, weapons on the wall are mentioned. The private apartments for the king's family were partly on the first floor. Also, we hear of storerooms and a treasury, as well as of a temple for the principal deity.[153]

Two of the earliest palaces or palatial houses to be found in Greece after the

Mycenaean period belong to this "Homeric" period, viz. those at Zagora in Andros, and Emporio in Chios, which date to the second half of the 8th century and to c. 700 BC, respectively.[154] Both were sited on the acropolis, in close proximity to the main temple of the town, but they are very different in layout, indicating that at least two models obtained in this early period. The palatial house of Zagora is a rather complicated structure covering c. 500 m^2: it consists of a courtyard surrounded by rooms with different functions, e.g. storerooms and kitchen. The main hall, a large square chamber with a hearth and benches, was reached, probably via a porch, from the courtyard as well. The "palace" of Emporio, on the other hand, consisted only of one hall (117 m^2), a megaron with three columns in the central axis, and a porch with two columns in antis. As mentioned above, this megaron-style building seems to have been especially popular in this and later periods in Anatolia, to which Chios was closely related, and is found in both Gordion and Larisa.[155] While Zagora was abandoned around 700 BC, Emporio remained in use for another century, and at both sites the temples continued to function even longer. The temple of Emporio was dedicated to Athena, who, as J. Boardman puts it, "was the patron goddess of the king before she ever became saviour of the people", that is, in the Ionian areas.[156]

From the Archaic period, i.e. the period of the tyrants, no palaces are preserved with certainty. In vase paintings, palatial buildings, albeit normally in a heroic or divine context, are presented as houses with a temple porch: two columns, typically in antis, an entablature, but no real pediment. One may cite as an example the François Crater (Fig. 38), which, incidentally, is contemporary with the early palaces of Larisa (Cat. 9), where the megaron type dominated (see p. 67).

It is possible, however, that in Athens we still have a surviving indication of how a tyrant's residence might have looked. The regrettable lack of sources for the Peisistratid reign makes it difficult even to be sure where in the city the palace was placed. The acropolis is an obvious choice, since we know that it was initially occupied by Peisistratos, but we have no evidence for a palace there. Perhaps, taking into account Peisistratos' comparative closeness to the people and his popularity in Athens, rather than looking for a fortified palace in the citadel (alongside the patron goddess of the city), we should look for the residence in the centre of main activity during the tyranny, namely the agora (Fig. 39).[157]

The buildings that we know were constructed there in this period are: the house called Building F, beneath the Tholos, and perhaps the complex C and D beneath

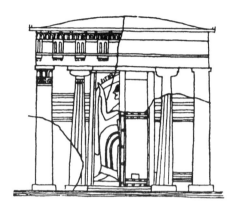

Fig. 38. The François Crater with depiction of a palatial front. (Lawrence 1967, fig. 53.)

the Old Bouleuterion. (This complex surrounds a courtyard and shares a common wall with Building F to the south (Fig. 40)). Also put up were the temples for Zeus Agoraios and Apollon Patroos; a courthouse (the "Helieia"), to the south; perhaps the Royal Stoa; the south-eastern fountain house; and, finally, the Altar of the Twelve Gods. Except for the two last mentioned, all these buildings were placed along the west side of the enormous new square created at this time, undoubtedly primarily in connection with the newly instituted Great Panathenaia (566 BC). As H. von Steuben has shown, these buildings along the western side are placed in a graceful arc, probably flanking the large *orchestra*, which we know dominated the area, and along which ran the Panathenaic street, serving also as a *stadion* (Fig. 39).

If we study the table of functions above (Fig. 1), we can see that all the elements belonging to a royal palace are in fact present here: the official sections (i.e. probably complex C-D, the Royal Stoa, and the "Helieia"), as well as the residence, which may well be identical with the large, but rather irregular Building F, occupying an area of c. 500 m². This was reached from the agora via a porch in the common wall of buildings C, D, and F (Fig. 40). The house itself was built around a courtyard with columns on two sides and flanked by rooms; there were other rooms also to the south and west. Apart from residential use, a banqueting function may be deduced from the two large cooking-pits found to the west of the courtyard; the Tholos complex that replaced this building after the Persian destruction in 480 BC served this purpose as well. The cult function was served

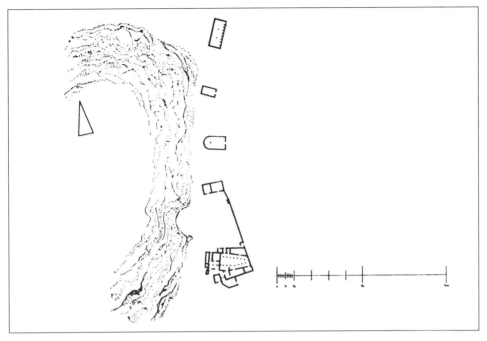

Fig. 39. Athens. Plan of the Agora during the reign of the Peisistratids. (von Steuben 1989, fig. 2.)

by the two temples, and the Altar of the Twelve Gods, probably including Hestia, was invested with the right of asylum, another royal prerogative.

I do not say that this complex was, in fact, a "palace complex", but if the tyrant did indeed reside in this area, the closeness of these different elements to his residence is thought-provoking and may, at least, indicate his control over these institutions. Added to this, various elements for the entertainment of the people, represented by the orchestra and the Panathenaic street/stadium, were related to this complex; and there are indications that the great feast of the Panathenaia was, if not instituted, then at least developed by the tyrants. One might even say that as far as the functional complexity of his palace and its "public" elements is concerned, Peisistratos and his sons anticipated the Hellenistic kings by around 250 years![158]

A second residence on the Athenian Acropolis, close to the tutelary deity, Athena, cannot, of course, be excluded; at least tyrants of other cities resided on the acropolis,[159] but again, we are sadly ill-informed about the residences of most tyrants. Much would be gained for example if we knew how a Polycrates lived in Samos! Taking into account the proximity of Anatolia, the appearance

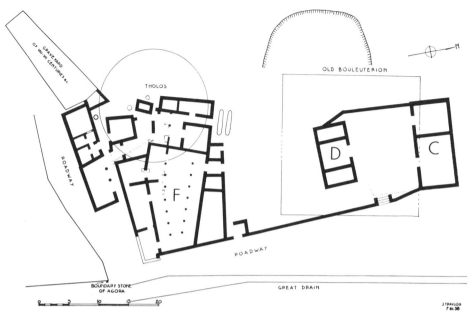

Fig. 40. Athens. Plan of Building F and complex D-C along the west side of the Agora during the reign of the Peisistratids. (Camp 1986, fig. 22.)

of his palace may perhaps be gleaned from the contemporary western Anatolian palaces, e.g. that of Larisa. Thus, a megaron would not have been at all out of place there.

Although these old palaces had disappeared by the time the Hellenistic kings began to build their palaces, the institutions which took over the official functions from the tyrant/king in the poleis, as well as the private houses of the rich, might at least have furnished the new kings with inspiration. In particular, the house-like *prytaneion* seems to have taken over many of these palatial functions. The prytaneion contained both the city hearth and a banqueting room for the *prytaneis*, which was also used for the entertainment of the city's guests; it was invested too with the right of asylum, and was a seat of the administration.[160]

The few prytaneia that have been identified with certainty normally contain a square or rectangular dining-room, with the Tholos of the Athenian Agora as the exception that proves the rule (below). The dining-hall opened onto a courtyard (which may be furnished with porticoes), as did the hearth-room and any other rooms. It is interesting that Building F in the Agora of Athens, here tentatively identified as the residence of the tyrant, agrees quite closely with this picture,

although the right of asylum was, in fact, attached to the Altar of the Twelve
Gods. Furthermore, one of the official functions, that of banqueting and the
reception of guests, was actually, in the form of the Tholos, placed over the old
residence of the tyrant, where one may imagine that many such dinner parties
might once have taken place.

Since a large part of the king's time was spent in the dining-hall, buildings
specifically for this purpose may also be adduced in this connection. One may
mention the banqueting houses, often placed in the sanctuaries, which normally
consisted of a large courtyard with square dining-rooms (compare Labraunda, see
p. 66). Early examples may be found at Argos (Heraion), Brauron, Troizen, and
Epidauros.

Finally, as far as the residential function is concerned, the private houses we
know best are the houses of Olynthus from the 5th-4th centuries BC, and a few
palatial houses in Eretria from the late Classical period. These houses, which were
regular in plan, were centred around one or sometimes even two courtyards. They
did not normally have a megaron or prostas as the main room, but instead the
pastas type was used, with several rooms facing a portico or corridor, which in
turn opened onto a courtyard.[161] Their androne were of the typical Greek
square shape, and two of the large houses in Eretria even had two androne of
different sizes. In Olynthus peristyles began to be introduced into the courtyards
of the finer houses in the early 4th century BC, while they existed from the outset
in the Eretrian houses, which had, moreover, often a smaller court with kitchen,
baths, and bedrooms besides the peristyle one, indicating that these houses, at
least, had both an official and a residential function.

From these buildings, and also from Building F in the Athenian Agora, one
may infer that the main element in future palaces could well be a central court,
invariably furnished with a peristyle, a conclusion that may also be drawn from
the study of preserved palaces elsewhere (above). Since the peristyle court will
also play a very important part in the following discussions, this may be the place
to treat this term in some detail.[162]

That the peristyle was not very familiar to the architects of Classical Greece
is perhaps shown by the ambiguity of the vocabulary. *Peristylos* may mean both
columns surrounding a building (i.e. externally), or placed around a courtyard (i.e.
internally). The confusion is compounded through the adjective's being adopted
as a substantive, a usage which arose in the 4th-3rd centuries BC. The modern
sense of the word, to mean an internal courtyard in a private house, is, in fact,
primarily a Latin adaptation (cf. Vitruvius). Polybius was the first to use it in this

sense, in connection with — and this may be significant — an Achaemenid palace in Media.[163] It may also, as mentioned previously, be used for structures with columns on only three sides.[164] M. Martin has proposed four types of peristyle; I quote his definitions verbatim: "1. La colonnade extérieure enveloppant une cella, type que nous appellerons, pour éviter toute confusion, la *péristasis*; 2. La colonnade et la cour caractéristiques d'un plan de maison défini, privée ou publique, demeure bourgeoise ou Prytanée; 3. L'ensemble des portiques qui entourent une cour associée à un parti plus complexe (gymnases, palestres, téménos etc.), mais considérée comme un élément d'un tout; 4. Les *stoai* enfermant une cour, le tout traité pour lui-même comme un parti architectural indépendant." As far as palaces are concerned, it is primarily type 2 that is of interest, and I may add a fifth type, namely the peristylar forecourt, placed in front of the main building (i.e. there are rooms on only one side, and these are reached through the court via a portal in the opposite side of the court, an arrangement often encountered, for example, in the Persian palaces and in Egyptian architecture). In the following treatment, I shall refer to peristyles of types 2 and 5 only.

The earliest examples of peristyle courts are to be found not in private houses, where, as stated above, they do not occur before the 4th century BC,[165] but in public buildings such as banqueting houses and gymnasia, i.e. Martin's type 3. The earliest example of a peristyle court in Greece in historical times, the "West Building" (probably a banqueting house), in the Heraion of Argos, dated either to the late 6th or late 5th century BC, is, however, a forecourt with rooms on only one side (i.e. type 5). Also in the Pompeion in Athens (c. 400 BC), rooms were almost exclusively placed on one side and the layout still gives the impression of a large forecourt with propylon. Alternatively, one may relate it rather to Martin's type 3. The above-mentioned later banqueting halls, especially those of Troizen and Epidauros, may, on the other hand, be compared more or less directly with the earliest preserved palace of Macedonia, that of Aigai (Fig. 41) (see pp. 81f) and thus belong to type 2. The earliest gymnasium with a peristyle seems to be that at Delphi, from the second half of the 4th century BC, i.e. contemporaneous with the private houses in Eretria.

C. Börker has advanced the theory that independent stoas and peristyles were developed specifically for use in the banqueting houses of sanctuaries, where they are often present.[166] In my opinion, already given above, it is more likely that peristyles of this second type originated in the palaces and were transferred thence to public and private buildings. For already around 500 BC the Palace of Vouni had a peristyle, or rather columns on three sides of the courtyard with a

monumental staircase occupying the fourth; and the Palace of Murlo in Etruria
had a courtyard with porticoes on three sides, and rooms behind them, as early
as the beginning of the 6th century BC (Figs. 29, 32) (see p. 61).

As was probably the case with the peristylar court and forecourt, other public
or religious building-elements may also ultimately go back to palatial architecture.
At least there can be no doubt that the Greek temple type goes back to the royal
meeting hall, the megaron, which also had religious functions. But as we are
dealing with very early times, it is impossible to determine in all cases in which
direction the inspiration for architectural expression travelled. Nor is it that
important as far as the Hellenistic period is concerned. The main thing is to
underline the many possibilities that the newly appointed kings had at their
disposal when they created their palaces.

Sicily

This area was never conquered by the Persians and had been less directly
confronted with Persian culture than Hellas. But there certainly was diplomatic
contact, and there is some indication that the Persian court in fact exerted a certain
direct influence here too. Thus Dionysius I laid out a *paradeisos* with plane trees
in Rhegion, a copy of the large parks belonging to the Persian kings, and Gelon
the tyrant had a famous garden containing an enormous pool with birds and fish
in Acragas, also an allusion to the paradeisos (above).[167]

In Sicily, the tyrants continued to reign until the Hellenistic period, and the
kingdom of Syracuse existed until the Roman conquest in 212 BC. We know that
palaces existed in the cities, but unfortunately none are known archaeologically.
From the written sources, we learn that King Dionysius I built a great palace on
the island of Ortygia at Syracuse in 404 BC. Diodorus tells us that this location
was chosen because it was easy to defend. It was separated from the adjacent city
by a massive wall with towers, and in front of this wall places for business
(*chrematisteria*) and stoas were built which could accomodate many people.
Perhaps they were used by the king for audiences and conducting business. On
the island was a fortified acropolis which probably housed the main palace, and
connected with it was a concealed harbour, Lakkios. There were also living-
quarters for the king's Friends and mercenary soldiers.[168] Unfortunately,
Diodorus does not describe the palatial buildings, but we hear of banqueting rooms
with thirty *klinai* during the reign of Dionysius the Younger.[169] From the letters
of Plato we know that there were large gardens in Dionysius' palace and that these
were divided into various sections with walls.[170] The innermost palace was,

at least in Cicero's time, situated on a small island: that is to say, it was surrounded by a canal spanned by a drawbridge.[171] Certain private houses found in Sicily, though from the early Hellenistic period, might also give an idea of how some of the palatial buildings looked. At any rate, the palatial house from Iato (House I) had a two-storeyed peristyle as well as Macedonian-inspired architectural elements;[172] but as early as during the reign of Dionysius there was close contact with the kingdom of Macedonia, primarily mediated through Epirus, and the "South-Adriatic *koiné*" was already being formed.

The Palace of Syracuse was destroyed by Timoleon, but was restored to even greater splendour by Agathocles in the late 4th century BC. Among other things, an enormous dining-hall called "*hexakontaklinos*" (i.e. the 60-kline hall), was added.[173] The palace was used in Hellenistic times, too, first by the Hellenistic king, Hieron II, later as the residence of the Roman provincial governor, for example the notorious Verres, and at that time it was called *regia maxima*.[174]

No remains of this palace have been found, but it is likely that it was sited between the Sanctuary of Athena, who was probably the tutelary deity, and the Temple of Apollo. Some structures in *opus quadratum*, found along the Via del Littorio, may belong to the palace.[175]

The models which the newly established Hellenistic kings had at their disposal when they built their royal palaces were both numerous and diverse. In the following chapters, the task will be to investigate how they used this heritage, beginning with the Macedonian dynasty, who were palace-dwellers from early on. It was from Macedonia that Alexander the Great began his conquests, and there too all the dynasties of the Diadochi originated.

III. MACEDONIA

Although unfortunately no palaces of the pre-Hellenistic period have been preserved in Macedonia, we know of their existence from the written sources: in the old capital of Aigai, present-day Vergina, a royal palace is indicated before the present one was built, probably in the late 4th century BC; and the palace that King Archelaus built around 400 BC, and which was decorated by Zeuxis, was very likely located at Pella, which became the new capital around that time.[176] Both are probably to be found under the later palaces, and since the present royal palace of Pella, built over a long period, is constructed partly from reused materials, these might well have come from the original palace.[177]

From the Hellenistic period, on the other hand, many palaces, both royal and private, have been found in Macedonia. This is very fortunate, for the royal palaces of this key area must form the point of departure for judging the palaces built in the new Hellenistic kingdoms. Typical features of these royal palaces were a commanding position above the city on a platform or terrace, the presence of a number of courtyards, and an emphasis on the view.[178] All of them were probably demolished or fell out of use after the Roman conquest in 168 BC.

Aigai, although in the Hellenistic period no longer the capital of the Macedonian kingdom, was still an important city and the place where the kings were traditionally buried. Its importance is underlined by the building of a new royal palace, probably in the second half of the 4th century BC; set on a terrace on the northern slope of the acropolis hill, it occupied an elevated position above the town and the plain (Cat. 10; Fig. 41, Pl. 10). Retaining walls supported the terrace and the steep slope above the palace. Built into the slope below the palace was a small theatre dated to the second half of the 4th century BC, the two buildings forming a single architectural unit. If this is the theatre in which Philip II was assassinated,[179] the palace must either have existed at that time, i.e. 336 BC, or have been oriented like the pre-existing theatre.[180]

The approach to the palace was monumental. The conspicuous 10-metre-wide entrance, or propylon, which could be reached via a ramp and faced a large plaza, was placed on the east side and had a pedimented façade of two storeys, flanked by stoas of one or two storeys. While the first storey of the façade had Doric columns, the second was formed by Ionic pillar half-columns resting on a plinth-

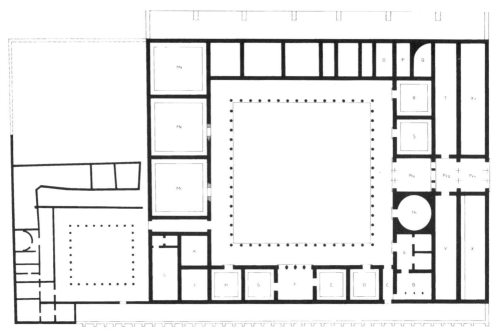

Fig. 41. Vergina/Aigai. Plan of the palace (Cat. 10). (Pandermalis 1976, fig. 1.)

zone, with blind windows of stone in the *intercolumnia* (Fig. 42).[181] The palace consisted of two sections: the main palace, and a peristylar service court to the west, which was only half as wide as the main palace, a planned enlargement to the north never having been carried out. This western part was definitely a later addition, since reused material and roof-tiles belonging to a restoration of the main building were used here. The main palace consisted of a large peristyle court surrounded by rooms on all four sides (Pl. 11). In front of the north wing, facing the city and the theatre, was a large terrace furnished with balustrades that rested on the retaining wall of the platform. Both this and the façade stoa to the east commanded a magnificent view of the land- and townscape (Fig. 42).

As far as the official part of the palace is concerned, one of the most conspicuous rooms is the tholos in the eastern wing (Pl. 12). Its function has been variously interpreted: the first excavators mention supports of marble along the wall and a kind of tribune or base with two steps, probably for a throne, statue, or altar. In addition, the recent discovery of an inscription with a dedication to Heracles has promoted the interpretation of the room as a combined sanctuary and throne-room.[182] Another interpretation, as a dining-room for seated guests,

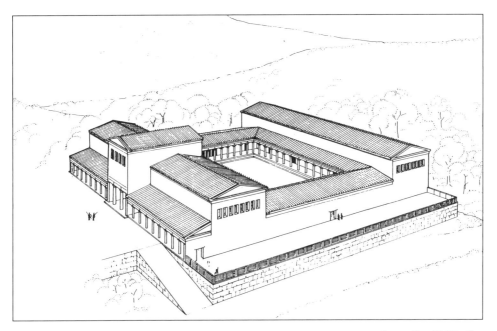

Fig. 42. Vergina/Aigai. Reconstruction of the main palace. (Pandermalis 1987, fig. 17.)

has recently been proposed by F. Cooper and S. Morris.[183] Perhaps one should envisage a multiple use of the room. If this hall was in fact the audience room, the access to it is not actually very impressive, since one would have had to turn sharp left after entering the monumental propylon. Another possibility, already proposed by L. Heuzey, is that the innermost hall of the vestibule could have been used both for audiences and as a waiting-room, with a *vestibulum regale* as an antechamber. As mentioned previously, such vestibules leading to audience halls are also met with elsewhere (e.g. in Ptolemy IV's Nile-barge, see p. 20), and the monumental porch would certainly suit an audience hall.[184]

As for the remaining official rooms, rooms for banquets dominate completely, and no wonder, for banquets, and drinking-parties, as we have seen, played a key role in life at court, not least among the Macedonians.[185] These rooms were used for traditional banquets, with the diners reclining on klinai. The dining-room function is revealed partly by the asymmetrically placed doorway, partly by tesselated bands in the mosaic floor indicating the positions of couches around the walls of the room ("*kline* bands"), and finally by the presence of drains. It is important to point out, however, that neither the presence of an asymmetrically placed doorway, nor that of a drain, is alone sufficient proof of a room's use as a dining-room, whereas the bands indicating klinai, on the other hand, do constitute such a proof (see Pl. 15). The dining-rooms of the southern wing, which, since the rooms were arranged symmetrically around a central axis, probably constituted the main wing, as was normal in Oriental palaces, were placed around an *exedra* with three double half-columns in antis, a Macedonian speciality. The exedra gave access to the two rooms flanking it, so that the three rooms formed an integrated group, which has been the source of some controversy (Pl. 13); I shall return to this below. The outermost rooms of this wing were reached from the peristyle. The west wing is dominated by three large rooms of identical size, without inner supports (each 295 m^2). Even though the thresholds are not preserved, the presence of "kline bands" and drains prove that they served as banqueting halls. In the east wing there are, in addition to the above-mentioned tholos, two dining-rooms opening onto the peristyle. The different sizes and positions of all these banqueting rooms undoubtedly reflect the social status of the various groups of people invited to the royal banquets. One may well imagine that the peristyle contained a formal garden, a view of which could be enjoyed from most of the dining-rooms.

Whether the poorly preserved north wing was official or residential is difficult to decide. The latter may well be the case, as it had direct access to the large terrace with balustrades. Three square rooms (each 115 m^2) and some smaller ones have been traced. Their function is uncertain. The large ones have been tentatively identified as banqueting rooms with room for nineteen klinai each. At any rate, the "*pastas* group" in the east wing, and the second storey of this part of the palace as well as that of the north wing, if present, were probably residential.[186] Thus in this early Hellenistic palace we see a rather close relation between the official and the residential function, which undoubtedly reflects the position of the king at that time.

In Pella, there is a problem as to which buildings should be included in our survey (Fig. 43). There is no doubt that the large palace on the acropolis was the royal palace: it probably already had this function at the time of Philip II, and may originally go back to the foundation of the city by Archelaus (above), although the present complex seems to be the result of rebuilding and enlargement carried out by Philip V. The large palatial houses in the central area of Pella were certainly not used by the king, but rather by his Friends. They were private palaces rather than mere houses, a part of them being definitely reserved for official purposes. Since they date from the late 4th century BC, they may, together with the contemporary palace of Aigai, give some hint of the appearance of the little-

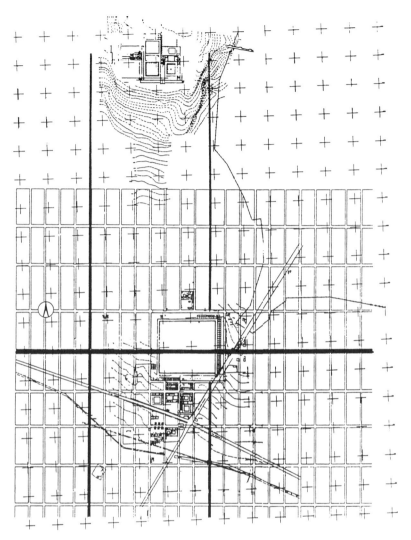

Fig. 43. Pella. General plan of the city. (Siganidou 1987, fig. 1.)

known palace on the acropolis, for at this time the royal palace does not seem to have differed much from the private ones, except in size. I have therefore decided to include the well-preserved private palace Pella I,1 (called the House of Dionysus), while excluding the others — Pella I,3, because of uncertainty as to its function and its poor state of preservation, and Pella I,5 (called the House of Helen), because of its ruinous condition, even though its splendid northern wing with large dining-halls certainly denotes an official function.

The House of Dionysus (Cat. 11) consists of three courtyards axially aligned

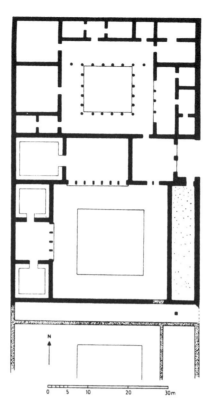

Fig. 44. Pella. Plan of the House of Dionysus, Pella I,1. (Cat. 11). (Lauter 1986, abb. 45a.)

from north to south in a rectangular *insula* (Fig. 44, Pl. 14). The house had a comparatively monumental propylon with a large vestibule towards the east, from which both the northern peristyle, constituting the private apartments, and the central peristyle, with an official function, could be reached. The southernmost courtyard has been only little excavated, but undoubtedly had a service function, as was the case with the western peristyle at Aigai. The poor preservation of the rooms of the residential peristyle precludes a fixed identification of them as, for example, dining-rooms, although V. Heermann gives this function to two rooms, an interpretation based, however, only on asymmetrically placed doorways. The "pastas group" of rooms, for bedrooms, baths, etc., in the east range of the residential court is also found in this position in the Palace of Aigai, as noted above, and perhaps in the "Anaktoron" of Demetrias as well (below).[187] The residential peristyle was in the Ionic style, and the northern portico, at least, had an upper floor with smaller Ionic columns, indicating the presence of a plinth-zone, as known also from Aigai, and from Pella I,3. In fact, it constitutes a feature that is typical of Macedonian architecture.[188]

In the central, official peristyle, two large rooms in the northern wing and one in the western wing had a demonstrable banqueting function, since bands for klinai were found (Pl. 15). The remaining rooms are too poorly preserved for the function to be discernible, but one may imagine guest apartments here, for such rooms were an integral part of the well-appointed Greek house, according to Vitruvius.[189]

At this juncture it would perhaps be appropriate to discuss the so-called "Flügeldreiraumgruppe", a term used by V. Heermann in her treatment of the Macedonian palaces. She regards this as one of their main palatial characteristics, a theory which has won general acceptance. This group consists of (*a*) a central room opening onto the courtyard with columns in antis (in the following called an exedra), and (*b*) two flanking rooms with klinai, opening with asymmetrically placed doorways to the exedra.[190] The problem with this typology is that in only one case has the existence of this group of rooms been clearly demonstrated, namely in the above-mentioned southern wing of the Palace of Aigai (Pl. 13). In every other instance where the group is identified by Heermann, it is at best a matter of interpretation, not of proof. This applies at Aigai, for example, to the three large halls in the western wing, where the central room is identified as an exedra, even though it is furnished with "kline bands" as well as a drain, and to the three westernmost rooms in the northern wing, even though only their foundations are preserved. In the House of Dionysus, Heermann sees a "Flügeldreiraumgruppe" in the three rooms of the western wing of the official peristyle, where there is absolutely no proof that the central room is an exedra, since only its foundations are preserved, and in the southernmost room, neither "kline bands" nor an asymmetrically placed doorway nor a drain have been ascertained.[191]

There are, on the other hand, several indications that many of Heermann's central rooms/exedrae were in fact closed rooms for banquets. One of the arguments which Heermann uses in favour of columns in antis and thus of an exedra is a stronger foundation to the wall facing the court. But, if the large "broad room" in the centre of the northern wing of the House of Helen, which is furnished with "kline bands", be included, this room opens only onto the peristyle with an asymmetrically placed doorway, although the foundations of the wall in question are stronger than in the rooms flanking it. Also the main room in the northern wing of the official part of the House of Dionysus, identified by Heermann as an exedra, even though only its foundations are preserved, had "kline bands" traced in the mosaics and was rather a closed banqueting room. The argument based on the asymmetrically placed doorway leading to the dining-room to the west must work both ways (Pl. 15). There is therefore no reason for an automatic identification of such "broad rooms" as exedrae merely because they have strong foundations towards the peristyle. That the exedra form was, in fact, an exiguous feature of the Macedonian palaces, is supported by their absence in the Palace of Pergamon (Cat. 14), which was strongly influenced by these palaces (see pp. 103ff).

One of the most important buildings to be excavated in Macedonia in recent years is the enormous Royal Palace of Pella, situated on the "acropolis" hill (Cat. 12). Little is known of this palace from the written sources, but Plutarch tells us that it contained a great library, probably already existing in Antigonus Gonatas' time, which the conqueror from Pydna, Aemilius Paullus, gave to his sons.[192] In the same connection, Polybius mentions that the Macedonian kings had large and well-appointed game reserves, probably inspired by the Persian paradeisoi and in general by the Oriental royal penchant for hunting.[193] But whether these hunting-grounds were in the vicinity of the palace is doubtful.

Excavation of this palace is still going on, but the overall layout, with its many courtyards, stoas, and corridors, has already been largely ascertained (Fig. 45), and an area of c. 60,000 m^2 for the entire complex does not seem unlikely. Unfortunately, the structure is seldom preserved above the foundations, and only a little dating material has been found. The palace was probably originally built in the second half of the 4th century BC, perhaps on a plan not very different from that of the Palace of Aigai and the House of Dionysus, and rebuilt and greatly enlarged probably by Philip V, whose scheme involved a terracing of the site towards the south.[194] The complex was built to fit in with the "Hippodamian" plan of Pella and was undoubtedly planned at the same time as the city (Fig. 43). It was flanked to the east and west by long streets and to the north was bounded by the city wall.[195] To the east, a theatre was probably dug into the slope, and, although hardly on the same axis as the palace, was nevertheless undoubtedly associated with the complex. It may well have been here that Euripides had his plays performed during his stay at Archelaus' court (see n. 176). A similar combination of palace and theatre in Aigai comes to mind.

The present complex seems to have consisted of two main sections, of which

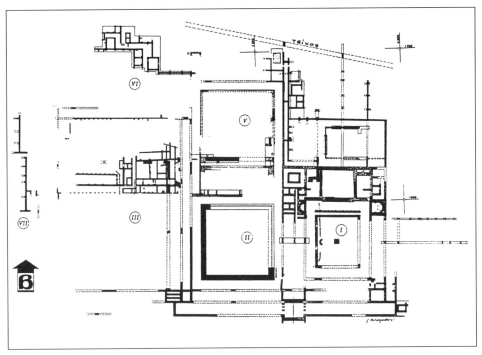

Fig. 45. Pella. Plan of the Royal Palace (Cat. 12). 1:3000. (Siganidou 1987, fig. 2.)

the eastern one, with four courtyards, constituted the main palace. The southern and most easily accessible part, peristyles I and II, probably built by Philip V, was for official purposes, while the northern part, peristyles IV and V, was undoubtedly residential. To the west, and separated by means of a long corridor from the eastern section, lay a large peristyle court (III), and an area to the north (VI), and west (VII), with smaller rooms, probably for service, administration, etc.

The official part of the palace had a commanding façade to the south and facing the city and consisting of a portico resting on a high terrace wall. In the middle was an appropriately monumental propylon with columns, which could be reached from the city by a broad ramp and gave access to a large vestibule. There was also undoubtedly another entrance from the east street, via a large forecourt. Peristyle I is the best preserved and constituted the most important part òf the palace. It had two storeys (Fig. 46); the lower columns were of the Doric order, while the upper storey had smaller Ionic columns, doubtless originally resting on a plinth-zone. At least on the northern side, the two-storeyed portico was only

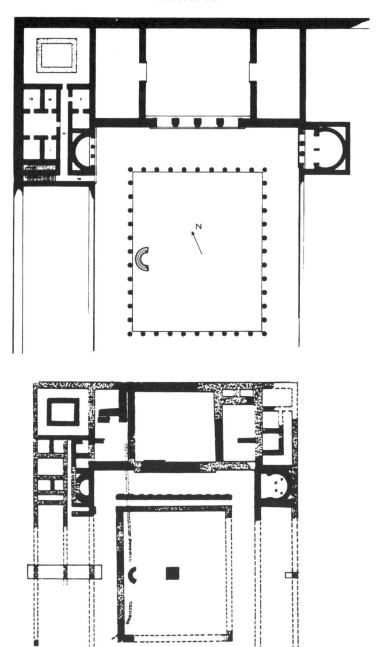

Fig. 46. Pella. A restored plan (above, after V. Heermann) and an excavation plan (below, after M. Siganidou) of Peristyle I of the Royal Palace. (Schmidt-Colinet 1991, Abb. 1a-b.)

a façade, the large rooms behind it reaching up through both storeys. The peristyle was probably furnished with a garden, as was the case in the houses of Dionysus and Helen, and perhaps also in the Palace at Aigai.

The large rooms of the north wing, which were fronted by a deeper portico than the others, were the most important ones (Pl. 16). Two "deep rooms" (Langräume) flanked a very large "broad room", with stronger foundations towards the yard than those of the other rooms. The monumentality of this range is underlined by the emphatic symmetry and in general by its axiality in relation to the peristyle. Heermann identifies it with a "Flügeldreiraumgruppe" solely on the grounds of symmetry and the above-mentioned strong foundation of the central room, for only the foundations of this wing are preserved. The two lateral rooms apparently had some kind of partition walls. These "deep rooms" have some affinities with the megaron, but this is probably a coincidence.

In my opinion, the most probable means of entry to all three rooms was through openings to the peristyle (without intercommunicating doorways), as is the case in the contemporaneous Palace of Pergamon (Fig. 52). The large central "broad room" probably had columns in front, but it may also have been a closed room, as in Pergamon. In this hall, fragments of a splendid scheme of wall decoration have been found, e.g. a stone plinth and fragments of three-quarter columns, which perhaps flanked niches for statues. One may imagine a decoration in two registers. This is probably the first example of interior decoration in stone known outside the sanctuaries, where it had been used in Macedonian buildings of the second half of the 4th century BC, namely in the Philippeion at Olympia and the Arsinoeion on Samothrace, both a kind of dynastic *heroon*.

As for the function of these rooms, the central one was undoubtedly used both as an audience and council hall, and perhaps as a banqueting hall as well. The latter function may also have been fulfilled by the lateral rooms, although a library is also a possibility. There is in this arrangement a clear development from the Palace of Aigai as regards the approach to the king. The enormous size (see Fig. 114) and lavish decoration of the audience hall alone denote an enhancement of the role of the king in relation to his subjects, and the placing of the hall at the far end of the main axis is known from palaces belonging to "absolute" monarchs. Also, one may well imagine that the very large Peristyle II to the west was used for major receptions, and compare it to the Megiston Peristylon of Alexandria (see p. 20).

Another element which may denote a change in the type of monarchy is the presence of two rounded rooms, to the east and west of the northern portico of

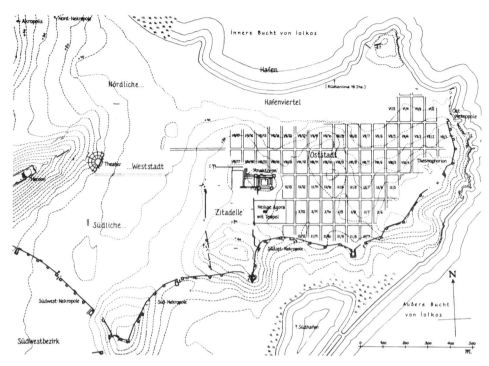

Fig. 47. Demetrias. General plan of the city. (Lauter 1986, Abb. 8.)

Peristyle I, respectively (Pls. 17-18). The possible function of these rooms has attracted much attention from scholars, and their use as a sanctuary as well as to display statues of the royal dynasty, a kind of dynastic sanctuary, has been proposed, although no statue bases have been preserved *in situ*.[196]

As far as the residential part of the palace is concerned, the two northern peristyles (IV and V) of the eastern section were undoubtedly used for that purpose. The investigations of recent years have done much to clarify this point. It seems that this part of the palace goes back to the 4th century BC. The two peristyles were flanked by rooms of which we do not know much, since only the northern wing of Peristyle V has been excavated in depth, revealing a bath complex with a small swimming-pool and heated rooms (Pl. 19). Large rooms were found in this wing, too. The excavators have proposed that this peristyle is a palaestra, which is possible, but a bathhouse belonging to the residence may be nearer the truth. In this case, the large courtyard may well have included a formal garden.

We do not know much about the service and administrative, perhaps also the defensive part of the palace; it occupied its western section with the large courtyard to the south, and took up a very large area in comparison with the corresponding section of the Aigai Palace, for example. But of course the Royal Palace of Pella, being the main palace and situated, as it was, in the capital, would obviously have been equipped with many more functions than a comparatively minor palace such as Aigai.

The last palace in Macedonia to be dealt with here is that of Demetrias (Cat. 13). This city was, from its foundation by Demetrius Poliorchetes at the beginning of the 3rd century BC, the second city of Macedonia after Pella. The palace was originally planned at the same time as the city itself, but only partly followed the Hippodamian plan (Fig. 47). The fortified palace that survives from Philip V's time is not the original one, a badly preserved precursor having been found beneath it. As at Pella, the complex was built partly of reused materials.

The palace was situated close to the citadel, on a hill with fine views in every direction. It was raised c. 7 m above the Sacred Agora, which the terrace in front of the southern façade overlooked (Fig. 48). The palace was probably reached from the agora via a ramp to a portal placed between the two easternmost courtyards of the three which constitute the present palace, an arrangement with close affinities to the contemporary enlargement of the Royal Palace of Pella. However, the area reached from the propylon in Demetrias in fact constituted a terrace in front of the west façade of the main palace, the courtyards to the west being placed at a lower level.

The main and best-preserved section of the palace had four corner-towers which dominated the building and endowed it with a defensive character that was underlined by the proximity of the citadel.[197] It had a peristyle court in Rhodian form, with two storeys on all sides except the northern one, and was reached via a small vestibule at the south-west corner. The general impression is that of a less monumental plan than the official Peristyle I of Pella.

As far as the functions of the individual rooms are concerned, it is problematic that the north wing, undoubtedly the main one, is so badly preserved.[198] Since most of the rooms of the other wings have their doorways placed asymmetrically, they might have been dining-rooms, although this is far from certain (above). The largest preserved rooms are two axially placed "broad rooms" in the west and east wings, respectively. The east room is the larger and may be interpreted as an audience hall, albeit of moderate size, if this was not in fact situated in the northern wing. The western room is certainly an exedra, with two double half-columns in antis, like the only safely identified exedra in the Palace of Aigai (Pl.

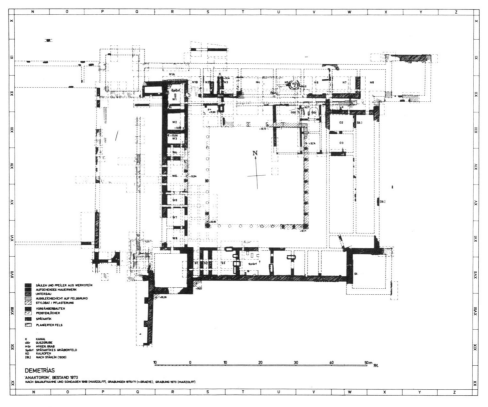

Fig. 48. Demetrias. Plan of the main court and part of the west court with the terrace of the palace (Cat. 13). (Lauter 1986, Abb. 46.)

13). From this western exedra there is a door to a room to the north, while the door to the south has been reconstructed so as to form a "Flügeldreiraumgruppe". The east wing has a double row of rooms, which made P. Marzolff see an apartment for guests; another possibility is an identification as private living-quarters for the king and his family. Perhaps the "broad room" mentioned above is in fact a "pastas corridor" instead. Also, the first floor of the western, eastern, and southern wings was undoubtedly for private use, as was probably the case in Aigai; so also were the upper floors of the towers, perhaps constituting a kind of pavilions (*diaitai*).

Summary
Some of the main characteristics of the Hellenistic royal palaces of Macedonia — their elevated position on hills and terraces, the emphasis on impressive

Fig. 49. Lefkadhia. The Great Tomb. Reconstruction of the facade. (Lauter 1986, Taf. 48.)

approaches, and their monumental propyleia and façades — are features typical of most of their precursors as well. As we have seen, façade and approach played a major role in royal palace architecture in the East, and these elements were, together with the decoration of the façade, of great importance in enhancing the prestige of the king. It is probably no coincidence that monumental façades turn up for the very first time in the West in the kingdom of Macedonia, more precisely in the east façade of the Palace of Aigai. The great affinity between this façade, particularly its propylon, and the façades of Macedonian chamber-tombs, especially that of the contemporary impressive Tomb of Lefkadhia (Fig. 49), supports the view that palace façades, with their porticoes (and, not least, their porches, the *portae regiae*, often leading to large vestibules and audience halls), served as a model for the royal tombs, as was the case in Achaemenid architecture.[199]

Moreover, since the tomb façades are decorated with paintings, both on friezes and behind the columns, one might argue that the same applies to palatial façades. Perhaps this is one of the places where one should expect depictions of the otherwise missing royal themes, such as audience and hunting scenes. At any rate, a hunting scene is rendered on the attic frieze of the so-called Tomb of Philip. In this connection one might also draw attention to the much later Second Style paintings, for instance in the villas of Boscoreale and Boscotrecase in Campania, which show a similar placement of figures in an architectural setting. Also, theatrical façades may help to elucidate the appearance of the Hellenistic palaces (see p. 19).[200]

Another feature typical of the Macedonian palaces is their compact layout, with large courtyards placed one beside the other, but with different functions. And again, a precedent can be found. Already Minoan and Mycenaean palaces had been planned in that manner, and in the Orient this layout had long been in use, with the Neo-Babylonian palaces and the Palace of Darius at Susa as the most recent examples. Such courtyards, now furnished with peristyles, were also the main feature in the Palace of Vouni (Cat. 8), as well as in the late Classical houses in Eretria. But innovative in connection with these Macedonian peristyles were the two-storeyed porticoes with plinth-zones carrying smaller columns in the upper storey, a feature which first appeared in the early Hellenistic private palaces of Pella. As to their origin, there has been much discussion concerning their relation to the two-storeyed stoa and the direction in which the inspiration went.[201] I think it not unlikely that they had their origin in palatial façades, for at Aigai we have a two-storeyed portico in the propylon of the façade, but not yet in the peristyle. In general, it was probably more often than not the royal architecture which set the trend for public/secular architecture.

Finally, enclosed gardens, in the courtyards, seem to have been widely used in Macedonian palaces. They may have been an importation from the East, where gardens were an important feature of royal palace architecture. Also the gardens of Greek gymnasia and sanctuaries may have made some impact, though generally these gardens were not placed in courtyards, but rather around the outside of the buildings.

A feature that is certainly foreign to the Oriental precursors is the close connection with the city theatre, which may be partly due to the fact that both palaces and theatres are traditionally placed on a hill or hillside; but as the proximity to or even inclusion of "public" buildings became one of the most typical features of Hellenistic basileia, the development might well have started in Macedonia.

Of the individual rooms and halls, the most characteristic and easy to recognize are those for banqueting. Architecturally, they have some affinities with the dining-rooms in the banqueting houses of the Greek sanctuaries,[202] which might originally have been inspired by local palaces, at least as far as their appearance is concerned (see p. 77). The large number of dining-rooms, especially in the early palaces, is an indication of the great importance of the banquet in Macedonian court life, a feature also mentioned by the ancient authors (see p. 21).

This social function in which the king ate and drank with his subjects in contrast to the Great King, who normally dined alone, isolated behind a curtain, is a reflection of the different status of the Macedonian king. The lack of an established canon of ceremonial architecture, i.e. for audience halls, in the early Hellenistic palaces, may support this interpretation. Although there is no doubt that there had already been moves towards a more "Asiatic" absolutist monarchy during the reigns of Philip II and not least of Alexander the Great, this position was apparently relinquished at least by the early Antigonids, according to E.N. Borza, and the appearance of the Palace of Aigai may support this view.[203]

There were definitely indications of something happening in this connection when Philip V, the king who began to seek his Friends outside his kingdom (see p. 18), greatly enlarged and monumentalized his main palace of Pella. This palace may thus illustrate a development both in architecture and function of the palace of the Macedonian kings, with a distinct shift from the *primus inter pares* palaces originally built in Aigai and Pella, perhaps by Philip II or the first Hellenistic kings, to a palace worthy of an "absolute" Hellenistic monarch. Philip V's building acitivities involved an impressive enlargement of the palace towards the south, necessitating extensive terracing works and a general monumentalization that included a very long and magnificent façade with a protruding columnar propylon in the centre, facing the city. Another of Philip V's creations was a purely ceremonial peristyle, from which the residential part of the palace was entirely separate. As mentioned above, terraces, approaches, and impressive engineering work were some of the means used by earlier monarchs, including the Great King, to emphasize their elevated position in relation to their subjects.

In this palace there is no doubt at all which room is the main one, namely the enormous hall (400 m^2 and two storeys high) placed in the north wing behind a deep portico, at the apex of the main axis of the two-storeyed peristyle. This "broad room", which was the main audience hall, could compete in size with the

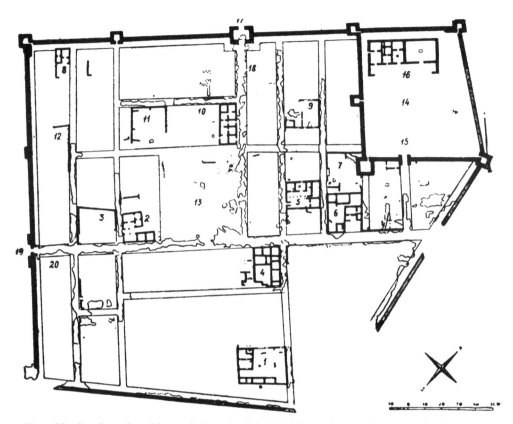

Fig. 50. Seuthopolis. Plan of the citadel (14-16) and its placement in the town. (Lauter 1986, Abb. 7.)

main halls of many models (see Fig. 114). It may have been used for banquets as well, but this was not its main purpose. The elaborate interior decoration in stone reminds one of the literary descriptions of marble-panelled dining halls (see p. 22). This decorative scheme, which was probably borrowed from sacred architecture (as were the pediments often used in royal architecture), acted as a further enhancement to the prestige of the hall and its owner. The two apsidal rooms flanking the portico may have served partly as dynastic, partly as tutelary, sanctuaries, and the long plinth placed in the portico may well have carried dynastic statues. All these new features point in the same direction, towards an absolute monarchy. The palace rebuilt by the same king in the second capital, Demetrias, is more modest, but the approach was still monumental, and the tetrapyrgion model, although a result of political necessity, would certainly have made an impression and commanded respect as well.

To judge from the Royal Palace of Pella, the monarchy of Macedonia thus underwent an important development between the time of Philip II and the early Hellenistic kings and that of Philip V, signifying increasing inspiration from the "personal kingdoms" of the Attalids, and especially the Seleucids and the Ptolemies.

Although only Hellenistic palaces are preserved, one has to remember that palaces had existed as long as the monarchy itself in Macedonia, and much of what we see in Aigai may well have been taken over from the earlier palace. The affinities to Oriental palaces should not surprise us, for Alexander the Great was far from being the first to come in close contact with the great empire to the east. Already the Macedonian king Amyntas I had been a vassal king under Darius I, or had at least an alliance with him, and the sojourn of the Persians in Macedonia and Thrace during and after their wars with the Greeks undoubtedly also made its mark, as did the Persian refugees at the Macedonian court. Generally, the eastern models, for palaces as well as gardens, are often overlooked in favour of the Greek models such as the Eretrian houses, the gymnasia, and the banqueting houses,[204] and of course, one should not underestimate the influence of Greek architecture on the palaces of these normally philhellene kings. Thus the architectural decoration and columnar orders bear witness to inspiration both from the Peloponnese and from Western Asia Minor. But the dimensions of the Macedonian palaces are truly regal, and certain aspects of their architecture are utterly foreign to Greek architectural traditions. Just as the word "eclectic" is often used in connection with Macedonian culture in general, so it is also fitting for palace architecture that draws upon Oriental, local, and Greek precursors as models; though the result is typically Macedonian.

Thrace and the Crimea

Two princely palaces have been excavated in the area north of Macedonia, one in Seuthopolis in Thrace, i.e. in the sphere of direct Macedonian influence, the other in Panticapeion in the Crimea, belonging to the Bosporan kingdom.

The Thracian palace in Seuthopolis (Fig. 50), the capital of a local principality, was built by Seuthes III in the late 4th century BC, i.e. at the same time as the palaces of Pella and Aigai.[205] The city was laid out according to Hippodamian principles, and the palace, located in a fortified area on the north-eastern fringe of the town, adhered to this city plan. The palace proper stood back in the citadel, the propylon of which was on the same axis as the palace, thus making the approach an impressive one. The palace itself is rather simple and unpretentious:

it had no peristyle, since it consisted of only one range (40 x 17 m = 680 m^2) with two storeys. The ground floor had a single row of rooms which all opened onto a stoa fronted by a large paved forecourt.

The main "broad room" took up almost the entire eastern half of the building and had a large stuccoed cult-hearth in the centre.[206] On the walls, fragments of stuccoed decoration are preserved. As the door of the hall was apparently placed asymmetrically, one may well imagine that this room was used both for audiences and banquets. The room to the west of this main room had a smaller cult-hearth, and an inscription found *in situ* proclaims that it was a sanctuary for the Great Gods from Samothrace, undoubtedly the tutelary deities of the king. The remaining rooms in the building, including the upper floor, were private living-quarters. One may remark that the megaron form was not used in this palace, nor was this the case in the Macedonian palaces. Both city and palace were probably destroyed during the Celtic invasion of the Balkans in 280-277 BC.

The second palace, in Panticapeion, has been excavated recently, and work is still going on.[207] The palace belonged to the Spartacidian dynasty and was built in the third quarter of the 4th century BC, being set on the acropolis, the so-called Mithridates Hill, of which it occupied the western part; the higher, eastern part was taken up by sanctuaries. The entire hill was fortified with a strong wall, and the two parts were separated by another wall. All the same, there is a close connection between fortification, palace, and temples.

The main palace measures c. 40 x 40 m = c. 1,600 m^2 and consists of an open court with rooms on three sides, including at least one dining-room. Towards the north, on the other side of a paved path running alongside the building, is a small temple and a larger building. The monumental entrance to the palace is towards the south and is flanked by two square towers (i.e. it is a dipyrgion). The courtyard was paved and had a two-storeyed peristyle, the lower columns in the Doric style, the upper in the Ionic with balustrades filling the intercolumnia.[208] The water supply, as was natural, had a high priority; there is a large reservoir in the courtyard, as well as a well and a large pool (5 x 5 m, 3 m deep) placed in the very deep eastern portico. The main wing with the largest rooms was the northern one, and there were smaller rooms in the western and eastern wings. Owing to the poor state of preservation, no doorways have been found, and the function of the rooms remains uncertain. The palace was rebuilt around 200 BC, perhaps in connection with a change of dynasty, according to V. Tolstikov.

There is no difficulty in placing this palace in a wider context that includes the contemporaneous palaces of Aigai and Seuthopolis. In addition, there are similari-

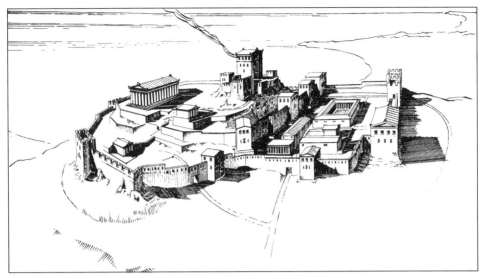

Fig. 51. Panticapeion. Reconstruction of the acropolis as it looked in the 3rd to 2nd century BC. (Tolstikov 1989, fig. 11.)

ties to the Palace of Pergamon (below), which was, however, not built until later. The close relation to the Macedonian palaces is underlined by the absence of the prostas (megaron) type of house in this area; instead houses of the pastas type predominate.[209] There is thus no resemblance to the late palace of Larisa from more or less the same period, which is dominated by the megaron form, although, if one accepts the Bit-Hilani façade of the late Archaic palace, the similarity to the dipyrgion façade of Panticapeion is great. Moreover, in the Palace of Panticapeion, pebble mosaics and fragments of paintings in the First Style from the 3rd century BC were found, elements that point to Macedonia. The combination on the acropolis of sanctuaries, palace, and fortifications, on the other hand, points in the direction of Anatolia, and the reconstructed layout of the Acropolis of Panticapeion made by the Russian excavators shows clear associations with both Larisa and Pergamon, especially the latter (Fig. 51).

IV. PERGAMON

Since no early Hellenistic palaces have been preserved in western Anatolia, the Palace of Pergamon (Cat. 14), built in the first half of the 2nd century BC, constitutes our only source for palace architecture in this area. True, Vitruvius mentions a palace called *domus regibus attalicis*, built in sun-dried brick by the Pergamene kings at Tralles, but nothing is preserved.[210]

The Pergamene kings had Macedonian roots, for Philetaerus' father bore the Macedonian name of Attalus, although coming from the Black Sea coast of Asia Minor. In their 150 years of supremacy, beginning when Attalus I took the title of king, they ruled over a population consisting mostly of Phrygians and Lydians, with a small admixture of Greeks. It is worth remembering that the Attalid kingdom was of the "personal" type, like the Seleucid and the Ptolemaic kingdoms, rather than of the "national" type, known from Macedonia. On the other hand, the Attalids were basically hellenophile in outlook, their ambition being to make Pergamon a new Athens and a centre of Greek culture. Also, their kingdom was small and well-defined, and this ensured a close relationship with their subjects.[211]

The royal palace was situated on a fortified acropolis together with the most important temples and some public buildings. This commanding position, created by means of a system of terraces with monumental substructures, made the palace complex highly visible and impressive (Pl. 20).

There has been some uncertainty as to which of the buildings on the acropolis belonged to the palace proper, since H. Schleif's 1932 reconstruction of a row of peristyle houses along the eastern side is not correct in every respect (Fig. 52).[212] The earliest palace of the Attalids was perhaps the northernmost structure, called "Baugruppe or Palast I" by the excavators (Fig. 53). Only a little remains of this, the building having been later replaced by another, but elements belonging to a large peristyle court with rooms and halls on most or all of its sides are preserved. Also, there have been suggestions that the main palace of the Attalids was, in fact, buried beneath the Trajaneum, and that the peristyle houses, which are rather modest in size, were used by the aristocracy only. Nothing in the recent excavations in the Trajaneum has so far supported this view, and the buildings found there rather indicate a service quarter; hopefully, further work in the area

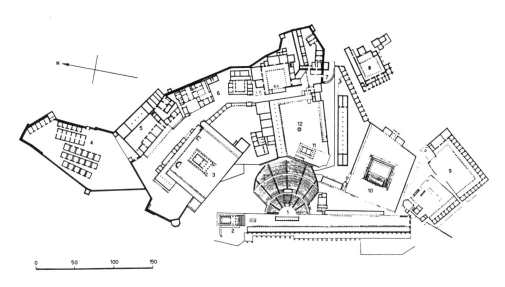

Fig. 52. Pergamon. General reconstructed plan of the acropolis (Cat.14) (by H. Schleif). (EAA s.v. Pergamon fig. 39.). 1. Theatre; 2. Temple of Dionysus; 3. Trajaneum; 4. Arsenal; 5. Barracks; 6. Palaces; 7. Entrance to the citadel; 8. Heroon; 9. Upper Agora; 10. Altar of Zeus; 11. Temple of Athena; 12. Temenos of Athena.

will bring clarification.[213] We are on safe ground only with the two southernmost buildings, the so-called "Baugruppe or Palast IV and V", both typical peristyle houses. These palaces date from the first half of the 2nd century BC.

The state of preservation of these buildings is very poor, but it may, all the same, be established that neither of them was axially or symmetrically laid out, elements that were normally used to create monumentality. The reason may lie in the morphology of the site, as well as in the position of earlier buildings, even though some were torn down to give room for Palace V.[214] The area of these palaces was limited by the acropolis wall to the east, and towards the south by the barracks for the guard ("Baugruppe VI"), while to the west the principal thoroughfare of the acropolis separated the palaces from the public buildings.

In general, Palace IV is considered to have been built before Palace V, which was almost certainly built by Eumenes II, since a discarded block from the Altar of Zeus, also built by him, was used in this palace. The argument for this slight

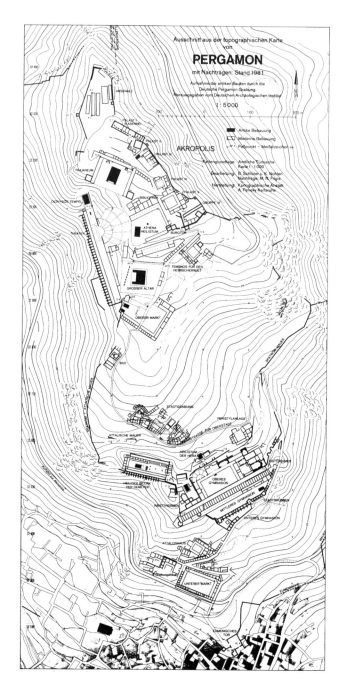

Fig. 53. Pergamon. General plan of the excavations. (Filgis & Radt 1986, Taf. 57.)

difference in age is based on the north wing of Palace V being adapted to the south wing of Palace IV, which, however, may merely indicate that IV was built before V, but during the same general building phase. The excavators, in fact, have not detected any great difference in age between them and date them both to the reign of Eumenes II. I find it most likely, therefore, that the two buildings belonged to the same complex and had different functions, the smaller, Palace IV, being used as a residence for the king, the larger, Palace V, for official purposes, a feature also known from Macedonia.

Palace IV had a paved courtyard surrounded by a peristyle, of which no column fragments have been found, though sockets cut in the underlying rock prove its existence (Fig. 54). The rooms on the western side and a large part of those on the south have disappeared. Fortunately most of the remaining rooms have their thresholds preserved, showing that they all opened onto the peristyle and were not interconnected. None of them were exedrae. The main wing was probably the northern one, where the rooms were largest and the portico deepest. Only the function of the eastern room has been ascertained. It had a very fine decoration in the First Style, with half-columns in stucco in the uppermost register and a rendering of ashlars below. Moreover, there was a mosaic floor with traces of a band in relatively coarse white tesserae around a central mosaic, which, like all the mosaics found in these palaces, was of a very high quality. This band and the fact that the room was square with the doorway placed asymmetrically make its function as a dining-room certain.

The largest room, located on the eastern side, is normally called a sanctuary, owing to the presence of an altar, which, however, was probably only placed there at a later stage. In its first phase, the room had fine mosaics and a channel along the north side, which might indicate that it was originally a banqueting hall as well. The remaining rooms in the east wing were used as living-rooms and bedrooms, etc. Perhaps the portico in front of them was partly closed, making a kind of "pastas group". Such groups also existed in the Macedonian palaces and afforded the king some privacy (above). Since this building probably had two storeys, the second one presumably had a residential function as well.

The official Palace V was, as was usual, the most monumental and had the finest decoration (Fig. 55). The dimensions were regal, the area being twice that of Palace IV. The square peristyle court had Doric stone columns, but there is no trace of a pavement. There were rooms only on three sides of the yard, there being none to the west. In the south wing, which is very poorly preserved, there was undoubtedly a monumental propylon with a staircase leading to it from the

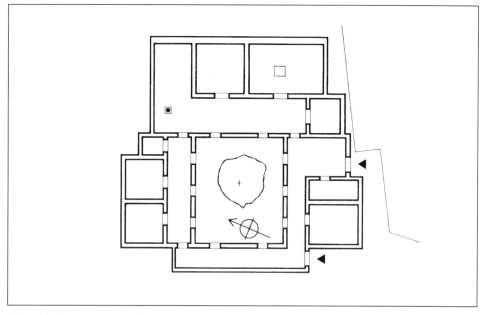

Fig. 54. Pergamon. Palace IV, reconstructed plan of the residential palace. 1:480. (Pinkwart & Stemmnitz 1984, Abb. 15a.)

area just inside the acropolis gate. The north wing was probably the main one, as usual, although the portico in front of it was not very deep.

One would certainly have expected a symmetrical layout here, but this is not the case. The largest room has a preserved threshold showing that it opened via a wide portal (2.39 m) onto the yard. The floor has disappeared, but part of the wall decoration may be reconstructed: it consisted of polychrome marble elements with socle, orthostats, etc., and an upper register probably in stucco. The room beside this had the same kind of marble decoration, and here part of the mosaic floor is preserved, and signed with the artist's name, Hephaistion. A broad white border surrounding the central motif indicates its use as a banqueting room (Fig. 56). The large room might have had the same function, but might also have been used exclusively as an audience hall (cf. Pella, p. 91).

In the east wing, the thresholds of the three northernmost rooms have been preserved. One room served as a small sanctuary and was furnished with the same kind of wall decoration as that of the northern rooms, and with a very fine mosaic floor. The remaining rooms on the east side and the poorly preserved ones in the southern wing were probably mostly banqueting rooms, their doors being placed

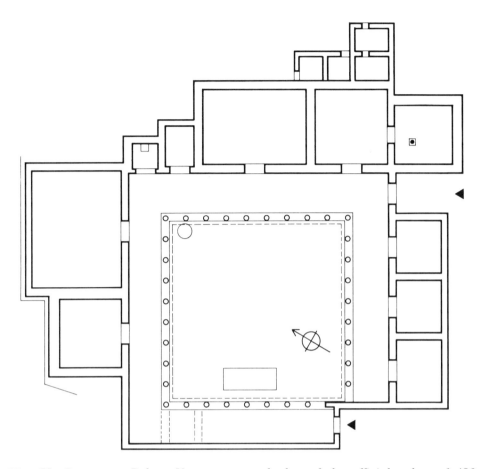

Fig. 55. Pergamon. Palace V, reconstructed plan of the official palace. 1:480. (Pinkwart & Stemmnitz 1984, Abb. 15b.)

asymmetrically. Behind the rooms facing the courtyard were small rooms, probably for service. This palace had undoubtedly two storeys, like the palaces of Macedonia and the contemporary private Pergamene houses. Since no pavement has been found in the peristyle, one might suggest a garden here; there are several cisterns in the building.

One notes the absence of a megaron element, which was present in the neighbouring Palace of Larisa (Cat. 9), in Labraunda, and in the prostas houses of Priene, indicating a wide use of megara in this area previously. Perhaps the structures of "Baugruppe III" in Pergamon itself might include an early megaron also (see n. 212). But on the whole, it seems that by the 2nd century BC this

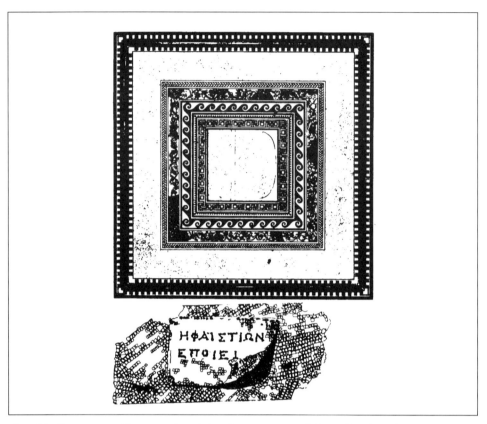

Fig. 56. Pergamon. The mosaic of the dining-room of the official Palace V, now in the Antikensammlung in Berlin. (Radt 1973, taf. 4.)

room-form that had been popular for official purposes had been abandoned in favour of the "broad room", perhaps on account of growing influence from Macedonia. The apparent lack of exedrae is surprising, largely because of the presence of this room type in the rich palatial houses near the Lower Agora, which rival the palaces in size. Exedrae are found, for example, in the west wing of the House of Consul Attalus, as well as in the main northern wings of Houses I and II (Fig. 57).[215] On the other hand, the existence of exedrae has very seldom been proved in the Macedonian palaces (see above). The peristyles of the houses near the Lower Agora were in two storeys, and here a lower order in the Doric style and an upper one in the Ionic style have been ascertained, making a similar

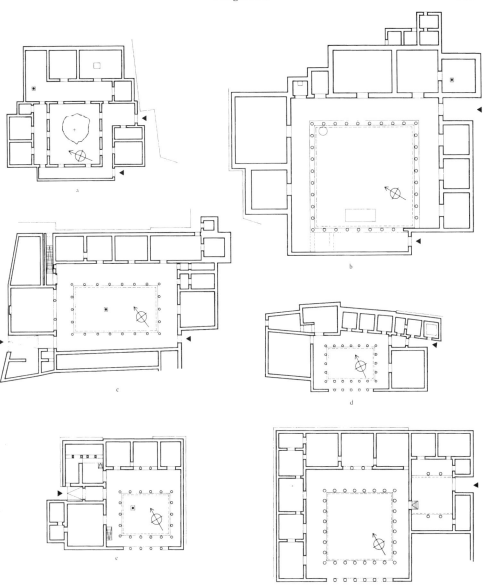

Fig. 57. Pergamon. Comparison of royal palaces (a-b) and palatial houses. (Pinkwart & Stemmnitz 1984, Abb. 15.)

arrangement very likely also in the peristyles of Palaces IV and V. Such peristyles, as well as the interesting arrangement of open porticoes with a view, built on the

southern sides of these houses, again show associations with Macedonian
architecture.[216]

The models for these Pergamene palatial buildings should probably be sought
primarily in Macedonia. A close parallel is to be found in the only slightly earlier
Royal Palace of Pella (Cat. 12), which shows clear affinities not only in layout,
but also in decoration, with the main hall of the official Peristyle I, which has
a marble embellishment very similar to that of Pergamon.

But in addition to the two palatial buildings, the Palace of Pergamon consisted
of many other elements, all placed on or close to the acropolis (Pl. 20). Of these,
among the most important is the Temenos of Athena Nicophorus, which was
embellished first sculpturally by Attalus I, and later architecturally by Eumenes
II. The latter thus surrounded the large court with porticoes of two storeys, except
on the west side where the temple was situated; this was placed asymmetrically
to the axis of the square, and here the landscape formed the backdrop. This
monumental temenos probably had a close resemblance to the great official
courtyards of Alexandria, and one can easily imagine large receptions taking place
here, with the king surrounded by his and his predecesssors' *anathemata*. The
impressive propylon, now restored in Berlin, would certainly have added to the
solemnity of the approach, and may also help us to envisage the vanished
propyleia of other royal palaces (Pl. 21).

Besides official and religious functions, the Temenos of Athena had other
functions related to the palace: to fulfil the intellectual and cultural ambitions of
the Attalids, the famous library was accomodated on the first floor of the northern,
double stoa, and in another hall behind the main stoa, there was probably a
museum of art, for statues from many periods have been found there. Finally the
temenos evidently housed an administrative sector too, since many inscriptions
reveal the presence of state archives in this area.

The general aspect of the temenos is perhaps informative too. Its stoas in two
storeys, the lower columns Doric and the upper Ionic, the balustrades with reliefs
between the upper columns, and finally the decoration of the back walls with
marble socles and paintings may all furnish a hint as to the possible appearance
both of the peristyles of Palaces IV and V in Pergamon, and of the almost contemporaneous official Peristyle I in Pella.

Various other palatial functions were also fulfilled on the acropolis. For
defensive purposes, the acropolis was at the same time a citadel, and there was
a large arsenal, as well as barracks for the guard. In addition to the main temple
of the city, that of Athena, a Temple of Dionysus, the tutelary deity of the dynasty,

was located near the palace, close beside a "public" building, namely the theatre. Finally, just outside the citadel lay the Heroon of the Attalid dynasty, and also the Upper Agora, which probably had administrative functions as well (Fig. 52).

All in all, one may find the inspiration for this Pergamene "palace complex" in many different places. For the complex as a whole, one should look first and foremost to Alexandria and perhaps Antiochia (below). But as mentioned above, there are also close affinities with Macedonia as far as the peristylar layout is concerned, and the royal palaces of Aigai and probably Pella included a theatre as well. Finally, the close connection with the cults of the city, in particular the city's deity Athena, and the very situation, on the acropolis, together with the complicated terraced construction of the whole, should be regarded as a heritage from the local western Anatolian palaces.

V. THE SELEUCID KINGDOM

After the struggle between Alexander's successors, the Seleucids emerged as the masters of a vast kingdom. To control it, the Seleucid kings had to travel continually, and they took with them to their various palaces not only the court, but also a limited bureaucracy. Some of the palaces they built themselves, in the new capitals of Antiochia and Seleucia on the Tigris, others, like those of Sardis, Babylon, Ecbatana, and Susa (both that of Darius and Artaxerxes), could be taken over from their Achaemenid predecessors without many changes. Also, many governors' palaces were built, while undoubtedly others were again taken over from the Persians.[217] However, most of these palaces were lost to the Parthians, together with the eastern part of the kingdom in the 2nd century BC, leaving only the Royal Palace of Antiochia and some governors' palaces in the hands of the Seleucids.[217a]

Royal palaces

The royal palaces in Seleucia on the Tigris and in Antiochia are very little known. The palace of Seleucia on the Tigris, the eastern capital founded by Seleucus I, is not documented archaeologically and is mentioned only briefly in written sources,[218] and we are only slightly better off with regard to the Palace of Antiochia (Cat. 15). Antiochia was founded by Seleucus I as well, but did not become the western capital (together with Ephesus) until the reign of Antiochus I; and it was Seleucus II who, after the loss of Asia Minor with Ephesus and Pergamon, enlarged the city, now the only western capital, and included as part of it the island in the River Orontes, joining it to the city on the left bank.

There has been much discussion concerning the precise site of the palace of the Seleucids in Antiochia. From the written sources we can adduce the following information, in chronological order. First of all, we are told of a library belonging to Antiochus II, probably located in his palace. In connection with the revolt of the Antiochenes against Demetrius II in 145 BC, which started near the palace (*ta basileia*), it is mentioned that it was fortified, consisted of several buildings, and was surrounded by a residential quarter with wooden houses. There is no hint as to the actual location of the palace in the city. However, we know that in 67 BC at any rate there was a palace on the island in the Orontes as well as a hippodrome, since both were built or more probably restored in that year by the new Roman proconsul of Cilicia, Q. Marcius Rex. Although the island is not actually mentioned in this context, the hippodrome has been located there, and one gets the impression that the two buildings were placed close together.[219] The original buildings may well have been constructed in the reign either of Antiochus I or of Seleucus II, who, as mentioned above, incorporated the island in the city. The island was probably also the scene of the revolt referred to above.

This palace no doubt continued to function throughout the Roman period, during which it was undoubtedly rebuilt and perhaps enlarged. At least, Cassius Dio relates that Trajan, when visiting Antiochia in 115 AD, had to flee the palace through a window during an earthquake and seek refuge in the hippodrome for several days. This palace must be the same as the one mentioned in connection with Alexander Severus, as well as the one described by later sources such as Libanius, Theodoret, and Evagrius from the 4th-5th centuries AD. Some scholars have, it is true, identified the palace from this late period with the one built by Diocletian, though there is, in fact, no evidence that his palace was situated on the island. But if so, it is not impossible that it was simply an addition to the already existing palace.[220]

If we dare to use the late descriptions of the palace from the 4th-5th centuries AD at all, they give the impression that it occupied a very large area — the western quarter of the island, in fact — that it was laid out orthogonally, that it consisted of several buildings (*oikoi*), and a *basileios stoa*, and that it was surrounded by walls with a monumental propylon, perhaps used for audiences (see p. 19). The relation of the hippodrome to the palace seems well established: it was located just east of the main palace. The area taken up by the basileia was then, to judge from the plan in the publication of Antiochia, around 25 ha (Fig. 58).

In addition to the evidence gleaned from these mostly very late written sources, one may advance another, "dynastic", argument for placing the Seleucid palace on the island and taking up a very large area (while not of course forgetting the purely defensive reason). In trying to visualize the appearance of this basileia, it is important to remember that the Seleucid dynasty was from the outset semi-Oriental, Seleucus I being one of the few of Alexander's generals to keep his Iranian wife, Apame from Bactria, after the death of Alexander. Also, Seleucus I stayed in the palaces of Babylon and Susa, and Antiochus I actually grew up in Babylon and had never visited the western part of the kingdom before he became king. In fact, the siting of the Palace of Antiochia on an island in the middle of the river would be very attractive from a Persian point of view: we

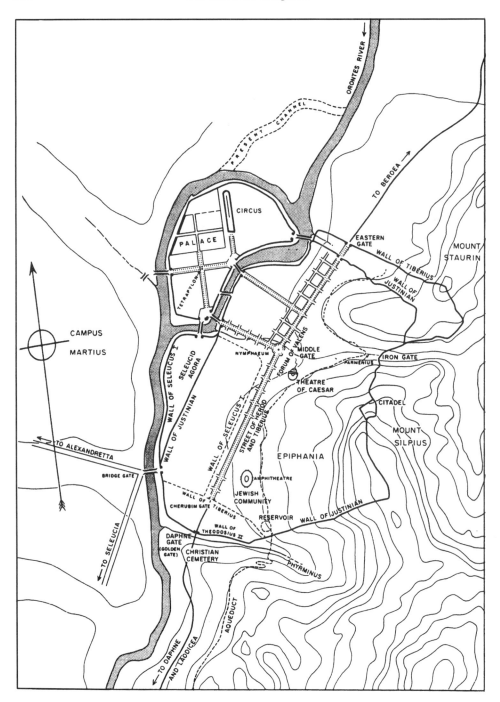

Fig. 58. Antiochia. General plan of the city with the palace on the island (Cat. 15). (By D.N. Wilberg) (G. Downey, Ancient Antioch, *Princeton 1963, fig. 3.)*

know for example that the Persian Palace of Kelainai was situated by two rivers, while that of Daskyleion was beside a lake, and a river ran through its paradeisos (see pp. 61ff). Also, the palaces of Seleucia and Babylon were both on riverside sites. Like the Persian palaces, the island palace in Antiochia was very large, and may already from the outset have taken up much of the aforementioned 25 ha. It undoubtedly consisted of many separate buildings set in a paradeisos, which embraced also the River Orontes.

In addition to the Palace of Antiochia, the Seleucids had another, primarily recreational palace at Daphne, a combined pleasure resort and royal sanctuary for the tutelary deity, Apollo, situated 8 km south of the city.[221] Daphne was famous for its abundance of water, for its villas, and for its paradisiac parks.[222] Great festivals took place there and the sanctuary included a stadium and theatre for use on such occasions; as we have seen Antiochus IV held some very famous games for Apollo in Daphne in 167 BC, which included procession and banquets for 6,000 and 9,000 guests respectively. There must have been room for such banquets in the palace (*aule*) or in tents in its park, and Antiochus IV thus did not fall short of Ptolemy II (see p. 22).[223]

Another indication that the Persian palaces with their paradeisoi were, in fact, one of the main inspirational factors in Seleucid palaces, is Plutarch's reference to the palace that Seleucus I placed at the disposal of Demetrius Poliorchetes at Apamea in Syria. It included *dromoi* and *peripatoi basilikoi* as well as a *paradeisos* with game; Plutarch's choise of words also indicates some influence from the Greek gymnasia. Again, one has the impression of a mainly recreational palace. Another kind of palace was built near Antiochia by Seleucus II, a *tetrapyrgion*, i.e. a fortified palace on a well-known model from Syria and Asia Minor (see p. 65). In general, one should probably not overestimate the Greek influence in this area.[224]

Governors' palaces

Since the royal palaces of the Seleucids are known only from the written sources, we have to resort to preserved governors' palaces to get an impression of their appearance, although of course certain elements closely associated with the royal power might well be missing from them. Such palaces have been preserved in the colonies of Dura Europos on the Euphrates and Aï Khanoum in Bactria (though this was later to become a royal palace), as well as in the city of Nippur in southern Mesopotamia.

At Dura Europos two Hellenistic palaces have been excavated (Fig. 59).[225] One,

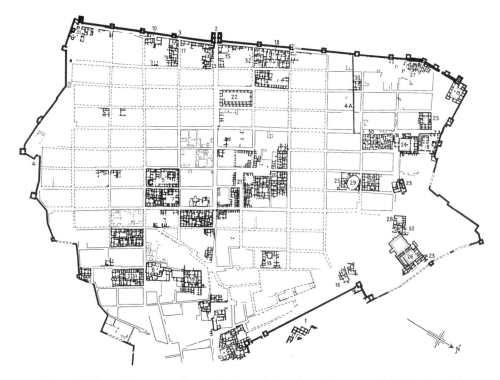

Fig. 59. Dura Europos. General plan of the city. (Rostovtzeff 1938, fig. 6.)

the so-called Redoubt Palace (Cat. 16), which was situated on the acropolis and
raised on a high terrace with an extensive view, was probably inhabited by the
main civic magistrate of the city, the *strategos*, and is also called the *strategeion*.
It was originally built in the middle of the 3rd century BC, and preserved its
original appearance in the second phase of building which dates from the first half
of the 2nd century BC, and was marked by the addition of a typical Oriental
temple for Zeus Melichios, placed in a large portico. This sanctuary was
presumably connected to the Strategeion by means of a large peristylar forecourt
linked to the palace's southern façade (Fig. 61).

The main palace was almost square. From the south, a "bent" entrance gave
access to a central courtyard surrounded by rooms, and there were other entrances
from the east and west (Fig. 60). No peristyle existed in the courtyard, while two
sets of two columns in antis to south and west marked the entrance to two ante-
rooms, which both opened into "broad rooms". In fact, there are two "andron
complexes" here, forming the official section of the palace. To the north and east
of the courtyard, several corridor-like rooms led to rooms placed behind them,

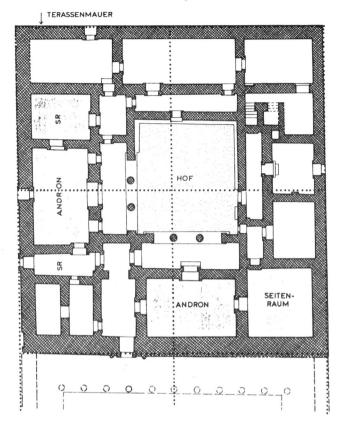

Fig. 60. Dura Europos. Redoubt Palace (Cat. 16). (Hoepfner & Schwandner 1986, Abb. 216.)

no doubt for service, etc., while the strategos and his family probably resided mainly on the first floor.

As far as the layout is concerned, there is a general resemblance to the private houses found in Babylon from the 6th to the 3rd centuries BC, and the same kind of private house occurred in Dura also. It normally had an "andron complex" to the south, the domain of the master, used for receptions, dining, and residence (Fig. 27).[226]

Probably the closest parallel to this Strategeion, however, is to be found in the Palace of Lachish in Palestine (Cat. 7), which was still in use in the early Hellenistic period. In addition to their identical function, there are similarities too both in the situation, on a terraced platform raised above the town, and in the plan —

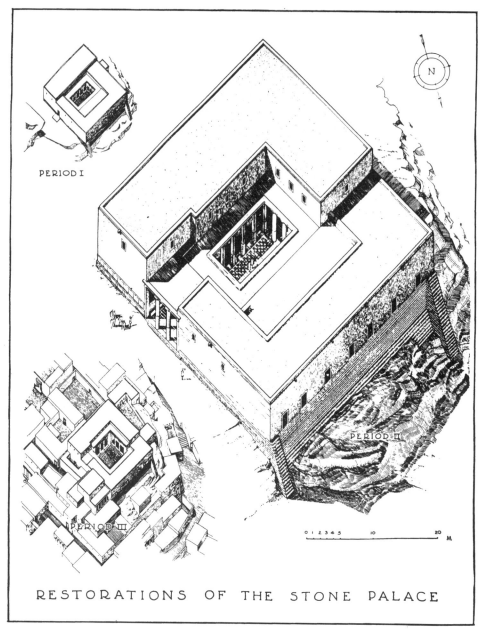

PERIOD I

PERIOD II

PERIOD III

0 1 2 3 4 5   10   20
                                        M

RESTORATIONS OF THE STONE PALACE

Fig. 61. Dura Europos. Reconstruction of the Redoubt Palace, periods I, II (the main palace period), and III. (Rostovtzeff 1938, pl. V.)

an interior courtyard with "andron complexes" in the south and west wings for official use (the Bit-Hilani model). In Lachish there is, however, no large forecourt, though such forecourts were very popular in Achaemenid architecture and many examples are found, e.g. in the palaces of Aï Khanoum.

It is remarkable that even the strategos of a Seleucid colony employed a local palace type when he built his abode, rather than a traditional Greek type with peristyle court(s) known for example from Macedonia. Since the inspiration for this palace probably came from the Seleucid capitals of Antiochia and Seleucia on the Tigris, this is an indication that the palaces of those cities, too, were strongly influenced by Oriental models. The combination with a temple is known from e.g. Lachish, Vouni, Larisa, and Pergamon.

The second preserved palace in Dura Europos, the Citadel Palace (Cat. 17), probably belonging to the Seleucid governor of Dura, was built over a previous palace dating from the middle of the 3rd century BC, but the traces of this first building are too fragmentary for its plan to be ascertained. The palace of the second phase, probably from the first half of the 2nd century BC, i.e. when the town was still in Seleucid hands, consisted of two parts: a Grecian section with a peristylar court, and, divided from it by a wide corridor, an apparently Oriental section. Only a smaller portion of the palace is preserved, and the reconstruction made by F. Brown, which is the one normally referred to by scholars, is far from reliable. It is safer to utilize M. Pillet's plan, showing only the actual remains (Figs. 62-63).

The most conspicuous element in the southern section of the palace is the peristyle, which has led to an interpretation of this part of the palace as a purely Greek building.[227] This may be true of the peristyle itself, at least at this late date, but instead of interpreting the large hall in the south wing as a vestibule (it has five inner columns (not on Brown's plan) and opens onto the courtyard with three columns in antis), I find it more likely that this was the main hall for audiences and councils; with the smaller rooms flanking it and accessible from it, it looks, indeed, like a kind of "andron complex". Also the rather large "broad room" in the western wing, flanked by side-rooms, probably had an official function, perhaps as a banqueting room. Thus again, we have the pattern of official rooms in the form of "andron complexes" in the south and west wings, with the main emphasis on the south wing. I see no reason, with Brown, to expect a symmetrical layout, with an identical east and west wing in this palace, rather one should expect private apartments and service rooms in the eastern wing. In general, this southern section of the palace has a great affinity to the Redoubt Palace, except

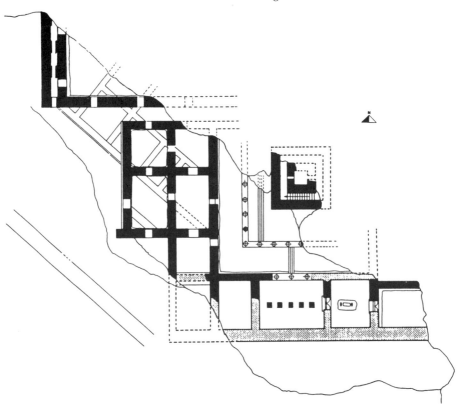

Fig. 62. Dura Europos. M. Pillit's plan of the Citadel Palace (Cat. 16). (Rep. II, pl. IV.)

that the ante-rooms with columns in antis and the corridors have been replaced by the peristyle. Thus the Greek elements are only superficial, and the layout basically Oriental; so that what we have here is a local type, originating probably in a combination of the Mesopotamian courtyard house and the North Syrian Bit-Hilani.

Nothing remains of the entrance to the palace, but it is likely that the peristyle was reached from the north, via the wide corridor, so that an axial approach to the main room was created, at the same time exploiting the element of surprise.

Most attention has been given by scholars to the northern part of the palace, separated from the peristyle part by the wide corridor and probably reached by means of this as well. Another, much narrower corridor is preserved on the western side of the northern section, with several doors opening inwards. This part has very thick walls, which has caused M.I. Rostovtzeff and Brown to

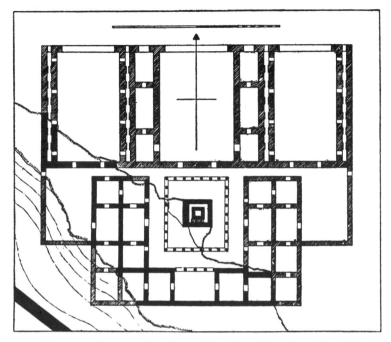

Fig. 63. Dura Europos. F. Brown's plan of the Citadel Palace (Cat.16). (Rostovtzeff 1938, fig. 9.)

interpret it as containing three *liwans*, a Parthian room type consisting of a large barrel-vaulted room completely open at one end. Each of the three reconstructed liwans would have a width of at least 20 m. A function as a kind of reception hall has been proposed. But this proposal is far from convincing, for the liwan has in fact not been identified elsewhere before the Parthian conquest, and the best-known examples, from Assur and Hatra, are much later.

I find S. B. Downey's reconstruction more acceptable. She sees here a large forecourt of Persian type, partly because a similar one was probably present in the Redoubt Palace, and partly because if this *is* the case, there would then be close similarities to the palaces, royal and private, in another Seleucid colony, Aï Khanoum.[228] Forecourts of this kind are often surrounded by corridors, as in a private palace outside the walls of Aï Khanoum, as well as in the gymnasium there (Fig. 68). Such large forecourts with corridors are known from Persepolis, and this type undoubtedly springs from Achaemenid architecture. A use for large receptions would then be a possibility.[229]

Both the palaces of Dura Europos have close similarities with the magisterial or princely Palace of Nippur (Cat. 18), probably built around 250 BC, although

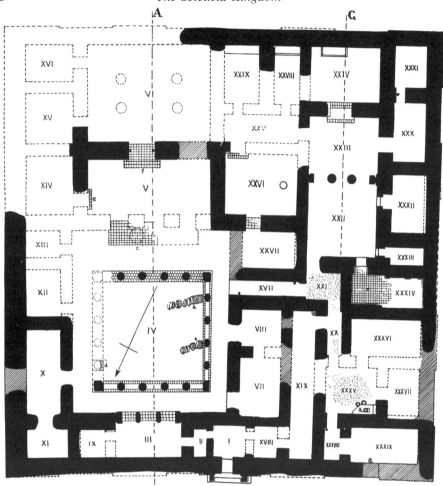

Fig. 64. Nippur. Plan of the palace (Cat.18). 1:475. (Fischer 1904, pl. XIV.)

this date is far from certain (Fig. 64).[230] However, the palace incorporates so many Greek, or rather Macedonian, features that a Seleucid date seems likely. What makes this building especially interesting is that it was situated in a provincial town and owned by a local dignitary, which means that the presence of Greek elements must signify the locals' general acceptance of them. The palace consists of two parts, connected only by a corridor. The larger, official part was reached from a "bent" entrance connected to a fine vestibule facing a peristyle court, which was surrounded by rooms and had a large main hall furnished with an ante-room to the south.[231] The residential part was centred round a small court without columns, and included a fine bathroom, a kitchen, and private living-rooms.

While the peristyle with the Doric tile columns placed on plinths, the heart-

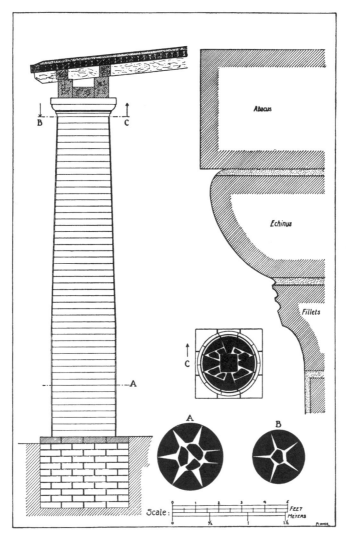

Fig. 65. Nippur. Drawing of one of the Doric tile columns in the peristyle court, with architectural details. (Fischer 1904, Pl. XV.)

shaped corner columns, and the double half-columns indicate a Greek, more specifically a Macedonian, influence (Fig. 65),[232] the layout of the palace is Oriental, primarily Mesopotamian: typical are the square plan with ressauts, the large "broad room" south of the main court, the "bent" entrance, the many corridors, the labyrinthine plan, and the building technique in sun-dried brick. Greek decorative elements have been incorporated in a basically Oriental architecture, as in Dura, and, as will be shown, also in the palace to be discussed next.

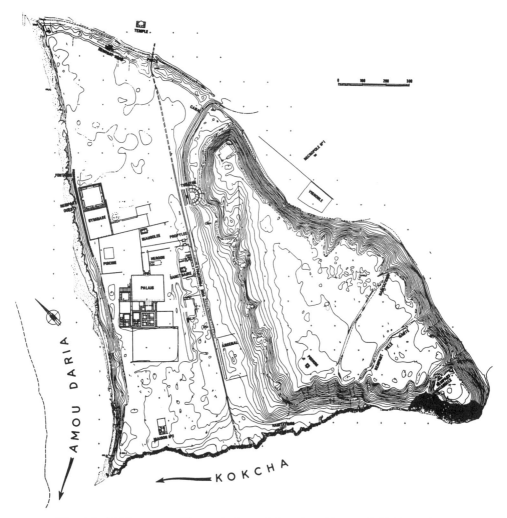

Fig. 66. Aï Khanoum. General plan of the city. (Bernard 1981, Taf. 44.)

This palace, found in the early Seleucid colony of Aï Khanoum in Bactria (Cat. 19), perhaps the metropolis of Alexandria on the Oxus, belongs in its present state to around 150 BC, but was originally built in the early days of the colony in the early 3rd century BC (Fig. 66).[233] The first phase was the work of the Seleucid governor, but to this period belong only the large peristyle forecourt and the hypostyle hall, with the bath section to the south of it. Later, the palace was taken over and greatly enlarged by a member of the local, independent dynasty which had replaced the Seleucids as early as the middle of the 3rd century BC, probably Eucrates (170-146 BC). Even in the original governor's palace, the general impression is that of an Oriental plan, while the architectural elements and decoration seem to be predominantly Greek, and these characteristics were further emphasized with its change of status.

The palace was located in the centre of the lower city, but with an orientation slightly differing from the surrounding Hippodamian plan. The area covered by the "palace complex" in its final phase, when it was the seat of a local dynasty and thus a royal palace, was very large, all in all c. 87,500 m^2 (Fig. 67). One entered this basileia from the main street via impressive propyleia of Persian type. A broad avenue, after making a 90-degree turn, led to the monumental propylon of the main palace, giving access to a huge forecourt with a peristyle, which in fact formed part of the original building. The 118 columns had Corinthian capitals of a Syrian/Phoenician type, but Persian bases. It is worth remarking that this peristyle is the earliest known example of a Rhodian peristyle, its southern portico towards the palace being raised above the others, and probably reaching the same height as the Grecian/Corinthian columns of the contemporaneous hypostyle hall behind it. Despite its name, one may well suspect that this kind of peristyle originated in Persian architecture, where it was particularly a feature of forecourts, another possibility is an Egyptian origin. In Aï Khanoum they might have chosen to heighten the columns along the south side, for the reason that the hypostyle hall was fully open to the portico, and creating an effective junction with a lower portico would have presented aesthetic difficulties.

The hypostyle hall, which was the only room opening onto the court, had eighteen columns and gave access to a large "broad room" behind it, and this in turn led to various side-rooms, for instance a bath wing, probably for the king's (earlier the governor's) use.[234] This section, which may be called a de luxe "andron complex", is very much the official part of the palace, together with the large forecourt and its propylon, in relation to which the hall was axially placed. The hypostyle hall or exedra constituted at the same time an impressive vestibule to the main hall, functioning as an audience hall and perhaps also as a banqueting hall.

Behind this ceremonial "king's suite", and divided from it by a wide corridor, was the residential part of the palace. This consisted of four smaller suites of rooms, the two eastern ones with finely decorated halls for receptions, the two western ones probably for private banquets. Since people in this region dined reclining on carpets on the floor, no "kline bands" are present to help the

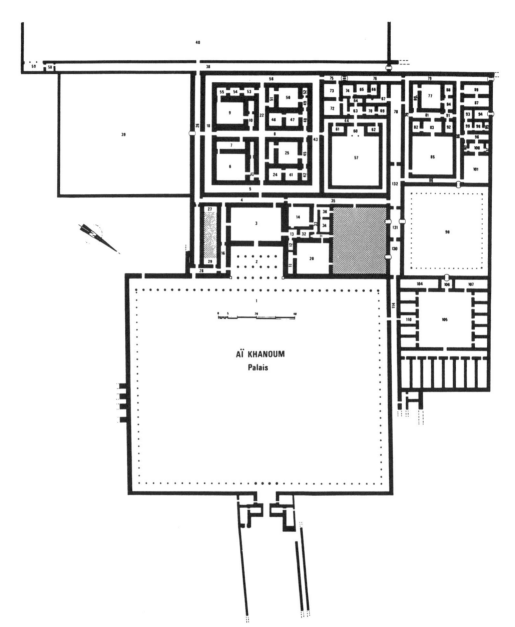

Fig. 67. Aï Khanoum. The palace area (Cat. 19). (Bernard 1981, Taf. 45.)

identification. Furthermore, the large apartment with a forecourt to the west of these suites may well have been for the king's private use. Finally, the westernmost part of this residence, which lay to the south of a secondary peristyle, probably housed the royal family. The identification of these residential buildings, especially "the king's house" and "the house of the royal family", is supported by their close affinities to the two private palaces found in Aï Khanoum, the "Maison du quartier Sud" and the "Maison hors-les-murs" (Fig. 68).

The administrative and service sectors were situated partly to the north of this secondary court (where there are traces of a treasury and archives) and probably partly to the east of the palace, but the area has not yet been excavated.

As one would expect in these eastern parts, the recreational element took up a considerable part of the palace. To the west, the area between the main palace and the river was probably laid out as a park. An enormous swimming-pool was constructed here in the last phase (the middle of the 2nd century BC), replacing an older bath suite (see n. 234). An esplanade led from the swimming-pool towards the propylon of the palace, but this area to the west could also be reached directly from the residential section. The swimming-pool, it is true, is normally considered to be part of the gymnasium, which lies to the north and dates from the same period, but in fact there is no direct connection between the two complexes. Moreover, the orientation of the pool follows that of the main palace, not that of the gymnasium. This gymnasium is of a highly unusual type with only a few rooms and corridors; it is, moreover, of a late date and perhaps was laid out rather as a formal garden. In that case, the whole area including the gymnasium would have formed part of the paradeisos of the palace, a theory that is supported by the presence of water, both natural (the river) and artificial (the swimming-pool). The same function may perhaps be attributed to the large walled areas south of the palace proper. If the palace was that extensive, it might even have included the Heroon of Kineas from the early years of the city, as well as the Mausoleum, perhaps in the form of a Greek temple, from the 3rd century BC. Finally, the city's theatre was situated near the palace. Whatever may have been the case here, all these elements were found again in the famous Alexandrian basileia (see pp. 130ff).

As P. Bernard has stated, this palace has very close affinities both to the Achaemenid and the Babylonian palaces, as far as the layout is concerned. The similarities to the former are mostly to be found in the official and administrative parts, i.e. partly in the hypostyle hall and the huge columnar forecourt, with its access via a monumental entrance with two great *pylones*, and partly also in the other Doric peristyle court, which had access to both private apartments and treasury. Moreover, the extensive gardens have precursors in the Persian

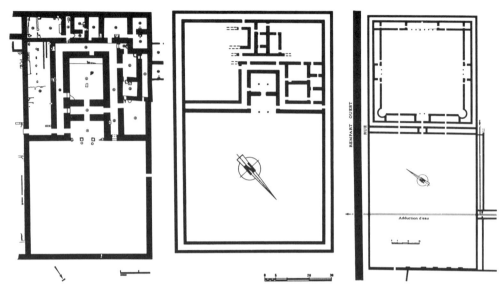

Fig. 68. Aï Khanoum. The two palatial houses, from the left, the "Maison du quartier sud" and the "Maison hors-les-murs", and the gymnasium. (Bernard 1981, Tf. 46.).

paradeisoi, and no wonder, when the climate and the general situation of Aï Khanoum are taken into account. Even the inclusion of a mausoleum is nothing new here. The residential parts of the palace, on the other hand, with their many rooms and corridors and flat roofs have a very great affinity with the Neo-Babylonian palaces of Babylon (Cat. 2; Figs. 5-7) and the Persian Palace of Darius in Susa (Cat. 5; Fig. 19). The mansions of the wealthy in Aï Khanoum have the same characteristics. Bernard proposes a certain degree of inspiration also from the Seleucid and the Ptolemaic palaces of the capitals, and this is undoubtedly so; and since they had the same sources of inspiration as that of Aï Khanoum one may legitimately use also this palace to throw light on these lost royal palaces.

Summary

One of the things that emerges from the study of Seleucid palaces is that they are a product of many different influences. In general, however, the Greek/Macedonian elements are mostly confined to the external, decorative, aesthetic, and formal aspects, while the function and content are basically Oriental. By the term Oriental I mean both Babylonian/Mesopotamian features, normally reflected in the primary residential parts, but embracing also the "andron complex", and North Syrian and Achaemenid features, almost invariably to be found in the official part, embracing respectively the Bit-Hilani and forecourts, portals, and hypostyle halls.

I think the architectural layout should be accorded great importance, where the hellenization/orientalization of the inhabitants of the Seleucid kingdom is concerned. Since architecture is basically conservative and functional, it must to some extent reflect the basic needs and cultural make-up of those who live with it. Since the palaces represented the élite, one should not be surprised that the houses of the lower classes bear even less witness to the Greek presence.

Thus to judge from the palaces, the hellenization of this large area was superficial, the new dynasty perpetuating both the architecture and the functions of its predecessors. Although only the Palace of Aï Khanoum may give us a glimpse of how a truly Seleucid royal palace looked, the re-utilization without major alteration of the Achaemenid palaces of Babylon and Susa undoubtedly reflects the fact that the Seleucid dynasty merely replaced the former dynasty, in this case the Achaemenid, as had always been the custom in the East.

VI. THE PTOLEMAIC KINGDOM

In contrast to the Seleucids, the Ptolemaic kings were normally resident in their only capital, Alexandria, although we know that in the old capital of Memphis they also had residences which replaced the Palace of Apries (Cat. 1) (see p. 27). Thus unlike the Seleucids, the Ptolemies apparently did not reuse the palaces of their predecessors.[235] Again, the royal palaces are known only from the written sources, which are fortunately very copious, at least as far as the Palace of Alexandria is concerned. But to get an impression of the architectural appearance of these palaces, we have once again to resort to the governors' palaces, which are to be found not in Egypt itself, but in the neighbouring provinces of the Ptolemaic empire.

Royal palaces

While very little indeed is known of the Memphis Palace, viz. only that it included an *akra*, a large park, and a lake, the royal Palace of Alexandria (Cat. 20), because of its great renown, was an obvious object of interest for ancient writers — though archaeologically, only fragments of some architectural elements have survived the city's turbulent history.[236] This palatial complex contained all the facilities needed for the numerous courtiers and the notorious and ever growing bureaucracy.

The important information with which Polybius furnishes us on this palace has already been used extensively in connection with the chapter on functions (see pp. 18ff): he calls the entire complex *aule*, and mentions the citadel, called *akra*, an entrance hall with a monumental portal, which could be used for large audiences, called *chrematistikon pylon*, suggesting a monumental palace façade, and a building called *megiston peristylon*, which may be identical with the forecourt in front of this façade. The name of the latter indicates that there were several peristyle buildings, of which the largest (*megiston*) was probably for official purposes. At least, it must have been very extensive, for the court could accommodate a great crowd; a tribune (*bema*) could be raised there, so that it could be used for receptions. Perhaps this important building contained the splendid banqueting hall, in which, as Lucan tells us, Cleopatra entertained Caesar; it might, in fact, be identical with the audience hall (see p. 22). Furthermore,

Polybius mentions a vaulted corridor (*syrinx*), which led from the palace to the theatre, sited on a somewhat higher level. A feature called *maiandros*, probably a winding water-channel or canal, perhaps for swimming, and the *palaistra* were close by.

While Diodorus tells us only that Alexander ordered the palace complex to be built, that it was famous for its size and wealth (*baros*), and that it was enlarged by most of his successors, Strabo's famous description is very detailed. The palace occupied a quarter or even a third of the city's area in his time, since each king had added his own complex (*oikesis*). These were, including the *akra* one on the Lochias peninsula (above), all connected with each other and with the harbour. Near this citadel were placed the finest guest houses (*katalumata*), according to "Aristeas"; they were probably on the landward side of the Lochias, where according to Strabo the inner royal palaces were situated. They were surrounded by a park (*alsos*) with many pavilions (*diaitai*), which perhaps included gazebos.[237] These pavilions undoubtedly belonged in the private sphere, and could be used as private dining-rooms, for instance. Below the inner palaces lay the king's concealed harbour. Across the mouth of the great harbour was the island of Antirhodos, which also contained a palace and itself had a small harbour.

The basileia also housed the famous *museion*. As this had a covered portico (*peripatos*), an *exedra*, and a dining-hall for users, it probably consisted of a peristyle court with surrounding rooms, which undoubtedly included the famous library. One might compare this with the situation in Pergamon, where the library was placed behind one of the porticoes of Athena's Temenos. The description of the Museion resembles that of a gymnasium in which philosophers and scholars worked, for gymnasia, it will be remembered, frequently had a library, and were often used for official banquets; also the placement in a park was typical of gymnasia (compare the Academy of Athens). The gymnasium at Alexandria, which Strabo calls the most beautiful building in the city, may have been placed nearby, or was perhaps even connected with the Museion. We know that it was used for official purposes, at least in the time of Cleopatra VII, since Mark Antony placed a tribune (*bema*) with thrones there, when he declared Cleopatra queen of a large part of the East. Also the famous vantage point, the artificial hill of the Paneion, was in the vicinity. Both it and the gymnasium were situated in the park (*alsos*), as was the Court of Justice.[238]

Moreover, temples and sanctuaries were present in the basileia: the *sema*, which housed the Tomb of Alexander and those of the Ptolemies, and which at the same time functioned as a dynastic heroon, was located there, and the possible remains

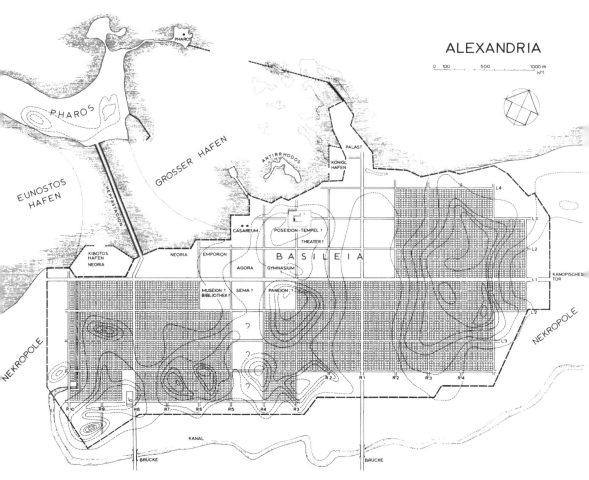

Fig. 69. Alexandria. Plan of the city with the basileia (Cat. 20). (Hoepfner 1990, Abb. 2.)

of the Sanctuary of Poseidon have been found near the harbour. Theocritus tells us that the royal park was open to the public during the festival of Adonis, which suggests that his sanctuary was situated in the basileia as well, undoubtedly in park-like surroundings.[239] Also, both Isis and Sarapis were present, partly as tutelary deities, and partly as protectors of the Museion and library; but their main sanctuary was the nearby Serapeion, which also housed a, probably public, library.[240]

As Alexandria from the begining was laid out on a grid pattern, and as one of the main streets led to the palace by the Lochias, it is very likely that the whole basileia, which was c. 2 km in diameter (estimated area, c. 200 ha!), was laid out regularly as well (Fig. 69).[241] That this was the case is supported by the fact that the palace was undoubtedly inspired by the Persian palaces with their paradeisoi. The water requirement was met partly by the sea, partly by an artificial channel or canal, Maiandros.[242] An interesting piece of information from Athenaeus, that Ptolemy VIII Physcon wrote a treatise on the breeding of birds in the palace area, also provides an association with the bird-filled Persian paradeisos,[243] as does the presence of zoological and botanical gardens. According to a Zenon papyrus, the Ptolemaic official Tobias of Transjordania sent rare animals to Ptolemy II for the zoo (below).[244] Another inspiration for such spacious parks, including zoological and botanical gardens, came from Pharaonic Egypt where they were also popular as an adjunct to the palaces e.g. in Tell el-Amarna (see p. 31).

Although it occurs in a mythical context and was inspired by Homer, one should perhaps in this connection draw attention to the description of the Palace of Aeëtes in Colchis, given in the *Argonautica* of Apollonius Rhodius.[245] Despite his name, Apollonius was an Alexandrian, and, after giving up his retirement in Rhodes, became the director of the Alexandrian library. Born in c. 295 BC, he was a contemporary of Ptolemy II and thus a witness to the main building period of Alexandria, including the basileia. Therefore, although it concerns the era of myth, his description of the palace at Colchis may well have reflected the famous "modern" Palace of Alexandria.

He stresses first of all the impressive *propyleia* of great height (one is reminded of Vitruvius'*vestibula regalia alta*, see p. 20), the finely decorated façade, and the wide vestibule with columns along the walls, which led to a garden with fountains. From the garden there was access to the *messaulos*, used in the Homeric sense of the word, to mean an inner court surrounded by rooms with doors and a gallery; of this the loftiest wing was reserved for the king and his queen, while the second finest was for the son and heir. The princesses and servants lived in the other wings.

Very important where royal palatial architecture is concerned are Callixenus' interesting descriptions, preserved by Athenaeus, of the Pavilion of Ptolemy II and of the sumptuous Nile-barge, the Thalamegos, belonging to Ptolemy IV, both already mentioned above (see pp. 22ff). Since the pavilion was erected in Alexandria and the boat had its base there, they may well help to throw light on the buildings of the Alexandrian basileia as well.

Ptolemy II's Pavilion was raised in 274-270 BC to house a symposium held in connection with a great religious procession in honour of Dionysus, the tutelary deity of the dynasty (Fig. 70).[246] It was a large tent-like structure which consisted of a main hall (*oikos*), with 4 x 5 very tall columns: Callixenus gives a hight of 26 m! On three sides were vaulted porticoes (*syringes*), from which the food for the banquet came, and these were separated from the main hall by hangings (*aulaiai*).[247] There was room for a hundred guests in the main hall, one side of which opened to the outside, and the many flowers and plants mentioned in the description afforded the diners a beautiful view, although the tent was placed in the *peribolos* of the Akra, not in the palace garden.

It is not difficult to guess where Ptolemy got the idea of constructing this pavilion. Tents have always been used in the Orient, among other things for royal banquets, their types varying slightly (see p. 46 and n. 247). A comparison which immediately suggests itself is with the marquee of Alexander, used both for banquets and for audiences (see p. 21). The main hall of this tent was supported by 50 columns, 10.5 m high, and surrounded by a probably lower *peribolos*, separated from the main hall by hangings (*aulaiai*). In front of it was a large yard (*aule*), four stadia in circumference. The tent was richly embellished, the columns with gold and precious stones. Probably the tent could also be placed in a paradeisos, since it is mentioned that *klinai* and a throne at one occasion were placed in such a park. One may here compare with the Great King, who often held court in his garden.[248]

Even closer to this description of Ptolemy II's Pavilion are the Persian official buildings, which in their turn were probably reflections of marquees (see pp. 46f).[249] The relatively few columns in the pavilion's main hall remind one especially of the apadana; the same applies to the unusual tallness of the columns. There is also a certain affinity with the Hall of 100 Columns in Persepolis, in respect of the surrounding corridors, for instance, but the hall's relation to Alexander's tent is much closer, in respect of the number of columns, its height, and the largeness of its forecourt. But of course we are speaking here of a lightweight structure in contrast to the Achaemenid stone architecture, and should therefore perhaps not focus too much on the number and height of the columns.

It could well be, too, that the pavilion was a reflection of a smaller banqueting hall in the basileia itself, perhaps one of the above-mentioned diaitai.[250] I thus find it very probable that one or more permanent buildings in the basileia of Alexandria were, in fact, constructed to a Persian model. It is worth remembering in this connection that the main builder of this basileia was Ptolemy I, who had

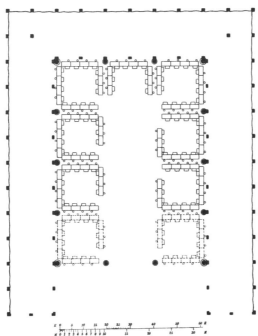

Fig. 70. The Pavilion of Ptolemy II. Reconstruction and plan. (Studniczka 1914, Taf. I and 3.)

stayed for long periods in Babylon and Susa with Alexander and who knew both the tents of Alexander and those of the Persian kings, as well as the Persian and Babylonian palaces, all of which which cannot have failed to impress and inspire him.

The Thalamegos, the palatial Nile-barge which Ptolemy IV had built for pleasure, inaugurated a long tradition of floating palaces, or rather it perpetuated an old Egyptian tradition for pleasure trips on the Nile (Fig. 71).[251] What strikes one is the amount of correlation with tents. The main saloon is in fact called a tent, *skene*, and its entrance a *proskenion*, while on the upper deck there was a tent-like dining-room. The very lightness of the structure also reminds one of Persian pavilions as well as of the Nile-boats of the Pharaonic period. Many of the functions normally associated with a royal palace could be dispensed with here. The official functions seem to have been placed mainly on the lower deck, and were characterized by a very elaborate propylon, perhaps for audiences, consisting of three elements reminiscent of the propylon of the Palace of Aigai (Cat. 10). The main hall, *oikos megistos*, was used primarily for banquets, but could probably also be used for audiences. The fact that the queen had her own apartment, including a *symposion* with nine *klinai*, is an indication of the important role played by the queens of the Ptolemaic dynasty (see p. 23). Taken as a whole, the Thalamegos positively abounded in banqueting rooms of varying sizes. The smaller ones on the lower deck were connected directly with bedrooms, both in the "*andronitis*" and the "*gynaikonitis*".[252] (cf. Fig. 72) Also on the upper deck there were both large and small *symposia*.

Another important feature of the Thalamegos was the close connection with the gods, represented by a *monopteros* for Aphrodite and the exedra (*anthron*), in the *bakchikos oikos* (see p. 23). Both were placed on the upper deck, indicating the private connection of the dynasty to these tutelary deities. The *anthron*, probably in the shape of a grotto, was built in natural stone with gilding, and has been the subject of much interest.[253] In it were statues of the royal family forming a kind of dynastic sanctuary or heroon. Because of the klinai, this exedra must have been raised somewhat above the floor.

As suggested recently by A. Schmidt-Colinet, there is a direct connection as far as function is concerned between the Bacchic *oecus* and the Philippeion, and probably also the apses of the official part of the Royal Palace of Pella (Cat. 12), both buildings belonging to the Macedonian dynasty. I may draw attention to yet another hitherto unnoticed predecessor, namely the androns of Mausolus and Idreus in Labraunda (Fig. 34, Pl. 8) (see p. 65). In the back walls of these androns, which functioned as royal dining-halls, was a large rectangular recess

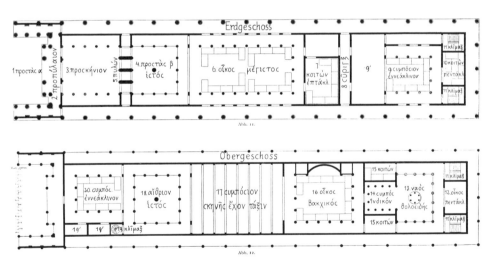

Fig. 71. The Thalamegos of Ptolemy IV. Reconstruction and plan. (Caspari 1916, Beil. p. 22 and 25.)

somewhat raised from the floor, where, as P. Hellström has convincingly proposed, statues of Mausolus and Artemisia, Idreus and Ada, etc., might well have been placed, perhaps flanking Zeus Labraundus. Conceivably, the Nile-boat of Ptolemy IV is in fact one of the "missing links" sought by Hellström, who sees another parallel in the great *triclinium* of the Flavian Palace on the Palatine.[254]

Before we leave Egypt, it is worth mentioning a fine private palace in Philadelphia belonging to a Ptolemaic court official, Diotimus, and described in some detail in a Zenon papyrus.[255] It had an entrance with *pylon* and *prostas* (compare the propylon of the Nile-boat, above), an official part with banqueting rooms, an *andron*, and an *exedra*, and a residential part centred around a light-well. The *loipa chresteria*, a service section, with among other things a bathroom, completed the building. In this description there are close affinities with the later Palace of Ptolemais (below).

Governors' palaces

To date, we have had only written evidence at our disposal in elucidating the palatial architecture of the Ptolemies. Outside Egypt, however, the areas governed by the Ptolemies furnish us with two preserved palaces, which might help us further to visualize the appearance of the basileia of Alexandria, since they were undoubtedly influenced by it: namely the princely palace of Hyrcanus in Transjordania, and the governor's palace in Ptolemais. Since these were, however, not royal palaces, many of the elements present in Alexandria are not to be expected here. Also the very different settings, the former set in a large domain, the latter taking up only a city insula, make these two structures very different both from each other and from the Alexandrian basileia.

The palace in Transjordania that belonged to the vassal king Hyrcanus the Tobiad is the earliest Hellenistic palace we know of in Palestine. The modern name of the estate is Araq el Emir (Cat. 21), but when Hyrcanus built a palace there in the beginning of the 2nd century BC, it was known as Tyrus.[256] Hyrcanus was a hellenized Jew and a Ptolemaic official and perhaps eventually even a semi-independent dynast, and the Tobiads had been the principal landowners of the locality for a long time. The palace was never finished, and after Hyrcanus' suicide, probably in 169/8 BC, the domain was expropriated by Antiochus IV. The preserved palace, called Qasr el Abd today, was situated in a large enclosed park which itself was set in a huge terraced agricultural estate that was well watered from the wadi by a complicated irrigation system (Fig. 73).

We are in the unusual position of having a rather detailed description of this

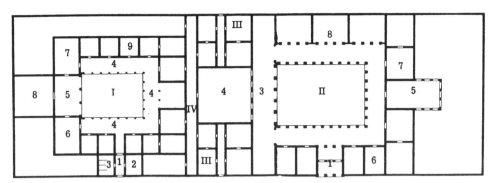

Fig. 72. Hypothetical reconstruction of Vitruvius' (6.7) Greek house: I. Gynaikonitis; II. Andronitis. (Raeder 1988, fig. 1.)

palatial complex as well: Josephus, after describing the main palace, mentions a network of caves used as living-quarters, and for dining, etc., with water laid on. Also, he refers to *aulai* placed in parks (*paradeisoi*).[257] While some of the caves, on two storeys, have actually been found at some distance from the main palace, there are problems with the aulai. As E. Will points out, only one building has been traced near the palace, beneath the modern village, but its plan is uncertain, although a courtyard at any rate has been identified. It is contemporary with the palace,[258] but Will finds no proof of large Persian-style parks in connection with it. He solves the problem by moving the aulai with their parks to other areas of the vast Tobiad domain.[259] This is possible, but on the other hand there are certain elements of the Tyrus site which bring a paradeisos to mind, for instance an artificial lake surrounding the palace, and the fenced park, where one should probably imagine pleasure gardens.[260] In this period, I do not think one has to imagine the paradeisos as a great hunting area, it could also be an extensive wooded park in which the palace was set, such as already existed in Pasargadae (see p. 38), and also, in my opinion, in Alexandria (above) and later in nearby Jericho, described in the next chapter.

The main or official palace, which Josephus calls *baris*,[261] was, for defensive reasons as well as to create an impression, placed high up on a large terrace and surrounded by an artificial lake, which among other things functioned as a kind of moat, and was undoubtedly also used as a reservoir for the irrigation system (Fig. 73). The building was reached from a propylon in the surrounding wall by means of a causeway crossing the moat. This palace — for with our present degree of knowledge there can be no doubt that this building is, in fact, a palace, although some scholars have identified it as a temple[262] — was never finished

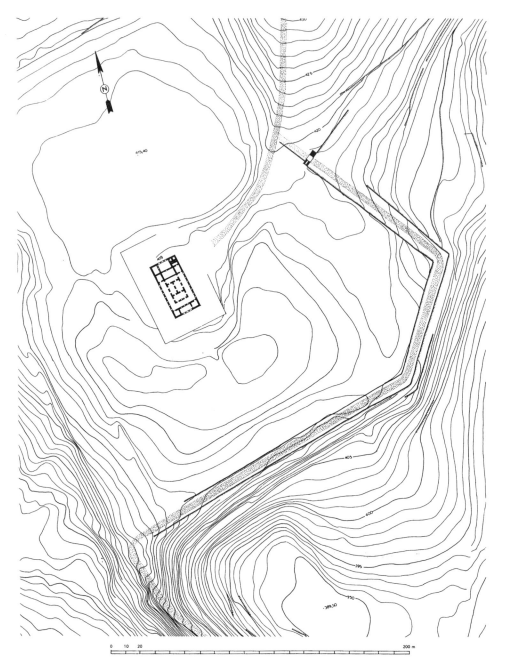

Fig. 73. Araq el Emir. General plan of the area. (Will 1991, pl. 3.)

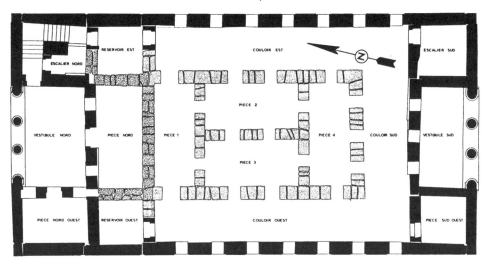

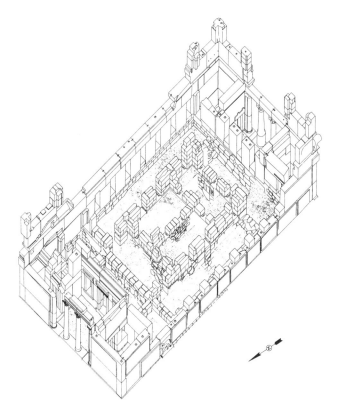

Fig. 74 Araq el Emir. Plan and isometric view of the lower storey of the main palace, Qasr el Abd (Cat. 21). (Will 1991, pls. 7-8.)

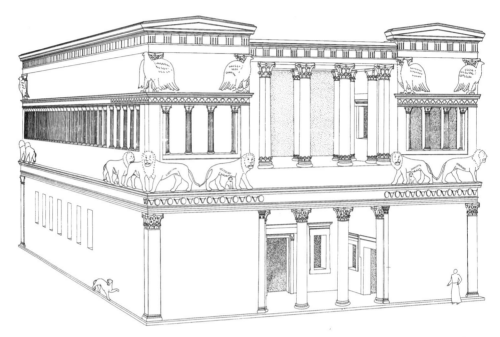

Fig. 75. Araq el Emir. Reconstruction of the main palace. (Will 1991, pl. 100.)

(Figs. 74-75). It is very compact and has a slightly forbidding appearance, reminiscent of a tetrapyrgion, a model often identical with the baris. It had two storeys, of which the lower one had highly placed windows, while the upper one had fine loggias and large windows flanked by columns on a continuous plinth decorated with lions. The actual placing of these lions is in the Oriental tradition, although their style is Greek.[263] The existence of many windows is also documented in the House of Diotimus (above), where no less than ten windows are mentioned. Finally, the *acroteria* were in the form of eagles.[264] Both lions and eagles connote royalty, although Hyrcanus was only a rich landowner and former royal tax collector of the Ptolemies; but he may, late in his career, have aspired to become an independent dynast. A general similarity between this palace and the Nile-boat of Ptolemy IV has already been noted by F. Caspari (above).[265]

We know only the plan of the lower storey, but the façades of both storeys have been ascertained. The main entrance was from the north, in the form of a wide porch leading to a vestibule with two columns in antis, and on the first floor was a loggia open to the sky, flanked by "towers" (Fig. 76). This entrance is probably reminiscent of the Bit-Hilani, found all over the area.[266] The vestibule, presumably the place for the guards, gave access to a staircase in one of the corner towers and led to a "broad room", which was perhaps, as Will proposes, for the chamberlain, although a use for audiences cannot be excluded, either. From the south, there was access only to a small "vestibule", again with two columns in antis, but not to the interior. On the first floor of this southern façade, there was probably a loggia or at least a range of windows, everything being topped by a pediment (Fig. 76). There was an impressive view from this side especially.

The interior of the ground floor, built in rather coarse materials and undoubtedly used for service purposes only, consisted of four interior rooms, reached from corridors along the long sides, as were the two cisterns flanking the "broad room". This plan was undoubtedly reflected in the first floor, for official purposes. This arrangement has strong affinities with the large private palaces of Aï Khanoum (Fig. 68), especially the one outside the city walls, since this also had an official part that was separate from the rest of the house. These houses had, however, only one floor and were moreover built in sun-dried brick.[267] The plan of the Tyrus palace is rather similar, too, to fortified residences in Iran from the Hellenistic period, e.g. one in Hecatompylos (Shahr-i Qumis) near Hamadan in Iran from the late 3rd to the 1st century BC, with a ground floor with storerooms and probably a first floor for residence.[268] And the structures in Babish Mulla from the 4th to the 2nd centuries BC,[269] and in Saksan Ochar in Bactria from the 2nd century BC, also show similarities.[270]

The upper floor could be reached partly by means of the monumental staircase in the north-east "tower", and partly by a service stair in the south-east corner. Instead of the four rooms on the ground floor, there was probably one large one, for audiences and banquets, to the north, perhaps reached from a vestibule, while the southern part may have been for residence, if this was not rather the purpose of the aulai. The main room was richly decorated with Grecian elements such as three-quarter columns with Corinthian capitals. The "towers", with their windows, were perhaps a kind of diaitai, which were known for example from Alexandria, though there they were independent buildings. Such built-in towers with diaitai seem to become popular later in the palaces of Judaea, and were perhaps also present in the contemporaneous Palace of Demetrias (Cat. 13) (see p. 93). On the other hand, the arrangement with large windows divided by small columns, especially on the long sides of the building, shows a similarity to the peristyles and façades of the Macedonian palaces, where the upper floor often had plinth-zones with smaller columns (see pp. 81ff), a system also seen in the large Lefkadhia

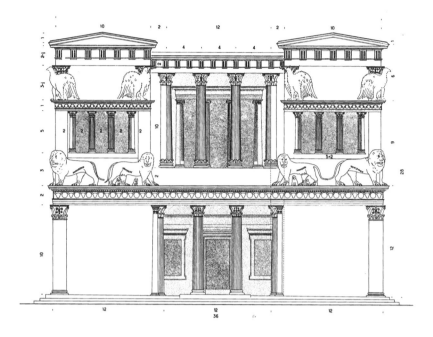

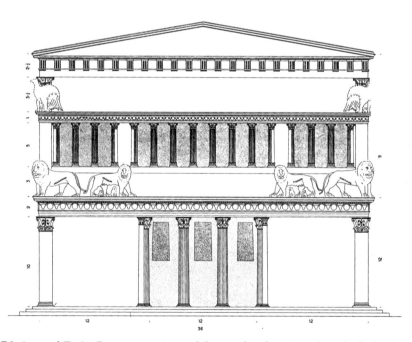

Fig. 76. Araq el Emir. Reconstructions of the north (above) and south (below) façades. (Will 1991, pls. 36-37.)

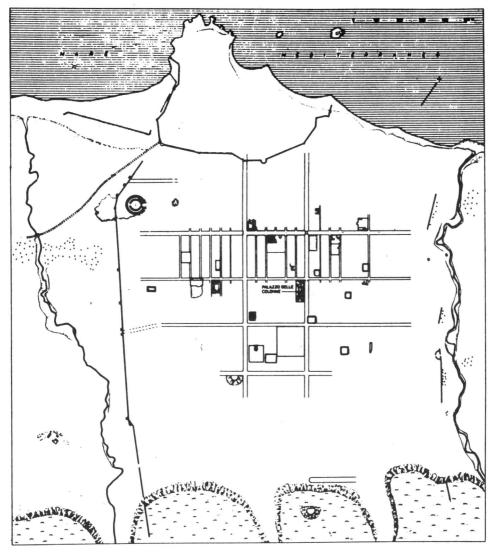

Fig. 77. Ptolemais. General plan of the city. (Greco & Torelli 1983, fig. 141.)

Tomb (Fig. 49). The attic-like structure above these columns in the Tyrus Palace may be compared to another Macedonian tomb, the so-called Tomb of Philip II in Vergina, where it is painted with the famous hunting scene. As a whole, however, the façades of this palace are unique.

Once again, this main palace represents an Oriental plan (and even to some extent Oriental decoration), combined with Greek architectural elements such as columnar orders, albeit hybrid Corinthian and Doric. The style, if not the position, of the animals is Greek as well (above). In fact, both architectural decoration and sculpture seem to point primarily to Alexandria, while the megalithic building method is by contrast local Syrian/Phoenician.[271] All in all, the building certainly gives an un-Greek, "barbaric" impression.

If we take into account the period with which we are dealing, namely the beginning of the 2nd century BC, the model for this remarkable building is most likely to be found in the royal Hellenistic palaces of the capitals. Since Palestine in the first hundred years of the Hellenistic period was dominated by the Ptolemies, and did not become Seleucid until around the time when this palace was built (and Hyrcanus was, incidentally, on the side of the Ptolemies), then the Palace of Alexandria is the obvious candidate: it had an abundance of water and was placed in a large park. When one considers Alexandrian structures like the Pavilion of Ptolemy II and the Nile-boat of Ptolemy IV, and the eclectic and unclassical architecture, which was typical even of the 100-year-younger Palace of Ptolemais (below), and finally takes into account that the architectural decoration and sculpture used at Tyrus was of the Alexandrian type, one may well imagine that Hyrcanus got the idea for the spectacular Qasr el Abd on one of his many visits to Alexandria as a Ptolemaic official.

Perhaps the well-preserved governor's palace, the so-called Palazzo delle Colonne at Ptolemais in Cyrenaica (Cat. 22) (Fig. 77), may also give an impression of the residential and official part of the Ptolemaic palatial buildings that we have lost, for Cyrenaica had long been ruled by the Ptolemies when the palace was built, probably by their governor, at the beginning of the 1st century BC (Figs. 78-79). There are, however, later additions. The palace consists of a large two-storeyed garden-peristyle with both official and residential functions, and a smaller peristyle, again in two storeys, used for various purposes, such as administration, service, etc. The building has a general resemblance to the Macedonian palaces. In particular, the two axially placed apses flanking the main northern wing and facing the official garden-peristyle have close affinities with the official Peristyle I of the Royal Palace of Pella (Cat. 12). In both cases these apsidal rooms were probably used for religious purposes.[272]

The most conspicuous hall is the large *oecus* on the central axis of the main wing to the north. It is completely open to the peristyle. This room type, with columns on three sides in two storeys with windows, and a lower, single-storey passage round the outside, may well have been developed in Alexandria, since it is called an Egyptian *oecus* by Vitruvius (6.3.9) (see n. 293); moreover, the

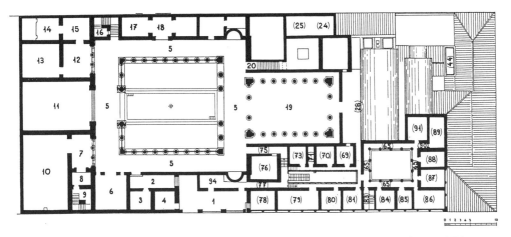

Fig. 78. Ptolemais. Plan of the palace (Cat. 22). (Pesce 1950, tav. XI.)

similarity to the description of the Egyptian-style *symposion* with nine *klinai* on the upper deck of the Thalamegos is considerable. There are certain affinities with the Pavilion of Ptolemy II as well, and a Persian room type may in fact underlie this oecus type. This hall was undoubtedly used for audiences, councils, and trials, and perhaps for banquets too, thus fulfilling the main official needs of the governor. It may both architecturally and functionally be compared to the Roman *basilica*, a term having a truly royal connotation (see p. 20). A comparison to the large hall in Pella with its wall decoration in stone consisting of columns in two storeys comes to mind also, although this room was still a "broad room". In fact the decoration in Ptolemais has merely been transformed into the original free-standing architecture.

The south wing of the large peristyle is only apparently symmetrical, the façade towards the peristyle concealing an irregularity in plan. The wing had three rooms opening onto the courtyard: thus the large central hall was flanked by two ante-rooms with two columns in antis, leading to other, anaxial rooms. The main hall, reached by four steps from the court, and the eastern room were primarily for banquets, if we may judge from the existing mosaics, but the central hall may have had other official functions as well. The rooms in the south-west corner were set aside for residential purposes, as was the first floor around the peristylar court. As far as the symmetry of the southern façade facing the peristyle is concerned, one may compare with the north wing of the official peristyle of Pella, which in my view has three rooms opening onto the peristyle as well (see p. 91).

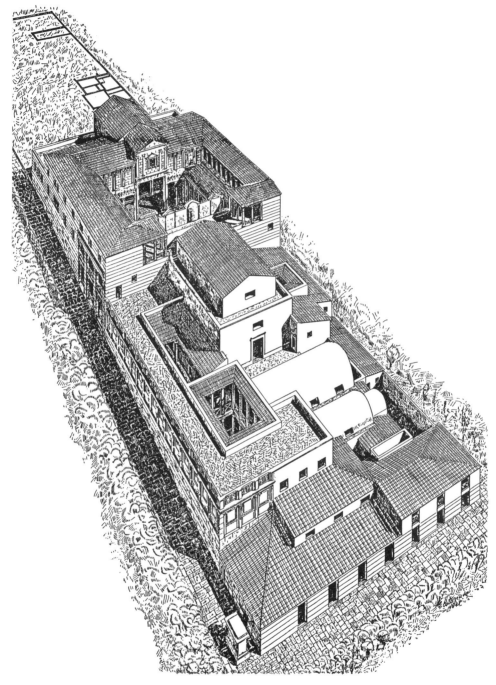

Fig. 79. Ptolemais. Reconstruction of the palace. (Pesce 1950, tav. IX.)

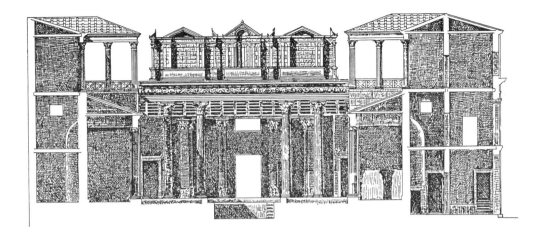

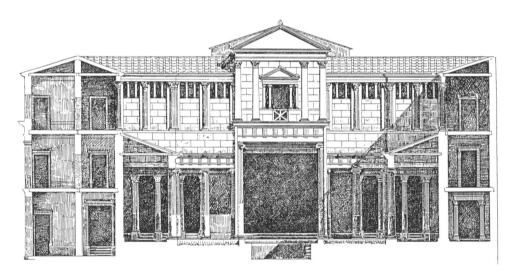

Fig. 80. Ptolemais. Reconstruction of the north (above) and south (below) façades facing the main peristyle. (Pesce 1950, tav. V and VI.)

In the garden of the main peristyle there is a pool lined with cement rendering and surrounded by a bench and balustrade on all sides. Two stairs led down to it.[273] This type of pool with benches has close affinities with the swimming-pools found in the Hasmonean and Herodian palaces of Judaea (see pp. 155ff, 182ff, and Pl. 26), where, however, they were not so closely associated with buildings as with gardens and parks. One may well imagine a common precursor in the Alexandrian basileia, e.g. the so-called Maiandros (above). A further development may be found in the many garden pools and fountains of the Italic private palaces. (see p. 170)[274]

The experimental architecture of this palace has justly been emphasized. Some scholars have seen it as a proof of a Roman date, but as C. Pesce and especially H. Lauter have stressed, there is no reason for not regarding it as a purely Hellenistic architectural expression, and recently the important investigation by J. McKenzie of Alexandrian architectural fragments and their dating has made a Hellenistic date even more likely. Although Pesce's reconstruction of the two-storeyed northern and southern façades towards the main peristyle may be incorrect in some details, all the elements have been determined by finds (Fig. 80). Broken pediments, "dwarf" architecture, curved entablatures, conchs, and a transition from architrave to archivolt, etc., are all elements which have been considered typically Roman, but which were, in fact, "invented" in Hellenistic times.

Lauter and Mckenzie have furnished evidence to show that these elements were probably also to be found in Alexandrian architecture. For example, temporary buildings such as pavilions, and even luxurious Nile-boats, as well as the use of light-weight materials, may have been inspirational sources. Moreover, many of these architectural features, e.g. the decorative style more usually associated with metal objects and the presence of many arches and apses, suggest wooden architecture or building techniques in sun-dried brick or even rush with stucco, rather than stone architecture. This means that the basically Greek architectural elements are used outside their original context: Lauter aptly calls it a "meaningless" architecture. Thus again, façade architecture is used to dignify the approach to the principal rooms and to give a certain prestige to the owner when receiving his subjects. Undoubtedly, façades of this kind were used in the basileia of Alexandria to enhance both the Chrematistikon Pylon and the main façades of the Megiston Peristylon (above). Such façades could be used both on the exterior and the interior of buildings according to need.

There is thus no doubt, in my opinion, that both the general layout and the style of the Palace of Ptolemais reflect buildings which could be found in the basileia

Fig. 81. Alexandria. The façade of the Moustapha Pasha Tomb I. (McKenzie 1990, Pl. 178.)

of Alexandria. The axiality and symmetry, which were reflected both in the southern peristyle façade and in the Egyptian oecus flanked by the apsidal rooms, seem to be features that may well have had their origin in the Palace of Alexandria. One can well imagine that a peristyle building of a similar layout existed in this palace. This argument is strengthened by the fact that a similar plan is found in the Palace of Herodium in Judaea (Cat. 31) (see p. 203 and Fig. 112). A direct inspiration from Macedonia to Ptolemais is at all events untenable, for chronological reasons alone.

In addition, the Palace of Ptolemais may give an impression of the appearance of the private palaces of the upper class in Ptolemaic Egypt, such as, for example, the House of Diotimus. As J. Raeder has pointed out,[275] there is also a close resemblance between the Palace of Ptolemais and the house which Vitruvius describes as being a typical Greek house (Fig. 72),[276] and Raeder suggests that this house should be located in Egypt and identified with a private palace. He sees another reflection of Alexandrian architecture in the houses on Delos, but as many of the houses of the Theatre District probably go back to the 3rd century BC, they may well also have been influenced from Macedonia directly. For in general there is a tendency to underestimate the influence of Macedonian architecture, because of the great and long-lasting success of Alexandria as a cultural focus and inspiration. Elements such as "dwarf" architecture, illusionist architecture, apses, peristyles in two storeys with balustrades and plinths, columnar façades with windows, etc., are known from the early Hellenistic period in Macedonia, and although they were undoubtedly later mediated through Alexandria, they were not necessarily invented there. But the baroque elements such as broken pediments, curved entablatures, segmental pediments, conchs, etc., were probably indeed an Alexandrian addition.

A further indication that Alexandria was, in fact, the centre of this kind of architecture is found in the tomb façades of Petra, in particular the so-called Khasneh, which most scholars now, probably rightly, date to the 1st century BC — and probably early in that century (Pl. 22).[277] It has often been compared with a palace façade, and rightly so, for the tradition of constructing rich tombs to resemble palace façades was not new; this feature made its appearance in the Achaemenid empire as well as in Macedonia and in Alexandria itself, where the façade of the Moustapha Pasha Tomb I, dating from the 2nd century BC at the latest, is especially illustrative (Fig. 81). Also, from the early 2nd century BC, the imagintive Palace of Qasr el Abd at Tyrus, with its original and impressive façades, presents itself for comparison.[278] Finally, there is a close connection with the architecture depicted in the wall-paintings of the Second Style.[279]

Summary

Although almost nothing of the famous Royal Palace of Alexandria has survived, we may, with the help of palatial buildings and even tombs in the Ptolemaic kingdom, whether known from archaeological or written sources, gain a clear impression of the architectural types and styles of which it was composed.

The inspirational sources for this "palace complex", which had such a long-lived importance, are legion. No doubt there was a strong inspiration from the precursors, the Persian palaces with their monumental portals, hypostyle ceremonial halls, and pavilions placed in paradeisoi. The siting of palaces in gardens with water and pavilions is also known from Pharaonic Egypt, of which the Palace of Apries was only the last-known representative (see p. 27). At the same time, the developed Greek/Macedonian peristyle building known from the early Macedonian palaces seems to have retained its role as an important palatial building, and in general many architectural features known from Macedonia are reflected here.

Even at a very early age, sacred elements formed an integral part in palatial architecture, both in the Orient and in Anatolia, although probably not in Macedonia originally. The placing of the king's tomb in the palace complex, i.e. Alexander's Sema reused by the Ptolemies and functioning also as a royal heroon, may be compared directly with the siting of the Tomb of Cyrus the Great in Pasargadae. Both were founders of the palaces and cities in which they were buried, and the tombs of both were placed in spacious paradeisoi.

What primarily distinguishes the Alexandrian basileia from its "models" is the associated cluster of cultural or "public" institutions, reflecting the king's hellenophile outlook and his role as protector of the Greek arts and sciences. We have already seen this association of cultural buildings with royal palaces in Aigai and Pella, which both had theatres connected to them from the outset, but in the Alexandrian basileia the repertoire was further extended, and it became a model for later Hellenistic palaces, such as that of Pergamon, as well as for Roman palaces.

Thus the Alexandrian basileia, which was partly open to the public, was at the same time an Oriental palace serving a personal monarchy and a kind of Greek town within the city. In Alexandria it was the palace, rather than the agora, that formed the centre of the city, which was first the capital of a monarchy, and only secondly a Hellenistic city. Thus the Alexandrian basileia is yet another proof of the validity of the axiom mentioned earlier, that the palace was a mirror of the monarchy it served. For a king of the Ptolemaic dynasty, like a Seleucid king, had two faces: the one turned towards his Egyptian subjects was that of an absolute monarch, a god-king like the Pharaoh, while the one turned towards his Greek and Macedonian subjects and Friends was rather that of a *primus inter pares*, at least in the early years of the dynasty; later, there was a tendency for this distinction to become blurred.

All in all, the general impression of the architecture of the Ptolemaic kingdom is that of a very thorough mixture of Greek/Macedonian and Oriental/Egyptian features. This mixture is very obvious in Qasr el Abd, where, with E. Will, we can conclude that "Le Qasr nous met en présence d'une situation en quelque sorte classique dans la région, celle de l'*interpretatio Graeca* d'un monument de tradition orientale".[280] The same conclusion was reached for the architecture of the Seleucid kingdom. On the other hand, the Palazzo delle Colonne in Ptolemais gives an impression of a primarily Greek/Macedonian architecture, but this building is also 100 years later than Qasr el Abd. From the sketch of the probable appearance of the Alexandrian basileia given above, however, although it is based mostly on written sources, one might well expect the presence of buildings there similar to both Qasr el Abd and the Palazzo delle Colonne. At the same time, one might argue for a development towards a predominantly western expression rather than an eastern one.

VII. JUDAEA

Judaea, like the rest of Palestine, had long been governed by foreign powers. After the Persians, came the Ptolemies, and at the beginning of the 2nd century BC the Seleucid dynasty became its masters. The reason for treating this region separately here is that for about a hundred years (168-63 BC), following the Maccabean revolt, Judaea was ruled by independent Jewish high priests and kings of the Hasmonean dynasty. Fortunately, this later part of the Hellenistic period is much better documented here than the early phase, both archaeologically and in the written sources, especially in the books of Maccabees and Josephus' works.[281]

The capital of the Hasmoneans was Jerusalem, where the Main Palace was situated (Fig. 82). Of this palace, nothing has been found, but we know, primarily from Josephus, that it was placed just opposite the Temple, on the north-east corner of the western hill beside the *xystos* (probably a gymnasium) (Pl. 23). Also, Josephus tells us that the palace towered above its surroundings and was connected with the Temple Mount by a bridge, and that there was a fortress (*baris*), placed on the site of the later Antonia fortress built by Herod (below), just north of the Temple Platform (see Pl. 29).[282] In addition to this Main Palace, the Hasmoneans had a Winter Palace in fertile Jericho; furthermore, the many fortresses founded by these kings in the Judaean desert were furnished with palaces.[283] While most of the Hasmonean palaces were reused and often completely rebuilt by that great builder, the Roman vassal king Herod the Great, whose work will be covered in connection with the early Roman palaces (see pp. 181ff), the original Palace of Jericho is still preserved, beside the Herodian ones.

The Winter Palace of Jericho (Cat. 23) was probably founded by Hyrcanus I, and was occupied and enlarged by his successors (Pl. 24). It was set in a large walled park, and the complex formed part of an extensive royal domain, which was well watered by many aqueducts, without which the area would have been a desert.[284] The abundance of water allowed many swimming-pools to be built, and these constitute the main characteristic of the palace.[284a] The palatial complex embodied many different elements, which were mostly laid out on a regular plan in the park.

Hyrcanus I's palace consisted of an apparently almost square main building (Fig. 83). It had a courtyard in the middle with corridors and rooms on two storeys

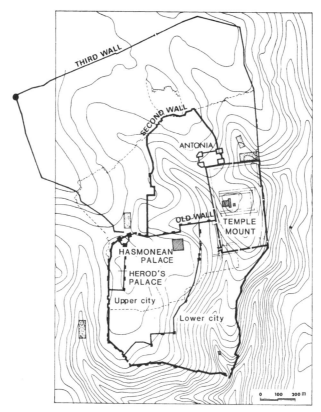

Fig. 82. Jerusalem. Plan of the city. (Jerusalem. 5000 years of History, 1992, p. 48d.)

around it; there were bath installations with both a Greek bathroom and a Jewish ritual bath, *miqveh* (Pl. 25), in the north wing, which probably had a residential function. A large room lavishly decorated in the First Style, perhaps for banqueting, was placed in the south wing, which was probably used for official purposes. The palace had a fortified element in the shape of a large tower built in ashlar, while the rest was in sun-dried brick. To the west of the palace lay two swimming-pools, which were probably surrounded by porticoes and gardens.

The greatest building activity occurred during the reign of Alexander Jannaeus, who came to power in 103 BC. His dramatic reign is reflected by changes in the make-up of the palace (Fig. 84). At first, he simply reused his father's palace, but east of it he laid out a very large recreational complex with a slightly different orientation and a common central axis, consisting of two large swimming-pools surrounded by a large paved square and gardens (Fig. 85, Pl. 26). North of this

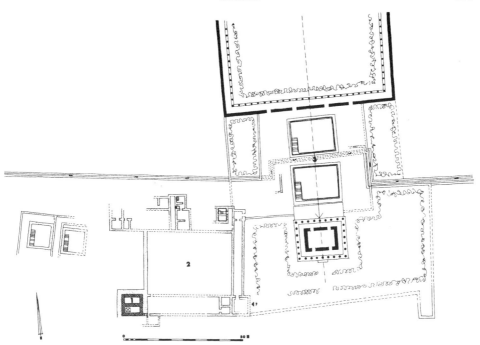

Fig. 83. Jericho. The early phases of the Hasmonean Winter Palace, reconstructed plan (Cat. 23): 1. Watch tower; 2. Hyrcanus' Palace; 3. The recreational complex built by Jannaeus. (Netzer 1990, fig. 1.)

was a large enclosed garden, probably surrounded by porticoes and opening via doors onto the area containing the swimming-pools. South of this area was a rectangular building, and on the basis of two rectangular foundations, one within the other, and fragments of architectual elements E. Netzer reconstructs this as a pavilion surrounded by a *peripteros* in the Doric style.

Late in Alexander Jannaeus' reign, in the turbulent years between 92 and 83 BC, the original main building was buried under a fill, which formed a kind of terrace for a fortified palace surrounded by a moat. The structure has some similarity to Qasr el Abd in Tyrus (Cat. 21), especially as far as the moat is concerned (see p. 139). The palace that was built inside the moat in Jericho was, however, quite different. Apparently it had several towers and a courtyard in the centre, which was perhaps surrounded by corridors or porticoes. The building as a whole might have had a certain affinity to a tetrapyrgion. Like its predecessor, it housed all necessary functions, and perhaps one or several of the towers had a second storey formed as a diaita; at any rate such structures were popular under Herod the Great. Only the foundations and, at the most, the lower part of the walls

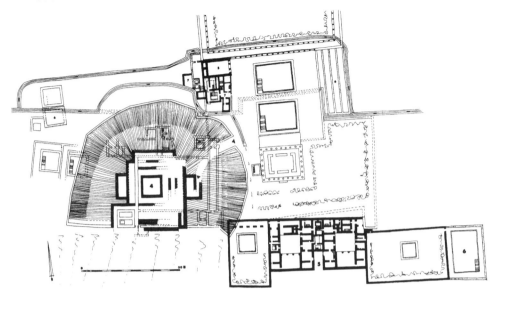

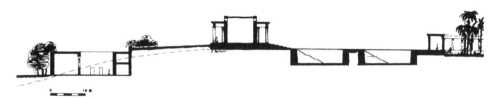

Fig. 84. Jericho. The later phases of the Hasmonean Winter Palace, reconstructed plan and section: 4. The palatial fortress built by Jannaeus; 5. The twin palaces and the oecus built by Alexandra; 6. Large swimming-pool; 7. Bath installations. (Netzer 1990, fig. 4-5.)

of this palace are preserved. One might perhaps get some impression of its appearance from the upper palace at Herodium, built by Herod the Great (Cat. 31) (see Fig. 113 and pp. 201ff). There is no doubt that the building of this fortress was a matter of urgency, since it was built with no regard for the paradeisoi and thus one of the old swimming-pools was covered over as well as part of the paved area around the new ones.

The next enlargement of the palace occurred during the reign of Jannaeus' widow, Alexandra (76-67 BC), and involved the building of the so-called Twin Palaces (Fig. 84). These two identical mansions are placed as mirror images of each other south of Netzer's pavilion, but sharing a common axis with the main fortified palace. The palaces were cut into the slope down to Wadi Qelt, probably

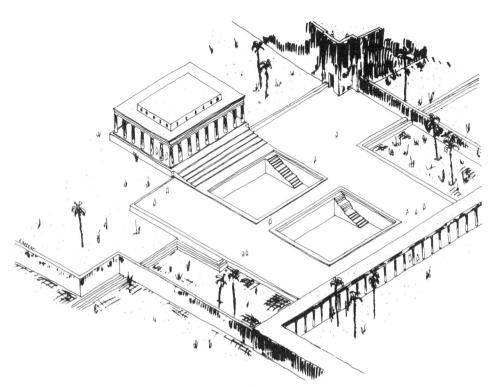

Fig. 85. Jericho. Reconstructed isometric view of the central area with the swimming-pools. (Netzer 1990, fig. 3.)

so as not to spoil the view from the pavilion, and consist of an inner courtyard without a peristyle, surrounded by rooms on two storeys. The main room took up the entire south wing, and (owing to the hot climate) opened northwards to the courtyard with two columns in antis. It probably served as a (private) reception and banqueting room, and there is a certain similarity to the Palace of Lachish (Cat. 7) as well as to the Citadel Palace of Dura Europos (Cat. 17), although the rooms of these palaces were "broad rooms" and the latter palace was furnished with a peristyle as well. Typical are the many bathrooms, both in the Greek and in the Jewish style (*miqvaot*). The Twin Palaces also had enclosed gardens with swimming-pools, and one of them was even furnished with a very modern garden triclinium, while the other had a garden pavilion. Probably during the reign of the last Hasmonean king, Hyrcanus II, an even larger swimming-pool was added to the eastern Twin Palace. These palaces were probably primarily residential.

Also to the time of Alexandra belong a group of rooms placed to the west of the paved area and laid out partly at right angles to it. A large, deep main room, perhaps with two columns in antis facing the swimming-pools, undoubtedly served as a banqueting room. It may be compared, for example, with the oeci of the same shape in the contemporary Palace of Ptolemais (Cat. 22), as well as in contemporary Italic palatial houses (see pp. 146f, 166). It had fine views both over the swimming-pools and over the enclosed garden to the north, which was now furnished with a portico to the south. South of this oecus, a group of Greek and Jewish bathrooms were built, among them a heated miqveh, which is unique. The difficulty of leading water up to the fortified palace may be one of the reasons for this arrangement. The presence of so many bath installations in the palace underlines the great importance attached to bathing, a feature which was even further accentuated in the Herodian buildings (see pp. 181ff). The site in general is lavishly provided with a rather confusing network of conduits, and in recent years an industrial area attached to the estate has been excavated east of the palace; it contains a number of pools, some of them large miqvaot used for the cleansing both of workers and of utensils used in the production of date wine and balsam. In a late phase, storerooms were added to the east of the recreational area.

As only one royal palace has been found in Judaea, it may be useful to include also a governor's palace, namely the one found at Tell Judeideh near Marisa (Fig. 86).[285] This was excavated around 1900 and tentatively dated to the second half of the 1st century BC, but it was probably somewhat earlier and belonged to a Hasmonean governor. The building, which measures only c. 14 x 33 m (= 462 m^2) had two sections: one was furnished with a courtyard with a primitive kind of peristyle; a deep pool measuring 5 x 4 m, perhaps a miqveh, lay in the middle of the court, which was surrounded by rooms all opening into the peristyle. A large "broad room", which took up the entire south wing and was furnished with an ante-room with two columns in antis, constitutes a well-known local element. The other section, separated from the first by a corridor, had a typically Oriental plan with a light-well surrounded by small rooms. The "Greek" section was undoubtedly the official one, while the Oriental one was for private use. Comparison with the basically Oriental palaces of Nippur, Dura Europos, and Lachish comes to mind, thus corroborating the impressions conveyed by the Jericho palace.

Summary

It is important to stress that the Winter Palace of Jericho was not the main palace of the king, which was in Jerusalem, but primarily a recreational retreat, so that elements like a monumental approach, and large ceremonial halls, as well as an

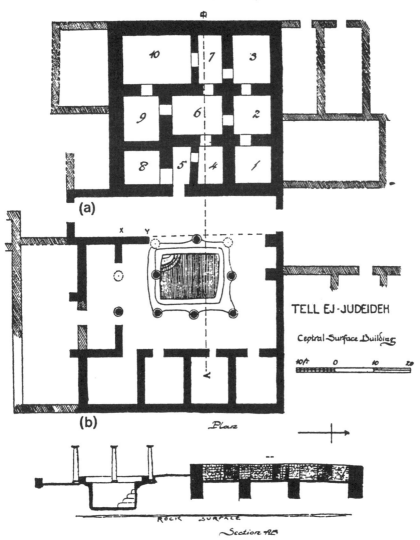

Fig. 86. Tell Judeideh. The palatial house, plan and section. (Bliss & Macalister 1902, fig. 15.)

administrative section, may well be missing here. Instead, the residential and recreational elements, along with the industrial elements, most probably assume more importance than was the case in the main palace in Jerusalem.

One may well ask where the Hasmonean kings looked to for inspiration when building their palaces. Both in the palaces of Jericho and Tell Judeideh, there are features belonging to the eastern as well as the western architectural tradition, a reflection of the history of Palestine before the Maccabean revolt. As a representative of the architecture of the Persian period, the Palace of Lachish (Cat. 7) and also the *paradeisos* in Sidon (known from written sources) may be mentioned (see p. 51), while the Qasr el Abd (Cat. 21) was built in the transitional phase between the rule of the Ptolemaic and Seleucid dynasties. As we have seen, there are certain affinities with these local precursors, but in its entirety the "palace complex" of Jericho seems to be an architectural innovation.

No doubt, the regular layout of the buildings in Jericho in paradisiac parks, with large enclosed gardens, and swimming-pools, was originally inspired by the Persian palaces, mediated through Alexandria and perhaps Antiochia. Also the nearby, defunct Palace of Tyrus had many of the same features. The rectangular pavilion put up by Alexander Jannaeus had antecedents in the Persian orbit as well; as we have seen, hypostyle halls surrounded by porticoes, and used among other things as garden pavilions, were popular there (see p. 40). Again, the direct inspirational source was probably the diaitai of the Alexandrian basileia, where towers were used in that way, too (see p. 134). Although the exterior and architectural elements of the pavilion at Jericho are Greek, the plan is thus basically Persian.

The fact that a crucial element in the royal palaces in Macedonia and Pergamon, namely the peristyle, is apparently absent from Jericho, although a primitive variety was used in the governor's Palace of Tell Judeideh, is an indication of the superficiality of the Greek influence, which is mostly limited to decorative architectural elements, to interior embellishment, and to the Grecian-style bathrooms, which were very popular in this period.[286] Although bathrooms were far from unknown in the East, where they were characterized by paved or stuccoed rooms with a drain and were probably equipped with movable bath-tubs,[287] the built-in immersion bath-tubs of the Hasmonean palaces are of a Greek type. All in all, in the period during which the Jericho Palace reached its final form, i.e. in the first half of the 1st century BC, the mixture of trends is so great that the cultural koiné at last seems to become a reality, as was the case in the contemporary Palace of Ptolemais (Cat. 22) (see p. 154).

Even if an inspiration from the Hellenistic royal palaces of Antiochia and Alexandria (Cats. 15, 20) may thus be imagined for Jericho, there is still a total absence of "public" buildings. The reason may be the basically recreational aspect of this palace; but it is worth remembering that the Hasmonean dynasty was, at least initially, an orthodox Jewish one and very anti-Hellenist. Greek polis institutions such as gymnasia, theatres, hippodromes, etc., were consequently unattractive to them.[288] Later, however, the dynasty became to some extent hellenized, and the siting of the Xystos near the Jerusalem Palace, is, especially if it was, in fact, a kind of gymnasium, revealing.

As for religious buildings, there was room for only one temple in the Jewish religion, namely the one in Jerusalem. The Jewish faith is, however, very much in evidence by virtue of the many miqvaot found in the palace, though these are often combined with a Greek bathroom. Also, the total absence of figural motives in the very fine and modern wall-paintings should be noted, as should the sheer number of swimming-pools. Although such pools were known both from the Hellenistic palaces of the East and from Greek gymnasia, this element was certainly very prominent here. The special emphasis on swimming may therefore be related to the Jewish ritual of bathing, and these pools may have been used for this purpose also.

All this may not seem surprising, but one has to remember that Judaea had been incorporated in the Hellenistic kingdoms for nearly two centuries, before the Maccabean revolt afforded the Jewish people a period of independence. Persian rule was already a thing of the past, and its stamp on the area has always been considered very weak. The basically non-Greek appearance of the Hasmonean palace in Jericho at least may therefore be used as an argument in favour of the hypothesis, already advanced in connection with the Palace of Tyrus, that the palaces on which they drew for inspiration (undoubtedly those of Alexandria and Antiochia), were perhaps not so heavily influenced and marked by Greek architecture as has generally been assumed. This again may support the assumption advanced earlier that these palaces were very much influenced by their precursors, the Persian palaces, with their independent halls, their paradeisoi, and their fondness for water.

As was the case in the Ptolemaic kingdom, the final phase of the palaces of Judaea, the second quarter of the 1st century BC, shows signs of an increasing westernization. The last two chapters, on early Roman palaces, will reveal whether this growing cultural koiné in the late Hellenistic period finally became a reality, at least as far as palatial architecture is concerned.

VIII. ITALY

Before dealing with early Roman palaces in Italy, it is important to try to appraise the cultural relationship between that area and the Hellenistic kingdoms during the Hellenistic period. For although not an actual part of these kingdoms, Italy was in close contact with them. Italy was hellenized gradually, over a long period: at first mainly through the Greek colonies in southern Italy and Sicily, but later, when Rome began to take a political interest in the Hellenistic kingdoms, the area entered the vortex of Hellenistic culture directly. As stated in the Introduction (p. 10), it is a moot point whether it is appropriate to term the culture(s) in Italy at that time, i.e. the 2nd-1st centuries BC, Hellenistic. I have preferred to use the term "hellenized" instead, since Hellenistic, in the way it is used here, covers the cultures which came, though seldom of their own volition, under the sway of the Hellenistic kings.

Culturally, Italy was highly regionalized in this period, and there were as many ways of being hellenized as there were regions. This is also the reason for the great difference as to their time of romanization. In most regions Rome did not make herself conspicuous culturally until after the Social War, and in some places, such as that stronghold of Hellenism, Campania, Rome continued to be more of a recipient than a contributor in this acculturation process, until the Augustan period.[289]

The direct hellenization of Rome and Italy in the 2nd-1st centuries BC meant that the cultural and moral character of the state was influenced, not merely its political one.[290] Direct knowledge of the official expression and luxurious living of the Hellenistic kings meant that the Roman élite, especially Roman generals, increasingly adopted the manners and customs of these monarchs. For example, they began building private palatial houses and villas after the model of Hellenistic palaces.[291] Moreover, without underestimating other inspirational sources, the influence of Hellenistic royal architecture on Italic religious and public architecture, represented partly by the great sanctuaries of Latium, partly by the splendid porticoes built in Rome by generals back from the East, is indisputable: the close relationship is reflected in the common use of, for example, rows of peristyles, often with gardens, an architectural rendering of nature through the medium of terracing, façade architecture, and a frequent use of rounded forms. While the role of Pergamon and Alexandria in this process has been well established, there has been a certain tendency to underestimate Macedonia's direct influence on Italy, owing to the relatively early fall of this kingdom; in fact, all the above-mentioned elements were already present in the early Macedonian palaces.

In this connection, I find it important to play down the rather sharp distinction which is generally made between the two major phases of hellenization in Italy (outside the Greek colonies, of course) mentioned above, namely the "indirect" hellenization, via Magna Graecia and Sicily in the 4th-3rd centuries BC, and the "direct" hellenization in the 2nd-1st centuries BC.

In respect of the first period, it is important to stress that even before the Second Punic War, Hellenistic inspiration did not derive exclusively from these Greek parts of Italy, although they may well have played an important role as mediators. For Magna Graecia and Sicily were very much stimulated by the contact with Epirus and Macedonia, as already mentioned in connection with the models in Sicily (see p. 79), in fact they seem together to have formed a kind of South Adriatic koiné. That this contact was far from new is shown by Dionysius I's activities in the Adriatic, and it was furthered by the frequent interference in Italian affairs of generals from Epirus, especially Alexander Molossa and Pyrrhus.

As for the second period, even if there can be no doubt about the dominant and massive cultural influence on Italy from the Hellenistic kingdoms at that time, we can establish a continuous influence on the rest of Italy from the regions with old Greek colonies as well. It was in Campania, where the two types of "influences" met, that the fashions and modes of the capital were to a certain degree created; this region flourished by virtue of its central position, its fine harbour, Puteoli (which communicated eastern customs to the rest of Italy and became the main port for Rome), and finally as a setting for the villas of the Roman upper class, which began to be built in increasing numbers in this period.[292]

Private palaces

There were, for very good reasons, no royal or governors' palaces in the Italian Peninsula in the Hellenistic period. From the 2nd to the 1st century BC we are, however, fortunate enough to have a good knowledge both of private town palaces in Pompeii, and of the rich country and coastal villas built by the Roman élite, primarily for recreational and social activities (*otium*), in Latium and especially Campania. In addition to the preserved monuments themselves, written sources as well as wall-paintings help to throw light on the appearance of these palatial

buildings. As far as Rome is concerned, we in fact owe most of our knowledge
of its luxurious private palaces, not least those on the Palatine, to the ancient
authors, although a few such houses have been found beneath the later palaces.
Vitruvius' description of a house suitable for a Roman aristocrat is illuminating:

For persons of high rank who hold office and magistracies, and whose duty it is to serve
the state, we must provide princely vestibules, lofty halls and very spacious peristyles,
plantations and broad avenues finished in a majestic manner; further, libraries and basilicas
arranged in a similar fashion with the magnificence of public structures, because in such
palaces, public deliberations and private trials and judgements are often transacted.[293]

The large *horti* owned by the élite just outside Rome's walls, which began to
appear in the late 2nd century BC, are also known only from the ancient authors.
The earliest *hortus* on which we have any information, that owned by the hellenophile Scipio Aemilianus, was already in existence in 129 BC.[294] Since we
know that he visited Alexandria, the inspiration for this villa garden may well have
come from the Alexandrian basileia, as was probably the case with the other horti
around Rome.[295] A drawing by Ligorio was earlier regarded as representing
Lucullus' great villa on the Monte Pincio, but the French excavations in this area
have not supported this view. A suggestion that his reconstruction was inspired
by the Sanctuary of Fortuna in Praeneste would give a reverse inspirational route
to the one suggested by F. Coarelli.[296] Of Pompey's great "hortus complex"
on the Campus Martius, which also included a villa, only the theatre and a small
part of the portico have been traced, but both are marked on the *Forma Urbis
Romae*.

Typical at least of the private town palaces in Pompeii is that they consist of
two parts, of which one is centred round the *atrium*, and the other round the peristyle (see Fig. 87); thus they illustrate very well the description of such houses
given by Vitruvius,[297] and may therefore be used with some confidence to illustrate the situation outside Campania too. The atrium section was for official use,
salutatio, etc., while the rooms around the peristyle court, if not the peristyle court
itself, were for private use, only invited guests having access, normally for dinner
parties. The new "Hellenistic" element in these houses was the peristyle, which
was — it is worth remarking — furnished with a garden, onto which dining-
rooms, picture galleries, libraries,[298] and exedrae, as well as bedrooms, etc.,
opened. Scholars have now definitely given up trying to find a precursor for this
peristyle section in the Greek/Hellenistic private house, and accept instead that

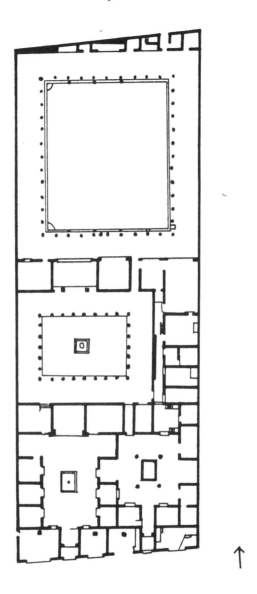

Fig. 87. Pompeii. Plan of Casa del Fauno (Cat. 24). 1:650. (Zanker 1979, Abb. 45a.)

the closest affinity is with the Hellenistic palaces. These had no atrium (although their vestibules had the same function), yet they often consisted, as we have seen, of rows of peristyles with gardens, partly for official use, including the social function of banqueting, and partly for residential purposes. In the Italic houses as well as in these palaces, the gardens were laid out formally, and were often furnished with basins and pools. Moreover, the Hellenistic non-royal palaces that we know of are more or less the same size as those of Pompeii. Thus the Casa del Fauno (Cat. 24; Fig. 87) has an area of 2,940 m²,[299] while the Palazzo delle Colonne in Ptolemais (Cat. 22), which was a governor's palace, amounts to 3,300 m², and only the palatial "House of Dionysus" in Pella (Cat. 11), at 5,240 m², is larger.

Turning now to the villas, the fortified ones probably constituted a special case. An example is Scipio Africanus' villa at Liternum, Seneca's description of which suggests an affinity with the tetrapyrgia of the East, and, for example, the contemporary Palace of Demetrias (Cat. 13). Seneca also mentions other villas in Campania that resembled camps. They belonged to famous generals such as Marius, Pompey, and Caesar and were situated on hilltops with a fine view of their surroundings, not by the coast.[300]

As far as pleasure villas in general are concerned, scholars normally identify two models, which may be designated "open" and "closed" or "portico" and "peristyle" villas.[301] The criterion is whether they were constructed around a peristyle, facing inwards, or open, with porticoes and terraces facing the landscape. One model does not, however, exclude the other; in fact features of both are often encountered in the same villa, as is the case in the Hellenistic palaces, where these models had their origin. Also, they were often placed on terraced platforms, as, for example, the Villa dei Misteri (Fig. 88).[302] In the "closed" and "mixed" villas the main focus was on the peristyle, which normally contained a garden like the city houses, usually formally laid out, and was reached directly from the entrance. There was not always an atrium, and if there was, it might be placed beyond the peristyle, probably because these villas did not have the same official function as the town houses, not being used for *salutatio*, for instance. But according to Cicero, this phenomenon was by no means unknown, even in villas, since many patrons combined business with pleasure.[303] At any rate they certainly had a social function, many friends often staying for long periods. Dining was one of the most important activities in villa life, and there were always several dining-rooms, which often included triclinia in the open.[304]

Since garden-peristyles were a very important innovation both in the palatial town houses and in the villas of Italy, this may be the place to discuss their origin, which has been much debated: most recently, M. Carroll-Spillecke,[305] like many before her, has found a pure Italic development to be the most probable, i.e. from

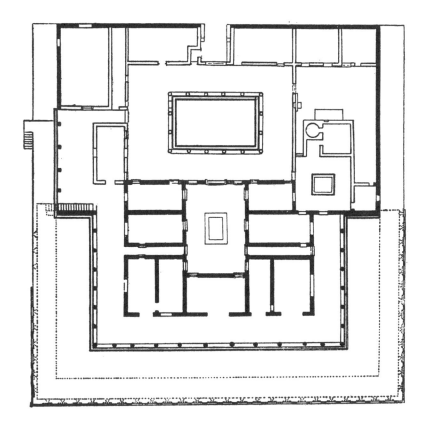

Fig. 88. Pompeii. Plan and reconstruction of Villa dei Misteri. (Drerup 1959, Abb. 1, Taf. 1.1.)

the horti which belonged to the old Italic houses. She argues, in my view not very convincingly, against the peristyles of the Hellenistic palaces having gardens at all. As another possible source of inspiration for the garden-peristyles, gymnasia have been suggested, as well as sacred groves.[306] However, I see no reason why Italic house-owners should resort to such disparate models to find inspiration for their gardens, when a model was at hand in the residential buildings of the Hellenistic kingdoms.

In the country and coastal villas, we meet with another kind of garden, or rather park, namely the grounds in which the villa was situated (Fig. 89).[307] To judge from the depictions of them in wall-paintings, these were frequently laid out on a regular plan, and embellished with pavilions, *i.a.* in the form of towers, and with artificial or natural streams that were sometimes combined with artificial grottoes as nymphaea.[308] In her investigations into the gardens of the Villa Oplontis, W.F. Jashemski has been able to show that at least the park in which this villa lay was laid out formally (Fig. 90).[309] One may compare the large park surrounding, for example, the Palace of Alexandria (Cat. 20), which for its part was inspired by the Persian paradeisoi and the Egyptian gardens of the pharaohs. Thus I do not agree with Carroll-Spillecke, when she brushes aside the gardens of the basileia of Alexandria as an exception and reduces the paradeisos to a mere plantation.

Of course, one cannot exclude an inspiration from the parks that were attached to the gymnasia, either. Undoubtedly the gymnasia and palaestrae mentioned in connection with the houses and villas of the Roman élite were actually gardens with porticoes for strolling in and for discussing philosophical or other matters (also called *ambulationes*) rather than for athletic activities.[310] The same may well have been the case with the palaestra of the Alexandrian basileia, located near the Maiandros, and perhaps the Museion also had a resemblance to that kind of gymnasium (see p. 132).

An interesting component in many coastal villas, and one which is very often referred to by the ancient authors, is the fish-pond. Much is said of the excessive lengths to which especially the late Republican pond-owners would go to keep their fish happy. Such fish-ponds were already in use in Sicily by the time of Gelon the Tyrant (see p. 80), and perhaps the many pools known from Hellenistic palaces, especially in Judaea, but probably also in Alexandria and Ptolemais, may have had a culinary function as well as serving as swimming-pools.[311] At least there is a great affinity to the lakes, rivers, and pools of the Persian palaces, which abounded with fish and birds. The purpose of these fish-ponds was primarily to

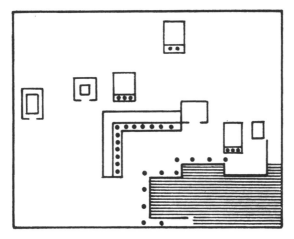

Fig. 89. Pompeii. Drawing from a wall-painting of coastal villas laid in parks, found in the Villa of Lucretius Fronto, and a reconstructed plan of the complex (after M. Rostovtzeff). (Grimal 1969, figs. 15-16.)

furnish the large and sumptuous dinner parties with the finest specialities. All in all, I think A. Boëthius has expressed the role of the Roman villa very aptly: "In Roman villas the love of nature, the old agricultural tradition of Italy, and the fanciful luxury and refinement of Hellenistic architecture and pleasure grounds (*paradeisoi*) met."[312]

Royal palaces

The only royal palace from the Hellenistic period in Italy was the old palace built in Syracuse by Dionysius I and renovated by Agathocles, which was used also by King Hieron II, and later by the Roman governor (see p. 79). Nothing of this

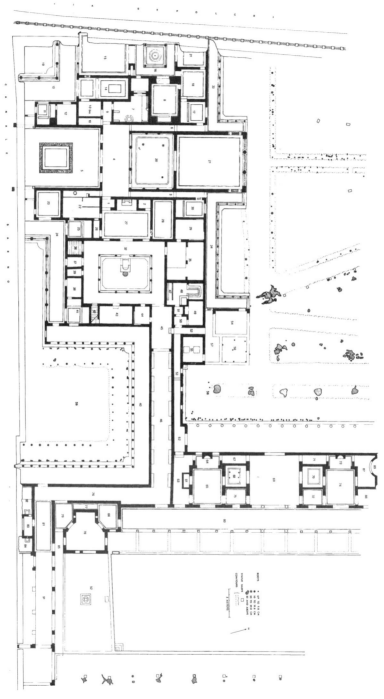

Fig. 90. Torre Annunziata. The Villa Oplontis, plan with gardens indicated.
(Jashemski 1979, foldout plan.)

palace has been preserved, but an impression of it may be gleaned from Moschion's description of the huge pleasure boat, the Syracusia, built by this king, which contained not only a *gymnasion* with *peripatoi* and gardens, but also a sanctuary of Aphrodite, a library, and a large bathroom, besides quarters for the crew. The rich embellishments included figural mosaic floors, panelled ceilings, paintings, and the lavish use of precious stones.[313]

Since palatial houses and villas clearly inspired by Hellenistic palaces also existed in Italy in the Hellenistic period, Augustus and his immediate successors had no difficulty in finding models when they began to build their imperial palaces. The splendid late Republican houses on the Palatine already included official functions and even several semi-public elements, such as porticoes and even "public" sanctuaries, a highly typical feature of the Hellenistic royal palaces.[314] On the Campus Martius, Pompey had gone a step further, including in his garden villa a complex consisting of a temple, a theatre, and a public portico with gardens and a *curia*. Augustus' immediate predecessor and adoptive father, Caesar, lived in the Domus Publica in the Forum Romanum, and to this were connected old sanctuaries for Vesta as well as the cults of the Regia. The house itself was distinguished by a pediment, connoting at the same time an official function and royalty (see p. 19).[315] In his capacity as dictator and Pontifex Maximus, Caesar had supreme religious as well as political power in Rome.

At this point, a discussion of Octavian/Augustus' relationship to the monarchical tradition, which Pompey and Caesar represented and which was partially a heritage from the great generals who had conquered the Hellenistic kingdoms, cannot be avoided. The issue is a complex one, and has in recent years attracted the attention of several scholars.[316] It has proved practical to divide Octavian/Augustus' reign into three phases. The first, from 43-27 BC, covers the triumviral phase and is dominated by a strong self-assertion on the part of Octavian; it ends with his disclaiming all powers and his acceptance of the title of Augustus. The second phase, from 27-12 BC, i.e. the period until Augustus became Pontifex Maximus and Agrippa died, is dominated by the notion of the restoration of the Republic. Finally, in the third phase, ending with his death in 14 AD, the dynastic aspect and the order of succession are the main issues.

In his ambition to be Caesar's sole successor, Octavian followed his monarchic policy in several respects. This applies to a continuation of Caesar's substantial reorganization of the Campus Martius, involving, for example, the building of the Mausoleum, a typical royal, dynastic monument, and of the Pantheon, which was the work of Agrippa and which F. Coarelli, probably rightly, considers to have originally been a kind of royal heroon. Also, the construction of the Temple of Divus Iulius in the Forum Romanum, and the completion of all the Caesarian buildings, primarily the Forum Iulium and the Saepta, as well as the building of his own forum, were all parts of this policy.[317] There is a direct line from the building projects of the Hellenistic kings to these Campus Martius projects; the combination of public, religious, official, and private architecture, which was typical of the great basileia, not least in Alexandria and Pergamon is, in fact, part of the very same tradition.

Octavian/Augustus' palace complex on the Palatine (Fig. 91), commonly known as the "Casa di Augusto" (Cat. 25), which was built between 36 and 28 BC, before he became sole ruler, may without any difficulty be associated with this development. The palace was the result of a major reorganization of a plot which Octavian owned, which faced the valley containing the Circus Maximus, and which was formerly taken up by late Republican houses. The whole complex was conceived and built at the same time and was laid out on two terraces with a difference in height of 9 m. All in all it covered an area of c. 12,000 m^2 (Figs. 92-93), and consisted partly of the main palace with official and residential quarters, and partly of religious and "public" buildings. (Fig. 92).[318]

The approach to the palace and its entrance are unfortunately not preserved, but taking into account the "royal vestibules" for private palaces mentioned by Vitruvius, a conspicuous entrance must certainly have existed. In fact, we have a description of the portal of the palace, crowned by a *corona civica* and flanked by laurels, of which Ovid says, "*conspicuos postes tectaque digna deo*" (Pl. 27).[319] It was undoubtedly surmounted by a pediment (see p. 19) and probably faced the street leading to the palace from the Area Palatina. It must have led to the vestibule, of which we hear that in 2 BC it was furnished with an inscription carrying Augustus'new title *pater patrias*.[320] Following the custom of the Roman élite, the atrium, the traditional place for the salutatio, was undoubtedly closely connected with the vestibule and entrance. While the palace proper, built on a slope and facing outwards, did not look much seen from this side, its appearance from the Circus Maximus valley must have been truly impressive. Since the Temple of Apollo also faced towards the Circus, one may well imagine that a main entrance not only to the temple (where the beginnings of an, albeit undated, construction of a monumental ramp from the valley have been identified) but also to the main palace from this side, was envisaged by Octavian (Fig. 91).[321]

The part of the main palace (Fig. 93) set aside as a private dwelling is rather poorly preserved; only two small rooms on the lower floor are left, but the finest

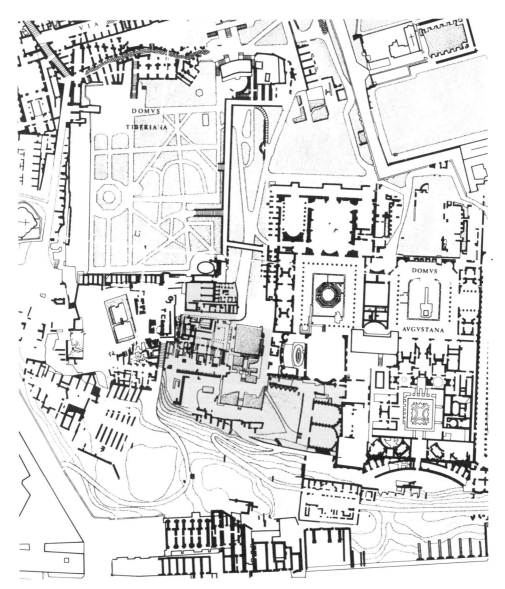

Fig. 91. Rome. General plan of the Palatine with the Casa di Augusto. (Grey shading)
(After Roma. Area Archaeologica centrale. 1983.)

rooms undoubtedly lay on the upper terrace, placed partly around a now almost
completely ruined small peristyle court and partly on the upper floor of large
peristyle. Among other things a very fine *cubiculum* has been found there, built
into the terrace of the Area Apollinis (below).

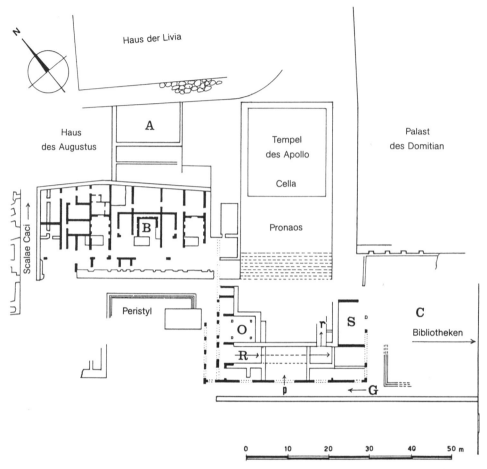

Fig. 92. Rome. Casa di Augusto. The entire complex (Cat. 25). (Carettoni 1983b, plan 1.)

The official section took up the main part of the ground floor of the large peristyle court, which was probably adorned with a garden. The main rooms were situated in the northern wing and placed symmetrically around a central axis, with the main focus on a large central hall. This hall, furnished with a continuous podium on three sides, with short flights of steps on the short sides, was probably a council- and court-room. Perhaps it was in this room that the secret meetings mentioned in the written sources were held, and judgement dispensed.[322] The main hall was flanked partly by two smaller halls, partly by two libraries. In the east wing, the main room was a tetrastyle oecus, which was furnished with a later walled-up apse in the back wall, and which probably functioned as a banqueting and perhaps audience hall.[323] Also from the eastern wing, a covered ramp led

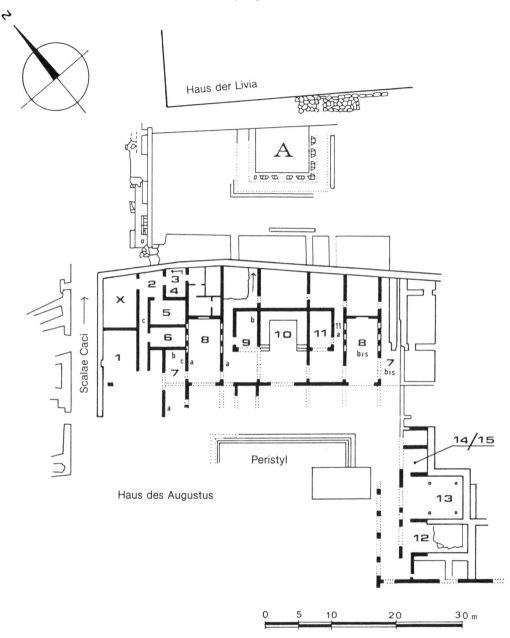

Fig. 93. Rome. Casa di Augusto. The main palace. (Carettoni 1983b, plan 2.)

up to the terrace of the Temple of Apollo (below).[324] The western side of the peristyle was undoubtedly lined by rooms as well, while its southern side, resting on the terrace wall, was open towards the Circus Maximus.

The main palace was decorated in the Second Style, which may be regarded as a pale reflection of the stone decoration of the Hellenistic palaces. One must, however, take into account that in Rome there was still an objection to the use of luxury materials in private buildings. But this did not prevent the use of stone in a floor decoration of *opus sectile* in the finer rooms, the less important rooms having mosaics. There seems to have been some difference in the painted decoration used in the official part and in the living-quarters.[325]

East of the main palace were the "public" and religious complexes (Fig. 92). The centrally placed and partly preserved temple of Octavian's tutelary deity Apollo had a commanding position. We know from the written sources that the temple was used as a meeting place for the senate and the emperor. Also, we are informed that the large plaza in front of it, the Area Apollinis, which was situated at a level with the upper terrace and could be reached by means of the above-mentioned ramp, was used for receptions; the emperor sat in state at the top of the staircase to the pronaos, while subjects and ambassadors crowded on the plaza below.[326]

To the east of the temple was the Portico of the Danaids, a garden-peristyle which could also be reached from the official peristyle. Its west wing contained, among other rooms, a large marbled hall for official purposes, while the east range was taken up by the now vanished libraries.[327] These libraries were open to the public, and Octavian here clearly followed Caesar's example, since the latter had planned to build libraries as an adjunct to his forum (they were completed by Asinius Pollio and carried his name). But there is also a major difference, for Octavian built his libraries into his palace, in the monarchic tradition of the Hellenistic kings, not into his forum, and probably used them for audiences.[328] The Portico of the Danaids was embellished with a great deal of sculpture, and, together with the marbled hall and the libraries, it contained all the elements mentioned by Vitruvius as belonging to the aristocratic *domus* (above). At the same time this portico was directly modelled on Pompey's portico in the Campus Martius (see n. 298).

Summary

When we compare this Palatine complex with the late Republican private houses and villas of the élite, the fundamental differences are thrown into relief. Although a comparison of single elements and rooms may well be made, the combination of residential, official, social, religious, and "public" elements is unique in Italy, even though Caesar and Pompey had certainly gone much of the way towards it.

Augustus' complex as a whole may be compared only with royal palatial buildings of the Hellenistic East. In fact, most of the elements known from the most multi-functional Hellenistic palaces, those of Alexandria and Pergamon, are present: if, as seems to be the case, a great part of the Palatine with its numerous sanctuaries, public buildings, and gardens in fact belonged to Augustus, it would compare well with the basileia of Alexandria. Also, there was the same close connection with the temenos of the tutelary deity, which could be used for royal receptions and which housed a library too, as found in the palace on the acropolis of Pergamon (Cat. 14) (i.e. the Temenos of Athena), now a part of the Roman empire (Pl. 20).

As we have seen, the façade and the approach were very important to Hellenistic palaces, often involving terraces and platforms. We have only minimal information on the approach to Augustus' complex from the Palatine, and although its portal was famous, is may not have been very impressive. Seen from the Circus Maximus, however, the palace must have been striking and no doubt reminded spectators of the great sanctuaries of Latium and the coastal villas of Campania, both of which were at least offshoots of Hellenistic royal architecture. Thus the terraced façade was dominated by the towering Temple of Apollo placed in the axis of the complex and flanked by the peristyles, the whole presenting a unified façade to the valley.

Even if Augustus' later policy, when his position was secure, was to avoid a monarchic title, and even if he endeavoured to appear as a restorer of the Republic, all the same, when he was Octavian and a triumvir, he nevertheless built his new house on the Palatine according to models found in the palaces of the Hellenistic kings. Although the size of his house has often been adduced as evidence of its modesty and "Republican" flavour, as has the decoration, 12,000 m^2 is not particularly small, and one must remember that the whole second storey of the large peristyle, and almost all the structures of the upper terrace, probably including the main reception hall, have disappeared. It is no coincidence, either, that he harks back to the first Roman monarchy by siting his palace beside the Hut of Romulus, and his Mausoleum beside the tomb of this first king.[329] The inclusion of the cult of Vesta in his palace, when he became Pontifex Maximus, and the erection of his palace close to the Sanctuary of Cybele, a link to the Trojan antecedents of the Julii, are yet other examples of this policy.[330]

Octavian's ambitions and aspirations are thus mirrored particularly in his private buildings, which also included his huge Mausoleum. If these private constructions are viewed in conjunction with the new works on the Campus Martius in the first two of the above-mentioned phases of Augustus' reign, partly undertaken by Octavian himself, and partly by Agrippa (i.e. the Pantheon, a theatre, a temporary stadium, Agrippa's Thermae,[331] with a swimming-pool (Stagnum) and a canal (Euripus) placed in a large park, and many sanctuaries, e.g. for Isis and Serapis), all the elements that characterize a Hellenistic basileia are found to be present.[332]

Eventually the Forum Romanum was the only spot not included in this great "basileia, Alexandrian style" (which also included the imperial fora), and this venerable area too underwent a metamorphosis from a political centre to a dynastic programmatic museum, a process that had already begun when the Temple of Divus Iulius was built and the triumphal arches flanking it raised. The Palatine Hill, which even as early as Augustus' time was probably mainly owned by the Imperial House, was further developed by Caligula, Nero, and Domitian.[333]

In this context, Nero's Domus Aurea, with its huge vestibule facing the Forum Romanum, seems less remarkable and revolutionary. In fact, Nero "merely" transposed the concept of the Alexandrian basileia to Rome, as his predecessors had tried to do to a lesser degree and in a less provocative manner.[334] Also, the concept of an official palace in the form of a peristyle building set on a platform on the Palatine (the Domus Tiberiana), and a residential palace, or villa (the Domus Aurea), set in a large park, supports this view.[335] Furthermore, the great villas on the outskirts of Rome, the former horti, were already in Julio-Claudian times all owned by the emperor and functioned as a sort of ancillary palaces.[336] The Domus Aurea forms a link to the country villas of succeeding emperors: for example, Domitian's huge villa in Albanum and Hadrian's beautiful villa at Tibur, where an element like the Canopus, in fact, gives direct associations with Alexandria.[337]

IX. ROMAN PALESTINE

Palestine, having been a battlefield during the many squabbles following Alexander's death, fell first to the Ptolemies, and then in 200 BC to the Seleucids. The important phase during which Judaea was an independent kingdom under the Jewish Hasmonean dynasty has already been covered in detail (see pp. 155ff). Pompey's conquest of Palestine in 63 BC meant its transformation into a Roman province, though Rome preferred to keep a dynasty of vassal kings in Judaea until 6 AD to avoid ruling this troublesome area directly. With the enthronement of the romanophile Herod the Great as vassal king (37-4 BC), the area entered a period of prosperity, which among other things manifested itself in extensive building activity. As Herod was a prolific and original builder, we are lucky enough in Palestine, primarily in Judaea, to have palaces preserved from both the late Hellenistic and the early Roman periods. In addition, Josephus' works are a mine of information.

In fact, these Herodian palaces, which were the direct successors of the Hasmonean ones, give us a unique opportunity to observe in which fields romanization was felt, and in which fields the Hellenistic models continued fairly uninterrupted. Since Hellenistic architecture in general is poorly preserved or not excavated in Palestine, the Herodian buildings may give some idea of what we have lost, for they were certainly not created out of nothing. When dealing with these Herodian palaces, it is important to remember that Herod, in contrast to the Hasmoneans, was only half Jewish, for which reason he had to take special measures to keep the Jewish population content.[338]

Royal palaces

Three kinds of royal palaces are known in Palestine from the Herodian period: first of all the main palaces, situated in the two most important cities, Jerusalem, the capital, and Caesarea, the new main port. Secondly there were palaces serving primarily recreational purposes, such as the three fine winter palaces in the oasis of Jericho, and the summer palace complex in Herodium, which was, at the same time, however, an administrative centre. Finally there were palaces in most of the desert fortresses which Herod either built or took over from the Hasmoneans. Best preserved are the two palaces in the largest fortress, Masada (below), while from

Cypros, just above Jericho, only two fine bath-buildings, belonging to the upper and lower palace respectively, have been excavated.[339] In the palace of Machaerus, also, on the other side of the Dead Sea, the bath-building constitutes the best-preserved part of the complex. Although we hear from Josephus that Herod proudly showed two other desert fortresses, those of Alexandrium and Hyrcania, to Agrippa on the latter's visit to Judaea in 15 BC, almost nothing has been found in either place.[340]

The Herodian Palace of Jerusalem, built in 24-23 BC and situated in the north-western part of the Upper City (Fig. 82), is unfortunately not preserved: only the great underlying platform, measuring c. 130 by 300-350 m (= 39,000-45,500 m²), with a height of 3-4 m, and consisting of a network of walls filled with earth, has been identified (Pl. 28).[341] By way of compensation, Josephus has given an enthusiastic description of the palace, mentioning, for instance, the lavish embellishment, several banqueting halls, one of them with room for a hundred guests, and round, connected peristyles, containing gardens with various kinds of trees and promenades flanked by canals and basins (see p. 24).[342] Particularly famous were the three mighty towers which protected the palace, their upper parts at the same time functioning as palaces in miniature, a kind of diaitai, and commanding a splendid view. The lower part of one of them, probably Phasael (now called the "Tower of David"), is preserved, built in ashlars. Such towers also formed part of the Hasmonean Palace of Jericho, and existed too probably in a smaller, recreational version, in Alexandria and Italy, this type being known both from written sources and from wall-painting. Moreover P. Grimal, probably rightly, draws parallels with the towers of the Persian paradeisos, and with the towers which often appear in scenes from Pharaonic Egypt.[343] A propagation via Alexandria is very likely, especially since Josephus himself compares the Herodian towers with the famous Pharos of that city.

Also the other features of this Herodian palace, such as garden-peristyles, an abundance of water, and large dining-halls, recur in the Hellenistic palaces. Of special interest is the mention of round peristyles, for round forms are a dominant feature in the architecture of this period, especially in Italy. Josephus' information that the palace included large buildings called after Herod's Roman friends, the Kaisareion and Agrippeion, underlines the Italian connection.

In addition to this main palace, Herod also built a fortified one, the Antonia, partly reusing the Hasmonean *baris*, on a an eminence north-west of the Temple Platform (Pl. 29). It was named after Mark Antony and thus built before 31 BC. It was a kind of palatial tetrapyrgion and, according to Josephus, contained among other things various courtyards (including one for the troops), apartments, and bath facilities. The two large Bethesda pools with their porticoes formed part of it. It was probably used by Herod as his main palace until the palace in the Upper City was built. One is reminded of the Hasmonean fortified palaces of Jericho and of the somewhat later Upper Herodium Palace (Fig. 113) (below).[344]

In this connection it is worth mentioning that palatial houses have been found in the Jewish quarter of Jerusalem in the last years. The largest one is the so-called "Palatial Mansion", which has an inner paved courtyard without columns, and a large reception hall, lavishly decorated with wall-paintings like the rest of the house. Perhaps it is a pale reflection of the halls to be found in the Royal Palace (Fig. 94). The house had a great many ritual baths (miqvaot), both on the ground floor and in the basement, but no Greek- or Roman-style baths: overall, it has greater affinities to Hasmonean than to Herodian buildings, but may be compared with the Western Palace of Masada (below). Other houses, however, had peristyles and Greek bathrooms, but everywhere miqvaot of different sizes predominate. Since the houses of this "Herodian Quarter" were situated directly opposite the Temple Mount, they were probably owned by rich priestly families.[345]

The recently discovered and only partly excavated Palace of Caesarea, Herod's seaport, built during the hectic years of 19-10 BC, was situated on a promontory on the southern outskirts of the city (Fig. 95). It was undoubtedly the palace in Caesarea referred to by Josephus.[346] The palace proper occupied an area of c. 5,000 m^2 and was dominated by a large pool measuring 35 x 18 m, which was surrounded by columns with flower-beds in between. The excavators are in favour of an interpretation of this as a swimming-pool with fresh water, since a water conduit has been found. However, a function as a fish-pond, like the ones known from the late Republican villas of Campania, has also been proposed on the basis of some channels connecting the pool with the sea (see p. 170).[347] Admittedly the excavators argue for dating these channels to the period after the palace had ceased to function, but since the palace was undoubtedly used also by the Roman provincial governor, as was the case with the Jerusalem Palace, a fish-pond function, which was so popular in Italy, cannot be entirely excluded. On the landward side of the pool was a row of rooms, the central one an oecus with two columns in antis and a fine mosaic floor, which probably served mainly as a private dining- and perhaps meeting-room. There are clear affinities with the main room of both the late Hasmonean residential Twin Palaces in Jericho (Cat. 23) (see p. 158). Thus this complex, with rooms facing a garden-peristyle, may have

Fig. 94. Jerusalem. Reconstruction of the major representative hall of the Palatial Mansion excavated in the Jewish Quarter. (Drawing by Leen Ritmeyer) (Avigad 1989, p. 63.)

been primarily residential, and the official part of the palace should probably be looked for elsewhere.

The position of a palace on a promontory is known, for example, from the basileia of Alexandria, and Herod's placing of the city theatre close to the palace also points to an inspiration from this famous palace, as does the newly excavated hippodrome or stadium found just north of the theatre and in close proximity to it.[348] A similar complex is seen in Jericho (below). A parallel to the swimming-pool surrounded by a peristyle courtyard is to be found in the Palace of Ptolemais (Cat. 22), which was again inspired by Alexandria.

But already before these city palaces were built, palaces had begun to appear elsewhere. The earliest Herodian palace was built in the fortress of Masada, where Herod had found refuge for his family in 40 BC, before he left for Rome. During the two first decades of Herod's reign two palaces were built, making Masada one large "palatial complex" (Fig. 96). There has been some uncertainty about the date of the earlier palace, the so-called Western Palace (Cat. 26; Pl. 30), as well as of the neighbouring small palatial houses, Buildings 11, 12, and 13. Before his recent stratigraphical excavations on the site, E. Netzer believed that these palaces belonged to the Hasmonean period, on account of their close resemblance

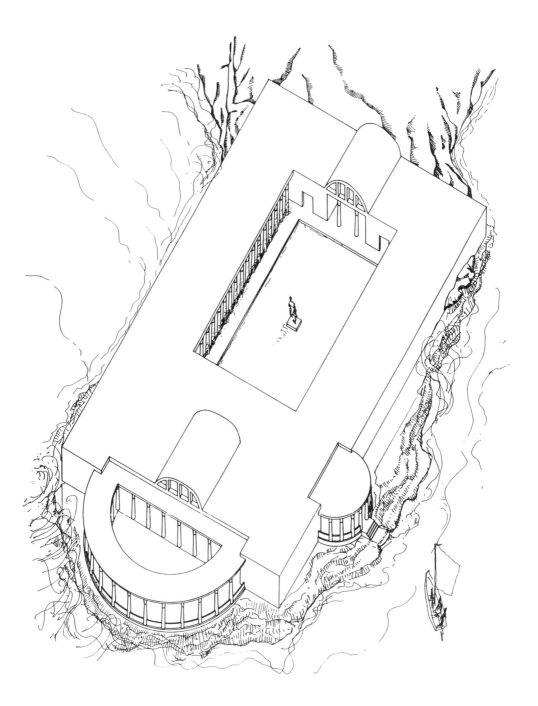

Fig. 95. Caesarea. Reconstruction of the Palace of Herod. (Drawing by E. Netzer.)

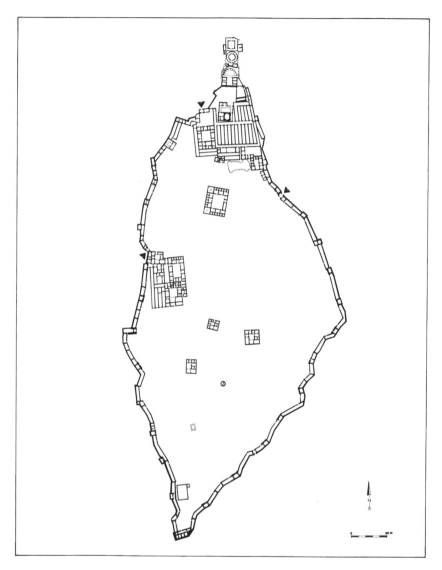

Fig. 96. Masada. General plan of the entire hill, last phase. (Netzer 1991, plan 75.)

to the Twin Palaces of Jericho (Fig. 99). The excavations have, however, made it clear that the palaces were, in fact, built early in Herod's reign, in the first building period at Masada (c. 37-30 BC). Since they reveal no features denoting any Italic/Roman influence, they were probably built by a team which had previously worked for the Hasmonean dynasty.[349]

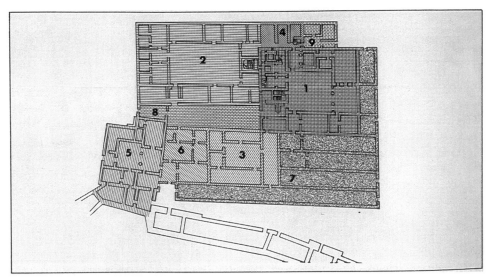

Fig. 97. Masada. Plan of the Western Palace, the nine phases (Cat. 26). 1:1050. (Netzer 1991, p. 234.)

According to the recent publication, the Western Palace had several building periods (Fig. 97): in the first period it consisted only of the "Core Palace", with both an official and a representative function, later it was gradually enlarged with courts for service and another one for vestibule. None of these courtyards had peristyles, not even the Core Palace ever acquired one, nor did the architectural concept change. The bathrooms, for example, are still of the Greek type, with no hypocaust.

The Core Palace (Fig. 98), reached through an unpretentious "bent" entrance from the north, had its most important rooms in the southern wing, namely a large room with two columns in antis giving access both to a large audience room, perhaps also a banqueting room, and to the living-quarters of the king; one might call it an "andron complex" (Pls. 31-32). In the western wing was a large room, not facing the courtyard but reached via an ante-room, which might have been for banquets.[350] The northern wing was taken up by bathrooms of both the Greek and the Jewish type, and had a first floor for residence. The splendid room with two columns in antis in the east wing, again reached only from a small ante-room, and with access through another corridor to the audience hall, was probably for private use also. In the later phases, a portal to the west led to a narrow vestibule court, which gave access both to the Core Palace and to every other part of the palace. In general the Oriental features, such as a "bent" entrance, lack of

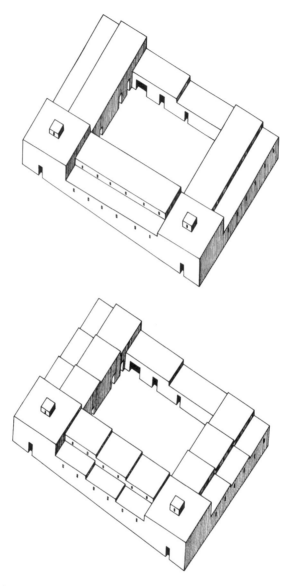

Fig. 98. Masada. The Western Palace, two alternative isometric reconstructions of the "Core Palace". (Netzer 1991, Ill. 912.)

peristyle, the "andron complex", and only a few rooms opening to the yard, predominate, the Greek features being found primarily in the bathrooms and the decoration.

Neighbouring the Western Palace were, as already mentioned, three small palatial houses belonging to important members of the court; these are of more or less

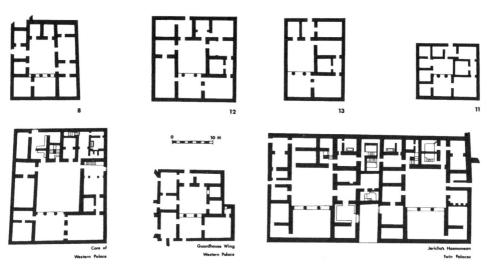

Fig. 99. Comparative plans of the early Herodian palaces of Masada and the Twin Palaces of Hasmonean Jericho. (Netzer 1991, Ill. 913.)

the same plan as the Core Palace and were built in the same, early phase. The same applies to a large pool at the southern end of the plateau, perhaps a swimming-pool, and three columbaria one of which was round and sited to the south of the palace (Fig. 96). Their presence reminds us of Josephus' mention of a dovecot in the Palace of Jerusalem, and that such towers have been found in a Hasmonean context in connection with the palaces of Jericho and Cypros. Perhaps they were used as watch-towers as well.[351] This southern part of Masada may originally have been covered by gardens, and thus already at this time the whole site may, in fact, be regarded as being one large "palace complex".

A major addition to this basileia was the building of the Northern Palace (Cat. 27), which Josephus describes and which in the recent publication has been dated to the main Herodian building period at Masada (30-20 BC). At the same time, the Western Palace probably became reserved for official, service, and perhaps administrative functions, the new palace taking over the residential function and perhaps also some official activities. A totally new architectural concept is evident here: the marvellous situation on three terraces down the steep northern slope of the mountain made great demands on the architect and craftsmen, and must have deeply impressed visitors (Figs. 100-3). Also the Large Baths from the same period, and built on the same axis, belonged to this complex, since the forbidding wall separating them from the palace was not built until the later period of Herod's reign, when more emphasis was placed on defensive measures.

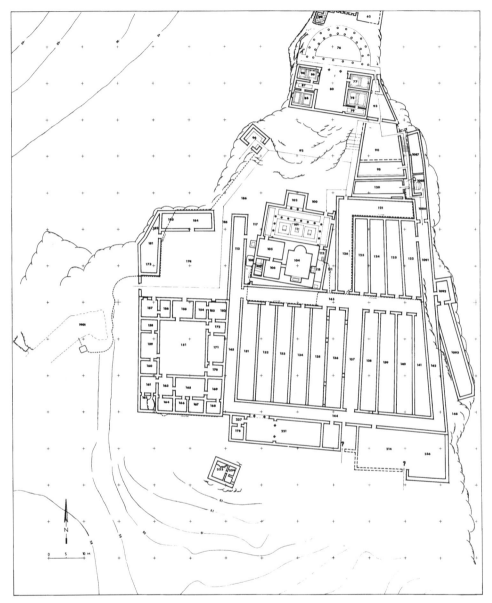

Fig. 100. Masada. Plan of the Northern Palace. The inner complex (Cat. 27). (Netzer 1991, plan 70.)

The lower terrace of the Northern Palace was occupied by a hypostyle hall with columns on plinths (earlier considered to be open to the sky). The hall was surrounded with covered porticoes, partly open to the north to take advantage of

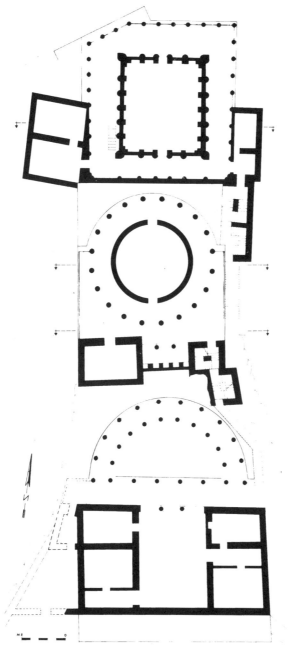

Fig. 101. Masada. The Northern Palace, reconstructed plan. (Netzer 1991, plan 60.)

Fig. 102. Masada. The Northern Palace, reconstruction of the palace from the west (above) and the north (below). (Netzer 1991, plan 61-62.)

the view, partly in the form of half-columns towards the rock (Pl. 34). There were rooms to the east and west, viz. a bath complex at a lower level, reached by stairs and including hypocausts and a miqveh (Pl. 33). One is reminded of the Hasmonean pavilion at Jericho, but also of Hellenistic reception halls. It was in fact a kind of Egyptian oecus known, for instance, from the Palace of Ptolemais (Cat. 22) and also present in other Herodian palaces (below). The hall was probably used for (private) audiences and banquets.

The middle terrace was dominated by a rotunda of which only the foundations, consisting of two concentric walls, remain. The function is unknown, but that of a combined pavilion and dining-room, like the one known from the Southern Tell of Jericho (below), which was also circular and more or less of the same size, seems the most reasonable guess (Pl. 35). A reconstruction as a tholos with columns seems the most likely, since a tholos in Lower Herodium is almost of the same size (below). Behind it were rooms, the main one being a large exedra with recesses raised 55 cm from the floor in the back wall; there are traces of shelves, and the room was entirely open to the rotunda, perhaps with two columns in antis: it might have functioned as a library (Pl. 36).[352]

The upper terrace, finally, had a large semicircular pavilion or rather balcony, since it was probably not roofed, with a superb view, and behind it were rooms placed around a large hall, of which the entire width was open to the balcony, perhaps with two columns in antis. This part of the palace was undoubtedly used primarily as a dwelling. The palace was finely decorated with wall-paintings in the Second Style and mosaics without human figures or animals, because of the Jewish faith of its inhabitants.

The extraordinary architectural expression inherent in this palace bears a striking resemblance to that of the façade of the Khasneh Tomb at Petra (Pl. 22), as well as to the experimental façades facing the garden-peristyle of the Palace of Ptolemais (Fig. 80); undoubtedly the same, Alexandrian, tradition is operating. The expanded use of round forms, however, is surely due to Roman influence.[353]

Moving to the old recreational area of the Hasmoneans, we find that Herod built three winter palaces in Jericho (Pl. 37). The First Winter Palace (Cat. 28) was built at more or less the same time as the Western Palace of Masada, namely in 35 BC, i.e. shortly after Herod's accession. It was situated on the southern bank of the Wadi Qelt, opposite, and with a different orientation from, the Hasmonean palace (Cat. 23), which was still used and owned by the Hasmonean family at that time. This new palace was probably used mainly as a recreational residence for Herod and his family, and resembles at first sight a large Hellenistic palatial

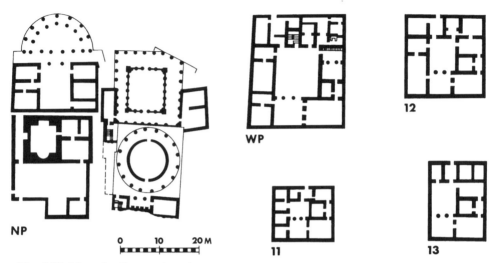

Fig. 103. Masada. Comparison betweeen an imaginary assembled plan of the Northern
Palace and the early Herodian palaces of Masada. (Netzer 1991, Ill. 904.)

house, being basically oriented inwards and having an Egyptian oecus facing a
large peristyle court with rooms on three sides (Figs. 104-5). The main part of
the building being only preserved in its foundations, the position of the doors is
often unknown. The same applies to the main entrance, which Netzer reconstructs
as leading directly into the peristyle from the north, facing the Hasmonean palace.

The plan of the main western wing with the oecus, which probably functioned
as the main reception hall, was unusual, since this hall was surrounded by a
corridor, which was itself surrounded by many small rooms. The entire northern
wing was residential, being taken up by small rooms, containing, for example,
Jewish miqvaot but also — and this is important — a bathroom of the Roman
type with a hypocaust. In the Western Palace of Masada there were only Greek-
and Jewish-style bathrooms; but the basic simplicity of the plan and the placing
of residential and administrative functions in the same building and around the
same court, are identical. Facing the oecus from the other end of the peristyle,
although not on the same axis, was a large, probably cruciform, hall, which gave
access to smaller, probably residential, side-rooms and may have been used for
banquets. Again, only a very few rooms faced the courtyard, and in general the
residential section with its many small rooms and corridors gives an impression
of an Oriental plan. The official part, i.e. the peristyle and the oecus, on the other
hand, points towards the West, and there is a general similarity to the somewhat

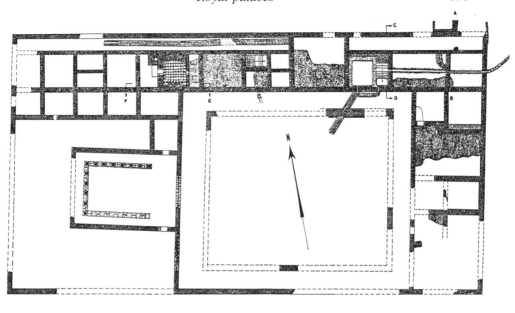

SCALE.

METERS. ⌊⌊⌊⌊⌊⌊⌊⌊⌊⌊⌊⌊⌊ ⌊ ⌊ ⌊ ⌊ ⌊ METERS.

Fig. 104. Jericho. Stone plan of the First Winter Palace (Cat. 28). (Pritchard 1958, pl. 63.)

earlier governor's palace in Ptolemais (Fig. 78) and to the palatial villas and houses of Italy.

Herod's recently discovered Second Winter Palace in Jericho (Cat. 29), built in c. 25 BC (and therefore more or less contemporary with the Palace of Jerusalem and the Northern Palace of Masada), had some resemblance to the First Palace, but follows the western tradition more closely (Fig. 106). It is built partially over the eastern part of the Hasmonean palace (Cat. 23), which was destroyed by the earthquake of 31 BC. It is more open to the outside than its predecessor, and is laid out on two levels, the upper one containing a large garden-peristyle with balustrades between the columns and surrounded by rooms on three sides. The two main rooms are placed on the central axis: to the north lies an exedra with two columns in antis, which perhaps was a reception room, and since it had access to two lateral rooms, the arrangement in fact resembles a "Flügeldreiraumgruppe" (see p. 87); to the south is a large oecus, probably for dining, facing both the peristyle and a portico, with a fine view of the wadi and the lower palace. The

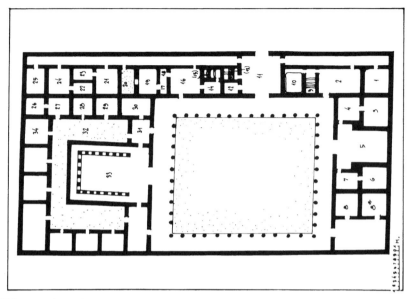

Fig. 105. Jericho. The First Winter Palace, reconstructed plan. (Netzer 1990, fig. 9.)

oecus was flanked by two groups of rooms symmetrically placed around the central axis. The lower part of the palace consisted of a large swimming-pool, reused from the Hasmonean period, but furnished with a new peristyle which also included a garden (Fig. 84). To the west, and connected with this complex, was an enclosed garden with a Roman bath-building that had miqvaot serving as cold rooms (*frigidaria*). Finally, the two large swimming-pools surviving from the Hasmonean period were amalgamated and surrounded with a newly laid out garden (Pl. 26). On the site of the ruined pavilion, a columbarium was built, perhaps supporting a new pavilion.

This palace probably had only one storey, and there were fewer rooms than in the First Palace, with greater emphasis being placed on the recreational aspect. Probably, the First Palace was still used primarily as a residence, while the Second Palace was used to a higher degree for social purposes and recreation, together with what was left of the Hasmonean palace.

While the Second Winter palace was placed in close relation to the Hasmonean palace and therefore partly dependent on its plan, the Third (and largest) Winter Palace in Jericho (Cat. 30) (30,000 m^2), which Herod built around 15 BC, was entirely his own project. This complex differed greatly from the earlier and still functioning first and second palaces, even if certain elements such as the basically recreational aspect were the same. Its main function was official, for which

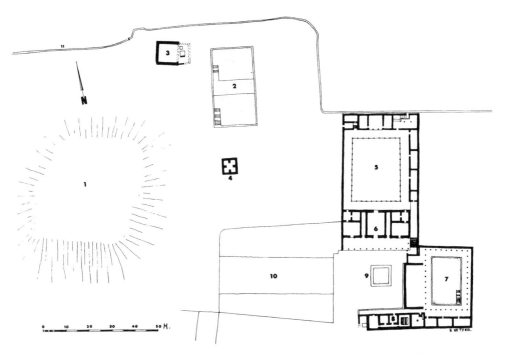

Fig. 106. Jericho. Plan of the Second Winter Palace (Cat. 29). (Netzer 1990, fig. 10.)

purpose the facilities of the earlier palaces were now felt to be too limited. The palace was laid out on a regular plan on both sides of the Wadi Qelt, and great emphasis was placed on making the most of the beautiful view towards the south by placing long porticoes alongside and to the west of the main palace, which was situated on the northern bank, an arrangement which also created an impressive approach. The view towards the north and the town, on the other hand, could be enjoyed from the pavilion on the Southern Tell (Figs. 107, 109).

The main palace was mainly official (Fig. 108, Pl. 38). The banqueting and audience hall to the west was enormous and had the shape of an Egyptian oecus with heart-shaped corner columns, a form taken over from the First Palace — and one is also reminded of the lower hall in the Northern Palace of Masada. It opened via a wide portal onto the above-mentioned portico.[354] The neighbouring garden-peristyle had to the north a finely decorated hall behind a large apse; it was undoubtedly used for minor audiences, etc., and the large apsidal exedra served perhaps as a vestibule to this throne-room, creating what was in fact a unique combination (Pl. 39).[354a] As mentioned earlier, such apses with official functions became important elements of Roman royal architecture (see n. 323). This part

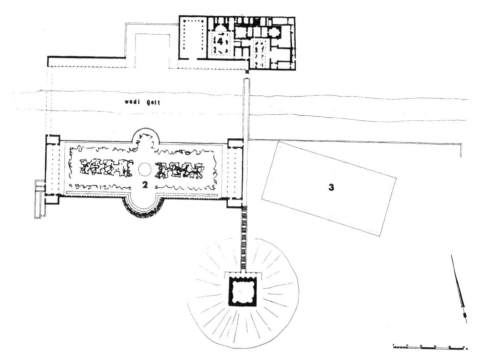

Fig. 107. Jericho. Plan of the Third Winter Palace (Cat. 30): 1. Pavilion on the Southern Tell; 2. The sunken garden; 3. Large swimming-pool; 4. Main palace. (Netzer 1990, fig. 11.)

of the main wing could be reached only through an inconspicuous entrance and by traversing two rooms, the outer one probably for guards, the inner one, which was beautifully decorated, for those awaiting audience.

A smaller, recreational part of this building to the east was dominated by another garden-peristyle, with a large cruciform hall of the same type as the one in the First Herodian Winter Palace. It was undoubtedly used as a private dining-hall and had service rooms behind it. The northern wing was taken up completely by a large and typical Roman bath-suite with a Vitruvian *caldarium* and a rotunda with apsidal niches, probably a *laconicum* (Pl. 40).[355]

Opposite this main palace, on the other side of the Wadi Qelt, i.e. on the same side as the First Palace (now probably exclusively residential) and reached by a bridge, were other structures belonging to the same complex. On top of the Southern Tell was a square structure enclosing a rotunda, of which only the foun-

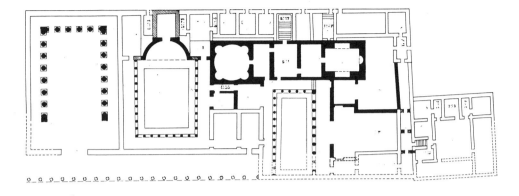

Fig. 108. Jericho. Plan of the main building of the Third Winter Palace. The walls in black are built in Roman building techniques, those in white in local techniques. (Drawing by E. Netzer.)

dations remain. Netzer's reconstruction of it as a rotunda with four apsidal niches is convincing, and is based on similar, contemporaneous rotundas in Italy: the Tempio di Mercurio at Baiae and the frigidarium of the Thermae of Agrippa in Rome. While these both contained large pools, this is not the case in Jericho, for no water supply has been found. But in the basement, a plastered cistern was discovered, indicating the use of water, and there was probably a small bath here as well. The upper floor undoubtedly took the form of a dining-hall, since there is a magnificent view over the entire oasis from there. With its subterranean bath-house and its fine view, this hall may be compared to the oecus on the lower terrace, as well as to the pavilion on the middle terrace of the Northern Palace of Masada.

Below this structure was a large formal, sunken garden surrounded by porticoes and walls with niches (140 x 40 m), and in the middle of the sides were very large semicircular exedrae, one of them arranged as a kind of theatre. A similar huge garden-peristyle probably also existed in the Hasmonean Palace (see p. 157), which supports the theory of an inspiration from, for example, the Palace of Alexandria. One may also compare it to the practically contemporaneous, very large garden-peristyle behind the Theatre of Pompey on the Campus Martius in Rome, measuring 180 by 135 m, and to the Portico of the Danaids connected to Augustus' palace (Cat. 25) (see p. 178); a similar structure was also later included in the Flavian palace on the Palatine, the so-called Stadium. Finally the complex south of the wadi embraced an immense swimming-pool, which was for some

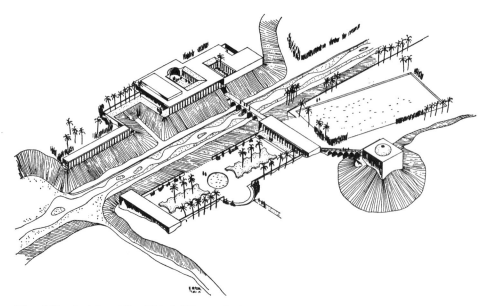

Fig. 109. Jericho. The Third Winter Palace. Reconstructed isometric view. (Netzer 1990, fig. 12.)

reason not placed at right-angles to the other structures. Only the corners have so far been located.[356]

In contrast to the earlier palaces, which were characterized by a linear architecture, rounded forms dominate this Third Palace, both in the shape of large apses and of rotundas with small apses; one is reminded of the round peristyles mentioned by Josephus in the Palace of Jerusalem (above). Although rounded forms certainly occurred in the Macedonian and Ptolemaic palaces as well, the elements of that type in Jericho seem to represent an Italic adaptation of these Hellenistic elements. This is certainly the case with the encapsulated rotunda with four apses, and also with the large dimensions of the rounded shapes. The same sphere of influence is felt in the lavish decoration, with floors partly in *opus sectile* and the walls with paintings in the Second Style, from which, however, themes with animals and human figures are again absent, out of respect for Jewish sentiment. The use of the typical Roman building techniques in *opus reticulatum* and *opus mixtum* in a large part of the building, and the general resemblance to Italic buildings, might well denote the presence of Italic craftsmen (Pl. 40).

Another Herodian complex in Jericho probably belonged to the domain of the palace, although situated some at distance from it (Pl. 24). It consisted of a hippodrome, uniquely combined with an auditorium in the form of a theatre, behind

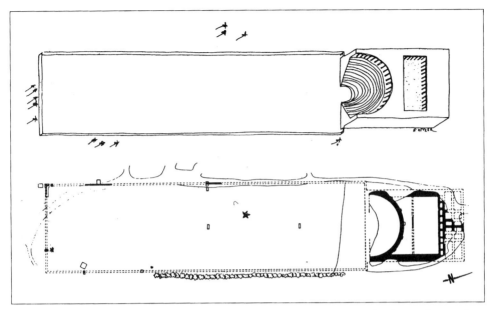

Fig. 110. Jericho. A reconstruction and plan of the hippodrome and "theatre" complex. (Netzer 1989, Abb. 11.)

which was a peristyle court, perhaps for receptions (Fig. 110).[357] The combination of palace and hippodrome is known both from the newly found complex in Caesarea (above), and from the Palace of Antiochia (Cat. 15), and even from Rome, where Octavian's palace on the Palatine was built close to the Circus Maximus (see p. 174). Theatres in connection with palaces are known from Aigai, Pella, Pergamon, and Alexandria, where there was, moreover, a palaestra in the vicinity, and Herod himself had used this combination in Caesarea at the same time. It has not, however, been ascertained whether the auditorium in Jericho in fact served as a theatre proper. A peristyle behind a theatre is known from Pompeii (2nd century BC), where it probably originally functioned as a palaestra.[358]

The third basileia built by Herod was the Palace of Herodium (Cat. 31), a complex situated 15 km south of Jerusalem, and begun in 23-20 BC, i.e. shortly before the Third Winter Palace of Jericho and at the same time as the Northern Palace of Masada, with which it had certain architectural affinities. It was at least partly finished in 15 BC, when Agrippa visited Herod there (Fig. 111). While the palace on the artificial conical hill had been known for a long time and was excavated in the early 1960s, the amazing complex on and below its northern slope has been excavated only in recent years (Pls. 41-42). Herodium was a combination

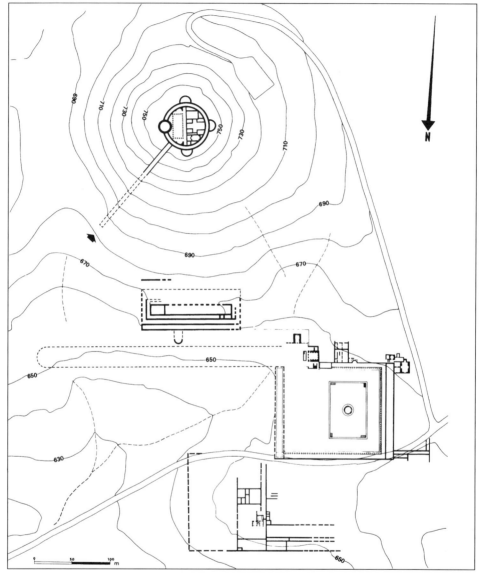

Fig. 111. Herodium. General plan of the palace complex (Cat. 31). (Netzer 1990, fig. 13.)

of a triumphal memorial to the victory over Antigonus in 40 BC, a summer palace, a fortress, an administrative centre (of the Toparchy), and burial place for Herod. But there was no real town there.

Again we see a division of functions among different buildings. The palace-fort on the Tell, which primarily functioned as a residence for Herod and his family and was used only to a limited degree for official purposes, was circular and provides another good example of the imagination exercised in Herodian architecture (Figs. 112-113). Apart from this unusual feature, it looked from the outside like a traditional fortress, such as the one Alexander Jannaeus built in Jericho or the Antonia in Jerusalem. Yet inside was a splendid palace: a close affinity to the palaces of Jericho is obvious, with the typically Roman bath-building containing a Vitruvian caldarium and a rotunda, the large private meeting- and banqueting-hall, here without columns, and the even larger cruciform hall, perhaps for banquets as well. Almost half of the area was taken up by a garden-peristyle with two apsidal exedrae facing each other and a third one built into the eastern wall (Pl. 43). As mentioned earlier, this element is found also in the palaces of Pella and Ptolemais (Cats. 12, 22). Moreover, this kind of peristyle court with symmetrically placed apsidal exedrae lived on in Roman architecture, e.g. in the House of Menander in Pompeii and the Forum of Augustus in Rome.[359]

Lower Herodium consists of several orthogonally placed elements, laid out on the northern slope of the hill (Fig. 111, Pl. 42). The uppermost building, of which only the foundations are partially preserved, is a large palatial structure, perhaps primarily for official purposes; one may compare it to the main building of the Third Winter Palace in Jericho. Belonging to the same general area was the unique complex located just below: this consisted of a long narrow terrace leading to a large hall with niches taking up its western end (Pl. 44). A typical royal approach was thus created, enhancing the importance of this hall, which was probably used *i.a.* as a throne-room and banqueting hall. E. Netzer has suggested that the long terrace was perhaps used for the funeral procession mentioned by Josephus, and sees the hall as a funeral triclinium. However, one interpretation does not preclude the other.[360] The tomb itself has not yet been found; the large hall with niches has been considered as a candidate, but the excavations have ruled out this identification. At the bottom of the hill was a very large recreational peristyle surrounded by walls and embracing a swimming-pool with a circular pavilion in the middle, used probably for dining (compare the middle terrace of the Northern Palace of Masada). Flanking the west side of this complex was a large Roman bath complex along with other buildings. Finally another, only partly excavated complex was placed further north, perhaps for administration.

Summary
Viewed as a whole, there is a clear development in Herodian palace architecture.

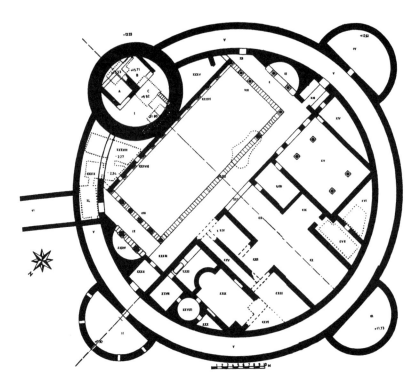

Fig. 112. Herodium. Plan of the upper palace. (Lauter 1986, Abb. 77.)

The early palaces, i.e. the Western Palace of Masada and the First Winter Palace of Jericho, seem highly traditional in relation to the three, later, experimental ones, the Third Palace of Jericho, the Palace of Herodium, and the Northern Palace of Masada, and, one might well add, those of Jerusalem and Caesarea. The Second Winter Palace of Jericho constitutes a kind of transitional phase. The early palaces are "compact palaces", characterized by a linear and closed architecture, many small rooms, often opening onto corridors, and few large main rooms, oeci. As previously stated, they encompassed all functions in one building, which resulted in a rather close relationship between the official and private life of the king. We should have no difficulty in finding the models for these palaces, in the local Hasmonean palaces as well as in the almost contemporaneous Palace of Ptolemais (Cat. 22), and other governors' palaces could well be adduced, e.g. the one in Lachish (Cat. 7) and perhaps even that of Tyrus (Cat. 21). The architecture is purely Hellenistic (in the sense used in this book), apart from the Roman bath-

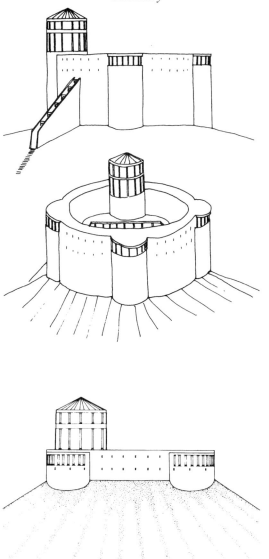

Fig. 113. Herodium. Reconstruction of the upper palace. (Netzer 1990, figs. 14-15.)

rooms in Jericho; in Masada a Greek type of bathroom was still used, but all were combined with miqvaot.

The contrast with the later palaces is striking. It is typical that in them, separate buildings are reserved for the various functions: thus we see purely residential buildings such as the Northern Palace of Masada and the fortress-palace of Herodium, and purely official ones, such as the main building in the Third Winter

Palace of Jericho and the large badly preserved building in Lower Herodium. Finally we see special areas set aside for recreation: in Masada the southern part of the hill, in Jericho the area south of the wadi, and even the entire Second Palace itself, and in Herodium the area below the hill. In all cases, large swimming-pools dominate the parks.

The question is, where did Herod find the models for these fascinating "palace complexes"? Of course there is a close relationship with the earlier palaces of the area, especially as far as the recreational parts and the "mixed" bathing arrangements are concerned. The theatrical layout with an organic use of the landscape and the great emphasis on views are features known from Hellenistic palaces in Macedonia and Pergamon, as well as from other kinds of Hellenistic architecture.

There are also, however, distinct differences, which make the late Herodian palaces the true representatives of a new epoch. For in many ways they were certainly inspired from the new centre of power, Rome. One should not underestimate the significance of Herod's visits to Rome and his friendly relations with Augustus' master-builder Agrippa. The Herodian palaces are certainly marked by this contact: both Lower Herodium and the Third Palace of Jericho had some affinities with the Campus Martius in Rome, the "metamorphosis" of which was completed by Agrippa (see p. 180). This area included extensive parks, garden-peristyles, villas, and an abundance of water, making possible the building of a big swimming-pool (Stagnum), as well as the great Thermae; and, from 28 BC, Augustus' prestigious Mausoleum was also sited there. Everything was laid out orthogonally.

Also, the central position of the Roman-style bath-buildings in these palaces is worth noting, as is the fact that the latest heating techniques were used here at almost the same time as in Italy, where they were developed.[361] The same applies to the building techniques, such as opus reticulatum and mixtum, that also denote the presence in Judaea of Roman architects and craftsmen, although the traditional building techniques, in ashlar or irregular stones and sun-dried brick, continue to dominate.[362] On the other hand, the use of decorative schemes such as opus sectile and the Second Style of painting again points to foreign craftsmen, as does the expanded use of rounded forms, which were very characteristic of the architecture of Italy in the 2nd-1st centuries BC. The great sanctuaries of Latium come to mind, and the axial planning, the use of landscape in the setting, and the many terraces and pavilions with a view, all suggest affinities with the Italic villas of the period as well; there are certainly also similarities to the Palace of Augustus on the Palatine (Cat. 25).

In connection with his publication of Masada, Netzer has emphasized that while the early, Western Palace was in the Hasmonean tradition, the new Northern Palace was a result partly of Roman influence (perhaps the architect was in fact Roman or had been trained in Rome), and partly of the "personal touch" of Herod himself, who now had the time to take a greater interest in his building projects.[363] The clear similarities between the later Herodian buildings and those of the same period in Italy indicate at all events a common heritage, the origin of which should probably be sought in the famous Alexandrian basileia.

Perhaps this change in architecture during Herod's reign also mirrored a change in the function, and thus in Herod's concept, of monarchy, a feature already mentioned for Macedonia (see p. 97). At first, Herod was very much a vassal king and may be compared with a governor rather than an independent, let alone "personal" king. He reigned over a "national" rather than a "personal" kingdom, as was the case with the Hasmoneans. Both dynasties tended to avoid stretching royal symbolism too far, and indeed eschewed the ostentation that typified Oriental monarchs; thus the elaborate approach to the palace with great avenues, stairs, monumental portals, etc., is seldom seen, and instead a "bent" or at least rather modest entrance to these palaces is typical. In his later palaces, however, Herod seems to show signs of approaching the role and lifestyle of the "personal" Hellenistic kings: one sees an increasing isolation from his subjects together with a monumentalization of his palaces that is expressed in the placing of the basic functions in different buildings, and not least in the great tryphe displayed. Thus, they began to resemble, for instance, the royal palace of Alexandria rather than, as was the case with the earlier palaces, the governor's palace of Ptolemais or the like.

In both periods, however, Herod laid emphasis on trying, not always successfully, to preserve good relations with his Jewish subjects, while at the same time following a policy of hellenization; thus he avoided the inclusion of human figures or animals in the Greek- and Roman-style paintings and mosaics of his palaces, and the presence of the many miqvaot is a sign that this respect was seriously meant.

If we accept the proposed division of Herodian architecture into an early, i.e. Hellenistic, and a late, i.e. Roman, phase, Palestine certainly furnishes us with one of the most convincing examples of the validity of the Actium date for the transition from one phase to the other. Presumably, Herod was leading developments rather than following them, and the new elements which occur in his buildings were destined to be echoed elsewhere, both in the East and in the

West. The existence of unquestionable affinities between what went on in architecture in Palestine and in Rome and Italy is a sign that the long-expected cultural koiné had at last begun to make considerable progress. E. Bickerman went even further, claiming that "The real hellenization of the Seleucid empire, outside Asia Minor, began only after the end of Seleucid domination, when the hellenizing process was taken over by the native rulers".[364]

X. CONCLUSION

One of the main objectives of this study has been to restore the Hellenistic royal palace to its rightful place as one of the principal cultural centres and cultural mediators of the period. The strong focus on the Greek polis has to some extent overshadowed the importance of this royal building type, since it represented a society antithetical to that of the polis. There can be no doubt, however, that the period of the independent Greek poleis constitutes only a parenthesis, however important, in the history of pre-industrial society, which was otherwise dominated by monarchy with its concomitant court society. Both before and after this parenthesis, it was the royal palace and the court which to a large degree set the trend, in architecture, in art, in science and learning, and in general behaviour. Of course this does not mean that the poleis of antiquity did not continue to influence these fields, only that the role of the palaces as trend-setters has been underestimated.

In the preceding chapters, I have tried to give a general picture of the palaces. The main stress has been on architecture; but the architectural expressions inherent in the palaces can be understood only if their multifarious functions are continuously taken into account. The royal palaces have been my primary concern. The governors' and private palaces, which played only a subordinate part in society, have mainly been used to help build up the picture of those poorly preserved royal palaces, of which they are but pale reflections. The leading role after all belonged to the royal palaces.

To answer the question, "How do we recognize a royal palace when we see one?", it is important to investigate the implications of this role: the prime purpose of the palaces, at least those belonging to the newly established dynasties, was to emphasize the omnipresence and the omnipotence of the king. The task of the architect was at the same time to express the king's visibility and accessibility to his subjects and his isolation from and superiority to them. To achieve this goal, the architect had various means at his disposal: an exhibition of great wealth, tryphe, was important; in the siting of the palace, a commanding position on terraces or platforms, reached by monumental ramps or staircases that led to impressive portals and vestibules, was crucial. This feature, involving great engineering skills, was intended to impress. An opening to the outside constituted by the monumental façade afforded the king a view from the palace over the land

Palaces		royal	governors'	private
Cat. 1	Memphis	1,155 m^2		
Cat. 2	Babylon	884 m^2		
Cat. 3	Pasargadae	1,170 m^2		
Cat. 4	Persepolis	3,600 m^2		
Cat. 5	Susa, Darius	3,600 m^2		
Cat. 6	Susa, Artaxerxes	1,190 m^2		
Cat. 7	Lachish		109 m^2	
Cat. 8	Vouni		68 m^2	
Cat. 9	Larisa		30/49 m^2	
Cat. 10	Aigai	100 m^2		
Cat. 11	Pella, Dionysus			100 m^2
Cat. 12	Pella, Royal	400 m^2		
Cat. 13	Demetrias	77 m^2 ?		
Cat. 14	Pergamon	133 m^2		
Cat. 15	Antiochia	?		
Cat. 16	Dura, Redoubt		69 m^2	
Cat. 17	Dura, Citadel		65 m^2	
Cat. 18	Nippur		180 m^2	
Cat. 19	Aï Khanoum	516/451 m^2		
Cat. 20	Alexandria	?		
Cat. 21	Araq el Emir		120 m^2	
Cat. 22	Ptolemais		227 m^2	
Cat. 23	Jericho, Hasmonean	?		
Cat. 24	Pompeii, Casa del Fauno			36/165 m^2
Cat. 25	Rome, Casa di Augusto	70 m^2 ?		
Cat. 26	Masada, West	53 m^2		
Cat. 27	Masada, North	289 m^2		
Cat. 28	Jericho, Winter I	234 m^2		
Cat. 29	Jericho, Winter II	80 m^2 ?		
Cat. 30	Jericho, Winter III	551 m^2		
Cat. 31	Herodium	158 m^2 ?		

Fig. 114. Table showing the size of the audience halls in the different types of palaces.

which he ruled, and at the same time drew attention to the main entrance, complete with columns, pediments, etc., which symbolized the communication between the king and his subjects. Neither the governors' palaces nor the private ones had any need of such features; they were therefore rather modest and less conspicuously situated, often closed to the outside and provided with quite simple entrances.

This theatrical setting of the palaces of the Hellenistic kings may be difficult to visualize today. But with the assistance of the Herodian palaces of Palestine and Augustus' palace in Rome, together with other kinds of monumental architecture, such as the great sanctuaries of Cos, Rhodes, and Pergamon, as well as those in Latium, and finally by taking into account tomb façades and wall-painting too, one may obtain a good impression of their effect on their surroundings.

In the layout of the royal palace, the architect had to consider the kind of monarchy it was destined to house. Two kinds of monarchies existed in the Hellenistic period: the "national", non-absolute monarchy already known from Macedonia, and the new "personal and absolute" one, which was created by the Diadochi for the conquests of Alexander and modelled on the Achaemenid monarchy. In fact there seems to be an interesting difference between the palaces belonging to the personal kings and those of the basically national, and not truly autocratic kings.

While the "personal" palaces, represented, for example, by Pergamon, Alexandria, Antiochia, and Aï Khanoum, were, as stated, very luxurious, very large, very monumental, and very visible, with separate accommodation for each function, the "national" palaces lacked most of these features: normally, a rather limited plot was set aside for palaces, and there is often a close combination of official and residential as well as other functions, even in the same building. Also, a preference for compact courtyard buildings and an avoidance of grand palace complexes in large parks are typical attributes. In fact, the same features characterize the governor's palace. A study of the audience halls, the main reception halls of the royal palaces, shows that their size in the "national" palaces is much closer to that of the main halls in governors' and even private palaces than of the audience halls in the palaces of absolute kings (Fig. 114). Good examples of such "national" palaces are the Palace of Aigai, the Hasmonean Palace of Jericho, and the early Herodian palaces, i.e. the Western Palace of Masada and the First Winter Palace of Jericho.

It is interesting that in both Macedonia and Palestine, where such "national" palaces are found, there seems to be a certain development from a national non-autocratic monarchy towards a personal monarchy inspired by those of the Attalids, Seleucids, and Ptolemies, a development which is reflected in the palatial architecture.[365] Thus the first Hellenistic palace of Macedonia, that of Aigai, is both smaller, and simpler in layout, with residential and official quarters close together, than the main Royal Palace of Pella in its latest form, dating from the period of Philip V. Here the monumentality is increased through sheer size, an even more impressive façade, and the axiality and symmetry of the main peristyle. The approach to the king has thus been rendered more imposing. A dynastic sanctuary, typical of the "personal" kingdoms, is probably present too, not merely one for the tutelary deity, as at Aigai, and we have evidence for the existence of a library, as well as the possibility of a game reserve in the neighbourhood.

In Palestine one sees the same tendency in the Herodian palaces. Herod's early palaces, built before he was securely in the saddle and confident in his relations with Rome, were rather modest, looking more like governors' and private palaces. Again, both official and residential functions were concentrated in the same building, and even the entrance was modest. Later, when Augustus became Herod's supporter after Actium, we see an increasing monumentality and a predilection for large complexes with separate buildings for each function, a feature known from the large "personal" palaces. Those new palaces are found in Jerusalem, Caesarea, Herodium, and Jericho, where the old palace was extended by the addition of two palatial buildings as well as an impressive recreational area.

There is something of a question mark over where the Palace of Augustus on the Palatine should be placed in this scheme of development. In fact, this structure seems to be a mixture of a "national" palace, with its rather modest private section and the placing of official and private elements close together, and a "personal" palace, reflected in the inclusion of "public" and religious buildings. The final result of palace development is represented by the "absolute" palace complexes of Nero and Domitian.

The functions that the palaces had to fulfil had of course a crucial effect on layout. The greater the number of functions, and the greater their differentiation, the larger and more complicated the palace. From the diagram based on these functions (Fig. 115), it appears that the royal Hellenistic and early Roman palaces included the most functions, and frequently all the nine groups that I use are represented. Compared to the models, the most obvious difference is that these precursors lack "public" functions, which must be considered a Hellenistic innovation. On the other hand, the absence of certain religious elements in the models, such as a sanctuary for the tutelary deity and a dynastic sanctuary, means only that the sanctity of the kings of the Egyptians, Babylonians, and Persians was expressed in a different manner. Because of the special requirements of the Jewish religion, the palaces of the Jewish kings had no religious installations of the kinds mentioned either, only the miqvaot denoting religious activity. In these palaces, the "public" aspect is seldom present, for the same reason.

In the governors' and private palaces, "public" buildings, large recreational parks, and religious elements are normally all absent, and the elements relating to the official function are rather limited. As might be expected, the governors' palaces have more variable functions than the private ones.

Finally, it is apparent that even the royal palaces differ among themselves in several ways. Thus while the main palaces of the various dynasties basically included all or most functions, the simply recreational or defensive palaces could make do with fewer functions: administrative and religious buildings could, for example, be dispensed with. Another distinction, between the "personal" and "national" palaces, has already been touched upon: dynastic sanctuaries and mausolea belong to the "personal" palaces, and in general these have more differentiated functions than the "national" ones.

We may thus conclude that whether we are considering royal, governors', or private palaces, there was not just *one* Hellenistic model. As far as royal palaces are concerned, they reflected the monarchical system of the dynasty they served. The elements which together constituted these palaces were found in palatial models in different areas: the governors' palaces of Anatolia, the old Macedonian palaces, and, not least, the Oriental palaces, i.e. those belonging to the Egyptian, the Neo-Babylonian and, most importantly, the Persian kings.

The life of the Persian court had made a great impression on the Greek and Macedonian mind from the early 5th century BC, and close contact between the cultures, sometimes diplomatic, sometimes antagonistic, continued right through the Classical period. Furthermore, the future Hellenistic kings acquired intimate knowledge of the Persian court and palaces from their participation in Alexander's campaigns, and the Seleucids even took over some of these palaces for their own use. Nothing would thus be more natural than to find in the new courts and palaces of the Diadochi many of the institutions, ceremonies, insignia, and architectural expressions that were characteristic of the Achaemenid monarchy, and, as I hope I have shown, this was in fact the case. To these models were added a new element, namely the "public" institutions, so that the palaces gradually took upon themselves many of the functions of the polis. At least in the capitals of the

	Function	Architectural expression	Models						Hellenistic royal palaces							
			Memphis	Babylon	Pasargadae	Persepolis	Susa Dar.	Susa Arta.	Vergina	Pella Royal	Demetrias	Pergamon	Antiochia	Aï Khanoum	Alexandria	Jericho Has.
1	official	portal, monu.	X	X	X	X	X	X	X	X	X	X?	X?	X	X	?
2	official	audience hall	X	X	X	X	X	X	X	X	X	X	X?	X	X	X?
3	official	reception hall	X	X	X	X	X	X	X?	X?	X?	X	X?	X	X	X?
4	social	banqueting halls	X?	X	X?	X	X	X?	X	X	X	X	X?	X	X	X?
5	religious	tutelary cult	-	-	?	-	-	-	X	-?	-?	X	X?	?	X?	-
6	religious	dynastic cult	-	-	-	-	-	-	-	X?	-	X?	X?	?	X	-
7	religious	mausoleum	-	-	X	X	-	-	-	-	-	-	?	?	X	-
8	defensive	precinct walls	X	X	X	X	-	-	-	-	-	X	X	-	X	?
9	defensive	citadel/akra	X	X	X	X	X	-	X	X?	X	X	-?	-	X	X
10	defensive	barracks/arsenal	X	X?	X?	X	X?	-?	X?	X?	X	X	X?	-	X	?
11	administrative	offices	-	X	?	X	X?	-	-	X?	?	X?	X?	X?	X?	?
12	administrative	archives	-	X?	X?	X	X	-	?	X?	?	X	X?	X	X?	-
13	administrative	treasury	-	X	X	X	X	-	?	-	X?	X?	X?	X	X	-
14	service	storerooms	X?	X	X?	X	X	X?	X?	X?	X?	X?	X?	X?	X?	X
15	service	kitchens, etc.	X	X?	X?	X?	X?	X?	X?	X?	X?	X?	X?	X	X?	X?
16	service	servants' quart.	X?	X?	X?	X?	X	X?	X	X?	X?	X?	X?	X?	X?	X?
17	A residential:	bedrooms	X	X	X?	X?	X	X?	X?	X?	X?	X?	X	X?	X?	X?
18	the king and	bathrooms	X?	X?	X?	X?	X?	X?	X?	X	X?	X?	X?	X	X?	X
19	his family	private dining	X?	X	X?	X?	X	X?	X	X?	X?	X	X?	X	X?	X
20		harem	X?	X	X?	X?	X	X?	-	-	-	-	-	X	-	-
21	B court/guests	apartments	-	X	?	X?	-?-	?	?	X?	X?	X?	X?	X	X	-?
22	"public"	gymnasium/pal.	-	-	-	-	-	-	-	X?	-	-	?	X?	X	-
23	"public"	library	-	-	-	-	-	-	?	X	?	X	X	X	X	-
24	"public"	theatre	-	-	-	-	-	-	X	X	-	X	?	-	X	-
25	"public"	hippodrome	-	-	-	-	-	-	-	-	-	-	X	-	-?	-
26	recreational	gardens	?	X	-	X	?	X	?	X	X?	X?	?	?	X?	X
27	recreational	parks	X	X	X	X	X	X	-	-	-	-	X	X?	X	X
28	recreational	pavilions	?	X	X	X	X	?	-	-	-	-	X?	?	X	X
29	recreational	(swimming-)pools	X?	-	?	X	?	?	-	-	-	-	?	X	X	X

Fig. 115. Table of palatial functions by type: models, Hellenistic royal palaces, governors' palaces, and private palaces.

	Roman royal palaces							Governors' palaces								Private palaces	
	Rome	Masada W	Masada N	Jericho W1	Jericho W2	Jericho W3	Herodium	Lachish	Vouni	Larisa	Dura Red.	Dura Cit.	Nippur	Araq Emir	Ptolemais	Pella Dion.	Casa Fauno
1	X	-	-	?	-	X	X	-	X	X	-	-	-	X	-	X?	X
2	X	X	?	X	-	X	X	X	X	X	X	X	X	X	X	X	X
3	X	?	-	X	-	?	X?	X?	X?	?	X?	X?	-	-?	X?	-	X
4	X	X	X	X	-	X	X	X?	X	X?	X	X	X	X?	X	X	X
5	X	-	-	-	-	-	-	-	-	-	-	-	-	-	-	-	-
6	-	-	-	-	-	-	-	-	-	-	-	-	-	-	?	-	-
7	-	-	-	-	-	-	X	-	-	-	-	-	-	-	-	-	-
8	-	X	X	-	-	-?	?	X	X	X	-	X	-	X	-	-	-
9	-	X	X	-	-	-	X	X	X	-	X	X	X	-	-	-	-
10	-	X	X	-	-	-?	X?	-	X?	X?	-	?	-	?	-	-	-
11	X?	X?	-?	-	-	-	X?	?	-?	?	?	?	-?	-	X?	-	-
12	-	?	-?	-	-	-	X?	?	-?	?	?	?	?	?	?	-	-
13	-	?	-?	-	-	-	X?	?	-?	?	?	?	X	?	?	-	-
14	X?	X	X	?	-	?	X?	X?	X	X?	?	X?	X	X	X	X?	X?
15	X?	X?	X?	X?	X?	X?	X?	X?	X	X?	X?	X?	X	X?	X	X?	X?
16	X?	X	X?	X?	?	X?	X?	X?	X	X?	X?	X?	X	X?	X	X?	X
17	X	X?	X	X	?	-	X?	X	X	X?	X?	X?	X	X	X	X	X
18	X?	X	X	X	X	X	X	X	X	X?	X?	X?	X	X?	X?	X?	X
19	X?	X?	X	X	X	X	X	?	X?	X?	?	?	X	X	X	X?	X
20	-	-	-	-	-	-	-	-	-	-	-	-	-	X?	-	-	-
21	-	X	X	?	?	?	X?	-?	-?	-?	-?	-?	-?	-?	X?	?	?
22	-	-	-	-	?	-	-	-	-	-	-	-	-	-	-	-	-
23	X	-	-	-	-	-	-	-	-	-	-	-	-	-	-	-	-
24	-	-	-	-	-	-	X	-	-	-	-	-	-	-	-	-	-
25	X	-	-	-	-	-	X	-	-	-	-	-	-	-	-	-	-
26	X	-	-	X	X	X	X	-	-	-	-	-	-	?	X	X	X
27	-	X?	X?	X	X	X	X	-	-	-	-	-	-	X	-	-	-
28	-	-?	X	?	X	X	X	-	-	-	-	-	-	X	-	-	-
29	-	X	X	X	X	X	X	-	-	-	-	-	-	X	X	-	-

Hellenistic kingdoms, it was the palace, rather than the agora, which was the centre of activity in the city.

To judge from these very important buildings, there is, it seems to me, no substantial evidence that Hellenistic culture, signifying the culture existing or developing in the areas ruled by the Hellenistic kings, had a uniform character. The more one moves away from the Greek heartlands, the more superficial the Greek/Macedonian features become, being mostly limited to architectural decoration, while the layout, and therefore the function, becomes increasingly Oriental/local.

Even if, as one might expect, the upper classes of the cities in the different Hellenistic kingdoms had plenty of opportunity and the ambition to create a uniform culture, the cultures represented by the kings and their court, which they imitated, differed very much, depending on which kingdom was concerned. It is well known that the further down one goes in the social hierarchy, the less foreign cultural influence is traceable. While a cultural koiné was on its way already in the late Hellenistic period (see the obvious "westernization" in the Palazzo delle Colonne and the late Hasmonean and early Herodian palaces), it was not until the time of Augustus that a cultural koiné became a reality (see, for instance, the later palaces built by Herod the Great in Palestine). This is not true of all areas covered by the former Hellenistic kingdoms, but in general one might say that it was left to the Roman emperors, rather than the Hellenistic kings, to give effect to Alexander the Great's idea of a fusion of Oriental and Western culture.

There can be no doubt that the Hellenistic royal palaces, especially those of Antioch, Pergamon, and, most importantly Alexandria, had a great influence on Hellenistic, as well as Republican and early Roman architecture in general. This is expressed in residential architecture as represented by private palaces and villas, with their peristylar courts, spacious halls, gardens, and parks, as well as through a general luxuria/tryphe; also, the monumental tombs of the élite drew inspiration from the royal palatial façades. But these palaces had a major effect on public and religious architecture as well. Thus certain kinds of heroa, libraries, porticoes, banqueting houses, perhaps even the stage-building of the theatres, and, not least basilicas, may have originated in or been inspired by the Hellenistic palaces. The same is true of the public parks and formal gardens, with their pavilions and pools, and features such as a theatrical layout and an architectural treatment of the landscape.

Only by not forgetting the existence of these poorly known or now vanished royal palaces can we begin to analyse Hellenistic, late Republican, and early

Roman architecture with any confidence. Their influence was not limited to antiquity. Through the Roman palaces in Rome, Constantinople, and elsewhere, and the late Persian and the Islamic palaces, they continued to exert their influence: even the Seraglio of Istanbul and the Palace of Versailles did not escape.

NOTES

1. Grimal 1969, 231f. This very important book was first published in 1943. Cf. in general Giuliano & Bisi, s.v. Palazzo, in *EAA* V, Roma 1963, 850ff.
2. E.g. Zanker 1979 and 1983, La Rocca 1986.
3. Heermann 1986, her dissertation of 1980.
4. Dura Europos: Downey 1985 and 1986; Aï Khanoum: Bernard *et al.* 1973, Bernard 1976 and 1981; Araq el Emir: Will 1991.
5. Especially Hoepfner & Schwandner 1986, Carroll-Spillecke 1989.
6. For the seminar in Leiden, see Le système palatial 1987. The results of the symposium "Hellenistische Paläste" held in Berlin in December 1992 has recently been published in: *Basileia. Die Paläste der hellenistichen Könige*, Mainz 1996.
7. E.g. Coarelli 1983b, La Rocca 1986, Wallace-Hadrill 1988, who are all indebted to Tamm 1963, and of course to Grimal 1969.
7a. This hellenocentric viewpoint is for example demonstrated by Hoepfner (1996) in his copious article which opens the publication of the "Basileia" conference in Berlin (see n. 6), and also other authors in this volume reflect this view. See also e.g. Murray 1996, who focuses on the Hellenistic royal *symposia*.
8. For this "school of research", see most recently the collection of articles in *Hellenism in the East*, eds. A. Kuhrt and S. Sherwin-White, 1987, with a useful bibliography; the new series, "Achaemenid History" I-VII, 1987-1991; and also the newly published book on the Seleucid empire, again by Sherwin-White and Kuhrt. For the works of P. Briant, another pioneer of this trend, see most recently Briant 1990.
9. For a discussion of the terms, see Bichler 1983, who also gives a general history of research in the period.
10. See, for example, the most recent major work on the period, Green 1990.
11. See, for example, Lauter in his book on Hellenistic architecture (1986, 5). Thus he devotes only 10 pages to the "Oriental" architecture of the period (pp. 276-86). Cf. Lauter 1987.
12. A. Giuliano, s.v. Palazzo, in *EAA* V, Roma 1963, 851.
13. The word *anaktoron* is primarily used for the dwellings of the gods in ancient literature (see Liddell & Scott); but in modern Greek, it often means "royal palace".
14. For court society in general, see Elias 1983. For the rather limited literature on the Hellenistic court, see esp. Bikerman 1938, 31ff (the Seleucids), Fraser 1972, 101ff and *passim* (the Ptolemies), Préaux 1978, vol. I, 179ff, Walbank 1984, 68ff, and various articles by L. Mooren, especially Mooren 1983 (the Ptolemies), with further sources and earlier literature.
15. It has been suggested that the original painting adorned a Hellenistic palace, perhaps that of Cassander at Pella, or, as C. Nylander has proposed, a palace in the formerly Achaemenid East (most recently Nylander 1993, 146, with references). As mentioned p. 21, Hieron II held audiences in a park in Syracuse.
16. Gabelmann 1984.
17. For Persian court life, see e.g. Eddy 1961, Root 1969, and Cook 1983, with references. The main sources are Herodotus, Ctesias (the Greek doctor who lived at the Persian court), and

Xenophon (who followed the pretender Cyrus the Younger). For the reliability of these Greek authors, esp. Ctesias, see Sancisi-Weerdenburg 1987.

18. Plut. *Art.* 22.4-6, *Them.* 27ff; cf. Philostratus *Imag.* 2.31; Xen. *Cyr.* 2.3.21, 2.1.30; Athen. 2.48d-f (cit. Heracleides). According to Athenaeus (12.525c-d)(cit. Democritus), the Great King was considered the originator of *tryphe*. Cf. Alföldi 1934, 47ff.

19. E.g. Plut. *Alex.* 45; Curt. 6.2.1, 8.7.12, 8.5.20, 8.5.19, etc.; Livy 9.18.3-4; Athen. 12.537d (cit. Ephippus); Justin. 12.7.1. Cf. Alföldi 1934, 9ff with further sources.

20. See Alföldi 1934 and 1935, reprinted together in Alföldi 1970; Wallace-Hadrill 1982, with earlier literature.

21. Alföldi 1935, 139. For the development of the official functions and their architectural expression at the court of the Roman emperors, see Tamm 1963.

22. For the role of the Hellenistic king in general, see Goodenough 1928 and Préaux 1978, vol. I, 179-294. For the Seleucids, see Bikerman 1938, 3ff; for the Ptolemies, the *Letter of "Aristeas"*, esp. the symposium discussion (187-300).

23. The use of the *proskynesis* in the audiences of these monarchies is but one example of this. See Gabelmann 1984 and *infra*.

24. For a general summary of the two main theories, see most recently Borza 1990, 230ff.

25. Cf. Plut. *Aem.* 8.2.

26. Walbank 1986, 85. This is also the impression one gets from Polybius, in his treatment of the reigns of Philip V and Perseus. For example, the former began to choose his "Friends" not only from the aristocracy of Macedonia, but from outside his kingdom, which placed him in a more independent position (see e.g. Polyb. 20.5.12).

27. This destinction between the ruler cult and the dynastic cult is not always made, as Walbank (1984, 84ff, and 1987) stresses. Cf. Bikerman 1938, 286ff; Préaux 1978, vol. I, 238ff. The dynastic cult was first introduced into Egypt by Ptolemy II, and probably not until almost a century later into the Seleucid kingdom, by Antiochus III.

28. See Eddy 1961. For a good summary of the discussion on divine kingship, see Nylander 1993, 150f, with earlier literature. As for the early Roman monarchy created by Augustus, it had both similarities to and differences from the various Hellenistic monarchies. At least at the outset, we probably have to deal with a *primus inter pares* model, rather than the absolute one which Caesar had tried to introduce with disastrous results, or that is doubtless what the early emperors wished us to believe. But this dissimulation was in any case directed only towards the subjects of Italy and especially the Roman senate: in the provinces, the Roman emperor had the same status as the Hellenistic autocratic king. For the ambiguous role of the Roman emperor, see Wallace-Hadrill 1982.

29. For the notion of *tryphe* and the ambiguous attitude of the Greek authors towards this phenomenon, see Athen. 12.510-550; Plut. *Demetr.* 41-42. Cf. Wallace-Hadrill 1982, 33ff. One is reminded of Xenophon's description of the means which Cyrus the Younger used to enhance his majesty (*Cyr.* 8.1.40-41, 8.3.1-23).

30. For the role of the Hellenistic queens, see Macurdy 1932, Pomeroy 1984, 3ff. For the Seleucid queens, see Bikerman 1938, 24ff.

31. See Gabelmann 1984.

32. Andronicos 1984. From Athenaeus (12.537d-f)(cit. Ephippus) we hear that Alexander dressed up as different gods, as well as assuming the costume of different countries. Cf. Augustus and his court dressed as gods at private parties, Suet. *Aug.* 70.

33. Diod. 18.60-61. A similar empty throne, of gold and ivory, with the king's insignia placed on it, is mentioned in Callixenus' description of the procession of Ptolemy II (Athen. 5.202b).

34. I Macc. 6.15.

35.   See Plut. *Ant.* 54.3-4, *Demetr.* 49.

36.   For this robe of Median or Persian origin, see Xen. *Cyr.* 8.1.40-41; Athen. 12.525c-d (cit. Democritus). For the Hellenistic royal robe, see Polyb. 26.1; Plut. *Mor.* 486a. Cf. Bikerman 1938, 32f.

37.   Athen. 12.535f (cit. Duris). Cf. Plut. *Demetr.* 18, 41-42, for the general pomp and circumstance surrounding this king. Cf. Alföldi 1934, 16ff for further literature. For the Roman use of the diadem, including the proffering of the diadem to Caesar by Mark Antony, see Alföldi 1935, 145ff.

38.   Plut. *Ant.* 54. For the lavish dinner dress of this queen, see Lucan, *BC* 10.136ff.

39.   Diotogenes *apud* Stob. *Ecl.* 4.7.62. He was only one of many philosophors who reflected on the nature and types of kingship from the 4th cent. BC onwards. Cf. the classic article by Goodenough, 1928, and, cautioning against some of his results, Wallace-Hadrill 1982, 33ff.

40.   Préaux 1978, vol. I, 183ff. For the attitude of contemporaneous and later ancient authors to royalty and the "correct" behaviour of a monarch, see Wallace-Hadrill 1982, 33ff, with earlier literature.

41.   For the triple grouping, see Le Bohec 1987.

42.   E.g. Athen. 2.48d-f (cit. Timagoras (?)) and 12.537d (cit. Ephippus); cf. the scene with the empty throne, Diod. 18.60-61 (*v.i.*). Also after Alexander's death, audiences in the field took place in tents, see e.g. Polyb. 21.1; Plut. *Demetr.* 50.1-2. For Cyrus the Younger's audiences, which often took all day, see Xen. *Cyr.* 7.37ff.

43.   "Aristeas" 172-186, 191. In the following, references to this letter, written by an Alexandrian Jew, are placed in parenthesis in the text. The dating of the letter to the 2nd cent. BC is now generally accepted. For a commentary on this source, see Pelletier 1962. For the Seleucid court, see e.g. Livy 35.16.1; Diod. 34.2. Cf. Bikerman 1938, 34.

44.   In Rome, we find the same system at quite an early date. Thus only his Friends had direct access to the emperor, others were split up into *prima et secunda admissio* (Sen. *Ben.* 6.3.3).

45.   Polyb. 5.56.10-11, 8.21.1.

46.   See e.g. Polyb. 5.42.7, 5.43.5; Plut. *Mor.* 790a.

47.   As at the Achaemenid court, one must imagine the presence of a dressing-room in connection with the audience hall. In fact, rooms of this description, and a bathroom or bath suite too, have been found in several palaces (see e.g. pp. 53, 124). This group of rooms is often called an "andron complex." It was important that the king could reach the official part of the palace from the residential part without being seen before he was ceremonially dressed.

48.   Vitr. 5.6.8-9, Loeb edn., trans. F. Granger.

49.   Polyb. 15.30.6 (*chrematistikon pylon*); Athen. 5.205ff (cit. Callixenus) (*thalamegos*, see p. 136); Vitr. 6.5.2 (*vestibula regalia alta*). Cf. Tamm 1963, 91ff for the ambiguous use of the words *vestibulum/atrium* in Roman literature.

50.   Lucan, *BC* 10.111-112. The pediment as a royal symbol was known in Rome also, for example from Caesar's house in the Forum (Cic. *Phil.* 2.43; Suet. *Caes.* 81.3, etc.). As for the resemblance of the audience hall to a temple, Caligula, in fact, used the Temple of Castor and Pollux in the Forum Romanum as a vestibule (Suet. *Cal.* 22; Cass.Dio. 59.28.5), and Augustus received embassies sitting in front of the Temple of Apollo on the Palatine (see p. 178). Cf. Alföldi 1935, 128ff. One may mention also the coin showing the vestibule of Domitian's Palace on the Palatine: with its pediment and columnar portico, it strongly resembles a temple. Cf. La Rocca 1986, 9, fig. 4.

51.   Vitr. 6.3.9. Vitr. 6.5.8 says that there ought to be basilicas in private houses belonging to Roman aristocrats. Cf. Tamm 1963, Wallace-Hadrill 1988, 58ff. Also the apse, present for

example in the Bacchic *oikos* of the Nile-boat (*v.i.* n. 66) and documented also both earlier and later, is an indication of this sanctity. Cf. Tamm 1963, 147ff.

52. See Polyb. 15.25.3 (*megiston peristylon*); Plut. *Ant.* 54.3-4 (*gymnasion*). Probably also the large open spaces (*eurychoriai*) in the Alexandrian palace, mentioned by Polybius (15.30.6), could be used for this purpose.

53. Athen. 12.542a (cit. Silenus of Calacte).

54. See Borza (1983) for a discussion of the various terms for this function. For the Hellenistic royal *symposia* and their setting, see recently Murray 1996; Nielsen 1998. For Roman imperial dining customs and dining-halls, see Tamm 1963, 189ff.

55. E.g. Athen. 4.145-146 (cit. Heracleides). Cf. Lewis 1987.

56. See for the Persian drinking-parties, Athen. 4.145 (cit. Heracleides), and for the Macedonian parties, Borza (1983) with references. That the Hellenistic kings were often drunk on these occasions is clear from e.g. Athen. 10.438c (cit. Phylarchus), 10.438d (cit. Ptolemy VII), and 10.439e (cit. Posidonius).

57. E.g. Athen. 4.153a (cit. Posidonius), on the Seleucid court. Cf. Bikerman 1938, 35.

58. See Athen. 12.537d-540a (cit. Chares); Aelian *VH* 8.7 (the wedding). Athen. 3.126e (cit. Duris), 5.211a (cit. Masorius) (entertainment). E.g. Diod. 17.68-73.1 (Persepolis). Athen. 1.17d-18a (cit. Duris) (the banquet of the 6,000). Athen. 4.146c (cit. Ephippus) (smaller dinner parties). Darius' tent, captured at Issus, was also used by Alexander for banquets (Diod. 17.36.5; Curt. 3.13.1-3; Plut. *Alex.* 20.7). Even before his eastern campaigns, Alexander had held a large banquet, in Dion, again using a tent holding 100 *klinai*, with the army dining outside (Diod. 17.16.4). Cf. Borza 1983.

59. Athen. 12.542c (cit. Silenus of Caracte); Ael. *VH* 9.9.

60. Athen. 5.196-197 (cit. Callixenus); Polyb. 31.3.7; see pp. 133f.

61. Polyb. 30.25-26; Plut. *Aem.* 28; Athen. 5.194ff (cit. Polybius). For the luxury of the Seleucid banquets, see e.g. Athen. 4.156c-d (cit. Antiphanes), cf. Bikerman 1938, 35. That these processions were reflections of similar Achaemenid processions is proved by the one arranged by Cyrus the Younger (Xen. *Cyr.* 8.3.1-23).

62. "Aristeas" 186. See also Lucan, *BC* 10.127ff, where particular attention is drawn to the multitude of attendants at the banquet which Cleopatra held in Caesar's honour. Cf. Diod. 17.36.5, on the pages of Darius preparing a reception in the Great King's tent.

63. Lucan, *BC* 10.111ff (Cleopatra's dining-hall); Joseph. *BJ* 5.4.4 (177-178) (Jerusalem). Cf. Lucret. 2.20ff for a description of luxurious halls in Roman villas, which resembled these royal halls. One may mention also the banquet that Metellus Pius held in 75 BC in Spain. It took place in a hall decorated to resemble a temple and may thus be compared with Cleopatra's dining-hall (Sall. *Cat.* 2.1-9; Plut. *Sert.* 22.2-3; Val.Max. 9.1.5). What Valerius Maximus finds particularly objectionable was that this did not take place in Greece or Asia, where such extravagance was only to be expected, but in provincial Spain. Cf. the feast of Mithridates held in the theatre of Pergamon in 88 BC (Plut. *Sull.* 11.1-2).

64. See Athen. 5.204ff (cit. Callixenus) (Thalamegos); Athen. 5.207 (cit. Moschion) (Syracusia). For Ptolemy II's Pavilion, see n. 60.

65. In Alexandria, the Temple of Adonis was in the palace (Theocr. *Id.* 15), and also that of Poseidon (Strab. 17.1.9 (794)), while the important Temple of Sarapis was close by.

66. Athen. 5.205d-e (cit. Callixenus). Also in the Syracusia, Hieron II' ship, there was a Temple of Aphrodite, which was used as a dining-room as well (Athen. 5.207e (cit. Callixenus)).

67. Thus, for example, in the palatial area of Memphis, there was a Temple of Arsinoe, Ptolemy II's queen. See Thompson 1988, 131 n. 118.

68. See Bikerman 1938, 286ff.

69.   For the religious role of the Roman emperor (already apparent in "Augustus", a title with a religious connotation), the imperial cult, and the worship of the *genius* of the emperor, see Alföldi 1934, 29ff, and p. 173. Cf. Ovid, *Fast.* 4.951-954, mentioning three gods in Augustus' palace: Apollo, Vesta, and the emperor.

70.   Caes. *BC* 3.112.3.

71.   E.g. Strab. 17.1.8 (793-94); Athen. 14.654c (cit. Ptolemy Physcon). Cf. in general, Sonne 1996.

72.   Joseph. *BJ* 5.4.4 (177-178). See p. 182. Also Roman villas with their spacious grounds may be mentioned in this connection, as may depictions of them in Pompeian wall-painting (see Fig. 89). See Grimal 1969, La Rocca 1986.

73.   Perseus' game reserve in Macedonia, which was taken over after Pydna by the Romans, who also enjoyed this sport, was probably an old royal estate (Polyb. 31.29.1-8).

74.   For instance, we hear of a citadel in Pella that is isolated from the palace (Livy 44.46.4-8).

75.   Polyb. 15.25.5, 15.27.8-9, 15.28.4 (*skenai*); cf. Philo *in Flacc.* 92 (arsenals).

76.   "Aristeas" 33, 80.

77.   See Bikerman 1938, 133ff, with sources.

78.   See the recent publication by Rapin 1992.

79.   For theatres: Aigai (Diod. 16.91.4-95); Alexandria (Polyb. 15.30.6; Caes. *BC* 3.112.3). For gymnasia/palaestrae: Alexandria (Polyb. 15.30.6). For library/museum: Pella (e.g. Plut. *Aem.* 28); Antioch (*Corpus Inscr. Indicarum* I, p. 48); Pergamon (Strab. 13.4.2 (624)); Alexandria (e.g. Athen. 5.203e; Strab. 17.1.8 (793)). For hippodrome: Antioch (Malalas 225.8; Cass.Dio 68.25.5). Cf. the Catalogue.

80.   Arr. *Anab.* 3.1.2-4; Ps.-Callisthenes 1.34.2.

81.   Arist. *Oec.* 2.2.33; Arr. *Anab.* 3.5.4; *FGrH* 239; Paus. 1.6.3. Cf. Thompson 1988, 107f.

82.   *Akra*: *P. Cairo Zeno* 59156.3 (256 BC). Park: *PSI* 488.12 (257 BC), and Strab. 17.1.31-32 (807-808), with general description.

83.   For the ancient Egyptian palaces, see in general Smith 1965; for the gardens, see e.g. Gallery 1978; Hugonot 1989 and 1992.

84.   The symmetrically arranged "three-room suite in depth" is a legacy from the Neo-Assyrian palaces, and continued to be used in Achaemenid architecture, e.g. in Susa (*v.i.*). See Amiet 1974.

84a.   The problem is that neither Koldeway's placement of these Hanging Gardens on the vaults, nor the new theory placing them along the Euphrates, fit in with the description given in the written sources (See Margueron 1992, 74ff). A new theory, that these garden were, instead, placed in Nineveh, has recently been propagated by Dalley 1994.

85.   For Khorsabad, see Loud 1936-38. For Near Eastern palaces in general, see e.g. Frankfort 1970.

86.   For the Khorsabad relief and the Nineveh relief, see Oppenheim 1965, Stronach 1989. For Near Eastern gardens in general, see Margueron 1992.

87.   For a penetrating treatment of this frieze, see Albenda 1976-1977. Cf. Deller 1987, who sets the banquet in a garden pavilion.

88.   Stob. *Ecl.* 16.1.5. Cf. Sherwin-White & Kuhrt 1993, 46, 157f. A gymnasium is mentioned as well.

89.   For this theatre, see Wetzel *et al.* 1957, 3ff. Cf. Sherwin-White (1987) for the fate of the city under the Seleucids (p. 20f for the theatre). For the hellenization of Babylonia, see van der Spek 1987.

90.   Besides these preserved palaces, Polybius (10.27.7-13) gives a description of the summer palace built by the Achaemenids in Ecbatana, the old capital of the Medes, as it appeared

in 210 BC. It consisted of a fortified citadel (*akra*), with the palace proper below; this was built entirely of wood and covered with precious materials, which had, however, been mostly removed by Alexander and his successors. As far as the position is concerned, one is reminded of Pasargadae. Columns belonging to stoas and peristyles are mentioned. The character of this building, however, may well reflect the original royal palace style of the Medes in Ecbatana. Cf. Diod. 17.110.7.

91. However, at least some of the Persian architects moved eastwards, to India, taking with them the traditions of Achaemenid palace and garden architecture. Thus Megasthenes, in his description (c. 300 BC) of the palace and court of Chandragupta and his new capital Pataliputra, mentions large parks with animals and cultivated plants, tanks for fish, etc., i.e. a true paradeisos. In excavations on the site, a hypostyle hall of Persian type has come to light. See Wheeler 1974, Sherwin-White & Kuhrt 1993, 91ff.

92. This is not the place to discuss this problem in detail, but see Nylander 1979, Root 1978, and the literature mentioned in the Introduction, n. 8.

93. For the role of Greek craftsmen in the construction of Persian palaces, see Nylander 1970.

94. These terraces are called *akra* by Diodorus (17.70-71).

95. For the definition of the *apadana* as a building type used here, see Stronach 1985.

96. Athen. 4.145-146, citing Heracleides of Kyme (c. 350 BC). We hear in the sources of very large banquets, with up to 15,000 guests; see Lewis 1987. These huge feasts took place in the open or in tents, either in the forecourts or in the palace park. Minor banquets took place indoors. Cf. Dentzer 1982.

97. Diod. 17.72. For a discussion of the extent of this destruction, see Sancisi-Weerdenburg 1993. (See p. 21.)

98. Diod. 17.66.3ff. We are told that the Persians considered the Greeks to be to be the very opposite of bons viveurs, because they finished their meals much too fast, which to them was a sign of poverty. Cf. Cook 1983, Ch. XIII. One may compare this with Herodotus' story about the Spartan general Pausanias, who after his victory at Plataea held a Persian banquet in Xerxes' tent and compared it with the primitive Spartan diet (Hdt. 9.80-82). Cf. Curtius Rufus (6.2.1), who says of Alexander that his magnificent banquets were a sign of his succumbing to Oriental vices. Cf. Borza (1983), who records that very little is known of what was eaten at this time at the Macedonian court, drinking being the main preoccupation.

99. According to Diodorus (17.70-71), there were living-quarters for the royal family and the high officials (*kataluseis basilikai kai strategikai*) spread over the terrace (*akra*). For arguments against a residential function for this part of the terrace, see Bernard 1976, Cook 1983. Nylander has expressed the same view orally.

100. Herzfeld (1941, 231) had some knowledge of these, but identified them as a temple complex. Schmidt (1953, 55) sees these structures, i.e. the "apadana" and the sunken garden, as residential buildings. Both these buildings and the many newly excavated ones figure on the plan in Kleiss 1980 (Fig. 14 in this volume), and were published in Persian, by Tadjvidi in 1976. Cf. Calmeyer 1990, who considers them to be private houses.

101. It was probably in such buildings and halls that the king dined with his family (Athen. 4.145d (cit. Heracleides)).

102. Scerrato 1966, esp. figs. 2 and 48. This locality is probably identical with the administrative capital of Dragana, Zranka. These private houses, dated to the 6th-5th cent. BC, are closely related to the contemporary houses in Persepolis, both on the terrace (the "Officer's House"), and on the plain below (Fig. 14). Typical is a square plan with a central court surrounded by square and rectangular rooms and corridors.

103.   Von Gall 1977, Nylander 1970. Also de Francovich (1966, 230f) thought an inspiration from Ionic buildings probable, especially in Pasargadae. Stronach (1978, 72f) in his discussion of this issue only partly supports Nylander's hypothesis. He finds the presence of local forerunners in Iran probable, but concedes that a peristyle around a central room might have been inspired by an Ionic peripteral temple. But this itself did not arise from nothing. That a close connection existed with e.g. Ephesus is demonstrated by the use of fluted bases in Palace P. Cf. De Angelis d'Ossat 1971.

104.   Nylander has elaborated on this theory in two important contributions (Nylander 1979, 1983). He stresses the symbolic value of Persian architecture, i.e. its combination of elements from many different parts of the vast kingdom. He sees it as a conscious choice on the part of the Achaemenid kings, and aptly uses the word "commonwealth" to describe the Persian attitude. He refuses to regard Persian architecture as provincial, as the "panhellenists" do. See for this comparatively new "Orientalist" trend, n. 92.

105.   For a discussion of this theory, see von Gall 1977, where he argues against Nylander's hypothesis. Nylander has told me that he thinks von Gall's tent theory has much to recommend it. Relevant tents are mentioned in the following written sources. In the Book of Esther (1.3-8), a marquee used by Xerxes or Artaxerxes for a large banquet for the people of Susa is referred to. This was set up in a large square in front of the park by the palace. Silver poles and marble columns supported the roof, and it housed *klinai* of gold and silver. Xenophon (*Cyr.* 5.5.2) describes the tent that Cyrus the Younger placed at Cyaxares' disposal. It had belonged to the Assyrian king, and he mentions *i.a.* that it incorporated women's quarters, and was richly appointed. Finally the tent of Darius III, abandoned after the Battle of Issus, is praised for its great size and height, and is said to have contained fine banqueting furniture. Also, it had a rich bathroom (*loutron*), with bath-tubs (*pyeloi*) in gold, connected to the main tent (Plut. *Alex.* 20.7). For the marquee belonging to Alexander, probably the one taken at Issus rather than the one mentioned at the feast of Dion, see p. 21.

106.   Hdt. 9.80-82. see n. 98. Cf. Vickers, forthcoming.

107.   Broneer 1944. Cf. von Gall 1979, and Francis 1980, 82f and n. 158, for a discussion of this theory.

108.   Plut. *Per.* 13.5-6. Cf. Vitr. 5.9.1, who mentions that besides stone columns this *odeum* contained elements from the Persian ships, i.e. masts (*mali*) and yards (*antemnae*). For its being a direct copy of the *skene* of Xerxes, see also Paus. 1.20.4. For a coin showing this Odeum with a pyramidal roof, see von Gall 1977, Abb. 5. Appian, *Mith.* 6.38 mentions that the Athenians themselves set fire to it, to prevent the wood of the building from being used by Sulla, which indicates a roof construction demanding much wood. For the excavations, see Travlos 1971, 387-391.

109.   Von Gall 1979.

110.   Von Gall 1977, 1979. Cf. De Angelis d'Ossat 1971.

111.   Athen. 12.534d (cit. Antisthenes); cf. Plut. *Alc.* 12.1. See for the influence of Oriental textiles including tents in Greece, Vickers, forthcoming.

112.   This was originally a Persian word. Although its original Persian meaning is uncertain, its later usage, especially in a biblical context, is very well known. Cf. Stronach 1989. For *paradeisoi* in general, see e.g. Xenophon, who at *Oec.* 4.13-14 emphasizes the interest that the Persian kings took in the layout of these parks and their cultivation. Cf. Ziegler (s.v. Paradeisos, *RE* 18, 1949, cols. 113-134) who deals mainly with the biblical meaning of the word, but also with the attitudes of the Greeks to the parks, which they identified with *kepoi* (cf. Carroll-Spillecke 1989). See also Grimal 1969, 79ff, and Gentelle 1981. Such gardens

continued in use under the Sassanids and the Arabs, and were also known in Iran much later; in fact they still exist. See Sackville-West 1953; Kawami 1992.

113. For hunting: Xen. *An.* 1.2.78, *Cyr.* 1.2.14. Park with utility trees: Xen. *An.* 2.4.14, cf. Nehemia 2.8-9 (wood for the building of the Temple of Jerusalem came from the royal *paradeisos*).

114. Another palace that is perhaps of similar layout has recently been found 3 km north of Persepolis at Takht-i-Rustam, near the unfinished tomb belonging probably to Cambyses, son of Cyrus. A building very similar to Palace S of Pasargadae has been traced, aligned with the tomb, c. 100 m away. Probably both were placed in a large paradeisos like the one at Pasargadae. See Tilia 1974, 1978, 73-80; Kleiss 1980.

115. Stronach 1989, 487. However, he does not include the western successors in his survey.

116. See in general Hanfmann 1975, Francis 1980, 68ff. Cf. Colledge 1987, 136ff.

117. Xen. *An.* 1.4.9-11.

118. Diodorus (16.41-45) mentions this *paradeisos* in connection with its destruction, in 350 BC. Cf. Clermont-Ganneau 1921, and, for Sidon in the Persian period in general, Elayi 1990.

119. The excavator, Tufnell (1953), recognized only one phase and dated it to the middle of the 5th cent. BC on the basis of the pottery. Aharoni (1975), after having examined the arguments thoroughly, dates this palace much earlier, around 700 BC, because of its unquestionable similarity to the palaces of that date in Northern Syria: e.g. the upper palace of Zinçirli and also Building 1369 in Megiddo; both were probably Syrian governors' palaces, suggesting a similar function for the Palace of Lachish. However, similarity of plan does not in itself give proof of synchronism, and Aharoni's stratigraphical arguments are not conclusive. Rather, I find that Stern (1982, 42ff, 57ff), who bases his arguments on the new excavation by Ussishkin (1977), is right in dating the first period to Persian times (middle of the 5th cent.-early 4th cent. BC) and the second period to early Hellenistic times. Cf. Arav 1989, 57f.

120. For these North Syrian palaces, and especially the Bit-Hilani, see Frankfort 1952 (with citation), and most recently Gregori 1982 and Fritz 1983.

121. See also Stern 1982, 57ff.

122. See Maier 1989 n. 24, with earlier literature.

123. Cf. Stern 1982, 59f.

124. E.g. Tosi 1959, 242ff. Cf. Boehlau & Schefold (1940, 33), who even consider the first phase of the Vouni Palace to have a Grecian megaron.

125. I.e. "Building 2", see Scerrato 1966, Genito 1986.

126. See Nielsen & Philips 1985, with earlier literature. The motifs on the terracottas seem rather to indicate a palatial function, see Rathje 1993. In this connection one may mention that a late source even makes the Etruscans the first to introduce a peristyle (*peristoa*) into the dwelling (Diod. 5.40); probably he means in Italy.

127. That three-sided peristyles were normal in domestic architecture is mentioned also by Vitruvius (6.7.1) in his description of the Greek palatial house.

128. Schäfer 1960, Maier 1989.

129. Cf. Ghirshman 1964, 353, fig. 454. For a general discussion of Cypriot palaces, see Maier 1989, who also stresses a close connection with the Near East, rather than with Greece. Recently, palatial structures have been found also in Amathus and Idalion. In Amathus, new excavations have revealed part of a royal palace on the top of the hill, in relation to the main temple of Aphrodite, i.e. in a similar position as the one in Vouni, and apparently of similar size. The remains of this structure, mostly storerooms, date from the Classical period, but

there are indications that the palace existed already before that time. It is interesting that a Hathor capital was found here as well. See for this palace, Aupert 1996, and, for the capital, Hermary 1985. The palace (or admimistrative building, as the excavators cautiously call it) of Idalion, of which partly storerooms, partly a very interesting archive containing Phoenician inscriptions have been excavated so far, dates in its present form to the Classical period. See Chronique des Fouilles à Chypre, in *BCH* from 1992 and onwards.

130. For a general survey of the situation in this area, see Colledge 1987, 136ff.
131. Xen. *An.* 1.2.7-9. Cf. Hanfmann 1975.
132. Xen. *Hell.* 4.1.15-16.
133. For the early excavations, see Akurgal 1956. Nothing further seems to have happened on the site, according to Malikhzade 1973, until the new excavations of the 1990s, see Bakir 1992.
134. Strabo (13.4.5 (625-626)) mentions a strong citadel (*akra*). See Hanfmann 1975, 1977 and Ratté 1989, 18ff and 218ff for the excavations.
135. For discussion of a possible Anatolian inspiration for Persian terrace and platform architecture, see Fehr 1969. Cf. n. 139.
136. Vitr. 2.8.10; Xen. *Oec.* 4.20-24.
137. Vitr. 2.8.10, 13. Lauter (1986, 54) interprets, in my view not very convincingly, the bricks as glazed, fired bricks of the Mesopotamian type.
138. E.g. Hornblower 1982, 302f. K. Jeppesen, the excavator of the Mausoleum, has informed me that he also regards this site as the most probable, as does P. Pedersen, the present director of the Danish excavations in Halicarnassus. Cf. Pedersen 1994.
139. I am grateful to P. Pedersen for this information. For the platform in Anatolian architecture, see most recently Pedersen 1991, cf. Fehr 1969.
140. See Bean & Cook 1957, 92f.
141. Hoepfner & Schwandner 1986, 169ff.
142. See Hellström 1989, 1990, 1991. He compares these buildings with the *triclinium* of Domitian's Palace on the Palatine, and suggests that dynastic statues were placed in the recess. See p. 136. The word *andron* normally designates a dining-room and constitutes an integral part of the Classical Greek private house. See Hoepfner & Schwandner 1986, 271f and *passim*. In areas where megara were used in palaces, they seem to be present in private houses also, here called *prostas*. Thus they occur in the private houses of Abdera, founded in the 370s BC and in Priene, founded in the 350s, but not in Olynthus, just as megara do not occur in the Macedonian palaces (see p. 101). However, Dunbabin (1998) is certainly right that the room in which Philip II entertained Menecrates of Syracuse, who considered himself a god, and his fellow "gods" (Athen. 7.289e), must have had a form akin to that of Andron A of Labraunda; thus it is emphasized that these "divine" guests reclined on the raised middle couch and were treated as gods with libations, while the rest of the company dined.
143. See Hellström 1994.
144. See Young 1962, 160ff pl. 42, Young 1964, 279ff pls. 85, 87. The largest megaron, M3, measured 30.40 x 18.30 m = c. 556 m^2, i.e. a palatial building. In many of the megara luxury goods were found, e.g. fine tableware; perhaps they were used for banquets as well as for living in.
145. Lauter 1975. His arguments have not, however, convinced one of the scholars who published the palace, K. Schefold, who sticks to an Oriental model for the late Archaic palace (Schefold 1978).
146. As suggested first by Anti 1947, 134ff. Cf. Marzolff 1976, 40ff.

147. Moreover, Archaic terracottas with banqueting scenes have been found in Larisa (Boehlau & Schefold 1940, 36ff). Cf. the megara in Gordion, see n. 144.
148. Boehlau & Schefold 1940, 88f.
149. Metzger 1963.
150. Metzger (1963, 15ff and 89ff) finds the closest comparative building in North Syrian Zinçerli, the contemporary so-called "Kleines Hilani", or "Building R-Z", probably built during the reign of the Assyrian king Asarhaddon (680-669 BC).
151. As also stated by Hanfmann 1975, Colledge 1987.
152. See p. 49. Cf. De Angelis d'Ossat 1971 for an inspiration from Achaemenid architecture to Greek architecture.
153. See e.g. Lawrence 1967, 81f, with references to the Homeric texts.
154. See Cambitoglou *et al.* 1971 (Zagora), Boardman 1967 (Emporio).
155. In nearby Lesbos, Alcaeus mentioned a large hall, probably a megaron, with fine decorations and weapons on the walls (cf. Homer, *v.s.*), albeit in an aristocratic context (Alcaeus, *Frag.* 357).
156. Boardman 1967, 249.
157. See Boersma 1970, 11ff; Shear 1978, 6f; Camp 1986, 38ff; Shapiro 1989; and especially von Steuben 1989.
158. There may even have been a library: at least the creation of one is mentioned in connection with Peisistratos (Athen. 1.3a (cit. Athenaeus); Gell. 7.17.1; Tert. *Apol.* 18; Isid. *Orig.* 6.3.3). Also, Polycrates of Samos is said to have had one (Athen. 1.3a). The inclusion of a library in the palace may be a loan from the Orient, since the first one known with certainty is that of Assurbanipal, found in his Palace of Nineveh, of the 7th cent. BC. Cf Dziatzko, s.v. Bibliotheken, *RE* 3.1 1897, cols. 406-423.
159. See e.g. Poll. *Onom.* 9.40. That may be the background for Demetrius Poliorchetes' turning part of the Parthenon of Athens into a palace (Plut. *Demetr.* 23.3-4). For the monarchies and tyrannies of Greece in general, see Andrewes 1958, Carlier 1984, esp. ch. 4, 485ff.
160. See Miller 1978, esp. 21ff.
161. For Olynthus, see most recently Hoepfner & Schwandner 1986, 271ff; for Eretria, see Auberson & Schefold 1972, 75, Reber 1990, and Ducrey *et al.* 1993. Recently, private palatial houses from the 4th cent. BC have been found on the northern outskirts of Athens (Walter-Karydi 1994). A late Classical palatial house (640 m²) with two courtyards, one with peristyle, found recently in Maroneia in Thrace, is very close to the houses of Eretria (Karadedos 1990).
162. See Martin 1951, 518-522, for a general discussion, on which I depend in the following.
163. Polyb. 10.27.7-13, see n. 90. In this connection one may mention the interesting Building 2 in Dahan-i Ghulaman. This building had a peristylar court surrounded by rooms, probably used as storerooms and as a treasury; it dates to the 6th-5th cent. BC, and is thus a testimony to the early presence of peristylar internal courts in the Achaemenid zone of interest. Cf. Scerrato 1966, esp. 22f, where he discusses this issue.
164. E.g. Athen. 5.196c (cit. Callixenus) on Ptolemy II's Pavilion, cf. pp. 133f. Cf. Vitruvius (6.7.1) on the Greek house.
165. I do not see the irregular court with columns on two sides in Building F in the Athenian Agora as a developed peristyle. See for these rich peristyle houses in the Greek area, Walter-Karydi 1994 and 1996.
166. See Börker 1983, with literature on these banqueting houses.
167. For Rhegion, see Pliny, *HN* 12.7; Theophr. *Caus. Pl.* 4.5.6. For Gelon's garden, see Athen. 12.541c-542a. Cf. Grimal 1969, 77.
168. Diod. 14.7.1-5.

169. Athen. 12.541c (cit. Satyrus).
170. Pl. *Ep.* 2.313a, 3.319a, 7.347a, 7.348e. The word *kepos* is used for garden.
171. Cic. *Tusc.* 5.59.
172. See Isler 1990, 57ff and 1996. One may also compare the early Hellenistic houses of Morgantina.
173. For the destruction by Timoleon, see Plut. *Tim.* 22. For the restoration by Agathocles, see Diod. 16.83. The hall with 60 *klinai* may be compared, for example, to the contemporary tent of Alexander the Great, which could hold 100 *klinai* (Diod. 17.16.4).
174. Cic. *Verr.* 2.4.54.
175. Coarelli & Torelli 1984, 224.
176. For the presence of an early palace at Aigai when this was the capital of Macedonia, see Diod. 16.3.5 (Aigai as seat of the king, 360 BC); Just. 7.1; Procop. *Aed.* 4.4, B279 (*basilike Amyntou*, undoubtedly in Aigai); Steph. Byz. s.v. Aigai. For an earlier palace at Pella, see [Scylax], *Periplus* 66. Aelian *VH* 14.17 is the source which mentions the fame of the palace (*oikia*) of Achelaus and its decorations by Zeuxis. Cf. Papakonstantinos-Diamantopos 1971, 55f. Heermann (1986, 432) proposes that the first palace of Pella was placed on the acropolis like the later one (*v.i.*). For the problems attending the founding of Pella as a capital, see Borza 1990, 166ff.
177. Ergon 1984. A position in the town itself, is, however, also a possibility for both palaces, given the probably limited size of the late 5th-cent. cities.
178. That a view over the land which they ruled was as important for the Macedonian kings, as it had been for the Great Kings, is seen in the story of Philip V told by Livy 40.21-22. Cf. Fehr 1969, 45ff for this aspect.
179. Diod. 16.91.4-95.
180. That this palace belonged to the same period as the palatial houses in the centre of Pella is proved by the same tile stamps being used in both localities. They probably date from before Alexander's reign, according to Pandermalis (1987).
181. As Heermann (1986, 372) stresses, this is one of the first instances of the basically un-Greek façade architecture, and she refers to its use in sepulchral architecture also.
182. Andronicos 1984, 42.
183. Cooper and Morris 1990, 75 n. 31, with earlier literature. Athenaeus (11.479d-e (cit. Hegesander) remarks that round rooms were suitable for the *kottabos* game. One may adduce Athenaeus 1.17-18a (cit. Duris), describing the banquet held by Alexander, where the diners sat on stools and couches. In Macedonia, only a man who had killed a boar was allowed to recline at dinner. Cf. Borza 1983.
184. Vitr. 6.5.2. For the *chrematistikon pylon*, mentioned by Polyb. 15.30.6, see p. 20 and 130.
185. Thus Tomlinson (1970) interprets the palace as primarily a house for banqueting, although he does not exclude a palatial function as well. Cf. Borza (1983) for the role of symposia in the time of Alexander.
186. Private "apartments" of the same pastas type have been found in the late Classical houses at Eretria, in the yard set aside for private use, see Auberson & Schefold 1972, 75ff, Reber 1990. Houses of the pastas type also predominated in Olynthus, see Hoepfner & Schwandner 1986, 27ff. For later examples, see n. 187.
187. Moreover, a "pastas group" is found in the private peristyle of the Palace of Pergamon (Cat. 14), also called Palace IV, again in the east wing, which seems to have been preferred for this function (see p. 105).
188. The building Pella I,3, which has been tentatively identified as a gymnasium, had a peristyle in the Doric order below, and the Ionic order with half-columns and false wall-zones in the

intercolumnia above. Since these half-columns are only 1.50 m high, there must have been a plinth-zone below them (Heermann 1986, 89ff).

189. Vitr. 6.7.4-5.

190. See Heermann 1986, 345-362, with a list of her examples of this room group (pp. 526-27). I shall not comment in detail on the proposed precursors, but merely point out that only in a very few cases, if at all, is the existence of this "Flügeldreiraumgruppe" demonstrated in architecture as well as in function. Again and again, we are told that the rooms in question are preserved only in their foundations. Moreover, the criterion of asymmetrically placed doorways is deemed sufficient to identify a dining-room function. As for the Macedonian palaces, the same method of identification is used (pp. 353ff); for instance all central rooms are identified as exedrae, despite the presence of "kline bands" (*v.i.*).

191. Other arbitrary identifications as "Flügeldreiraumgruppen" are to be found in the house in area IV at Pella, where room f, part of the "group" d-e-f, has no "kline bands", and the doors are not preserved (see Heermann 1986, Abb. 1). As an argument in favour of a wider use of this "group", however, a banqueting house found in Antigoneia in Epirus may be adduced. This had a stoa from which an exedra flanked by two dining-rooms could be reached. See Budina 1990, Abb. 3.5. Also, House I and II at Iato in Sicily, with many Macedonian features, may have had such a group of rooms, although "kline bands" are absent, the interpretation being based on asymmetrically placed doorways (Isler 1990 and 1996).

192. It was a favourite sport of Roman generals to move libraries from Hellenistic cities to Rome. The Apellikon in Athens, for example, containing the last remnants of Aristotle's famous library, went the same way, thanks to Sulla (Strab. 13.1.54 (609)).

193. See Borza 1990, 261ff, who also includes the frieze from the "Tomb of Philip" in Vergina in this connection.

194. Livy (42.51.1-2) refers to a meeting held by Perseus here in 171 BC, "*in vetere regia Macedonum*".

195. Siganidou 1990. The city might in fact well have been laid out according to the hill housing the royal palace.

196. Heermann (1986, 369) rightly emphasizes the similarity to the Palace of Ptolemais (see p. 146). Since then, Schmidt-Colinet (1991) has written about these apsidal rooms, stressing among other things their similarity to the Herodian Palace of Herodium and drawing parallels also with the Philippeion at Olympia (see also p. 136).

197. This kind of building with four towers at the corners is commonly called *tetrapyrgion* (see p. 65). It is also known from palaces and estates in the country, e.g. in Asia Minor, the Crimea, and the East (Marzolff 1976, 41 n. 103, 1996). Xenophon describes a fortified villa near Pergamon owned by a Persian, Azidatos (*An.* 7.8). Also, one may compare the Bit-Hilani of the Palace of Larisa, as does Marzolff (*v.s.*) — if this is indeed a correct reconstruction (see p. 67) — and the *dipyrgion* of Panticapeion (*v.i.*). Perhaps these towers were used also as pavilions, e.g. for dining (compare the Herodian towers, see p. 182).

198. A channel in one of these northern rooms could indicate a banqueting room here. One may imagine a layout like that in the official Peristyle I of the Royal Palace of Pella, where a central audience hall was perhaps flanked by two dining-rooms (*v.s.*).

199. See e.g. Schmidt 1953, 83.

200. See Miller 1971, 149ff.

201. Heermann 1986, 371.

202. See Börker 1983. However, I find that in his treatment of the development of banqueting rooms he underestimates the importance of the earlier Oriental banquets, stressing only the religious banquet as a model for the royal Macedonian one.

203.   Borza 1990, 248ff, with earlier literature.

204.   See Heermann 1986, 423ff, and, for gardens, Carroll-Spillecke 1989 and 1992. The same pan-hellenic viewpoint is shown by Lauter (1986) in his treatment of the palaces.

205.   See Dimitrov & Cicikova 1978. See for palatial structures in the Black-Sea area in general, Bouzek 1996.

206.   Such cult-hearths are also known from the private houses of Seuthopolis, as well as from other towns in the area, and moreover from the Scythian area (Ukraine) from as early as the 7th-6th cent. BC. They are very similar to those known from the Minoan and Mycenaean palaces. In the latter they were placed in the throne-room, the megaron. Even the size and the decoration are almost identical. See Dimitrov & Cicikova 1978, 48-52.

207.   The director of the excavations is Dr. V. Tolstikov, to whom I am grateful for his lecture and for further information on this palace communicated during his visit to Copenhagen in April 1992. Dr. Tolstikov will shortly publish his results in German in *Xenia*, and in Russian in *Vestnik drevnei istorii (VDI)*. Cf. Tolstikov 1989.

208.   One may compare the stoas of the Temenos of Athena in Pergamon, which exhibit the same feature. Will (1991, 280) draws attention to a stele, probably belonging to the 2nd cent. BC, found in the necropolis of Panticapeion. It probably depicts a two-storey tomb façade of the same type as that at Lefkadhia. This may thus be another example of the close connections with Macedonia. The stele may also give an impression of how the façade of the Palace of Panticapeion looked at that time.

209.   See Rolle *et al.* 1991, 187ff, Abb. 5-6. Cf. n. 186.

210.   Vitruvius (2.8.9) includes it in his treatment of building materials, together with Croesus' Palace of Sardis and Mausolus' Palace of Halicarnasssus.

211.   See, for the way the Attalids ruled, Polyb. 18.41.3.

212.   In pointing this out, Radt (1988, 90f) mentions the so-called "Baugruppe III", of which only a little is preserved. Rather than resembling a peristyle house, there is a certain similarity to the Palace of Larisa (Cat. 9), either the one on the disputed Bit-Hilani model (see p. 67), or that of the very frequently used megaron type. If the "Baugruppe III" does include a megaron, it might, as Radt proposes, constitute the ruins of the first palace on the spot, belonging to the Gongylian dynasty.

213.   For the theory of the palace beneath the Trajaneum, see most recently Hoepfner 1990, 281 and n. 10; but already Studniczka (1914) had advanced this view in connection with his work on Ptolemy II's Pavilion. For the new, in fact negative, results, see Radt 1988, 83. But B. Gossel-Raeck has kindly informed me that monumental walls have recently been found south-east of the Trajaneum.

214.   These probably belonged to the barracks of "Baugruppe VI". See Kawerau & Wiegand 1930, 34f, Radt 1988, 83ff.

215.   See Pinkwart & Stemmnitz 1984, cf. Radt 1988, 119ff. One may compare these houses with the large Hellenistic villa (c. 80 x 80 m = 6,400 m²) found in Samos, sited so as to command a view of its surroundings and with one side of the peristyle opening to the landscape (Tölle-Kastenbein 1974). Also, the large house filling an entire insula just below the Acropolis of Rhodes may be mentioned in this connection. It had, among other things, a large garden with a *nymphaeum* (Dreliossi-Herakleidou 1996). Another comparison which presents itself is with the Casa del Fauno in Pompeii (Cat. 24), thus underlining the cultural *koiné* that was gradually emerging in the late Hellenistic period.

216.   See Pinkwart & Stemmnitz 1984. One notices that in the north wings of Houses I and II there are affinities with Heermann's "Flügeldreiraumgruppe", although the placing of the

doorways of the side rooms seems to differ. Also, their function as dining-rooms is unlikely, since large andrones are also present.

217. Palaces are mentioned in Sardis (Vitr. 2.8.10; Xen. *Oec.* 4.20-24, see p. 63), Mopsuhestia (Joseph. *Ant.* 13.13.4 (368)), Gabae (Strab.15.3.3 (728)), and Tambrax/Tape in Hyrcania (Polyb. 10.31.5; Strab. 11.7.2 (508)), some of them undoubtedly originally Persian royal and satraps' palaces. The royal Persian Summer Palace of Ecbatana was probably used only by the early Seleucids, if at all (Polyb. 10.27.7-13, see n. 90). Cf. most recently for this kingdom in general, Sherwin-White & Kuhrt 1993, where the important status of the Babylonian palaces during the reign of the Seleucids is stressed (pp. 156-58).

217a. One may, in this connection, also refer to the Hellenistic palaces found in present day Georgia and Armenia. In eastern Georgia, a palace of the Achaemenid period has recently been found in Gumbati (Furtwängler et al. 1995, 1996), and in the early Hellenistic independent kingdom of Iberia several palatial buildings have come to light, primarily in the capital of Amasziche, but also in Dedopolis Mindori. See for these palaces, and for pertinent literature, Lordkipanidse 1991, passim.

218. E.g. Strab. 16.1.5 (739). He says that Seleucus Nicator moved the royal residence from Babylon to Seleucia. For Seleucia on the Tigris, see e.g. Invernizzi 1993.

219. For the excavation of the hippodrome, see Campbell (1934, 40-41), who considers the identification with Rex's building probable. The building is dated from coins and building technique to about the 1st cent. BC. For the written sources, see the Catalogue.

220. See Malalas 306.21, who says that Diocletian built his great palace on foundations laid by Gallienus. For a discussion of this source, see Downey 1961, 644.

221. This palace is not mentioned specifically, but the account of the murder of Queen Berenice and her son by Seleucus II, which took place in Daphne, is undoubtedly placed here, where the queen had taken refuge (Just. 27.1.4-7; Polyaen. 8.50; *FGrH* 160). Cf. Downey 1961, 642f. At least in the Roman period, Daphne was an imperial possession, and a palace was built there.

222. Strabo 16.2.4-5 (750) uses the word *alsos*.

223. See Polyb. 30.25-26 for this feast.

224. Plut. *Demetr.* 50.1-2 (Apamea); Joseph. *AJ* 13.2.1 (40-42) (*tetrapyrgion*). As for the Greek influence in Syria in general, Millar (1987) stresses that in Syria/Palestine cities were not established outside the Tetrapolis, only military colonies. The hellenization, if any, did not derive from the colonies, and we have no proof of any massive immigration of Greeks, either.

225. The date of both palaces in Dura is, however, rather uncertain, as stressed, for example, by Allara (1986).

226. For Babylonian houses, see Reuter & Koldewey 1926. For the houses in Dura, see most recently Allara (1986), who concludes that although most belong to the Roman period or are impossible to date, they are basically of the local Mesopotamian type with only a few Greek features, e.g. profiled door frames. Cf. Hoepfner & Schwandner 1986, 236ff. No Parthian *liwan* element is present, either. It is interesting that the andron in the shape of a "broad room" appears even at Delos, albeit in a modified form, in the 2nd century BC, but here, because of the climate, it is placed on the north side of the yard (Hoepfner & Schwandner 1986, 243ff).

227. Downey (1986) compares this southern part with Greek peristyle houses from the Hellenistic period.

228. Downey 1985, 1986. On account of the poor preservation, one cannot exclude the possibility

that there were, in fact, rooms here, especially since the palace is in a rather isolated position, and the forecourt would have been difficult to reach. But perhaps this court should not be interpreted as one opening directly to the outside, for in a private palace at Aï Khanoum (Fig. 68) this is not the case, the yard being reached only from the house.

229.   Even the palace of the Roman legate, Dux Ripae, had such a forecourt, combined with a peristyle house. See Detweiler & Rostovtzeff 1952.

230.   Fischer (1904) has a good description of the palace, although he dates it to Mycaenean times, which indicates how little evidence we have for a secure date. See most recently Colledge 1987, 148. His plan (fig. 7) is incorrect. Hopkins (1972) considers the palace to be Parthian.

231.   Hopkins (1972, 32ff) proposes a reconstruction with two columns in antis instead of a closed ante-room, comparing it to the contemporary houses of Seleucia on the Tigris. In that case there would also be great affinities with the palaces of Dura. If columns were used to support the roof of the main hall, we have a hypostyle hall, but there is no proof of columns here.

232.   Cf. Lauter 1986, 281f. Heart-shaped corner columns are seen in many places in the Hellenistic area. The earliest example is to be found in the decoration of the Macedonian chamber tomb in Dion. Moreover such columns are present, for example, in the Temple of Arsinoe (= Aphrodite Zephyris) (Studniczka 1914, 36, Abb. 7) near Alexandria, from early Hellenistic times, and in Asia Minor at Priene and Magnesia on the Maeander; also in Macedonia in the Palace of Demetrias (Cat. 13), in Cyrene e.g. in the Palazzo delle Colonne in Ptolemais (Cat. 22) (*v.i.* and Stucchi 1975, 190f), and in Judaea in Masada and Jericho (*v.i.*) Column-plinths are found also in Ptolemais and in the Northern Palace of Masada (Cat. 27).

233.   This palace should resemble a palace in Saxanokhour, also in Bactria, probably from the same period (Pougatchenkova 1990, 62, fig. 2). To me this looks more Babylonian, with its rooms on all sides of the yard.

234.   This bath suite was very large, with rooms equipped with drains, and paved with a primitive kind of pebble mosaic. No traces of bath-tubs have been found, either here or in the Babylonian bathrooms, and they are also absent from the fine bathroom in the Nippur Palace, mentioned above. They were probably portable. In a later phase, several rooms changed function and one of them got a floor of stone slabs instead of mosaic tesserae. Another bath suite was found to the west of the palace proper, destroyed when a swimming-pool was built over it in the middle of the 2nd cent. BC (Bernard 1978). This baths-building consisted among other things of a tholos, an unusual form in these areas, and undoubtedly borrowed from the Greek *balaneion*. A relationship to the palace is uncertain, but not unlikely.

235.   A princely palace already existed in the Ammon Oasis, when Alexander visited the place in 331-330 BC. Thus we have to do with a local palace type. The palace, termed *ta basileia*, consisted of a citadel/acropolis surrounded by three walls. In the innermost ring were the living-quarters of the ruler, in the second ring those of the harem and children; the famous Sanctuary of Ammon was located here as well. We hear nothing of the situation of the official part of the palace. The outermost ring was reserved for soldiers and guards (Diod. 17.50.3; Curt. 4.7.20-21). H. H. Schmitt (1994) has pointed out that the description of this palace has a great similarity to Plato's description of Atlantis (*Tim.* 24e ff).

236.   In the Museum of Alexandria some elements in stucco from the mid-Hellenistic period give evidence of an experimental architecture. The elements from early Hellenistic times are closely related to Macedonia, as might be expected. See Adriani 1932-33a, Hoepfner 1971, 88ff. Very important is J. McKenzie's recent treatment of all published fragments from the Ptolemaic period in Alexandria (McKenzie 1990, 61ff, with earlier literature). Very little is still known of the recent under-water investigations by Franck Goddio along the eastern

shore of the large harbour. His sensational ideas, including his identification of the "palace of Cleopatra", are far from based on fact; the ruins and architectural fragments discovered by him rather belong to the later history of the city, before the Arabian conquest of it in the 640s (see Grimm 1996b). More convincing are the results of the, scientific, under-water investigations around the island of Pharos, by J-Y. Empereur, where large blocks have been found, which have been tentatively related to the famous lighthouse, ruined by an earthquake in the 14th century. See Grimm 1996a.

237. Cf. Grimal 1969, 251f. See p. 24.

238. See Strab. 17.1.10 (795). As far as the Paneion is concerned, one is reminded of the royal custom of viewing one's realm from an elevated spot, see n. 178. Cf. Fehr 1969.

239. For Adonis, see Theocr. *Id.* 15. For the Poseidon Sanctuary, see Hoepfner 1971, 54ff, 1990, 277. The layout of the surroundings of the temple was never finished, and Hoepfner sees it as a picturesque ruin. Strabo (17.1.8-9 (793-94)) says that the temple did in fact function. In the vicinity, Mark Antony built a royal pavilion (*diaita*) on a jetty.

240. Epiph. *p. Metr.* c.11. Cf. Dziatzko, s.v. Bibliotheken, *RE* 3.1, 1897, col. 410.

241. This is also shown by the finds made in the district, see Adriani 1932-33a, Hoepfner 1990, 275ff.

242. One may compare the fashion for giving an artificial watercourse the name of a real one with the custom in the palatial villas of Italy of naming canals after Egyptian rivers: the Euripus, the Nile, the Canopus. Cf. Grimal 1969, 296ff, Zanker 1979, 470ff, La Rocca 1986, 10.

243. Athen. 14.654c (cit. Ptolemy Physcon).

244. *P. Cairo Zeno* 59075, of 257 BC.

245. Ap. Rhod. *Argon.* 3.164ff.

246. Athen. 5.196-197. Studniczka (1914) has analyzed this description in detail and proposed a reconstruction of the pavilion (Fig. 70). Recently, Salza Prina Ricotti (1988-89) has, however, challenged this generally accepted reconstruction. She emphasizes that all tents seen on depictions had sloping roofs, and rather sees the pavilion as akin to a modern circus tent with an open space in the centre and a raised *ouranos*, or canopy, with a diam of c. 31 m, carried by the tall columns mentioned by Callixenus. The surrounding tent she thinks was much lower.

247. These *syringes* have caused some controversy. Von Gall (1977, 129) mentions an Assyrian tent type with barrel-vaulted ceilings and concludes that the Mesopotamian/Assyrian tent type differed from the Achaemenid one without a barrel vault. Studniczka (1914) proposes a segmental vault made on a wooden frame. This kind of vault is often seen in Alexandrian chamber tombs, and it was very popular in the wall-paintings of the Second Style, which itself was undoubtedly inspired by Alexandrian architecture, as is also shown by the presence of very tall and very slim columns modelled on plant-forms. Cf. McKenzie 1990, 85ff. For the hangings and the importance of such textiles, including tents, in the palaces of the Hellenistic kings, as well as in those of their predecessors, see Vickers, forthcoming.

248. Athen 12.538b-c (cit. Chares), 12.537d (cit. Ephippus). Cf. Salza Prina Ricotti 1988-89, who estimates Alexander's tent to have measured c. 50 x 50 m.

249. Studniczka (1914) underestimates the Persian influence on this pavilion, although he mentions certain affinities with both the Apadana and the Hall of 100 Columns in Persepolis. He tries instead to find precursors in Greece, e.g. in the Telesterion of Eleusis (in fact the inspiration probably went the other way, see von Gall 1979), and in Pharaonic residential architecture, which utilized light materials, as may be seen, for example, in the Nile mosaic of Praeneste. Cf. Lauter 1971, McKenzie 1990, 99ff.

250. The canopies found in a funerary context, for example painted on the roofs of the Alexandrian tombs and also of Lyson and Kallikles' tomb in Lefkadhia, may be reflections of this kind of pavilion; such canopies were also used in a funerary context for funeral banquets. See Tomlinson 1986.
251. Athen. 5.203-206. Caspari (1916) has dealt with the Thalamegos in detail and given a convincing reconstruction of it (Fig. 71) As for other floating palaces, one may mention the contemporary one built by Hieron II of Syracuse (see p. 173), a combination of a ship for transport and pleasure, which he presented as a gift to Ptolemy IV. Its residential part included gymnasium, garden, promenades, library, bathroom, and a sanctuary for Aphrodite (see Athen. 5.207, esp. d-f)(cit. Moschion). Furthermore, one may mention the boats belonging to Cleopatra and Caligula, and it seems that the Hasmonean dynasty of Judaea had such barges for pleasure cruises on the Dead Sea as well (see Netzer 1990, 42f).
252. Raeder (1988) compares this boat to Vitruvius' description of a "Greek" house or rather private palace (6.7) (Fig. 72). But in the Nile-boat the two parts, the *gynaikonitis* and the *andronitis*, probably still had their original function, while in Vitruvius' house one should perhaps rather interpret the *gynaikonitis* as the residential and the *andronitis* as the official part of the house. In fact, Vitruvius' description is more informative when considered in comparison with another private palace, that of Diotimus in Philadelphia, and with the governor's palace of Ptolemais (*v.i.*).
253. See Schmidt-Colinet 1991. He, however, considers the recess in the Nile-Boat as only one part of an "exedra duplex", a suggestion which I do not find convincing, since if a second recess existed, it would undoubtedly have been mentioned in the very detailed description. As Schmidt-Colinet stresses, such dynastic exedrae are found later, too, e.g. in the Forum of Augustus, but there in a public context. One may compare this grotto-like recess with the decorative grottoes that were very popular in the villas of the élite in Italy, in the late Republic and later (Grimal 1969, 302ff; Tamm 1963, 147ff). It is interesting that Tamm sees there grottoes as a kind of precursor of the apse.
254. Hellström 1990.
255. *P. Cairo Zeno* 59764. Cf. Préaux 1947, 42f, Raeder 1988, 365f.
256. According to Zenon papyri from 259-257 BC, *P. Cairo Zeno* 59075-76, Tobias, Hyrcanus' grandfather, was already at that time a major landowner in this area as well as probably a Ptolemaic official, as was his son Joseph, the famous tax collector who had close contacts with the Ptolemies. See Will 1991, 10ff (F. Zayadine) for a discussion of the sources.
257. Joseph. *AJ* 12.4.1 (228-236). For a penetrating treatment of this source, see Will 1991, 20f (F. Zayadine), and 25ff.
258. See Lapp 1963, 17-20; it is called "the Plastered Building".
259. Will 1991, 27f.
260. Gentelle (1981) also sees this area as a paradeisos, as does F. Zayadine, in disagreement with E. Will (in Will 1991; see n. 257.)
261. For a discussion of the meaning of this word, see Will 1991, 31ff.
262. For conclusive arguments, see Will 1991, 255ff. But H. Lauter (1986, 279), for example, sees this building as an old-fashioned Greek temple type with *pronaos* and *opistodomos*, another example of Lauter's panhellenic viewpoint. I find it difficult to understand this identification, since Josephus' description of the *baris* is completely in accordance with the present building. The word *baris* is also used, for example, for the Antonia in Jerusalem (see p. 182).
263. These lions are unusual in being placed between two storeys rather than at the base as a socle frieze, as is usual in Oriental examples. Will proposes a possible inspiration from Asia

Minor, mentioning the position of the friezes on the monumental tombs there (Will 1991, 280). For this frieze, see Will 1991, 219ff (F. Queyrel).

264. For a detailed treatment of these eagles, see Will 1991, 243ff (F. Queyrel). They may be compared to the eagles on the Pavilion of Ptolemy II (Athen. 5.197a) (cit. Callixenus) (*v.s.*). Moreover they are found in a similar position in the paintings from the tombs at Marisa of the 3rd century BC, and the tradition continues in the Khasneh tomb of Petra, probably of the 1st century BC (Pl. 22). Cf. Studniczka 1914, 61ff.

265. Caspari 1916.

266. See Will (1991, 270ff) for a discussion of the models, including both Bit-Hilani and tetrapyrgion. Perhaps the Persian apadana model is behind both these types. See p. 40.

267. Bernard 1971, 1976.

268. Will 1991, 274, fig. 30.1. The system with service/residence on two storeys is known both earlier and later, see *ibid.* 270ff.

269. Colledge 1987, fig. 6.

270. Lauter 1986, 284.

271. See Will 1991, 141ff (J. Dentzer-Feydy) and 209ff (F. Queyrel). Both conclude, however, that the architect was probably local rather than Alexandrian.

272. See Schmidt-Colinet (1991) for statues found in the vicinity of these rooms in Ptolemais.

273. Pesce (1950, 107) considers it at least a possibility that the pool and the peristyle may be contemporaneous, although the former may also be a Roman addition.

274. See especially Grimal 1969, 293ff. In Rhodes, a similar pool has been found in a newly excavated palatial house below the acropolis (Dreliossi-Herakleidou 1994).

275. Raeder 1988.

276. Vitr. 6.7.

277. For this tomb, which is in the Classical Style, and its date, see most recently McKenzie 1990, *passim*. One might, with Browning (1982), place it in the reign of Aretas II the Philhellene (84-56 BC), when the Nabataean kingdom was at its largest and most flourishing.

278. For the Moustapha Pasha Tomb, see McKenzie 1990, 64ff. She recognizes many elements from Alexandrian architecture in the Palace of Tyrus (p. 77).

279. This style must be considered a good source of contemporary architecture, as proposed by Lauter 1971, 149ff, Fittschen 1976, and most recently by McKenzie 1990, 85ff, who argues convincingly for Alexandria being the primary source for this baroque architecture. She also sees the gardens of many Second Style paintings as being inspired by Egyptian gardens.

280. Will 1991, 285.

281. See e.g. Ovadiah 1983, Arav 1989, Rajak 1994 and, for the character of the Hasmonean kingship, Rajak 1996.

282. Joseph. *BJ* 2.16 (344), *AJ* 20.8 (189-192). Cf. Vincent & Steve 1954, 232-35.

283. For these desert fortresses, see Tsafrir 1982; cf. Netzer 1990, 42.

284. Large parks were known from early on in Judaea. In Jerusalem a royal garden is mentioned in relation to the Babylonian attack (II Kings 25.4). From the Persian period, we hear of a royal *paradeisos* belonging to the Persian king, from which timber for the rebuilding of Jerusalem was to come (Nehem. 2.8-9) (see pp. 181ff).

284a. One may, in this connection, refer to the great importance of pools in the Egyptian Gardens from far back both for practical purposes, i.e. irrigation, and with a religious significance (see n. 83). These garden pools were taken over also in Ptolemaic Egypt (see p. 131).

285. See Bliss & Macalister 1902, 47-50. No private palaces have been dated with certainty to the Hasmonean period. Thus none of the mansions which have recently been excavated in the Jewish quarter of Jerusalem, seem to be earlier than the Herodian period (see p. 183).

The Jewish houses belonging to the lower classes appear eastern rather than western. They have been found, for example, at Gezer and Marisa, and are normally furnished with an inner courtyard without columns, a "bent" entrance, and rather irregular rooms around the yard. Miqvaot may be included in them. This type of house dates back to a very early period in this area. Naturally, the situation is different in the Greek cities outside Judaea, such as Samaria and Tell Anafa, where the larger houses are basically of the Greek type.

286. See Nielsen 1990, 7, 103.

287. Bath-tubs in bronze have been found in bathrooms in the North Syrian palace of Zinçerli, see Frankfort 1952, 124. Also such *pyeloi* are mentioned in connection with Darius III's tent, which was abandoned after his defeat at Issus (Plut. *Alex.* 20.7). See n. 105.

288. The building of a gymnasium in Jerusalem by the hellenophile high priest Jason was, in fact, said to be one reason for the Maccabean revolt (II Macc. 4.9).

289. See e.g. Hellenismus in Italien 1976, especially Castrén 1976. Cf. Aspects of Hellenism in Italy 1994. Some of this has already been touched on in a recently published article (Nielsen 1994a).

290. Hölscher 1990.

291. Clinias, Pyrrhus' legate, called the Roman senate an assembly of kings (Plut. *Pyrrh.* 19.5). For the architectural influence of the Hellenistic palaces, see Zanker 1979 and 1983, La Rocca 1986, Nielsen 1994a. Others consider the inspiration for these palatial houses and villas to come primarily from religious or public buildings; see, for example, Coarelli 1983b, Wallace-Hadrill 1988.

292. See D'Arms 1970, Frederiksen 1984.

293. *Nobilibus vero, qui honores magistratusque gerundo praestare debent officia civibus, faciunda sunt vestibula regalia alta, atria et peristylia amplissima, silvae ambulationesque laxiores ad decorem maiestatis perfectae; praeteria bybliothecas, basilicas non dissimili modo quam publicorum operum magnificentia comparatas, quod in domibus eorum saepius et publica consilia et privata iudicia arbitriaque conficiuntur* (Vitr. 6.5.2, edn. Loeb, trans. F. Granger). Note the "royal" choice of words. As mentioned earlier (pp. 20 and 147), it is very probable that the basilica developed from the central hall of the royal palaces of Ptolemaic Egypt, i.e. the Egyptian oecus known from Vitruvius (6.3.9) (cf. Gros 1978), which the basilicas greatly resemble in plan: We know of such Egyptian oeci from the Nile-boat of Ptolemy IV, from the Palace of Ptolemais, and later from the Herodian palaces. Rather than the basilica of rich Roman houses being a loan from public architecture, as Wallace-Hadrill believes (1988), it was probably the other way round: both the public and the private basilica were directly inspired by the main hall of the Hellenistic palaces. In the palace this served as a room for audiences, councils, and banquets (see p. 20). Also the other elements which Wallace-Hadrill judges to indicate a "public" function, i.e. columns, peristyles, and pediments, are royal elements which may have reached the houses directly from the Hellenistic palaces. Cf. Vitruv. 5.6.9. For houses and villas in general, see D'Arms 1970, McKay 1975, Mielsch 1987, Wallace-Hadrill 1988, Reutti 1990, and Clarke 1991. Zanker (1979) has investigated the influence of luxury villas on the embellishment of the private houses owned by the bourgeoisie; cf. Wallace-Hadrill 1990. For houses in Rome, see Tamm 1963, 28ff, Degrassi 1966-67, Grimal 1969, 102ff, Coarelli 1983b, La Rocca 1986.

294. Cic. *Rep.* 1.14, *Amic.* 25.

295. See La Rocca 1986, 5.

296. See Coarelli 1983b. For the French excavations, see Broise & Jolivet 1987 and annual reports in *MEFRA*.

297. Vitr. 6.3.5.

298. Such libraries belonging to the élite were to be found both in their *domus* in the city and in their country villas. The first we know of belonged to Lucullus; both Cicero and Atticus had private book-collections too (Plut. *Luc.* 42.1-4; Cic. *Att.* 2.6.1, 4.14.1, 13.31.2, 13.32.2), and, as already mentioned above, the library that Scipio Aemilianus received from his father had earlier belonged to the Macedonian king (Plut. *Aem.* 28, see p. 88). In Seneca's time, the library was as essential to a house as a bathroom (*Tranq.* 9), and Trimalchio, doing everything he could to copy the Roman upper class, had both a Greek and a Latin one (Petr. *Sat.* 48). Libraries, as well as picture galleries and basilicas (all, according to Vitruvius, (*v.s.*) to be met with in the houses of the élite), were also to be found in the Republican public porticoes mentioned above (the one in Pompey's complex being the final example), as well as in their successors, the imperial fora, beginning with Caesar's Forum. See Tamm 1963, 119ff.

299. A house by the Clivus Carinae in Rome, remains of which were found behind Maxentius' Basilica and which is probably Julio-Claudian, had an area of perhaps 3,800 m² although only 1,430 m² have been excavated; see Pisani Sartorio 1983. It was physically impossible for the houses on the Palatine to be very large owing to lack of space; see Tamm 1963, 28ff.

300. Seneca, *Ep.* 51.11-12, 86.4. Cf. Mielsch 1987, 45f.

301. Swoboda (1969) was the first to make this distinction, which is still the one generally used. Cf. Grimal 1969, 203ff; but see Mielsch (1987, 58ff) for a discussion of this distinction and the doubt he expresses about the existence of the portico villa in late Republican Italy.

302. One is reminded of the large Hellenistic villa in Samos, which, placed on a hill with a view, is a combination of a peristyle and a portico villa. It is dated to around 125 BC and is thus contemporary with the earliest pleasure villas of Italy (Tölle-Kastenbein 1974) (see n. 215). Villas placed on platforms were called *basis villae* (Cic. *QFr.* 3.1.5; Tac. *Ann.* 14.9).

303. E.g. Cic. *Att.* 5.2.2, 10.16.5. Cf. D'Arms 1970, 54. According to Vitruvius (6.5.3), the difference between the city house and the villa is that in the former, the *atrium* is placed near the entrance, while in the latter, it is placed beyond the peristyle, being surrounded by paved colonnades and opening onto palaestrae and walks.

304. See e.g. Cic. *Fam.* 9.24.2-3, who entreats a friend not to give up dinner parties, which were a main source of pleasure. Cf. D'Arms 1970, 51, Zanker 1979, 508, La Rocca 1986, 20ff. Compare also the prominent role that the dining-rooms (*oeci*) play in Vitruvius' desciption of the houses of the Roman élite (6.3.9).

305. Carroll-Spillecke 1989, 65 and *passim*, with earlier literature.

306. E.g. by Grimal 1969, 203ff, cf. Carroll-Spillecke 1989, 64. We know only of very few such sacred groves, but Jashemski (1979) argues convincingly for one surrounding the Doric temple of Pompeii. The ones known from the Hephaisteion in Athens, and from the Sanctuary of Diana at Gabii, are both laid out formally around the temple. As for the gymnasia, there were not, actually, gardens in the peristyles (the palaestrae), only in connection with the running-tracks.

307. See for these parks Jashemski 1979, 289ff, La Rocca 1986.

308. See e.g. Hor. *Carm.* 2.15; Cic. *Leg.* 2.1, *QFr.* 3.1.5; Varr. *RR* 2.5.8-17. Cf. Grimal 1969, 203ff. It is interesting that the description of the Cyzicene *oecus* by Vitruvius (6.3.10) (a type of room not very usual in Italy), reminds one of such pavilions; thus Vitruvius mentions folding doors and windows and the importance of the view of the garden. The general impression of this room is that of a tall and light structure. An imitation of a pavilion is, perhaps, the subterranean Auditorium of Maecenas, consisting of an exedra with steps and niches with garden scenes painted on the walls. Cf. La Rocca 1986, 4.

309. Jashemski 1979, 289ff.

310. Thus Cicero's house on the Palatine was furnished with a *palaestra* (*Att*. 2.4.7), and in his villa in Tusculum he had both a Lyceum and an Academy (*Tusc*. 2.9). As Varro rightly says (*RR* 2, *Proem*.), while in the old days there were no gymnasia of the Greek type, now they (the élite) are not satisfied unless their villas teem with Greek names.

311. For fish-ponds in a Greek context, see Pl. *Resp.* 264e and Arist. *Hist. An.* 8.2.592a. For preserved ponds in Roman villas, see Jashemski 1979, 315ff. Cf. D'Arms 1970, 41. See also in general Banti, s.v. Piscina in *RE* 20, 1950, cols. 1983-1985.

312. Boëthius & Ward-Perkins 1970, 162.

313. See p. 22. Athen. 5.206d-209b (cit. Moschion). Cf. the description of the Thalamegos belonging to Ptolemy IV (see p. 23, 136).

314. This was the case, for example, with the house of Catullus and also with that of Clodius, which had a portico and a Temple of Libertas. See Tamm 1963, 120ff.

315. See Suet. *Caes.* 81.3; Flor. *Epit.* 4.2.91. For the use of such pediments in the major Pompeian houses, see Wallace-Hadrill 1988.

316. See especially Paul Zanker and Filippo Coarelli's contributions to the seminar "Città e Archittura nella Roma Imperiale", Rome (Zanker 1983, Coarelli 1983a), and Henner von Hesberg and Coarelli's articles in the catalogue of the exhibition "Kaiser Augustus und die verlorene Republik", Berlin (von Hesberg 1988, Coarelli 1988). For the perennial discussion of the royal or Republican status of Octavian/Augustus and the early emperors, see Alföldi 1970, and Wallace-Hadrill 1982.

317. Richard 1970 (Mausoleum), Coarelli 1983a, 1988 (Pantheon). One is reminded of the Alexandrian Sema. Another reflection of Alexander is to be seen in the Forum of Augustus, where there are many references to this king and to Augustus as his heir through the Ptolemies. See Zanker 1968, Castagnoli 1984. Cf. Schmidt-Colinet 1991, 52ff.

318. It is likely, as Degrassi (1966-67) proposes, that Octavian/Augustus owned other houses on the Palatine, too. Apart from the so-called "House of Livia", many other houses in the area, which was later named the Domus Tiberiana, seem to have belonged to him. Also the designation of the Palace of Augustus as the "Palatium", might indicate that he in fact owned property that took up the major part of the hill. The palace was built on a plot that along with the older houses that stood on it was bought up for the purpose (Vell. Pat. 2.81.3), and Hortensius' House was incorporated in the palace (Suet. *Aug.* 72.1-2). Furthermore, Suetonius (*Gram.* 17) mentions that Gaius and Lucius Caesar used the *atrium* of the House of Catullus as their classroom, and that therefore this also formed part of the palace, called *domus palatinae* (Suet. *Aug.* 57.4; *CIL* VI 8656, 8659). See Wiseman 1987, Corbier 1992. Cf. Frézouls 1987, who, however, plays down the monarchic aspect of the complex.

319. *Mon. Anc.* 34.2; Ovid, *Fast.* 4.951-54, *Tr.* 3.1.33-34 (citation).

320. *Mon. Anc.* 35. Cf. Tamm 1963, 94ff, for a discussion of this entrance and of the interpretation of the designations *atrium/vestibulum* in general.

321. The same idea is put forward by Wiseman (1987), who bases the proposal on Virgil's *Aeneid* and the mythical past of the Palatine as well as Octavian/Augustus' exploitation of it. He suggests that the turning of the entrance, perhaps after the fire of AD 3, should be seen as a part of Augustus' "Republican" policy.

322. For court-rooms in the houses of the élite, also, see Wallace-Hadrill 1988.

323. Such apses are sometimes seen in the royal banqueting halls, e.g. in the andrones of Labraunda and in the Nile-boat of Ptolemy IV, where they house dynastic statues. In a Roman context, they enjoyed considerable popularity; thus there is one in the Auditorium Maecenatis and in the Aula Isiaca, as well as in both the audience hall and the triclinium

of Domitian's palace. Cf. Tamm 1963, 147ff. For the apse's probable origin in sacred architecture, see Ganzert 1990.

324. This corridor was later closed, owing to the construction of the large monumental staircase in front of the temple, the precise date of which is not known (Carettoni 1988).

325. Cf. Fittschen 1976. Wallace-Hadrill (1988) has noticed a similar difference in the palatial houses of Pompeii.

326. Josephus (*AJ* 19.1.13-14 (84-113)) furnishes us with an interesting piece of information in connection with his description of the assassination of Caligula during the Ludi Palatini, for he mentions a temporary theatre built near the palace during the festival. Tamm (1963, 66f) proposes that it was raised on the Area Appolinis, the terrace in front of the Temple of Apollo. One is reminded of the close connection between the theatre and royal palace in the Hellenistic period.

327. See Suet. *Aug.* 29.3, where it is mentioned that the senate met there with the emperor.

328. See Corbier 1992.

329. Cass. Dio. 53.16.5 (for the hut).

330. See Coarelli 1983a; Wiseman 1984, cf. Lauter 1987. As Degrassi (1966-67) has proposed, this Sanctuary of Vesta probably consisted simply of a statue in a niche rather than a proper temple like the one in the Forum.

331. It is worth remarking that at this very period the gymnasium part of the *thermae* was first introduced into Rome, although the designation already existed in those earlier Republican villas, here named after famous Athenian institutions such as the Academy and the Lyceum; but *their* main purpose, of course, was as a venue for philosophical discussions, not for sport (see n. 310). See Nielsen 1990, 43ff. Palaestrae were also present in the palaces of Alexandria and perhaps in the Royal Palace of Pella.

332. Coarelli (1988) directly compares the Campus Martius as it looked at this time with the Alexandrian basileia; both were laid out orthogonally as well. Cf. Castagnoli 1984. One may also compare Herod the Great's contemporaneous palaces in Jericho and Herodium: they both included large swimming-pools, many baths, and formal gardens, and Jericho incorporated public structures too, e.g. a hippodrome with a kind of theatre and portico, perhaps a palaestra. Agrippa and Herod knew each other well, and visited each others' native cities (see p. 182).

333. I find plausible Degrassi's (1966-67) proposition that it was Augustus, rather than Tiberius, who developed the north-western part of the hill. His theory that Nero or Domitian were better candidates than Tiberius for making the so-called Domus Tiberiana an integrated whole, and that before their time, older houses filled the area, has recently proved correct; see Krause *et al.* 1985, Krause 1987. It was Nero who after the fire of AD 64 built the platform and made it an integrated part of his Domus Aurea. Cf. Wiseman (1987), for this development of the Palatine and the approaches to the imperial palace.

334. Suet. *Nero* 31.1-2. Cf. Tamm 1963, 192ff, Voisin 1987.

335. Krause *et al.* 1985.

336. La Rocca 1986, 24ff.

337. See Frézouls 1987.

338. For Herodian architecture in general, see Netzer 1977b, 1981a, 1996, and Levine 1981. See also the various articles in the publication of the conference: *Judaea and the Graeco-Roman World in the Time of Herod*, from 1996.

339. For Cypros, see Netzer 1975b. The site will be published in the forthcoming *"Hasmonean and Herodian Winter Palaces at Jericho. Final Report"*, vol. II, Jerusalem.

340. Joseph. *AJ* 16.2.1 (22) (Agrippa's visit). See in general for these desert fortresses, Tsafrir 1982.
341. See Amiran & Eitan 1970 and 1972.
342. Josephus *BJ* 1.21.1 (401-402), 5.4.3-4 (161-183); *AJ* 15.9.3 (318). Cf. Vincent & Steve 1954, 222-32.
343. Grimal 1969, 261f.
344. Joseph. *BJ* 1.21.1 (401-402), 5.5.8 (238-247) (Antonia), John 5.2 (Bethesda). Cf. Vincent & Steve 1954, 222-32. In this connection it is worth mentioning that a Herodian "palace complex" should probably be envisaged in Samaria-Sebaste, situated in the western part of the acropolis. Begun around 27 BC, it consisted of a richly decorated peristyle building for residence, an apsidal building, probably for official purposes, a bath-building, a Temple of Augustus with a large forecourt, also well suited to official use, and storerooms, all of which was fortified. There was a monumental approach from the east, and perhaps also from the north, and the area was heavily terraced to allow for the enlargement of the acropolis. For this theory, see Barag 1993. Cf. Netzer 1987b. The general comparison, made by G. Foerster and cited by Barag, to Augustus' palace complex on the Palatine in Rome, seems convincing. See p. 174.
345. See Avigad 1975, 1983, and 1989.
346. Joseph. *AJ* 15.9.6 (331), *BJ* 1.21.5 (408). For the excavations, see Levine & Netzer 1986, 149-182. For the latest theories on its reconstruction, see Netzer 1993.
347. See Flinder 1982.
348. I am grateful to the excavator, Dr. Y. Porath, for information on this new site.
349. Netzer 1991, 651.
350. For the functions of this palace and its decoration, see G. Foerster 1995.
351. For the swimming-pool, see Netzer 1991, 481ff; for the columbaria, see Netzer 1991, 370, 637f. Such columbaria were also built in the villa gardens of Italy, as well as in Egyptian gardens, see Grimal 1969, 288.
352. G. Foerster has informed me that he, also, considers a library a possibility. See also Foerster 1995.
353. The theatrical siting of the palace has caused Netzer (1981b, 60) to compare it to Tiberius' villa on Capri. This feature, however, had occurred in Italy at a much earlier period, in the sanctuaries of Latium, e.g. in Palestrina, Tivoli, and Terracina (see Coarelli 1987).
354. Netzer (1975a) has tentatively identified this room and the rotunda on the Southern Tell (*v.i.*) with, respectively, the Agrippeion and the Augusteion mentioned by Josephus (*BJ* 1.21.4 (407)) as belonging to Herod's palace at Jericho. Such halls, named after his two benefactors, were also to be found in his Main Palace in Jerusalem (*v.s.*).
354a. The garden peristyle has recently been excavated by K. L. Gleason, revealing a row of large trees along the apsidal room and smaller bushes placed in pots in rows in the rest of the garden. See Gleason 1987-88 and 1993.
355. For the problems attending the identification of this room, see Nielsen 1990, 103f and n. 60. When I visited Jericho in 1992, E. Netzer told me that he is now convinced that it is a laconicum.
356. In one of these swimming-pools in Jericho the young high priest Aristobolus II was drowned, deliberately, according to Josephus (*AJ* 15.3.3 (53-56)).
357. Another suggestion, also promoted by E. Netzer (1981a, 1989), was that this complex served as a gymnasium, but the raised position on a platform, as well as the lack of water, seems to make this identification doubtful.
358. Zanker 1987, 9ff.

359. See Schmidt-Colinet 1991.
360. Joseph. *BJ* 1.33.9 (670-673). Cf. Netzer (1987a, 37f), who compares the funeral triclinia known from Petra.
361. Nielsen 1985, 1990, 14f, 103f.
362. Tsafrir (1981) has advanced the opinion that in contrast to other Roman building techniques, the introduction of concrete vaulting had a lasting effect on the architecture of the area, although it was not much used in Herod's buildings. Also, he regards the introduction of Roman technology as one of Herod's most important contributions to the architecture of Palestine. I can only go along with his remark (p. 72) that rather than Pompey's conquest of Palestine in 63 BC, it was Herod's seizure of power in 37 BC that marked the beginning of the Roman period here.
363. Netzer 1991, 651.
364. Bickerman 1988, 302.
365. For a further development of this theory, see Nielsen 1997 and, specifically for the reflection of status in the context of dining, Nielsen 1998.

CATALOGUE OF PALACES

Introduction

Not all palaces mentioned in the text are found in this Catalogue: thus while all known royal palaces are included, this applies to only some of the best known governors' palaces, and to just two private palaces. The best-preserved models and the early Roman palaces are included as well.

Each catalogue entry is divided into three main parts: the first gives general information on traditional name, locality, category, i.e. whether a royal, governor's or private, main or recreational palace is concerned, further situation, and area of the complex. The second part treats the architecture of the palace, dealing with building technique, treatment of the façade, type of gateway, type of courtyard/s, and order of columns. The third and main part focuses on the function of the palace: the nine main functions referred to in the first chapter are repeated here, i.e. official/ceremonial, social, religious, defensive, administrative, service, residential, "public", and recreational. Each registration closes with practical information on state of preservation, time of excavation, date and period of use, and on written sources, each being marked with an asterisk and followed by a number referring to similar indications in the Catalogue. Finally, there are references to modern literature: if a publication exists, (P) is appended, if only a preliminary report, (Pr). If nothing is appended, the palace is treated in a wider context. The last rubric gives references to the text and illustrations.

Some of the items used in the catalogue may require a clarification: the *gateway* is the one leading to the palace area, and may, or may not, be identical with the *portal* of the official palace. The former is normally the case with "compact palaces", the latter with "palace complexes".

As for the distinction between the *audience hall* and the *reception hall/area*, it tends to float. In general, one may say that the audience hall is more personal, i.e. there is a more direct contact between the king and the supplicant individual or group, than in the reception hall/area, where a great crowd could be received by the king all at the same time. Thus the reception hall is normally larger than the audience hall, and receptions frequently took place in the open.

Finally there may be problems with *parks* and *gardens*. In my definition, a garden is smaller than a park, forms an integrated part of the buildings, and is invariably enclosed, while the park surrounds the palatial buildings. The gardens may belong to all kinds of palaces; they are normally present in "compact palaces" and are found in both governors' and private palaces. The park, on the other hand, is limited to the large royal "palace complexes".

Different signs are used to clarify the status of the various items. A question mark indicates that the element in question might well have been present, despite not being found or mentioned in the sources. The use of a dash, on the other hand, denotes that this element was absent from the palace. To further differentiate the possibilities, "X?" indicates that the item was undoubtedly present, although not mentioned or identified with certainty, while "-?" indicates that an item was probably not present, although the possibility cannot be entirely ruled out.

These signs are used in the same way in the diagram at the end of the book, based on the nine functions (Fig. 115, pp. 214-15). The order of the palaces is, however, different there, being governed by categories, royal, governors' and private, and only then following the order used in the Catalogue.

List of catalogued palaces
Cat. 1: Memphis. Palace of Apries. A royal Pharaonic palace.
Cat. 2: Babylon. Südburg. A royal Neo-Babylonian palace.
Cat. 3: Pasargadae. The royal Palace of Cyrus the Great.
Cat. 4: Persepolis. The royal Palace.
Cat. 5: Susa. The royal Palace of Darius.
Cat. 6: Susa. The royal Palace of Artaxerxes II.
Cat. 7: Lachish. The governor's Palace.
Cat. 8: Vouni. The princely or governor's Palace.
Cat. 9: Larisa. The princely Palace.
Cat. 10: Vergina/Aigai. The royal Palace of Palatitsa.
Cat. 11: Pella. The private House of Dionysus (Pella I,1).
Cat. 12: Pella. The royal Palace.
Cat. 13: Demetrias. Anaktoron. A royal palace.
Cat. 14: Pergamon. The royal Palace.
Cat. 15: Antiochia. The royal Palace.
Cat. 16: Dura Europos. Redoubt Palace. A governor's palace.
Cat. 17: Dura Europos. Citadel Palace. A governor's palace.
Cat. 18: Nippur. The magisterial or princely Palace.

CAT. NO. 1

Traditional name: Palace of Apries.
Kingdom: Egypt.
Locality: Memphis.
Category: Royal palace.
Situation: Northern part of the city on a hill by the river, on an artificial platform, h. c. 12 m.
Area: Palace proper without forecourt: 72 x 92 m = 6,624 m². 1 ha. excavated.
General characteristics: Occupied only part of a large fortified terrace.

Architecture

Building technique and material: Sun-dried brick partly covered with stone slabs in the finer rooms.
Façade: To the south, with a large forecourt.
   gateway: Monumental, reached from a broad avenue.
Courtyards/forecourts: Forecourt surrounded by a wall.
   peristyles/order of columns: —

Functions

Official/ceremonial:
   portal: Entrance portico to forecourt and "broadway" to the main hall.
   audience/council/court hall: The central tetrastyle hall (33 x 35 m = 1,155 m²) and the large poorly preserved hypostyle hall to the north, the so-called *mandara*.
   reception hall/area: Forecourt for large receptions.

Social:
   banqueting hall/s: Probably one of the above-mentioned halls.
Religious:
   temple for the tutelary deity: —, but there were sanctuaries in the palace quarter.
   dynastic sanctuary: —
   mausoleum: —
Defensive:
   precinct walls: The palace area was surrounded by a wall.
   citadel/akra: The palace was situated in a large fortified area, 15 ha.
   barracks and arsenal: In the citadel.
Administrative: —, a quarter of the city was set aside for this purpose.
   offices: —, ditto.
   archives: —, ditto.
   treasury: —, it was placed in the Temple of Ptah in Memphis.
Service: The rooms to the north and south of the main hall.
   storerooms: X?
   kitchens, etc.: Near the entrance, south of the central hall.
   servants' quarters: X?
Residential for the king/governor and his family: The area to the east.
   bedrooms: Probably located to the east of the main hall, facing away from it.
   bathrooms: X?
   private dining-rooms: X?
   harem: Probably the rooms to the east of the central hall.
Residential for the court/guests:
   apartments: —, they probably lived in the city.
"Public":
   gymnasium/palaestra: —
   library: —
   theatre: —
   hippodrome: —
Recreational:
   gardens: ?
   parks: A sloping park to the north is mentioned *1-2.
   pavilions: ?
   (swimming-)pools: A lake in relation to the park is mentioned *1.

Miscellaneous: The Ptolemaic palace was built nearby, probably reusing the park and lake *1-2.
State of preservation: Rather poor, only partly preserved.
Time of excavation: Early this century.

Date and period of use
Built by Pharaoh Apries (588-563 BC) (inscriptions), reused by the Persians and the last

pharaohs as well as by Alexander (finds). This palace, or its Ptolemaic successor, was in ruins in the 1st century BC *1.

References

Written sources: For Egyptian inscriptions, see Petrie 1909. *1: Strab. 17.1.31-32 (807-808); *2: *PSI* 488.11 (257 BC).
Modern literature: Petrie 1909 (P); Kemp 1977; Thompson 1988, 9ff.
This volume: pp. 27ff; Figs. 2-3.

CAT. NO. 2

Traditional name: Südburg, Kasr.
Kingdom: Neo-Babylonian kingdom.
Locality: Babylon.
Category: Royal palace.
Situation: By the eastern river bank, on a fortified hill on the northern outskirts of the city.
Area: 183 x 273 m = 49,959 m^2.
General characteristics: The palace consisted of a row of interconnected courtyards.

Architecture

Building technique and material: Sun-dried brick, covered with glazed tiles. Roofs either vaulted or covered by wooden beams.
Façade: Monumental, to the east.
   gateway: Monumental, flanked by towers.
Courtyards/forecourts: Five courts without peristyles or gardens.
   peristyles/order of columns: Perhaps peristyles were added in the Seleucid period.

Functions

Official/ceremonial: "Haupthof".
   portal: Monumental portal partly to the courtyard, partly to the "broad room", with decoration in glazed brick (Pl. 2).
   audience/council/court hall: The "broad room" to the south of the "Haupthof" (52 x 17 m = 884 m^2).
   reception hall/area: Perhaps the courtyard served this purpose.
Social:
   banqueting hall/s: Both courts and the large "broad room" were probably used for banquets.
Religious:
   temple for the tutelary deity: —, but there were sanctuaries in the vicinity.
   dynastic sanctuary: —
   mausoleum: —
Defensive:
   precinct walls: Heavily fortified, to the north by the inner city wall.

citadel/akra: Together with the "Nordburg", the complex constituted a fort.
    barracks/arsenal: ?
Administrative: In the "Osthof" and "Mittelhof".
    offices: Ditto.
    archives: X?
    treasury: A treasury is mentioned in relation to Alexander's takeover *6.
Service:
    storerooms: The vaulted chambers in the north-eastern angle of the palace.
    kitchens, etc.: X?
    servants' quarters: X?
Residential for the king/governor and his family: "Westhof" and "Anbauhof".
    bedrooms: South of the courtyards, the king's apartments were probably planned in connection with the large southern rooms (a "three-room suite in depth").
    bathrooms: X?
    private dining-rooms: Probably the large halls south of the courtyards. Also the garden pavilion could be used.
    harem: The six apartments south of the two courtyards.
Residential for the court/guests:
    apartments: Probably the many rooms north of the courts.
"Public":
    gymnasium/palaestra: —
    library: —
    theatre: —
    hippodrome: —
Recreational:
    gardens: The famous Hanging Gardens are thought to have been located west of the palace, terraced down to the river *1-5.
    parks: A park is mentioned *2.
    pavilions: The "Persian Building" in the west garden.
    (swimming-)pools: —

State of preservation: Poor, but the plan is quite clear.
Time of excavation: Beginning of this century.

Date and period of use
Built by Nebuchadnezzar (605-562 BC) *1, reused by the Persians (the "Persian Building"), and by the Seleucids (roof-tiles for porticoes). The same was the case with the other two palaces of Babylon.

References
Written sources: For Babylonian sources, see Koldewey 1931, 29-32. Diodorus (2.8.3-7) describes all three Babylonian palaces, basing his description on Ctesias. His figures for the circumference of the various palaces are grossly exaggerated. *1: Joseph. *Cont. Ap.* 1.19

(128-141); *2: Joseph. *AJ* 10.1.3 (11); Arr. *Anab.* 7.25.3; *3: Diod. 2.10; *4: Strab. 16.1.5 (739); *5: Curt. 5.1.32-33; *6: Arr. *Anab.* 3.16.3.

Modern literature: Koldewey 1931 (P); Koldewey 1932, 6ff (Northern Palace) (P); Koldewey 1932, 41ff (Babil Palace) (P); Bergamini 1977; Wisemann 1985; Heinrich 1984, 198-229. For the Hanging Gardens: Fehr 1969, 67; Nagel 1979; Wisemann 1983; Dalley 1994. For the "Persian Building": Koldewey 1931, 121ff; Haerinck 1973, who dates it to the reign of Artaxerxes I. For activities during the reign of the Seleucids, see Wetzel *et al.* 1957, 3ff. *This volume:* pp. 31ff; Figs. 4-5, 8-9; Pl. 2.

CAT. NO. 3

Traditional name: Palace of Cyrus the Great.
Kingdom: Achaemenid.
Locality: Pasargadae.
Category: Royal palace.
Situation: Laid out on a large plain.
Area: Tell-i Takht: c. 6,460 m^2; Palace S: 54 x 44 m = 2,376 m^2; Palace P: 76 x 42 m = 3,192 m^2; the whole park: c. 20-30 ha.
General characteristics: The palace consists of many isolated buildings laid out regularly in a large park and on a terraced platform.

Architecture

Building technique and material: Built of large ashlars in local stone, with wooden ceilings and walls in sun-dried brick.
Façade: —
   gateway: A large gate, R, with a hypostyle hall and four portals, the main one guarded by Assyrian-style animals, led to the park with the palatial buildings.
Courtyards/forecourts: ?
   peristyles/order of columns: —, but the columns in the palaces had Ionic-style bases and shafts, and Persian capitals.

Functions

Official/ceremonial: Palaces S and P.
   portal: Both Palaces S and P had entrances in the form of porticoes flanked by projecting corner rooms.
   audience/council/court hall: The hypostyle hall of Palace S (c. 39 x 30 = 1,170 m^2). Also the hall of Palace P (30 x 21 = 630 m^2) may have had this function.
   reception hall/area: The southern portico in antis facing the garden had a throne and benches and could perhaps be used for receptions, the people assembling in the garden.
Social:
   banqueting hall/s: Perhaps in Pavilions A and B, and in the park, perhaps in tents. Also, the platform Tell-i Takht may have housed structures for this purpose.

Religious:
    temple for the tutelary deity: ?, but a sacred precinct with two altars was situated in the palace area *2.
    dynastic sanctuary: —
    mausoleum: Cyrus the Great's tomb was placed in relation to the palace, surrounded by a park (*paradeisos*) *1,*4.
Defensive:
    precinct walls: The park was surrounded by a wall.
    citadel/akra: The terraced hill called Tell-i Takht may have served this purpose, among other things, and certainly this was the case with the fortified area connected with it, compare Persepolis.
    barracks/arsenal: Probably in tents, or on the Tell-i Takht.
Administrative: Probably buildings planned on the Tell-i Takht.
    offices: Ditto.
    archives: X?
    treasury: A treasury is mentioned *3. The mysterious Zendan near the palace in the park was perhaps used to house ritual and/or royal effects.
Service:
    storerooms: X?
    kitchens, etc.: X?
    servants' quarters: X?
Residential for the king/governor and his family: Perhaps in tents in the park, perhaps on the Tell-i Takht, which was reached by monumental staircases. This could perhaps also be used for ceremonial purposes.
    bedrooms: X?
    bathrooms: X?
    private dining-rooms: X?
    harem: X?
Residential for the court/guests:
    apartments: ?
"Public":
    gymnasium/palaestra: —
    library: —
    theatre: —
    hippodrome: —
Recreational:
    gardens: —
    parks: The park is a typical Persian paradeisos, laid out regularly with water canals.
    pavilions: Two have been found, Pavilions A and B.
    (swimming-)pools: ?

Miscellaneous: There has been much discussion on the function of Palaces S and P. The residential character normally suggested is doubtful, since they were not practical to live in, but well suited for official functions. The location of the rest of the palace is uncertain, perhaps on the terrace, perhaps in tents in the park.

State of preservation: Partially rather well preserved.

Time of excavation: Various investigations in the first half of this century, and from the early 1960s regular excavations.

Date and period of use

Built by Cyrus (inscriptions) and probably used by Cambyses and Darius I, at least. Not reused by the Seleucids.

References

Written sources: For Persian inscriptions, see Stronach 1978. *1: Strab. 15.3.7 (730); *2: Strab. 15.3.14 (732-33); *3: Arr. *Anab.* 3.18.10; *4: Arr. *Anab.* 6.29.5-6.

Modern literature: Stronach 1978 (P); Nylander 1970. For the park, see Stronach 1989.

This volume: pp. 35ff; Figs. 10-13.

CAT. NO. 4

Traditional name: Palace of Persepolis.

Kingdom: Achaemenid.

Locality: Persepolis.

Category: Royal palace, perhaps primarily ceremonial.

Situation: Partly on a large terrace, partly probably on the plain below.

Area: The terrace: 125,000 m^2; Apadana: 112 x 112 m = 12,544 m^2.

General characteristics: The palace consisted of many independent buildings, placed in a regular arrangement, partly on the terrace, partly on the plain.

Architecture

Building technique and material: Built of stone in large ashlars, wood was used for the ceilings and sun-dried brick for part of the walls.

Façade: The main façade was the tall western one, dominated by the monumental staircase and the front of the Apadana.

　　gateway/s: Three monumental portals: "Gate of All Nations" with "Assyrian"-style animal guardians, leading to the Apadana, the never finished "Gate of the Army", leading to the "Hall of 100 Columns", and finally the "Tripylon" or "King's Gate", which led to the southern complex.

Courtyards/forecourts: Forecourts in front of the Apadana and the Hall of 100 Columns. Smaller forecourts to Darius' and Xerxes' palaces.

　　peristyles/order of columns: —, but the columns of the halls, which were mostly of stone, had Egyptian bases and Persian capitals.

Functions

Official/ceremonial: Most buildings on the terrace.

portal: Access to the Apadana after passing through the "Gate of All Nations" was via monumental staircases decorated with reliefs, and two doorways. The access to the Hall of 100 Columns was less monumental, leading through a double portico flanked by rooms, again with two doorways.

audience/council/court hall: The hall of the Apadana (60 x 60 m = 3,600 m²), and probably the Hall of 100 Columns (68.5 x 68.5 m = c. 4,692 m²) (reliefs).

reception hall/area: The Apadana and the Hall of 100 Columns, the latter probably mostly for the army (reliefs). The forecourts in front of this and the Apadana could also be used for this purpose. Also the western terrace of the Apadana was undoubtedly used in connection with processions below the terrace.

Social:

banqueting hall/s: According to the motifs of the reliefs, the "Palace of Xerxes" (*hadish*) had this function. Perhaps this was also one of the functions of the "Palace of Darius" (*tachara*) (reliefs) and the badly preserved structures in the area (Palaces D and G). Large banquets could also be held in the open air, in the huge forecourts, perhaps also in tents on the plain below.

Religious:

temple for the tutelary deity: —

dynastic sanctuary: —

mausoleum: Artaxerxes II and III had rock-cut tombs in the hill above the terrace.

Defensive:

precinct walls: The terrace was fortified.

citadel/akra: The terrace was connected to the fortified hill to the east, constituting the citadel *1.

barracks/arsenal: Barracks were probably in the rooms east of the forecourt to the Hall of 100 Columns. The arsenal has been identified with the area just in front of the "Gate of the Army" *1.

Adminitrative:

offices: Probably in the treasury and the so-called Harem.

archives: Ditto.

treasury: Treasury in the south-east part of the terrace *1. It was later moved to Ecbatana *3-4.

Service:

storerooms: In the south-east part of the terrace.

kitchens, etc.: X?

servants' quarters: X?

Residential for the king/governor and his family: This part may have been situated on the plain below. Many complexes have been found, with courts and hypostyle, apadana-like halls, placed regularly in a garden. But, according to *1, also on the terrace.

bedrooms: Perhaps in Buildings H, G, B on the plain.

bathrooms: Ditto.

private dining-rooms: Perhaps Building F.

harem: Perhaps Buildings H, G, B.

Residential for the court/guests:
   apartments: Perhaps all or part of the buildings on the plain were for this purpose.
"Public":
   gymnasium/palaestra: —
   library: —
   theatre: —
   hippodrome: —
Recreational:
   gardens: Perhaps the sunken court in connection with Building C on the plain had a garden. There may also have been gardens on the terrace, south of the Palace of Darius.
   parks: The buildings on the plain were laid out regularly in a large park, a paradeisos with canals.
   pavilions: Some of the buildings on the plain.
   (swimming-)pools: A pool and an artificial lake have been traced on the plain.

Miscellaneous: It is, as mentioned above, also a possibility that some of the southern buildings of the terrace served residential purposes, e.g. the so-called Harem, which could have had precisely this function, the apartment in connection with it, and the palaces of Darius and Xerxes.
State of preservation: Partially well preserved.
Time of excavation: 1931-39 (mostly the terrace). In the 1970s reconstructions were made. Excavations are still going on in the plain.

Date and period of use
Begun by Darius I, continued by Xerxes and mostly finished by Artaxerxes I (inscriptions, foundation tablets). Destroyed by Alexander *1-2 and not reused by the Seleucids.

References
Written sources: For inscriptions and foundation tablets, see Schmidt 1953. *1: Diod. 17.70-71; *2: Curt. 5.6.1ff; *3: Strab. 15.3.9 (731); *4: Arr. *Anab.* 3.19.5-8.
Modern literature: Herzfeld 1941; Schmidt 1953 (P); Krefter 1971; Tilia 1972, 1978 (P); Kleiss 1980; Calmeyer 1990; Sancisi-Weerdenburg 1993.
This volume: pp. 35ff; Figs. 14-17; Pl. 3.

CAT. NO. 5

Traditional name: Palace of Darius.
Kingdom: Achaemenid.
Locality: Susa.
Category: Royal palace.
Situation: Placed on a large terrace, h. 18 m.
Area: C. 50,000 m^2; palace without Apadana, 246 x 155 m = 38,130 m^2; the Apadana: 109 x 109 m = 11,881 m^2; the terrace covered 13 ha.

General characteristics: Placed exclusively on the terrace, no part laid out on the plain below. It consisted of two parts: an Apadana and a compact courtyard palace.

Architecture

Building technique and material: Sun-dried and fired brick, only the Apadana was built partly in stone.

Façade: To the east.

> *gateway/s:* Two portals, one on the terrace proper, "Porte de Darius" (40 x 30 m), reached by an avenue from "Propylon de Darius" in the "Ville Royale".

Courtyards/forecourts: Four large courtyards without columns.

> *peristyles/order of columns:* —, but the columns of the Apadana were in Persian style.

Functions

Official/ceremonial: East court.

> *portal:* Large portal to the east, towards "Porte de Darius".
>
> *audience/council/court hall:* The hall of the Apadana (60 x 60 m = 3,600 m²) and the hall located to the south of the east court, a "three-room suite in depth", the "broad rooms" each measuring 52 x 7 m = 364 m² *2.
>
> *reception hall/area:* The Apadana, the area in front of it, and probably the east courtyard.

Social:

> *banqueting hall/s:* The audience hall and some of the halls in connection with the east court and perhaps the court itself could be used for this purpose.

Religious:

> *temple for the tutelary deity:* —
>
> *dynastic sanctuary:* —
>
> *mausoleum:* —

Defensive:

> *precinct walls:* The palace was placed on a high terrace.
>
> *citadel/akra:* The terrace was protected by a fortified acropolis.
>
> *barracks/arsenal:* X?

Administrative:

> *offices:* Probably rooms in connection with the east and central court.
>
> *archives:* Ditto.
>
> *treasury:* Probably south of the central or the west court. It is mentioned *i.a.* in relation to Alexander's conquest *3-6.

Service:

> *storerooms:* Located south of the central and west courts *6.
>
> *kitchens, etc.:* X?
>
> *servants' quarters:* In the central and east courts.

Residential for the king/governor and his family: The interior court and the five apartments south of the three western courtyards, isolated by a long corridor. It is mentioned that each king built on the acropolis for himself a separate habitation, *oikesis* *6.

> *bedrooms:* Ditto.

bathrooms: X?

private dining-rooms: Probably at least one of the three halls south of the interior court and opening onto it with a large arch.

harem: The above-mentioned five apartments.

Residential for the court/guests:

apartments: Probably in the "Ville Royale".

"Public":

gymnasium/palaestra: —

library: —

theatre: —

hippodrome: —

Recreational:

gardens: ?

parks: The large unbuilt area south of the palace was laid out as a park.

pavilions: A pavilion for dining is mentioned in the sources *1.

(swimming-)pools: ?

State of preservation: Poor.

Time of excavation: First in 1909-10, and then again in 1968-78.

Date and period of use

Built by Darius I (foundation tablets and inscription), with only few restorations; used by all the Achaemenid kings as well as by Alexander and the early Seleucids. It went out of use during the 3rd century BC.

References

Written sources: For foundation tablets and inscription, see Perrot & Ladiray 1972. *1: Book of Esther 1.3-8 (it may also concern the palace of Artaxerxes, (Cat. 6)); *2: Diod. 17.66.3ff, *3: Arr. *Anab.* 3.16.6-8; *4: Diod. 17.65.5-66; *5: Strab. 15.3.9 (731); *6: Strab. 15.3.21 (735).

Modern literature: Perrot & Ladiray 1972 (P) with all earlier literature; Perrot 1981; Boucharlat 1990.

This volume: pp. 35ff; Figs. 18-20.

CAT. NO. 6

Traditional name: Palace of Artaxerxes II.

Kingdom: Achaemenid.

Locality: Susa.

Category: Royal palace, perhaps primarily residential.

Situation: On the plain, on the other side of the Shaour Stream from Darius' palace, built on the same axis.

Area: 200 x 150 m = 30,000 m^2; the Apadana: 60 x 70 m = 4,200 m^2.

General characteristics: The palace consisted of several independent buildings placed around a courtyard.

Architecture
Building technique and material: Sun-dried brick with some stone elements, e.g. column bases.
Façade: The eastern façade of the Apadana, with a forecourt facing towards the Palace of Darius.
    gateway/s: Probably one leading to the forecourt of the Apadana.
Courtyards/forecourts: One large courtyard and a forecourt in front of the Apadana.
    peristyle/order of columns: —

Functions
Official/ceremonial: The Apadana.
    portal: Access from the east via a portico flanked by two towers, and via two doorways.
    audience/council/court hall: The hall of the Apadana (34.5 x 34.5 m = c. 1,190 m^2).
    reception hall/area: The Apadana or the forecourt.
Social:
    banqueting hall/s: X?
Religious:
    temple for the tutelary deity: —
    dynastic sanctuary: —
    mausoleum: —
Defensive:
    precinct walls: —
    citadel/akra: Probably the citadel of the acropolis protected this palace also.
    barracks/arsenal: —?
Administrative: Probably not present in this palace.
    offices: —
    archives: —
    treasury: —
Service:
    storerooms: Perhaps in Building II.
    Kitchens, etc.: Ditto.
    Servants' quarters: Ditto.
Residential for the king/governor and his family: Probably Building III raised above the garden, and perhaps Building II with an interior courtyard with rooms.
    bedrooms: X?
    bathrooms: X?
    private dining-rooms: X?
    harem: X?
Residential for the court/guests: Probably in the "Ville Royale".
    apartments: —

"Public":
  gymnasium/palaestra: —
  library: —
  theatre: —
  hippodrome: —
Recreational:
  gardens: Garden in the court.
  parks: The palace was probably situated in a paradeisos, near the river.
  pavilions: ? *1.
  (swimming-)pools: ?

Miscellaneous: Since only part of the palace is preserved, locations for all functions have not been ascertained. But probably it was not exclusively a residential palace, because of the Apadana.
State of preservation: Partly preserved, only the plan of the Apadana is clear.
Time of excavation: 1970-76.

Date and period of use
Built by Artaxerxes II (inscriptions on columns), probably used by his successors as well as by the Seleucids.

References
Written sources: For the inscriptions on columns, see Boucharlat & Labrousse 1979. *1: perhaps Book of Esther 1.3-8, if not the Palace of Darius (Cat. 5).
Modern literature: Boucharlat & Labrousse 1979 (P).
This volume: pp. 35ff; Figs. 18, 20-22.

CAT NO. 7

Traditional name: Palace of Lachish.
Kingdom: Achaemenid.
Locality: Lachish/Tell ed-Duweir, Palastine.
Category: Governor's palace.
Situation: On a fortified hill, built on a terrace larger than the present palace, formed by the ruins of an earlier palace.
Area: Terrace: 2,630 m²; palace proper: 48 x 36.5 m = 1,752 m².
General characteristics: Typical are the two Bit-Hilani units, an inspiration from the palace architecture of Northern Syria.

Architecture
Building technique and material: Small roughly cut ashlars with mortar; stone arches carried the roof.

Façade: Non-monumental.
   gateway: In the fortification wall.
Courtyards/forecourts: Central court and forecourt to the north, probably.
   peristyles/order of columns: —

Functions

Official/ceremonial: Two Bit-Hilani units, south and west of the court.
   portal: A "bent" entrance from the north.
   audience/council/court hall: Probably the southern "broad room" (16.5 x 6.6 m = c. 109 m²) and perhaps the western one.
   reception hall/area: The courtyard could probably be used for this purpose.
Social:
   banqueting hall/s: Probably the southern "broad room".
Religious:
   temple for the tutelary deity: —, but there was a temple near the palace.
   dynastic sanctuary: —
   mausoleum: —
Defensive:
   precinct walls: The palace was situated on a fortified acropolis.
   citadel/akra: The acropolis.
   barracks/arsenal: —, but rooms for guards near the entrance.
Administrative:
   offices: ?
   archives: ?
   treasury: ?
Service: Probably the east and north wing.
   storerooms: X?
   kitchens, etc.: X?
   servants' quarters: X?
Residential for the king/governor and his family:
   bedrooms: In connection with the southern Bit-Hilani, an "andron complex".
   bathrooms: Probably room B to the south, and a water closet in room A.
   private dining-rooms: ?
   harem: —
Residential for the court/guests:
   apartments: —?
"Public":
   gymnasium/palaestra: —
   library: —
   theatre: —
   hippodrome: —
Recreational:
   gardens: —

parks: —
pavilions: —
(swimming-)pools: —

State of preservation: Preserved in foundations, except for parts of the west and north side.
Time of excavation: 1930s, 1960s and 1970s.

Date and period of use
Built in the Persian period over an earlier palace, probably by the governor, reused in early
Hellenistic times, when ruled by the Ptolemies.

References
Written sources: —
Modern literature: Tufnell 1953, 131ff, 168 (P); Starkey 1933 (Pr.); Aharoni 1975;
Ussishkin 1977; Stern 1982.
This volume: pp. 51ff; Figs. 24-26.

CAT. NO. 8

Traditional name: Palace of Vouni.
Kingdom: Achaemenid or local principality.
Locality: Vouni, Cyprus.
Category: Princely or governor's palace.
Situation: On a terrace just below the summit, "acropolis". The palace was included in a
large fortified area.
Area: C. 81 x 69 m = 5,589 m²; the terrace including the small sanctuaries surrounding
the palace: c. 9,000 m².
General characteristics: The palace consists in its present state of a main peristyle building
and several service courtyards and wings.

Architecture
Building technique and material: Foundations in ashlars in local limestone, superstructures
in sun-dried brick.
Façade: Non-monumental.
    gateway: Access from a monumental, 7.7 m wide staircase, reached by a ramp, to a portal
    leading to a "bent" entrance.
Courtyards/forecourts: 1st phase: one peristyle court, a kitchen yard and a small
multifunctional yard. In the 2nd phase, a large service courtyard was added.
    peristyles/order of columns: Porticoes on three sides of the court, a monumental staircase
    to the official wing on the fourth side. The capitals were a Cypriot variety of the
    Egyptian Hathor capital.

Functions

Official/ceremonial: The southern wing.

> *portal:* Monumental access by a broad staircase from the courtyard to the official part.
>
> *audience/council/court hall:* The central hall of this wing (9.40 x 7.25 m = c. 68 m²),
> and the inner one.
>
> *reception hall/area:* Probably the courtyard.

Social:

> *banqueting hall/s:* Either the same southern complex (direct access from the kitchen)
> or the large "broad room" to the west in the first phase (12 x 7.3 m = c. 88 m²).

Religious:

> *temple for the tutelary deity:* —, but a Temple and Sanctuary of Athena was situated
> on the summit just above the palace and not separated from it by a wall.
>
> *dynastic sanctuary:* —
>
> *mausoleum:* —

Defensive:

> *precinct walls:* The palace was placed in a large fortified area, and could be reached only
> via small staircases.
>
> *citadel/akra:* —
>
> *barracks/arsenal:* X?

Administrative: Probably located in the residential area included in the fortification.

> *offices:* —?
>
> *archives:* —?
>
> *treasury:* —?

Service:

> *storerooms:* 1st phase: rooms in west annex; 2nd phase: rooms in east wing of the new
> courtyard.
>
> *kitchens, etc.:* One kitchen was placed in the south-eastern complex.
>
> *servants' quarters:* In the 1st phase the western and eastern annexes to the main peristyle,
> in the 2nd phase also in the new courtyard.

Residential for the king/governor and his family: Partly probably the rooms on the northern
and eastern sides of the peristyle, including the baths, partly the south-western complex,
with apartment and baths. In the 2nd phase also the second storey of the main peristyle.

> *bedrooms:* Ditto.
>
> *bathrooms:* In the north-eastern corner of the main palace, and in the south-western
> complex.
>
> *private dining-rooms:* X?
>
> *harem:* —

Residential for the court/guests:

> *apartments:* —?, probably they lived in the residential area below the palace in the
> fortified area.

"Public":

> *gymnasium/palaestra:* —
>
> *library:* —

theatre: —
    hippodrome: —
Recreational:
    gardens: —
    parks: —
    pavilions: —
    (swimming-)pools: —

Miscellaneous: There has been much discussion about the function of the main wing to the north and the placement of the entrance.
State of preservation: Rather well preserved; the plan is clear.
Time of excavation: 1928-1929.

Date and period of use
1st main phase: first half of the 5th century BC; 2nd main phase: second half of the 5th century BC. The palace was destroyed in the early 4th century BC.

References
Written sources: —
Modern literature: Gjerstad 1932 and 1933 (both Pr.), Gjerstad *et al.* 1937, 76-229 (P); Müller 1932, 1933; Maier 1989.
This volume: pp. 54ff; Figs. 28-31; Pl. 4.

CAT. NO. 9

Traditional name: Palace of Larisa.
Kingdom: Achaemenid (partly).
Locality: Larisa, Asia Minor.
Category: Princely palace.
Situation: On the acropolis.
Area: The acropolis: 7,500 m²; new palace from the 4th century: c. 30 x 21 = 630 m².
General characteristics: The complex in its latest phase consisted of a newly built palace and an older, still functioning palace from the middle of the 5th century BC. The main element in all palaces on the site is the megaron.

Architecture
Building technique and material: Stone and rubble masonry.
Façade: Non-monumental.
    gateway: In the acropolis wall.
Courtyards/forecourts: A large courtyard in the new palace, and a small one in the old one. In between, a service yard of irregular plan.
    peristyles/order of columns: No peristyle, but columns in antis in front of many rooms.

Functions

Official/ceremonial:

portal: Propylon to the new palace.

audience/council/court hall: In the first three periods, the hall of the Bit Hilani (c.7 x 7 m = 49 m^2) and/or the hall of the megaron in the old palace (c. 6 x 6 m = 36 m^2). In the fourth period, one of the megara in the northern wing of the new palace, of more or less the same size.

reception hall/area: Perhaps the courtyard of the new palace.

Social:

banqueting hall/s: Perhaps megara in old and new palace.

Religious:

temple for the tutelary deity: —, but the main temple of the city, probably for Athena, was situated on the acropolis as well.

dynastic sanctuary: —

mausoleum: —

Defensive:

precinct walls: Situated on the fortified acropolis.

citadel/akra: The acropolis functioned at the same time as a citadel.

barracks/arsenal: X?

Administrative:

offices: ?

archives: ?

treasury: ?

Service: The courtyard between the two buildings.

storerooms: X?

kitchens, etc.: X?

servants' quarters: X?

Residential for the king/governor and his family:

bedrooms: X?

bathrooms: X?

private dining-rooms: X?

harem: —

Residential for the court/guests:

apartments: —?

"Public":

gymnasium/palaestra: —

library: —

theatre: —

hippodrome: —

Recreational:

gardens: —

parks: —

pavilions: —

(swimming-)pools: —

Miscellaneous: There has been some discussion of the identification of the eastern part of the 500 BC palace, whether as a megaron or a Bit-Hilani.
State of preservation: Poor.
Time of excavation: 1933-34.

Date and period of use
The palaces of Larisa existed from the 6th century BC to the destruction of the city at the beginning of the 3rd century BC. Four main periods: A. c. 500 BC, with megaron and perhaps Bit Hilani; B. c. 450 BC, a courtyard added to the megaron with rooms; C. 430/20 BC, stoas added to the north; D. c. 350 BC, a new courtyard palace added.

References
Written sources: —
Modern literature: Boehlau & Schefold 1940 (P); Schefold 1978; Lauter 1975.
This volume: pp. 66ff; Figs. 35-37.

CAT. NO. 10

Traditional name: Palace of Palatitsa.
Kingdom: Macedonia.
Locality: Aigai, present-day Vergina.
Category: Royal palace, perhaps a summer palace.
Situation: Placed on a terrace on the slope of the acropolis, included in the Hippodamian plan of the city.
Area: Main palace: 104.5 x 88.4 m = c. 9,238 m^2.
General characteristics: Two peristyle courtyards and another probably planned; the main courtyard is asymmetrically laid out.

Architecture
Building technique and material: Built in Ashlar in local stone and sun-dried brick.
Façade: Monumental columnar façade towards the east i.e. towards the city.
   gateway: The propylon was distyle in antis, and had two storeys, Doric below, Ionic above. In depth a triple propylon. Width 10 m. It was reached from a ramp along the façade.
Courtyards/forecourts: Main courtyard and service courtyard.
   peristyles/order of columns: Peristyles in both courtyards, the order in the main one was Doric.
Functions
Official/ceremonial:
   portal: Monumental propylon.
   audience/council/court hall: Probably the tholos (diam. 11.25 m) and/or the innermost propylon hall (10 x 10 m = 100 m^2).

reception hall/area: Large receptions were perhaps held in the open area in front of the propylon, the first floor of which could be used by the king. Also the theatre could perhaps be used for official purposes.

Social:
> *banqueting hall/s:* The dominant feature in the main peristyle, different sizes for different groups of people. The finest rooms were probably those to the south.

Religious:
> *temple for the tutelary deity:* The tholos might have had this function also, an inscription mentioning Heracles having been found.
> *dynastic sanctuary:* —
> *mausoleum:* —, although Aigai was the traditional burial place for the kings, their tombs were not placed in direct connection with the palace *1-2.

Defensive:
> *precinct walls:* Included in the city's defences.
> *citadel/akra:* The citadel was situated on the top of the hill behind the palace.
> *barracks/arsenal:* X?

Administrative: Probably limited, since it was a secondary palace, perhaps a summer palace.
> *offices:* —
> *archives:* ?
> *treasury:* Perhaps located in the long halls flanking the propylon's central hall.

Service:
> *storerooms:* X?
> *kitchens, etc.:* Probably in connection with the dining-rooms of the main peristyle.
> *servants' quarters:* The second courtyard, to the west. Another yard for the same purpose was planned to the north of this one.

Residential for the king/governor and his family: Probably part of the east wing, with "*pastas* corridor", and part of the north wing, and also the first floor.
> *bedrooms:* Probably on the first floor.
> *bathrooms:* X?
> *private dining-rooms:* Behind the "pastas corridor".
> *harem:* —

Residental for the court/guests:
> *apartments:* ?

"Public":
> *gymnasium/palaestra:* —
> *library:* ?
> *theatre:* A theatre was built on the same axis as the palace, down the northern slope. Perhaps it was also used for assemblies and festivals, since the orchestra was very large in relation to other theatres (diam. 28.5 m) *3.
> *hippodrome:* —

Recreational:
> *gardens:* ?
> *parks:* —

pavilions: —
(swimming-)pools: —

State of preservation: Partly well preserved.
Time of excavation: First excavated in 1855, then in 1938-56, and finally in 1959-74.

Date and period of use
From the second half of the 4th century BC to the fall of the Macedonian dynasty in 168 BC. The service yard was added probably in the first half of the 3rd century BC.

References
Written sources: For the inscription in the tholos, see Andronicos 1984, 38. *1: Diod. 19.52.5; *2: Pliny, *HN* 4.33; *3: Diod. 16.91.4-95.
Modern literature: Heuzey & Daumet 1876, 184-226 (P); Andronicos 1984, 38ff (Pr); Pandermalis 1976, 1987 (Pr); Heermann 1986, 239ff; Hoepfner 1996, 9ff.
This volume: pp. 81ff; Figs. 41-42; Pls. 10-13.

CAT. NO. 11

Traditional name: Pella I,1 or House of Dionysus.
Kingdom: Macedonia
Locality: Pella, the capital of the kingdom.
Category: Private palace.
Situation: In the centre of town, near the agora, laid out in a Hippodamian pattern, filling one insula.
Area: 47 x 111.5 m = c. 5,240 m².
General characteristics: The palace consisted of three courtyards.

Architecture
Building technique and material: Local rubble stone and sun-dried brick.
Façade: To the east, non-monumental.
  gateway: A propylon, perhaps with two columns in antis.
Courtyards/forecourts: Three courtyards.
  peristyles/order of columns: The two northernmost yards had peristyles, the northern one in two storeys, both with Ionic columns.

Functions
Official/ceremonial: The official peristyle was the central one.
  portal: The propylon led to a large vestibule.
  audience/council/court hall: Probably the vestibule (10 x 10 m = 100 m²).
  reception hall/area: —

Social:
  banqueting hall/s: In the official peristyle three banqueting halls were ascertained, the two largest ones being in the north wing.
Religious:
  temple for the tutelary deity: —
  dynastic sanctuary: —
  mausuleum: —
Defensive:
  precinct walls: —, located in a fortified city.
  citadel/akra: —
  barracks/arsenal: —
Administrative:
  offices: —
  archives: —
  treasury: —
Service: In the southernmost courtyard.
  storerooms: X?
  kitchens, etc.: X?
  servants'quarters: X?
Residential for the king/governor/owner and his family: The northernmost peristyle.
  bedrooms: On the first floor and perhaps in the "pastas group".
  bathrooms: X?
  private dining-rooms: X?
  harem: —
Residential for the court/guests:
  apartments: Perhaps in the official peristyle, west wing.
"Public":
  gymnasium/palaestra: —
  library: —
  theatre: —
  hippodrome: —
recreational:
  gardens: Some or all courts had gardens.
  parks: —
  pavilions: —
  (swimming-)pools: —

Miscellaneous: The house was finely decorated with mosaics.
State of preservation: Mostly only foundations.
Time of excavation: 1957-61.

Date and period of use
Built in the second half of the 4th century BC, contemporary with the Palace of Aigai (Cat. 10). It was destroyed by the Romans in 168 BC, but later reused.

References
Written sources: —
Modern literature: ADelt. 16, 1960, 72-83; 17, 1961/62, *Chron.* 209-13 (Makaronas) (Pr); Makaronas & Giouri 1989 (P); Heermann 1986, 9-65. Walter-Karydi 1996, with reconstruction (Abb. 3).
This volume: pp. 85ff; Figs. 43-44; Pls. 14-15.

Cat. no. 12

Traditional name: Pella II or Royal Palace of Pella.
Kingdom: Macedonia.
Locality: Pella, the capital of the kingdom.
Category: Royal palace.
Situation: On the "acropolis" hill above the city to the north. The palace was laid out in accordance with the Hippodamian plan of the city and flanked by two streets to the east and west, and by the city wall to the north.
Area: At least 60,000 m². Peristyle I: c. 98.6 x 77.5 m = c. 7,642 m², yard 42.8 x 54 m = c. 2,311 m²; Peristyle II: yard 50 x 50 m = 2,500 m²; Area III: c. 90 x 90 m = 8100 m².
General characteristics: A "compact palace" with large courtyards and various structures connected to them.

Architecture
Building technique and material: Ashlar in local stone and sun-dried brick, partly built in reused material.
Façade: Monumental façade towards the south, facing the city, with columnar porticoes resting on a high terrace wall.
  gateway: Monumental tetrastyle prostyle propylon, 15 m wide and 10 m deep, in the middle of this façade. It was reached from the city via a broad ramp. It was placed in the axis between the two main peristyles, I and II, and led to a large vestibule.
Courtyards/forecourts: Six courtyards, of which at least four had peristyles. Perhaps there was a forecourt to the east.
  peristyles/order of columns: The main Peristyle I had two storeys, Doric below, Ionic above. Doric columns found in Courtyard III.

Functions
Official/ceremonial: The south-east Peristyle I and the large Peristyle II to the west.
  portal: The entrance to the main Peristyle I has not been found, but was undoubtedly to the south.

audience/council/court hall: The central hall in the north wing (22 x 18 m = 396 m²)

reception hall/area: Probably the large Peristyle II.

Social:

banqueting hall/s: The large hall might have been used, as well as the flanking halls.

Religious:

temple for the tutelary deity: —?, but a Temple of Athena Alkidemos is mentioned *1.

dynastic sanctuary: Probably in one of the apsidal rooms flanking the northern wing of Peristyle I. The eastern one had a small ante-room and a diam. of 7.5 m, depth 5 m, that to the west a diam. of 6.4 m with traces of *antae* and two supports. Both were well suited for statues, as was the long base in the northern portico (31 x 1.5 m).

mausoleum: —, the kings were buried in Aigai.

Defensive:

precinct walls: —, the palace was included in the walls of the city.

citadel/akra: —?, but a citadel, Arx Phaecus, situated just outside the walls towards the marshes, with a moat, is mentioned *2.

barracks/arsenal: X?, perhaps in the poorly known western part of the palace.

Administrative: Ditto.

offices: X?

archives: X?

treasury: —, located in the citadel of Phaecus *2, cf. *3.

Service: Undoubtedly to be found in the western area. The peristyle in Area III was never finished.

storerooms: X?

kitchens, etc.: X?

servants' quarters: X?

Residential for the king/governor and his family: The northern peristyles in the eastern part, i.e. Peristyles IV and V.

bedrooms: X?

bathrooms: North of Peristyle V is a fine bath suite with a small swimming-pool (7 x 5 m) and a heated room.

private dining-rooms: X?

harem: —

Residential for the court/guests:

apartments: ?

"Public":

gymnasium/palaestra: A palaestra with bath facilities may have been included in the palace, taking up Peristyle V, though in that position undoubtedly private. More likely is a garden in connection with the residential palace.

library: Mentioned in the written sources, perhaps one of the rooms in Peristyle I *3-5.

theatre: The city's theatre was probably built on the slope of the hill carrying the palace.

hippodrome: —

Recreational:

   gardens: At least Peristyle I, and probably several of the peristyles had gardens. A large altar (4 x 3 m) and a semicircular structure with water supply and drain were found in Peristyle I.

   parks: —, but perhaps the royal game reserves known from the written sources were placed in the vicinity *6.

   pavilions: —

   (swimming-)pools: —

Miscellaneous: The large hall in Peristyle I had a lavish decoration in stone. In the lower city was a heroon for the ruler cult.

State of preservation: Badly preserved, mostly only foundations.

Time of excavation: 1960-62 and from 1981, still in progress.

Date and period of use

Originally built perhaps by Philip II, it was much enlarged, probably during the reign of Philip V, according to the style of the architectural elements. The first royal palace of Pella, built when the city became the capital in c. 400 BC, was placed here as well, since *spolia* have been used. In 171 BC the palace is called old: *"in vetere regia"* *1.

References

Written sources: *1: Livy, 42.51.1-2; *2: Livy, 44.46.4-8; *3: Plut. *Aem.* 28; *4: *Corpus Inscr. Indicarum* I, p. 48; *5: Isid. *Or.* 6.5.1; *6: Polyb. 31.29.1-8.

Modern literature: Siganidou 1984 (1988); *Ergon* 1984, 38-39, 1987, 65-67; *BCH* 1985, 815, 1986, 718f, 1987, 547-9, 1988, 651-54 (G. Touchais); Siganidou 1987; Misaelidou-Despotidou 1988; Chrysostomou 1988; Siganidou 1989 (all Pr). Heermann 1986, 123-238, and n. 381 for the early excavations; Siganidou 1996; Hoepfner 1996, 26ff.

This volume: pp. 88ff; Figs. 43, 45-46; Pls. 16-19.

CAT. NO. 13

Traditional name: "Anaktoron" of Demetrias.

Kingdom: Macedonia.

Locality: Demetrias.

Category: Royal palace.

Situation: On a hill in the centre of the city, in connection with the citadel, raised c. 7 m above the "Sacred Agora". It is included in the Hippodamian city plan, but the orientation is slightly different.

Area: 59.8 x 61.3 m = c. 3,666 m^2 for the main building. The maximum length E-W is c. 200 m, N-S at least 100 m, i.e. c. 20,000 m^2.

General characteristics: The palace is fairly compact and consists of three large courtyards. Four towers flank the peristyle main building. The main palace faced terraces to the south and west. The palace is closely connected with the citadel.

Architecture

Building technique and material: Foundations and socle in ashlars in local stone, the rest in sun-dried brick, partly reused materials.

Façade: The entrance façade was probably to the south, facing the Sacred Agora.

> *gateway:* Probably placed between the main palace and the first western courtyard, it was reached from the Agora via a ramp to the "west-terrace 1" in front of the main palace.

Courtyards/forecourts: Three courtyards, the main one to the east.

> *peristyles/order of columns:* A peristyle with two storeys, both with Doric columns and the lower with heart-shaped corner columns, have been ascertained in the main courtyard (27.1 x 27.1 m = 734m²). The peristyle was probably of the Rhodian type.

Functions

Official/ceremonial: Probably part of the main peristyle and the one flanking it to the west.

> *portal:* The one mentioned above. A vestibule in the southern part of the west wing led from the "west-terrace 1" to the peristyle.

> *audience/council/court hall:* Perhaps the central hall in the eastern wing (7 x 11 = 77 m²), although a larger hall placed in the badly preserved north wing seems more likely.

> *reception hall/area:* Perhaps the large courtyard flanking the main one to the west served this purpose.

Social:

> *banqueting hall/s:* Many of the rooms were probably banqueting rooms, having asymmetrically placed doorways, although no other characteristics have been noticed.

Religious:

> *temple for the tutelary deity:* —?, but the temple of Artemis Iolkia in the Sacred Agora was situated close to the palace *1.

> *dynastic sanctuary:* —

> *mausoleum:* —, the kings were buried in Aigai.

Defensive:

> *precinct walls:* —, included in the city's defences and connected to the citadel towards the west.

> *citadel/akra:* The main palace, having towers in the corners, formed a kind of tetrapyrgion. The large citadel in connection with the palace had an area of 10 ha.

> *barracks/arsenal:* In the citadel.

Administrative:

> *offices:* ?, probably in the Sacred Agora.

> *archives:* ?

> *treasury:* X?

Service: Probably the courtyard to the west, placed at a lower level than the main palace and thus not blocking the view from it.

> *storerooms:* X?

> *kitchens, etc.:* X?

> *servants' quarters:* X?

Residential for the king/governor and his family: Probably the east wing, with two storeys and rooms in two rows, as well as the second storey of the south and west wing.

    bedrooms: X?

    bathrooms: X?

    private dining-rooms: X?, one might imagine that the top storey of the towers, which probably had three storeys, was used for this purpose. Large halls are concerned, since the towers measured 12.75 x 12.75 m = c. 163 m².

    harem: —

Residential for the court/guests:

    apartments: X?, perhaps the eastern wing.

"Public":

    gymnasium/palaestra: —

    library: ?

    theatre: —

    hippodrome: —

Recreational:

    gardens: Perhaps one in the main peristyle.

    parks: —

    pavilions: —

    (swimming-)pools: —

Miscellaneous: Perhaps a royal heroon situated at some distance from the palace above the theatre on the acropolis was for the city's founder, Demetrius Poliorchetes *2.

State of preservation: Generally preserved poorly or not at all.

Time of excavation: 1970s and 1980s.

Date and period of use

The present palace was built by Philip V *3, upon older palaces and other buildings, perhaps from Demetrius Poliorchetes' reign *4. Antiochus III held court in Demetrias *5. Destroyed around 168 BC, part of it was used thereafter for other purposes.

References

Written sources: *1: *IG* V, 2 no. 367, XI, 2 nos. 1105-1106; *2: Plut. *Demetr.* 53.2-3; *3: Livy, 35.31.9; *4: Strab. 9.5.15 (431); *5: Diod. 29.2.

Modern literature: Milojcic & Theocharis 1976 (P); Marzolff 1976, 1979, 1987 (all Pr), 1996.

This volume: pp. 93ff; Figs. 47-48.

CAT. NO. 14

Traditional name: Palace of Pergamon.

Kingdom: Attalid kingdom.

Locality: Pergamon.

Category: Royal palace.

Situation: On the acropolis.

Area: The entire *basileia:* c. 30.000 m²; Peristyle IV: 30 x 35 m = 1,050 m²; yard: 11.45 x 13.45 m = 154 m²; Peristyle V: c. 52 x 46.5 m = 2,420 m²; yard: 22.5 x 22.5 m = c. 506 m².

General characteristics: The palace area consists of an agglomeration of many different buildings.

Architecture

Building technique and material: Built in ashlars in local stone and sun-dried brick.

Façade: No monumental façade to the palace proper.

    gateway: Portal to the acropolis and the palace, monumental.

Courtyards/forecourts: Two courtyard buildings, one for official purposes, V, one for residence, IV.

    peristyles/order of columns: Both courtyards had peristyles; in Peristyle V, with two storeys, the lower one was in the Doric style.

Functions

Official/ceremonial: Peristyle V, richly decorated.

    portal: Not preserved, probably to the south, with staircase.

    audience/council/court hall: The large hall in the north wing (14.8 x 9 m = c. 133 m²).

    reception hall/area: Probably the Temenos of Athena Nicophoros with its monumental propylon was used for this purpose (the court measures 72 x 40 m = 2,880 m²).

Social:

    banqueting hall/s: One in the north wing, beside the audience hall, and at least the large hall in the east wing; finally probably some or all the rooms in the south wing.

Religious:

    temple for the tutelary deity: A small sanctuary of the divine ancestor of the Attalid dynasty, Dionysus, was in the east wing of Peristyle V. Also, there was a temple of this god on the lower terrace of the theatre.

    dynastic sanctuary: The exedra reused in the Trajaneum, but dedicated by Attalos II, was perhaps for dynastic statues.

    mausoleum: —

Defensive:

    precinct walls: Walls surrounding the acropolis.

    citadel/akra: The entire acropolis, but especially its northern part constituted a citadel.

    barracks/arsenal: Situated in the northern part of the acropolis hill, with separate defences. Also there were barracks for the guards north and south of the palace buildings ("Baugruppe" VI).

Administrative: Perhaps rooms in the Temenos of Athena.

    offices: X?

    archives: Rooms behind the portico in the Temenos of Athena.

    treasury: X?

Service: Probably now beneath the Trajaneum.
  storerooms: X?
  kitchens, etc.: X?
  servants' quarters: X?
Residential for the king/governor and his family: Peristyle IV.
  bedrooms: In the eastern wing, and on the second storey. One of them was furnished
  with a collection of Archaic statues *2.
  bathrooms: X?
  private dining-rooms: The easternmost room in the north wing and the east wing.
  harem: —
Residential for the court/guests:
  apartments: X?
"Public":
  gymnasium/palaestra: —
  library: In the Temenos of Athena, behind the northern portico *3. It was offered to
  Cleopatra by Mark Antony *4.
  theatre: In connection with the acropolis, on the western slope.
  hippodrome: —
Recreational:
  gardens: Probably in Peristyle IV.
  parks: —
  pavilions: —
  (swimming-)pools: —

Miscellaneous: The palace buildings were richly decorated with First Style wall decoration
partly in stone, and with coloured mosaics. The Royal Heroon was situated just outside the
entrance to the acropolis, as was the Upper Agora.
State of preservation: The palaces proper are very badly preserved.
Time of excavation: 1878-1886.

Date and period of use
Built at the beginning of the 2nd century BC, it was in use at least until 133 BC *1.

References
Written sources: *1: Horace, *Carm.* 2.18.5-6; *2: Pausanias, 9.35.6-7; *3: Strab. 13.4.2
(624); *4: Plut. *Ant.* 58.5.
Modern literature: Kawerau & Wiegand 1930 (P); Radt 1988, 83-105; Hoepfner 1990,
279ff; 1996, 17ff.
This volume: pp. 102ff; Figs. 52-57; Pls. 20-21.

Cat. no. 15

Traditional name: Palace of Antiochia.

Kingdom Seleucid.
Locality: Antiochia.
Category: Royal palace.
Situation: On an island in the River Orontes *3-4, 6-8.
Area: probably around 25 ha., c. 500 x 500 m.
General characteristics: The palace probably consisted of many isolated buildings *1-2, 6-8. Known only from written sources covering a long period.

Architecture
Building technique and material: ?
Façade: ?
   gateway: Probably a monumental propylon *6-8.
Courtyards/forecourts: ?
   peristyles/order of columns: ?

Functions
Official/ceremonial: Perhaps the Basileios Stoa *6-8.
   portal: A monumental propylon is mentioned *6-8.
   audience/council/court hall: X?
   reception hall/area: X?
Social:
   banqueting hall/s: X?
Religious:
   temple for the tutelary deity: X?
   dynastic sanctuary: X?
   mausoleum: ?
Defensive:
   precinct walls: The palace was surrounded by walls *1-2.
   citadel/akra: —?
   barracks/arsenal: X?
Administrative:
   offices: X?
   archives: X?
   treasury: X?
Service:
   storerooms: X?
   kitchens, etc.: X?
   servants' quarters: X?
Residential for the king and his family: Oikoi are mentioned *6-8.
   bedrooms: X?
   bathrooms: X?
   private dining-rooms: X?
   harem: —

Residential for the court/guests:
  apartments: X?
"Public:
  gymnasium/palaestra: ?
  library: A library, probably in the palace, existed already during the reign of Antiochus
  II *9.
  theatre: ?
  hippodrome: A hippodrome has been traced on the island, connected with the palace *3-4.
Recreational:
  gardens: ?
  parks: Probably the various buildings were scattered in a large park, since a quarter of
  the island was perhaps occupied by the palace *6-8.
  pavilions: X?
  (swimming-)pools: ?

State of preservation: Unknown.
Time of excavation: Not excavated.

Date and period of use
Built by Antiochus I, and used by all his successors including the Romans. It is mentioned
in connection with the revolt of the Antiochenes against Demetrius II in 145 BC *1-2. The
palace was restored together with the hippodrome by the Roman proconsul, Marcius Rex
in 67 BC *3; it was still in use during the reign of Trajan *4, and Alexander Severus *5,
and also in late Antiquity, as it is mentioned in sources from the 5th-6th cent. AD *6-8.

References
Written sources: *1:I Macc. 11.45-47; *2: Joseph. *AJ* 13.5.3 (137); *3: Malalas, 225.8; *4:
Cass. Dio, 68.25.5; 5: S.H.A. *Alex. Sev.* 54.6; *6: Liban. *Or.* 11.206; *7: Theodoret, *Eccl.
Hist.* 4.26.1-3; *8: Evagrius, 2.12; *9: *Corpus Inscr. Indicarum* I, p. 48.
Modern literature: Downey 1961, 640-50 for the sources for this palace; Campbell 1934
(the hippodrome).
This volume: pp. 112ff; Fig. 58.

CAT. NO. 16

Traditional name: Redoubt Palace.
Kingdom: Seleucid.
Locality: Dura Europos.
Category: Governor's palace, for the *strategos* of Dura.
Situation: On a high terrace towering over the ravine, on the acropolis, included in the Hip-
podamian city plan.
Area: Palace proper: 36.5 x 38 m = 1,387 m^2; courtyard: 17.1 x 12.1 m = c. 207 m^2.
General characteristics: The palace consisted of one compact courtyard house.

Architecture

Building technique and material: Built in ashlars in local stone.

Façade: No monumental façade. The palace was reached by way of a forecourt.

    gateway: ?

Courtyards/forecourts: The main palace had a courtyard, and a forecourt flanked the palace to the south.

    peristyles/order of columns: No peristyle in the main building, only columns in antis. The forecourt may have had a peristyle.

Functions

Official/ceremonial: Probably the southern wing.

    portal: The main entrance, a "bent" entrance from the forecourt, led to the courtyard.

    audience/council/court hall: A "broad room" behind an ante-room in the south wing (10.47 x 6.57 m = c. 69 m^2).

    reception hall/area: Probably the forecourt to the south.

Social:

    banqueting hall/s: Probably the room east of the audience hall, and the "broad room" to the west.

Religious:

    temple for the tutelary deity: —, but the Temple of Zeus Melichios, added in a second phase, was probably identical with Zeus Olympios, a tutelary deity of the Seleucids, especially Antiochus Epiphanes.

    dynastic sanctuary: —

    mausoleum: —

Defensive:

    precinct walls: Placed on a terrace inside the town's defences.

    citadel/akra: The acropolis had the appearance of a fortress.

    barracks/arsenal: —, but guard rooms near the entrance to the palace were present.

Administrative:

    offices: ?

    archives: ?

    treasury: ?

Service: In the east wing.

    storerooms: ?

    kitchens, etc.: X?

    servants' quarters: X?

Residential for the king/governor and his family: The strategos may have lived on the ground floor, while the family lived on the first floor over part of the palace.

    bedrooms: X?

    bathrooms: X?

    private dining-rooms: ?

    harem: —

Residential for the court/guests:

apartments: —?
"Public":
  gymnasium/palaestra: —
  library: —
  theatre: —
  hippodrome: —
Recreational:
  gardens: —
  parks: —
  pavilions: —
  (swimming-)pools: —

State of preservation: Partly well preserved.
Time of excavation: 1930s.

Date and period of use

Built in the middle of the 3rd century BC, it was restored in the first half of the 2nd century BC, when the temple with the large portico was added.

References

Written sources: —
Modern literature: Dura Europos Rep. IV, 1933, 21-27 (Pr); Rostovtzeff 1938, 35-37; Hoepfner & Schwandner 1986, 220ff; Mouton 1992.
This volume: pp. 116ff; Figs. 59-61.

CAT. NO. 17

Traditional name: Citadel Palace.
Kingdom: Seleucid.
Locality: Dura Europos.
Category: Governor's palace.
Situation: In the citadel.
Area: The southern peristyle court: 47 x 27 m = 1,269 m^2; peristyle proper: 20 x 20 m = 400 m^2.
General characteristics: The palace consisted of a courtyard house and probably a large forecourt.

Architecture

Building technique and material: Built in ashlars in local stone.
Façade: Probably no monumental façade.
  gateway: To the citadel.
Courtyards/forecourts: One peristyle court surrounded by rooms and perhaps a large forecourt to the north.

peristyles/order of columns: A Doric peristyle in the southern part, cistern in the centre.

Functions

Official/ceremonial: The southern and western wings of the peristyle.

portal: Probably this part was reached from the large corridor to the north, with entrance from the west.

audience hall: The southern large hall with columns in antis and internal columns (9.5 x 6.8 m = c. 65 m²).

reception hall/area: Perhaps the reconstructed large forecourt to the north.

Social:

banqueting hall/s: Probably the audience hall and/or the large room flanking it to the east.

Religious:

temple for the tutelary deity: —

dynastic sanctuary: —

mausoleum: —

Defensive:

precinct walls: Situated in the citadel.

citadel/akra: Ditto.

barracks/arsenal: ?

Administrative:

offices: ?

archives: ?

treasury: ?

Service:

storerooms: X?

kitchens, etc.: X?

servants' quarters: X?

Residential for the king/governor and his family: Probably the eastern wing, which, however, is not preserved, or the western one, where the walls were decorated with paintings.

bedrooms: X?

bathrooms: X?

private dining-rooms: ?

Harem: —

Residential for the court/guests:

apartments: —?

"Public":

gymnasium/palaestra: —

library: —

theatre: —

hippodrome: —

Recreational:

gardens: —

pavilions: —
parks: —
(swimming-)pools: —

Miscellaneous: There has been some discussion as to how the northern part of the palace should be reconstructed.
State of preservation: Only partly preserved.
Time of excavation: Late 1920s.

Date and period of use
Built in the middle of the 3rd century BC, it was totally rebuilt in the first half of the 2nd century BC. The function of the earlier building is uncertain.

References
Written sources: —
Modern literature: Dura Europos Rep. II, 12-15, 20-22, 53-57 (Pr); Rostovtzeff 1938, 46f; Downey 1985, 1986.
This volume: pp. 119ff; Figs. 59, 62-63.

CAT. NO. 18

Traditional name: Palace of Nippur.
Kingdom: Seleucid?
Locality: Nippur in Mesopotamia.
Category: Magisterial or perhaps princely palace.
Situation: ?
Area: 52.5 x 52.5 m = 2,756 m².
General characteristics: Compact building with two inner courtyards.

Architecture
Building technique and material: Sun-dried brick.
Façade: To the north, non-monumental.
  gateway: The portal was symmetrically placed with stairs on the north side.
Courtyard/forecourt: One peristyle court, one without peristyle.
  peristyle/order of columns: In the peristyle, the Doric columns were built in tile. The corner columns were heart-shaped.

Functions
Official/ceremonial: The peristyle court.
  portal: A "bent" entrance led to a vestibule with two columns.
  audience hall: The large hall to the south (15 x 12 m = 180 m²), located behind an ante-room probably with two columns in antis and reached by steps.
  reception hall/area: —

Social:

    banqueting hall/s: Probably the main hall also used for audiences.

Religious: An altar was placed outside the anteroom.

    temple for the tutelary deity: —

    dynastic sanctuary: —

    mausoleum: —

Defensive:

    precinct walls: Situated inside the city walls.

    citadel/akra: —

    barracks/arsenal: —

Administrative:

    offices: —?

    archives: ?

    treasury: Probably the small room in the southwest corner of the peristyle court.

Service:

    storerooms: Two rooms to the south flanking the corridor which separated the two courts.

    kitchens, etc.: In the north-western corner of the building.

    servants' quarters: In the north-west area of the building.

Residential for the king/governor and his family: Placed around a small courtyard.

    bedrooms: The one belonging to the master was probably situated in connection with the private audience hall (an "andron complex"). Also some rooms around the main court may have served this purpose.

    bathrooms: In connection with the kitchen.

    private dining-rooms: Probably the main hall of the small courtyard, reached by steps.

    harem: This part may have been reserved for the harem.

Residential for the court/guests:

    apartments: —?

"Public":

    gymnasium/palaestra: —

    library: —

    theatre: —

    hippodrome: —

Recreational:

    gardens: —

    parks: —

    pavilions: —

    (swimming-)pools: —

State of preservation: The plan is only partly preserved.

Time of excavation: Around 1900.

Date and period of use

Uncertain, probably built around 250 BC.

References

Written sources: —
Modern literature: Fischer 1904 (P); Hopkins 1972, 32ff; Lauter 1986, 281f.
This volume: pp. 121ff; Figs. 64-65.

CAT. NO. 19

Traditional name: Palace of Aï Khanoum.
Kingdom: Seleucid, later Bactrian.
Locality: Aï Khanoum in Bactria, present-day Afghanistan.
Category: Governor's, later royal palace.
Situation: In the southern part of the town.
Area: 250 x 350 m = 87,500 m²; large forecourt: 137 x 108 m = 14,796 m².
General characteristics: The palace proper consisted of one compact building, but laid in
a park with annexes.

Architecture

Building technique and material: Sun-dried brick.
Façade: Marked only by the propylon.
   gateway: Monumental portal to the palace area from the main street, a monumental
   approach via an avenue to the propylon leading to the forecourt.
Courtyards/forecourts: Large forecourt and a smaller courtyard, between treasury and
residence both had peristyles. A smaller forecourt, to "the king's house", had none.
   peristyles/order of columns: The peristyle in the large forecourt with 118 columns had
   Corinthian capitals but Persian bases.

Functions

Official/ceremonial: The part just south of the large forecourt, with a hypostyle hall leading
to a "broad room".
   portal: Monumental propylon to the large forecourt from the avenue.
   audience/council/court hall: The large hypostyle hall (27.5 x 18.75 m = c. 516 m²), and
   the "broad room" behind it (17 x 26.5 m = c. 451 m²). Perhaps the halls of the two
   apartments to the south served this purpose as well.
   reception hall/area: Probably the forecourt.
Social:
   banqueting hall/s: Probably the large "broad room". Large banquets could take place
   in the forecourt. Also the halls of the two eastern apartments might have had this function. People dined reclining on rugs, therefore there is no sign of "kline bands".
Religious:
   temple for the tutelary deity: Perhaps the "Temple à Redans" close to the palace.
   dynastic sanctuary: ?
   mausoleum: Perhaps the one just north of the avenue.

Defensive:

precinct walls: —, placed inside the city walls, no independent defences. Nor was it raised on a platform.

citadel/akra: —, the citadel on top of the mountain served the whole city.

barracks/arsenal: —, undoubtedly in the citadel, but with rooms for guards in the palace.

Administrative: The western part of the building north of the western peristyle, and the unexcavated area east of the main palace.

offices: Probably east of the excavated area, towards the main street.

archives: In the rooms added to the north of the western peristyle in the last phase.

treasury: Ditto.

Service:

storerooms: X?, probably located east of the excavated area.

kitchens, etc.: E.g. in the western two apartments.

servants' quarters: X?

Residential for the king/governor and his family: The part flanking the official part to the south and west, including the apartment with the large forecourt, "the king's house" and the westernmost residence, "the house of the royal family".

bedrooms: Ditto.

bathrooms: A large official bathroom west of the audience hall, probably for the king/governor (an "andron complex"). Private bathrooms in the houses mentioned above.

private dining-rooms: Halls in the two eastern apartments and in "the house of the royal family".

harem: "The house of the royal family" (late phase).

Residential for the court/guests:

apartments: X?

"Public:

gymnasium/palaestra: A gymnasium close by, perhaps it also had another function.

library: North of the western peristyle, south of the treasury.

theatre: ?, but the theatre of the city was located just on the other side of the main street from the palace.

hippodrome: —

Recreational:

gardens: In the gymnasium?

parks: Probably a large park to the west, towards the river, and perhaps also to the south.

pavilions: ?

(swimming-)pools: A huge swimming-pool placed in this park, 41.5 x 44 m, depth 2.1 m. It had the same orientation as the main palace.

Miscellaneous: The Heroon of Kineas close to the palace might also have had connotations of a seat for the ruler cult.

State of preservation: The plan is quite clear.

Time of excavation: 1970s.

Date and period of use

First built in the early 3rd century BC, at the same time as the colony, for the Seleucid governor, to which period belonged only the large forecourt and the hypostyle hall and the baths. Taken over and much enlarged by the local dynasty around 150 BC, it was destroyed by the locals after the Greek population left in 145 BC.

References

Written sources: —

Modern literature: Bernard *et al.* 1973 (P); Bernard 1976, 1981; Rapin 1992 (treasury) (P).

This volume: pp. 123ff; Figs. 66-68.

CAT. NO. 20

Traditional name: Palace of Alexandria.

Kingdom: Ptolemaic.

Locality: Alexandria.

Category: Royal palace.

Situation: Placed near the harbour and including the peninsula of Lochias as well as a large part of the city, "District B" *3,*6. Its layout follows that of the city's Hippodamian plan.

Area: All in all around 200 ha., c. 2 km in diam.

General characteristics: The palace consisted of many buildings situated in a large park, probably laid out regularly. It is known only from the written sources.

Architecture

Building technique and material: ?

Façade: ?

   gateway: A large portal and hall, called Chrematistikon Pylon, i.e. used for audiences, is mentioned *1. The palace was reached from one of the main streets of the city, leading directly to the Lochias, i.e. a monumental approach to the palace must be envisaged.

Courtyards/forecourts: A large courtyard with a peristyle, Megiston Peristylon is mentioned *1.

   peristyles/order of columns: The reference to a large peristyle implies the existence of many *1.

Functions

Official/ceremonial: The Chrematistikon Pylon and undoubtedly the Megiston Peristylon were used for official purposes.

   portal: The Chrematistikon Pylon *1

   audience/council/court hall: The Chrematistikon Pylon was, as the word says, used for audiences *1, and this audience hall was probably situated in connection with the Megiston Peristylon. See in general *12.

   reception hall/area: The courtyard of the Megiston Peristylon was used for large receptions; a *bema*, or tribune, was present. Also public buildings could be used for receptions *11.

Social:

banqueting hall/s: A banqueting hall is mentioned e.g. in the *Letter of "Aristeas"* in connection with the Septuaginta project *13, and in connection with Caesar's visit to Alexandria. The latter hall is described as being decorated with marble and precious stones, and with a wooden roof *2. Banquets also took place in the courtyard of the citadel, where Ptolemy II's Pavilion was raised *8, and undoubtedly in the park.

Religious:

temple for the tutelary deity: X?, but a Temple of Poseidon was probably present, as was the Sanctuary of Adonis *7, and also Isis was worshipped there *19.

dynastic sanctuary: Perhaps the Sema had this function as well *3.

mausoleum: The Sema, i.e. the Tomb of Alexander and the Ptolemies *3.

Defensive:

precinct walls: The large park was undoubtedly surrounded by a wall.

citadel/akra: There was a citadel on Lochias, the Akra *1.

It contained a large courtyard. Below it and the inner palaces was the king's harbour *3,*8.

barracks/arsenal: The palace guard had their quarters just outside the Chrematistikon Pylon, in *skenai* *1. Also arsenals are mentioned *9.

Administrative:

offices: X?

archives: X?

treasury: The treasury is mentioned in the sources *14.

Service:

storerooms: X?

kitchens, etc.: X?

servants' quarters: X?

Residential for the king/governor and his family: Probably in peristyles in the park (inner palaces, *oikeseis* *3), and on the island of Antirhodes *1-2.

bedrooms: X?

bathrooms: X?

private dining-rooms: Probably the pavilions, or *diaitai*, in the park, were also used for this purpose *3.

harem: —

Residential for the court/guests:

apartments: *Katalumata* are mentioned near the Akra *5, *15.

"Public":

gymnasium/palaestra: A *palaistra* is mentioned *1. The large Gymnasium of Alexandria might have been placed in close relation to the basileia as well *3,*11.

library: The famous library was placed in relation to the Museion *18, which consisted of a portico, an exedra and a dining-hall for the users *3 and *16-17.

theatre: The theatre could be reached from the palace directly via a *syrinx*, a corridor
*1,*5.
hippodrome: —?
Recreational:
  gardens: X?
  parks: The palace was placed in a large park, laid out regularly. Here, birds were bred
  *11.
  pavilions: Pavilions (*diaitai*) are mentioned in the park *3.
  (swimming-)pools: The Maiandros, probably a canal, may have had this function also.

Miscellaneous: Of other institutions mentioned in connection with this enormous basileia
were the Paneion, an artificial vantage point, and the Court of Justice *3.
State of preservation: Unknown.
Time of excavation: Not excavated.

Date and period of use
The palace was commissioned and laid out by Alexander *4, and each Ptolemaic king built
onto it *3. It is described as it appeared in 203 BC, in connection with Agathocles' activities
*1. During the reign of the last Ptolemaic queen, Cleopatra VII *2, we have Caesar's report
on his stay there *5. It was also used by the Romans.

References
Written sources: *1: Polyb. 15.25.3, 15.28.4, 15.30.6, 15.31.2-4; *2: Lucan, *BC* 10.111ff;
*3: Strab. 17.1.8 (793-794); *4: Diod. 1.50, 17.52; *5: Caes. *BC* 3.112.3; *6: Pliny, *HN*
5.62; *7: Theocr. *Id.* 15; *8: Athen. 5.196-197; *9: Philo, *In Flacc.* 92; *10: Athen. 14.654c;
*11: Plut. *Ant.* 54.3-4; *12: "Aristeas" 81 and 172-186; *13: "Aristeas" 180-300; *14:
"Aristeas" 33, 80; *15: "Aristeas" 181; *16: e.g. *Corpus Inscr. Indicarum* I, p. 48; *17:
Athen. 5. 203e; *18: Athen. 1.22d; *19: Plut. *Ant.* 72-74.
Modern literature: Adriani 1932-33a, 1932-33b; Hoepfner 1971; Fraser 1972; La Rocca
1986; Hoepfner 1990; McKenzie 1990, 61ff; Grimm 1996a and b.
This volume: pp. 130ff; Fig. 69.

CAT. NO. 21

Traditional name: Araq el Emir/Tyrus (area), Qasr el Abd (main palace).
Kingdom: Seleucid.
Locality: Araq el Emir/Tyrus near Amman.
Category: Princely palace.
Situation: In a private domain. The main palace was placed on a large terrace surrounded
by an artificial lake, or moat.
Area: Main palace: 37.5 x 19 m = c. 713 m²; the terrace: 46 x 67 m = 3,082 m².
General characteristics: Isolated buildings situated on a terrace in a large enclosed park

of which only one, the Baris, is well preserved, others being known from written sources *1.

Architecture
Building technique and material: Built in ashlars in very large local stones.
Façade: The monumental north façade of the Qasr el Abd, or the Baris, had a pavilion on top of the portal and was decorated with animals in high relief.
   gateway: A monumental propylon with Grecian decoration led into the park.
Courtyards/forecourts: None in the main palace, but *aulai* in the park are mentioned, probably, but not certainly indicating peristylar houses *1.
   peristyles/order of columns: ?

Functions
Official/ceremonial: Main palace, the Baris *1.
   portal: Monumental portal and vestibule from the north, two columns in antis.
   audience/council/court hall: Probably the large hall in the upper floor (c. 12 x 10 m = 120 m²), decorated with Corinthian three-quarter columns, reached by means of a stair-case from the vestibule, which could perhaps also be used for audiences.
   reception hall/area: —?
Social:
   banqueting hall/s: Probably the inner rooms in the upper floor, including the large hall.
Religious:
   temple for the tutelary deity: —
   dynastic sanctuary: —
   mausoleum: —
Defensive:
   precinct walls: The park was surrounded by walls, and the main palace by an artificial lake functioning as a moat.
   citadel/akra: —
   barracks/arsenal: ?, but probably the guard was placed in or near the vestibule.
Administrative:
   offices: —
   archives: ?
   treasury: ?
Service: In the ground floor of the Baris.
   storerooms: Ditto.
   kitchens, etc.: Ditto.
   servants' quarters: X?
Residential for the king/governor and his family: Caves with these functions are mentioned, and also the *aulai* in the park *1, of which one, the Plastered Building, has been found.
   bedrooms: I.a. in the caves *1.
   bathrooms: X?

private dining-rooms: I.a. in the caves *1.
harem: —
Residential for the court/guests:
  apartments: —?
"Public":
  gymnasium/palaestra: —
  library: —
  theatre: —
  hippodrome: —
Recreational:
  gardens: ?
  parks: The palace was set in a large park, *paradeisos* *1.
  pavilions: The first floor of the Baris had the appearance of a pavilion.
  (swimming-)pools: A large lake (c. 270 x 150 m, depth 2-3 m) surrounded the main palace *1.

State of preservation: The main palace is rather well preserved.
Time of excavation: 1976-1987.

Date and period of use
Built by Hyrcanus the Tobiad at the beginning of the 2nd century BC *1, it was never finished.

References
Written sources: *1: Joseph. *AJ* 12.4.1 (228-236).
Modern literature: Will 1982, 1987 (both Pr). 1991(P), and 1996; Lapp 1963 (The Plastered Building) (Pr); and Netzer 1997, who draws attention to the impression given by the palace's reflection in the surrounding lake.
This volume: pp. 138ff; Figs. 73-76.

CAT. NO. 22

Traditional name: Palazzo delle Colonne.
Kingdom: Ptolemaic.
Locality: Ptolemais in Cyrenaica.
Category: Governor's palace.
Situation: In the city, occupying one insula, incorporated in the Hippodamian city plan.
Area: 90.4 x 36.5 m = c. 3,300 m^2; main courtyard: 24.1 x 28.9 m = 697 m^2.
General characteristics: A compact palace was a necessity because of its situation in the city, therefore also no parks.

Architecture
Building technique and material: In ashlars in local stone.

Façade: To the east, facing the street, non-monumental.

    gateway: Monumental, in two storeys, pillars in antis.

Courtyards/forecourts: A large main courtyard and a much smaller courtyard for service, etc.

    peristyles/order of columns: The main courtyard had a Rhodian peristyle with two storeys, Ionic below (except on the north side, Corinthian), Corinthian above. The Doric peristyle of the small courtyard also had two storeys.

Functions

Official/ceremonial: The large peristyle court.

    portal: "Bent" entrance from the street, entering the side of the peristyle via a large vestibule.

    audience/council/court hall: The large Egyptian oecus had this function (17.6 x 12.9 m = c. 227 m²).

    reception hall/area: Ditto, and perhaps the garden; speeches could be made from the first floor balcony.

Social:

    banqueting hall/s: In the south wing, two large halls were used for this purpose: room 11 (see Fig. 78) in axis with the peristyle and with the oecus (9 x 12.6 m = c. 113 m²), and room 10 (8.25 x 14.1 m = 116 m²), reached via an ante-room with two columns in antis. Also the Egyptian oecus might have been used for banquets.

Religious:

    temple for the tutelary deity: —

    dynastic sanctuary: The apses of the large peristyle might have had some kind of cultic function, especially if the excavated statues of dignitaries from the Ptolemaic court stood here.

    mausoleum: —

Defensive:

    precinct walls: Placed inside the city walls.

    citadel/akra: —

    barracks/arsenal: —

Administrative: Perhaps some of the rooms centred around the small Doric peristyle.

    offices: Ditto.

    archives: ?

    treasury: ?

Service: Probably some rooms on the ground floor of the large peristyle, in the eastern part of the house and around the small peristyle.

    storerooms: In the extensive cellars.

    kitchens, etc.: E.g. room 6 in the east wing of the main peristyle.

    servants' quarters: In the north-eastern part of the house.

Residential for the king/governor and his family:

    bedrooms: For the master the south-westernmost room of the main peristyle (14). For the rest of the family probably the first floor or the main peristyle was used.

bathrooms: The fine bath suite is a later addition, probably Flavian, but one must have been present also originally.

private dining-rooms: Probably the small dining-room in the west wing of the main peristyle (room 18).

harem: —

Residential for the court/guests:

apartments: X?

"Public":

gymnasium/palaestra: —

library: —

theatre: —

hippodrome: —

Recreational: There was access to a large terrace above the northern part of the house.

gardens: In the main peristyle, a formal garden.

parks: —

pavilions: —

(swimming-)pools: In the garden of the main peristyle (16.4 x 4.6 m).

Miscellaneous: The large number of architectural fragments have enabled a reconstruction of the main peristyle with two storeys, a highly experimental architecture.

State of preservation: Rather well preserved.

Time of excavation: 1937-42.

Date and period of use

Probably built in the early 1st century BC for the Ptolemaic governor, it was reused by the Roman governor and rebuilt, *i.a.* with a bath building, in Flavian times. Also reused probably by Byzantine governors. Destroyed by an earthquake.

References

Written sources: —

Modern literature: Pesce 1950 (P); Lauter 1971; McKenzie 1990, 75ff.

This volume: pp. 146ff; Figs. 77-80.

CAT. NO. 23

Traditional name: Hasmonean Winter Palace of Jericho.

Kingdom: Hasmonean.

Locality: Jericho.

Category: Royal palace.

Situation: Set in a park adjacent to a large agricultural domain (50 ha.), but near the town.

Area: The Palace of Hyrcanus I: 60 x 50 m = 3,000 m^2; the Fortress Palace of Jannaeus: c. 1,500 m^2; the Twin Palaces, each 25 x 25 m = 625 m^2.

General characteristics: The buildings and structures are situated in the park and were built successively during the Hasmonean period.

Architecture
Building technique and material: Ashlars (tower), and sun-dried brick.
Façade: ?
 gateway: ?
Courtyards/forecourts: Hyrcanus' Palace had a court surrounded by corridors and rooms; also a court in Jannaeus' Fortress. The Twin Palaces had internal courtyards without peristyles.
 peristyles/order of columns: Perhaps there was a peristyle in the Jannaeus' Fortress (foundations).

Functions
Official/ceremonial: Probably the southern part of the ground floor of Hyrcanus' Palace.
 portal: There was probably access to this palace from the south-eastern corner, non-monumental.
 audience/council/court hall: Perhaps the large decorated hall.
 reception hall/area: Perhaps the courtyard.
Social:
 banqueting hall/s: The finely decorated hall in Hyrcanus' Palace. Also probably the the large hall, or oecus (perhaps with two columns in antis) from Alexandra's reign, which faced the western garden with swimming-pools, and the pavilion in the southern part of the garden from Jannaeus' reign. The many bathrooms built south of the oecus and from the same time may have connection to the use of this dining-hall.
Religious:
 temple for the tutelary deity: —
 dynastic sanctuary: —
 mausoleum: —
Defensive:
 precinct walls: ?
 citadel/akra: Hyrcanus' Palace was built on a hill, but was protected only by one tower. Jannaeus' fortified Palace was built upon it, the old palace having been filled in to form a terrace and surrounded by a moat. Jericho was protected by two fortresses, Tryx and Tauros, mentioned by Strabo *3 (probably today's Cypros and Nuseib Dag).
 barracks/arsenal: ?
Administrative:
 offices: ?
 archives: —
 treasury: —
Service:
 storerooms: There are storerooms to the east of the recreational area from a late Hasmonean phase.

kitchens, etc.: X?

servants' quarters: X?

Residential for the king/governor and his family: Under Hyrcanus I, the north wing of the ground floor and the first floor. Under Alexander Jannaeus, in the fortress. The Twin Palaces were probably primarily residential.

bedrooms: X?

bathrooms: In Hyrcanus' Palace were both a Jewish-style and a Greek-style bathroom, ditto in the Twin Palaces.

private dining-rooms: In the Twin Palaces the large halls with two columns in antis in the south wing.

harem: —

Residential for the court/guests:

apartments: —?

"Public":

gymnasium/palaestra: —

library: —

theatre: —

hippodrome: —

Recreational:

gardens: A large enclosed garden (70 x 60 m) was laid out to the north in the time of Alexander Jannaeus. In connection with the Twin Palaces were two enclosed gardens with swimming-pools.

parks: There were parks both to the east and the west of the main palace.

pavilions: In the eastern park was a raised pavilion, (21 x 17 m). There was also a pavilion in relation to the western swimming-pool complex, and one in the western Twin Palace's garden.

(swimming-)pools: In the park to the west of Hyrcanus' Palace were two swimming-pools (8 x 9 m) probably surrounded by porticoes. In the park laid out by Alexander Jannaeus east of this palace were two large swimming-pools (each 18 x 13 m) surrounded by a paved square and a garden. Finally in the Twin Palaces two enclosed gardens with swimming-pools.

Miscellaneous: A fine wall decoration in the First Style without figures has been ascertained.

State of preservation: Partly well preserved.

Time of excavation: 1970s and 1980s.

Date and period of use

Built probably by Hyrcanus I, rebuilt and much enlarged by Alexander Jannaeus, and further enlarged by Queen Alexandra *1-2. It was used at least until the fall of the Hasmonean dynasty, and destroyed by the earthquake of 31 BC *4.

References

Written sources: *1: Joseph. *AJ* 15.3.3 (53-56); *BJ* 1.6.6 (138-140); *2: Pliny, *NH* 12.115-

118, 13.44-46; *3: Strab. 16.2.40 (763); *4: Joseph. *AJ* 15.5.2 (121-122).
Modern literature: Netzer 1975a, 1977a (both Pr), 1982, 1986, 1989, 1990, 1996; Netzer *et al.* forthcoming (P).
This volume: pp. 155ff; Figs. 83-85; Pls. 24-26.

CAT. NO. 24

Traditional name: Casa del Fauno.
Kingdom: Roman empire.
Locality: Pompeii.
Category: Private palace.
Situation: In the northern quarter (Reg. VI), filling an entire insula.
Area: C. 33.5 x 87.7 m = c. 2,940 m².
General characteristics: The house consisted of two atria and two peristyle courts.

Architecture
Building technique and material: *Opus incertum* and *opus quadratum* in tufa.
Façade: Non-monumental, towards the street.
   gateway: The main door led to a finely decorated small vestibule and from there to the main *atrium*.
Courtyards/forecourts: Of the two peristyles, the central one was surrounded by rooms, the one behind it almost without rooms.
   peristyles/order of columns: In the central peristyle, Doric columns, later replaced by Ionic ones, in the large one behind, Doric columns. A small order in Ionic half-columns probably belonged to the first floor, perhaps in the Tuscan atrium.

Functions
Official/ceremonial:
   portal: The aforementioned vestibule and porch to the street.
   audience/council/court hall: The main atrium (16.5 x 10 m = 165 m²) and perhaps the *tablinum* (6 x 6 m = 36 m²).
   reception hall/area: The main atrium.
Social:
   banqueting hall/s: Several triclinia facing the central peristyle and also the large one behind it.
Religious:
   temple for the tutelary deity: —
   dynastic sanctuary: —, but a *lararium* is preserved in the small vestibule.
   mausoleum: —
Defensive:
   precinct walls: —, placed in a walled city.
   citadel/akra: —
   barracks/arsenal: —

Administrative:
  offices: —
  archives: —
  treasury: —
Service: Around the small atrium and along the east side of the central peristyle.
  storerooms: X?
  kitchens, etc.: X
  servants' quarters: Ditto.
residential for the king/governor/owner and his family: The tetrastyle atrium and part of the peristyles.
  bedrooms: On the first floor of the tetrastyle atrium and perhaps around the Tuscan atrium.
  bathrooms: In the eastern wing of the central peristyle.
  private dining-rooms: The same triclinia as those mentioned above.
  harem: —
Residential for the court/guests:
  apartments: ?
"Public":
  gymnasium/palaestra: —
  library: —
  theatre: —
  hippodrome: —
Recreational:
  gardens: In both peristyles.
  parks: —
  pavilions: —
  (swimming-)pools: —

Miscellaneous: The house was finely decorated, originally in the First Style and with polychrome mosaics, of which the Alexander Mosaic is famous. Façade architecture with Ionic half-columns has been found, albeit *ex situ.*
State of preservation: Very well preserved.
Time of excavation: 1830-32, 1961-63.

Date and period of use
Built around 180 BC and restored and enlarged with a second peristyle court around 100 BC, it was destroyed in 79 AD.

References
Written sources: —
Modern literature: Mau 1908, 300ff (with earlier literature); Hoffmann 1978 and 1996.
This volume: pp. 166ff; Fig. 87.

CAT. NO. 25

Traditional name: Casa di Augusto, Domus Augusta/i.
Kingdom: Roman empire.
Locality: Rome.
Category: Royal palace.
Situation: On the Palatine, raised above the city.
Area: The whole complex: c. 150 x 80 m = 12,000 m²; the main palace: c. 55 x 84 m = 4,620 m² (excl. Casa di Livia).
General characteristics: Placed on a slope with two terraces, great emphasis on a view towards the city.

Architecture

Building technique and material: Opus quadratum, in tufa.
Façade: Probably two façades, one towards the Palatine, one towards the valley.
  gateway: Though not preserved, the portal is mentioned in the written sources, decorated with a *corona civica* and flanked by laurels *1. It faced the Palatine.
Courtyards/forecourts: Two courtyards in the main palace, one, on the upper terrace, for residence, the lower primarily for official purposes. The Portico of the Danaids also belonged to the palace *14.
  peristyles/order of columns: All three courts had peristyles, and at least the official one had two storeys.

Functions

Official/ceremonial: The lower peristyle, the Sanctuary of Apollo, and the Portico of the Danaids.
  portal: See above (gateway). The lower peristyle could be reached partly from the Scalae Caci, partly from the Portico of the Danaids. None of them monumental entrances.
  audience/council/court hall: The main audience hall was probably placed in relation to the entrance and vestibule. In the preserved palace, the large central hall in the northern wing (10.5 x 6.7 m = c. 70 m²) was probably for councils. A hall which could be used for private meetings is mentioned in the sources *2-3. Perhaps this hall was also used as a court room, since the small steps leading to the podium indicate a placing of stools upon it *3,*5. Similar functions could be envisaged for the large marbled hall with niches (10 x 6.6 m = 66 m²) opening with two pilasters to the Portico of the Danaids, as well as for the libraries facing it *6.
  reception hall/area: We know from the written sources *7-8 that the Area Apollinis, i.e. the plaza (35 x 25 m = 875 m²) in front of the temple, was used for this purpose, the emperor sitting in the pronaos of the temple receiving his subjects.
Social:
  banqueting hall/s: Probably the tetrastyle oecus with a later walled-up apse, and halls in the western wing. Perhaps also the large hall facing the Portico of the Danaids could be used for this purpose.

Religious:

   temple for the tutelary deity: The Temple of Apollo placed centrally in the palace *9-10, also used for meetings *8. Later, a Sanctuary of Vesta was added *11-12.

   dynastic sanctuary: —, but originally the Pantheon probably had this function.

   mausoleum: —, Augustus' Mausoleum was placed on the Campus Maximus.

Defensive:

   precinct walls: —, the palace was placed inside the city walls.

   citadel/akra: —

   barracks/arsenal: —

Administrative: During Augustus' reign this function was mostly separated from the palace, and in connection with the Forum.

   offices: X?

   archives: —, in the Tabularium facing the Forum Romanum.

   treasury: —, the *fiscus* was placed in the Temple of Saturn.

Service: Probably *i.a.* the rooms behind the north wing.

   storerooms: X?

   kitchens, etc.: X?

   servants' quarters: X?

Residential for the king/governor and his family: The upper peristyle, a few rooms to the west of the lower peristyle, and probably rooms on the first floor of the lower peristyle.

   bedrooms: I.a. the isolated room on the first floor to the east of the official peristyle.

   bathrooms: X?

   private dining-rooms: X?

   harem: —

Residential for the court/guests:

   apartments: —?

"Public":

   gymnasium/palaestra: —

   library: There were libraries both in connection with the official peristyle, flanking the main hall to the north, and in connection with the Portico of the Danaids, only the latter for "public" use as well as for meetings for the senate, etc. *9-10, *12-13.

   theatre: —

   hippodrome: The Circus Maximus was situated directly below the palace.

Recreational:

   gardens: Probably both the official peristyle and the Portico of the Danaids had gardens.

   parks: —

   pavilions: —

   (swimming-)pools: —

Miscellaneous: The palace was lavishly decorated with Second Style paintings and floors in mosaic and opus sectile. The Portico of the Danaids was at the same time a gallery for sculpture. A heroon for the ruler cult was probably planned by Agrippa in the Pantheon.

State of preservation: Partly well preserved, partly not at all.

Time of excavation: 1956 through the 1960s and 1970s.

Date and period of use

Built by Octavian/Augustus 36-28 BC and used by Augustus *1, *9, burned down in 3 AD and restored *14, of which restoration there is no trace. Perhaps Augustus' immediate successors used it, but they also built palaces in other parts of the Palatine. It burned down again probably in 64 AD, not to be rebuilt, and was filled in and partly built over with Domitian's Palace.

References

Written sources: *1: *Mon. Anc.* 34.2; *2: Cass. Dio, 53.19.3; *3: Sen. *Clem* 1.9; *4: Cass. Dio, 55.33.5; *5: Suet. *Aug.* 33; *6: *POxy.* 25, 2435 verso; *7: Verg. *Aen.* 8.720ff; *8: Joseph. *AJ* 17.11.1 (301), *BJ* 2.2.4 (25), 2.6.1 (81); *9: Cass. Dio, 53.1.3; *10: *Mon. Anc.* 19; *11: Cass. Dio, 54.27.3; *12: Ovid, *Fast.* 4.949-56, *Met.* 15.864-65; *13: Suet. *Aug.* 29.3; *14: Solin. 1.8.
Modern literature: Carettoni 1966-67, 1978, 1983a (all Pr); 1983b, 1988. Cf. Tamm 1963, 46ff; Lauter 1987; Zanker 1983 (Portico of the Danaids); Corbier 1992.
This volume: pp. 171ff; Figs. 91-93; Pl. 27.

CAT. NO. 26

Traditional name: Western Palace.
Kingdom: Herod the Great's.
Locality: Masada.
Category: Royal palace.
Situation: Placed on a fortified hill.
Area: Core Palace: 28 x 24 m = 672 m²; entire complex: 75 x 50 m = 3,750 m².
General characteristics: The palace was compact and was gradually enlarged, with more and more wings.

Architecture

Building technique and material: Opus quadratum in local stone.
façade: To the north, non-monumental.
  gateway: Not very impressive, led in the last phase to a vestibular courtyard.
Courtyards/forecourts: Originally only one courtyard, later enlarged with three for service and one as vestibule.
  peristyles/order of columns: —

Functions

Official/ceremonial: Parts of the Core Palace.
  portal: "Bent" entrance to the north-west.
  audience/council/court hall: The large hall in the southern wing (8.8 x 6 m = c. 53 m²), reached by a vestibule with two columns in antis.

reception hall/area: Perhaps the courtyard.

Social:

  banqueting hall/s: Perhaps the large room in the western wing served this purpose. The rooms in the southern wing could probably be used for dining also.

Religious:

  temple for the tutelary deity: —

  dynastic sanctuary: —

  mausoleum: —

Defensive:

  precinct walls: The palace formed part of a large fortress.

  citadel/akra: Ditto.

  barracks/arsenal: Elsewhere on the hill, but partially also in the north-east and north-west wings.

Administrative: Ditto.

  offices: X?

  archives: ?

  treasury: ?

Service: The wings added to the north, east and west.

  storerooms: Long rooms in the western and southern parts of the final palace.

  kitchens, etc.: Probably in the courtyard to the north.

  servants' quarters: In the northern wings added.

Residential for the king/governor and his family: Part of the Core Palace, primarily the first floor, the north wing and perhaps the south-western rooms, but the king may also have resided in the southern wing. Later the residential function was mostly taken over by the Northern Palace (Cat. 27).

  bedrooms: Probably on the first floor covering the northern part of the palace.

  bathrooms: In the northern wing, both Grecian and Jewish-style baths.

  private dining-rooms: Perhaps the finely decorated room in the western wing.

  harem: —

Residential for the court/guests:

  apartments: The palatial houses spread over the hill and the north-eastern building.

"Public":

  gymnasium/palaestra: —

  library: —

  theatre: —

  hippodrome: —

Recreational:

  gardens: —

  parks: The southern part of the fortress might have been laid out as a large park.

  pavilions: —?

  (swimming-)pools: A very large one was found in this southernmost part of the fortress (12.4 x 18.4 m, depth 2.6 m).

Miscellaneous: Fine decoration, with mosaics and First Style painting.
State of preservation: In general well preserved.
Time of excavation: 1960s.

Date and period of use
Built by Herod the Great early in his reign, the first building phase of Masada being 37-30 BC, to which belong the Core Palace, the palatial buildings on the same model, spread on the hill, and the swimming-pool. The palace was enlarged in another eight building periods, all during Herod's reign. After the building of the Northern Palace (Cat. 27), the Western Palace was used primarily for official purposes, service, and administration.

References
Written sources: —
Modern literature: Yadin 1965 (Pr), 1966; Netzer 1991, 232ff, 599ff (P); Foerster 1995 (P) and 1996.
This volume: pp. 184ff; Figs. 96-98; Pls. 30-32.

CAT. NO. 27

Traditional name: Northern Palace.
Kingdom: Herod the Great's.
Locality: Masada.
Category: Royal palace.
Situation: On a fortified hill.
Area: C. 60 x 18 m =1,080 m^2.
General characteristics: The palace was situated in the northern point of the cliff, on three terraces *1.

Architecture
Building technique and material: Opus quadratum and sun-dried brick.
Façade: Non-monumental.
   gateway: Non-monumental.
Courtyards/forecourts: A forecourt between the palace and the bath building.
   peristyles/order of columns: —

Functions
Official/ceremonial: Both the Western Palace (Cat. 26) and the Northern Palace were used for official purposes, most intimate in the Northern palace.
   portal: Non-monumental.
   audience/council/court hall: Perhaps the lower hall, which, however, was rather difficult to reach (16.5 x 17.5 m = c. 289 m^2).
   reception hall/area: —

Social:

> *banqueting hall/s:* The lower hall, and the pavilion on the middle terrace could probably also be used for minor banquets.

Religious:

> *temple for the tutelary deity:* —
> *dynastic sanctuary:* —
> *mausoleum:* —

Defensive:

> *precinct walls:* The palace was situated in a citadel. In the late Herodian period a wall isolating the palace from the rest of the hill was built.
> *citadel/akra:* The palace formed part of the citadel.
> *barracks/arsenal:* In the citadel.

Administrative: In buildings in the citadel, e.g. probably in the Western Palace.

> *offices:* —?
> *archives:* —?
> *treasury:* —?

Service: Mostly concentrated in the Western Palace, but also present in this palace.

> *storerooms:* Near the palace.
> *kitchens, etc.:* X?
> *servants' quarters:* X?

Residential for the king/governor and his family: The buildings on all three terraces, the habitation being mostly concentrated on the upper terrace, with several rooms centred around a large hall, and a large balcony (diam. 19 m) with a fine view.

> *bedrooms:* On the uppermost terrace.
> *bathrooms:* A Roman-style bath suite is placed in connection with the dining-hall on the lower terrace, but the main baths were the Large "public" Baths south of the upper terrace. Both had miqvaot instead of frigidaria.
> *private dining-rooms:* Probably the large dining-hall in the form of an Egyptian? oecus taking up the whole lower terrace served this purpose, as well as being used for limited official purposes. Also the rotunda on the second terrace probably served this end, being a kind of pavilion.
> *harem:* —

Residential for the court/guests:

> *apartments:* The palatial houses scattered on the terrace.

"Public":

> *gymnasium/palaestra:* —
> *library:* —, but perhaps there was a private library on the middle terrace.
> *theatre:* —
> *hippodrome:* —

Recreational:

> *gardens:* —
> *parks:* The southern part of Masada was perhaps laid out as a park.
> *pavilions:* The rotunda on the second terrace (diam. 13.5 m).

(swimming-)pools: In the southern part of the fortress (12.4 x 18.4 m).

Miscellaneous: The palace was finely decorated with mosaics and Second Style paintings.
State of preservation: Rather well preserved.
Time of excavation: 1950s and 1960s.

Date and period of use
Built 30-20 BC, the main Herodian building period of Masada.

References
Written sources: *1: Joseph. *BJ* 7.8.3-4 (280-300).
Modern literature: Yadin 1965 (Pr), 1966; Netzer 1991, 134ff, 575ff (P); Foerster 1995 (P) and 1996.
This volume: pp. 189ff; Figs. 96, 100-102; Pls. 33-36.

CAT. NO. 28

Traditional name: First Winter Palace.
Kingdom: Herod the Great's.
Locality: Jericho.
Category: Royal, mainly recreational palace.
Situation: On the southern bank of the Wadi Qelt, opposite the Hasmonean palace which was still partly in existence, in a domain outside the town.
Area: 87 x 46 m = 4,002 m²; the courtyard: 42 x 35 m = c. 1,470 m².
General characteristics: A compact rectangular building orientated inwards and closed to the outside.

Architecture
Building technique and material: Only foundations, in stone, the rest in sun-dried brick.
Façade: Entrance probably from the north, not preserved.
 gateway: ?
Courtyards/forecourts: A large courtyard with peristyle dominated the palace; it was surrounded by rooms on three sides and a wall on the fourth.
 peristyles/order of columns: The large peristyle is preserved only in foundations.

Functions
Official/ceremonial: Only in the early phase, later taken over by the Second and the Third Winter Palace (Cat. 29, 30).
 portal: ?
 audience/council/court hall: The large oecus to the west (18 x 13 m = 234 m²).
 reception hall/area: Ditto.
Social:
 banqueting hall/s: Probably the cruciform hall in the eastern wing, but also the oecus.

Religious:
   temple for the tutelary deity: —
   dynastic sanctuary: —
   mausoleum: —
Defensive:
   precinct walls: —
   Citadel/akra: —, but Jericho was protected by two fortresses, Tryx and Tauros, probably today's Cypros and Nusieb Dag *1.
   barracks/arsenal: —
Administrative:
   offices: —
   archives: —
   treasury: —
Service: Perhaps behind the oecus.
   storerooms: ?
   kitchens, etc.: X?
   servants' quarters: X?
Residential for the king/governor and his family: The palace may have been primarily residential from the outset, perhaps except for the two main halls. Later it was probably used exclusively for residence.
   bedrooms: Probably the many small rooms behind the oecus facing a corridor, and the northern wing, and also the rooms to the east, flanking the cruciform hall.
   bathrooms: In the northern wing are bathrooms in the Jewish and the Roman style, i.e. with hypocaust.
   private dining-rooms: The oecus and the cruciform halls after the Third Winter Palace was built.
   harem: —
Residential for the court/guests: Near the large pool (Birket Musa) south of the palace, some well-appointed houses from the Herodian period have been found, which probably belonged to the aristocracy.
   apartments: Ditto.
"Public":
   gymnasium/palaestra: —
   library: —
   theatre: —
   hippodrome: —
Recreational:
   gardens: A garden in the peristyle seems very probable.
   parks: The palace was probably set in a large park.
   pavilions: ?
   (swimming-)pools: Perhaps the very large (swimming-)pool (180 x 150 m) (Birket Musa) found to the east with the same orientation, belonged to this palace.

State of preservation: Only foundations, no longer visible.
Time of excavation: 1951.

Date and period of use
Built by Herod in c. 35 BC.

References
Written sources: *1: Strab. 16.2.40 (763).
Modern literature: Pritchard 1958, who interpreted it as a gymnasium (P); Netzer 1989, and 1990, 44 (new interpretation as a palace).
This volume: pp. 193ff; Figs. 104-105; Pl. 37.

CAT. NO. 29

Traditional name: Second Winter Palace.
Kingdom: Herod the Great's.
Locality: Jericho.
Category: Royal recreational palace.
Situation: In a large domain, just beside the Hasmonaean Winter Palace (Cat. 23) which was partly reused.
Area: 33 x 57 m = 1,881 m^2 (main palace); all in all c. 4,050 m^2.
General characteristics: This palace was a combination of an introvert and an extrovert building. It was combined with the eastern Twin Palace's garden and open towards the south - a new feature. It is placed on two terraces.

Architecture
Building technique and material: Stone foundations, thereover sun-dried brick.
Façade: —
  gateway: —
Courtyards/forecourts: A large courtyard with garden-peristyle on the upper terrace dominated the palace; it was flanked by rooms on three sides.
  peristyles/order of columns: The large courtyard had a peristyle. Another surrounded the large swimming-pool on the lower terrace.

Functions
Official/ceremonial: This palace was primarily recreational.
  portal: —
  audience/council/court hall: —
  reception hall/area: —
Social:
  banqueting hall/s: —?
Religious:
  temple for the tutelary deity: —

dynastic sanctuary: —
mausoleum: —
Defensive:
  precinct walls: —
  citadel/akra: —, but two fortresses protected Jericho *1.
  barracks/arsenal: —
Administrative:
  offices: —
  archives: —
  treasury: —
Service: Some of the rooms around the large peristyle.
  storerooms: —, in the Hasmonean Palace nearby (Cat. 23).
  kitchens, etc.: North-east of the peristyle, probably.
  servants' quarters: ?
Residential for the king/governor and his family: Only a few rooms, the only candidates being those flanking the large hall to the south and opening to the southern portico. The main residential function was undoubtedly fulfilled by the still existing First Winter Palace (Cat. 28).
  bedrooms: Ditto.
  bathrooms: A fine Roman bath building is placed to the south of the lower garden.
  private dining-rooms: The south hall with a view in two directions and perhaps the northern hall with columns in antis.
  harem: —
Residential for the court/guests: Again, the above-mentioned mansions traced to the south of the First Winter Palace could be used for this purpose.
  apartments: Ditto
"Public":
  gymnasium/palaestra: —
  library: —
  theatre: —
  hippodrome: —
Recreational:
  gardens: There was a raised garden in the large peristyle on the upper terrace. On the lower terrace there were probably two gardens, both reused from the Hasmonean period, the eastern one now being furnished with a peristyle.
  parks: The palace was set in a large park, in which also the two large swimming-pools from the Hasmonean Palace (Cat. 23), now made into one, were included.
  pavilions: Perhaps the columbarium built at this time above the ruined Hasmonean pavilion had a pavilion on top.
  (swimming-)pools: Both lower gardens had swimming-pools, the larger one measuring 12.5 x 20 m. Also the two Hasmonean swimming-pools, made into one (32 x 18 m) were included.

Miscellaneous: This palace was not an independent structure, since it had almost exclusively a recreational function. It must be seen in relation to the two other Winter Palaces built by Herod (Cats. 28, 30).
State of preservation: Partly well preserved.
Time of excavation: 1970s.

Date and period of use
Herodian, built around 25 BC.

References
Written sources: —
Modern literature: Netzer 1989 (Pr), 1990, 44-45, Netzer *et al.* 1994 (forthcoming) (P).
This volume: pp. 195ff; Fig. 106.

CAT. NO. 30

Traditional name: Third Winter Palace.
Kingdom: Herod the Great's.
Locality: Jericho.
Category: Royal, mainly recreational palace.
Situation: In a large park on both sides of the Wadi Qelt.
Area: C. 30,000 m² (= 3 ha.); main palace: 90 x 38 m = 3,420 m².
General characteristics: A "palace complex", consisting of a main building on the northern bank and several additional recreational buildings on the southern bank of the wadi.

Architecture
Building technique and material: A mixture of local sun-dried brick founded on rubble and the Roman techniques *opus reticulatum* and *opus mixtum.*
Façade: The main palace had a fine columnar façade towards the wadi.
   gateway: ?
Courtyards/forecourts: Two peristyle courts in the main palace, both with gardens.
   peristyles/order of columns: Both peristyles have only three porticoes; in the western peristyle the northern one is replaced by a large apse, in the eastern peristyle it is the southern one, towards the valley, which is missing.

Functions
Official/ceremonial: Probably the western part of the main palace was set aside for this purpose.
   portal: The various parts were reached from the portico running all along the palace front to the south; a "bent" entrance led to the apsidal court, a large portal to the huge oecus.
   audience/council/court hall: Primarily this oecus (29 x 19 m = 551 m²), but perhaps also the smaller room (c. 4 x 5 m = 20 m²) behind the apse flanking the northern side of the western garden peristyle.

reception hall/area: —, but perhaps the peristyle court behind the "theatre" was used for this purpose (below).

Social:

banqueting hall/s: The large oecus had this function as well, as revealed by the floor decoration.

Religious:

temple for the tutelary deity: —

dynastic sanctuary: —

mausoleum: —

Defensive:

precinct walls: —?

citadel/akra: — but Jericho was protected by two fortresses, mentioned above (Cat. 28).

barracks/arsenal: —?

Administrative:

offices: —

archives: —

treasury: —

Service: The rooms to the north and east of the main rooms had this function.

storerooms: ?

kitchens, etc.: X?

servants' quarters: Probably spread around in the three palaces.

Residential for the king/governor and his family: Probably, the First Winter Palace (Cat. 28) was still used for this purpose.

bedrooms: —

bathrooms: A very large typically Roman bath wing to the north of the eastern court.

private dining-rooms: Probably the large cruciform hall to the east of the courtyard. In the recreational and primarily private complex on the southern bank of the wadi was a large round hall (diam. c. 16.8 m) on the top of the Southern Tell, which was undoubtedly used for dining also. One may call it a diaita.

harem: —

Residential for the court/guests: Again, the mansions south of the palace.

apartments: Ditto.

"Public": A complex placed at some distance from the palace but nevertheless probably part of it.

gymnasium/palaestra: Perhaps the portico raised on a platform behind the "theatre" (70 x 70 m); if this complex is, in fact, related to the palace; it is placed 2 km north of the palace. It may also have been used for receptions.

library: —

theatre: The theatre-shaped auditorium facing the hippodrome was probably used in connection with both equestrian and theatrical performances *1.

hippodrome: Perhaps this could also be used as an amphitheatre, mentioned by Josephus *2-3.

Recreational:

> *gardens:* Both peristyles had gardens. On the other bank of the Wadi a huge sunken formal garden was surrounded by halls, with porticoes and apsidal structures (140 x 47 m).
>
> *parks:* The palace was set in a very large park.
>
> *pavilions:* A large circular hall on the Southern Tell may be interpreted as a kind of diaita.
>
> *(swimming-)pools:* An enormous swimming-pool on the southern bank of the Wadi Qelt (90 x 40 m).

Miscellaneous: The palace was plastered white externally and lavishly decorated internally with opus sectile and mosaic floors, and wall-paintings in the Second Style. Since all three Winter Palaces existed and were used at the same time, they should not be regarded as isolated palaces, but rather as complementary. The entire area taken up by them was c. 12 ha.

State of preservation: Partially well preserved.

Time of excavation: 1950s and 1970s.

Date and period of use

The complex was built by Herod the Great around 15 BC. It was burned down in connection with Herod's death, restored by his son Archelaus and used by him (4 BC-6 AD); totally destroyed around the middle of the 1st century AD.

References

Written sources: *1: Joseph. *AJ* 17.5.5-6.3 (115-162); *2: Joseph. *AJ* 17.6.5 (174-179); *3: Joseph. *AJ* 17.8.2 (193-195).

Modern literature: Kelso & Baramki 1955 (P); Netzer 1975a, 1977a (both Pr); Gleason 1987-1988 (Pr); Netzer 1990, 45-46, Netzer *et al.* 1994 (forthcoming) (P).

This volume: pp. 196ff; Figs. 107-110; Pls. 37-40.

CAT. NO. 31

Traditional name: Palace of Herodium.

Kingdom: Herod the Great's.

Locality: Herodium, 15 km south of Jerusalem.

Category: Royal summer palace.

Situation: The "palace complex" consists of a palatial fortress, placed inside an artificial hill, and various buildings, placed on the northern slope of this hill and on the plain below. Not part of a town, but it formed an administrative unit.

Area: The upper palace was 63 m in diam; the main palace measured 130 x 58 m = 7,540 m²; the whole complex covered 15 ha.

General characteristics: The palace was spread in a large park, consisting of many different buildings for different purposes.

Architecture

Building technique and material: Opus quadratum, rubble and sun-dried brick.
Façade: ?
   gateway: ?, but probably to the north-west.
Courtyards/forecourts: In the upper palace a peristyle court took up a large part of the fortress. In Lower Herodium a large peristyle court surrounded a formal garden with a
swimming-pool. Probably also courtyards in the other buildings.
   peristyles/order of columns: Two peristyles are preserved.

Functions

Official/ceremonial: The buildings serving this purpose were undoubtedly placed both in
the fortress and in Lower Herodium, probably mostly in the uppermost badly preserved
building here, the main palace. It had a connection with a complex consisting of a long
processional avenue (350 x 25 m), leading to a large hall with niches (8 x 10 m = 80 m^2).
   portal: One in the wall of the upper palace, reached by a ramp.
   audience/council/court hall: Probably in the main palace, but also the large hall in the
   upper palace (15 x 10.5 m = c. 158 m^2) and perhaps the hall with the niches.
   reception hall/area: X?, probably in the main palace.
Social:
   banqueting hall/s: Partly in the main palace, partly in the upper one, and the hall with
   niches, placed at the end of a large processional avenue could have served this purpose
   as well as other official ones.
Religious:
   temple for the tutelary deity: —
   dynastic sanctuary: —
   mausoleum: The tomb of Herod was situated in Herodium but has not been found. The
   hall with the niches could perhaps also have been used as a funeral triclinium in connection with the funeral procession of Herod the Great *1.
Defensive:
   precinct walls: ?
   citadel/akra: The circular upper palace was protected by a large wall and a huge tower
   and thus constituted a citadel as well.
   barracks/arsenal: Undoubtedly placed in Lower Herodium.
Administrative: In the "northern area" of Lower Herodium. We know from the written
sources that Herodium was the administrative centre of Herod's kingdom *2.
   offices: X?
   archives: X?
   treasury: X?
Service: Buildings for this purpose were present both in Lower and Upper Herodium, partly
in the round corridors of the latter, partly in the "northern area" of the former.
   storerooms: X?
   kitchens, etc.: X?
   servants' quarters: X?

Residential for the king/governor and his family: Upper Herodium was probably used primarily by Herod and his family and close friends, although it could also have been used for minor receptions.

    bedrooms: X?

    bathrooms: A fine bath wing in Roman style is preserved in the northern corner. Another, for the court, was placed by the large peristyle in Lower Herodium.

    private dining-rooms: The large oecus, here without columns, had probably among other things this function but could also be used for minor official banquets. The same may be the case with the cruciform hall.

    harem: —

Residential for the court/guests:

    apartments: X?

"Public":

    gymnasium/palaestra: —

    library: —

    theatre: —

    hippodrome: —

Recreational:

    gardens: A garden was present in the large peristyle in Lower Herodium (120 x 105 m) with a swimming-pool and a Roman bath wing.

    parks: The whole complex was placed in a large park.

    pavilions: Beside the upper storeys of the towers of Upper Herodium which probably had this function, there was a circular pavilion (diam. 13 m) in the middle of the large swimming-pool.

    (swimming-)pools: A huge swimming-pool (70 x 46 m) was placed in the peristyle garden of Lower Herodium.

Miscellaneous: The palace was plastered white externally.

State of preservation: Partly well preserved, especially Upper Herodium, partly not excavated.

Time of excavation: 1962-67 (Upper Herodium), 1970s and 1980s (Lower Herodium).

Date and period of use

The complex was built by Herod in 23-20 BC and used also by Archelaus.

References

Written sources:'*1: *BJ* 1.33.9 (670-673); *2: Joseph. *BJ* 1.21.9-10 (418-421), cf. *AJ* 16.2.1 (12-14) (Agrippa's visit).

Modern literature: Corbo 1963, 1967 (P); Netzer 1981b (P), 1987a, 1990, 46-50.

This volume: pp. 201ff; Figs. 111-113; Pls. 41-44.

BIBLIOGRAPHY

The German system of abbreviations as used by the *Archaeologische Bibliographie* is employed throughout.

Achaemenid History I-VII, ed. H. Sancisi-Weerdenburg *et al.*, London 1987-1991.

Adriani, A. 1932-33a. "Saggio di una pianta archeologica di Alessandria", *Annuario del Museo Greco-Romano* 1, 1932-33, 55-96.

Adriani, A. 1932-33b. "Alessandria. Scoperta di costuzioni greche nel quartiere dei Basileia", *Annuario del Museo Greco-Romano*, 1, 1932-33, 11-18.

Aharoni, Y. 1975. *Investigations at Lachish. The Sanctuary and the Residency* (*Lachish V*), Tell Aviv 1975.

Akurgal, E. 1956. "Les fouilles de Daskyleion", *Anatolia* 1, 1956, 20-24.

Albenda, P. 1976-77. "Landscape Bas-Reliefs in the *Bit-Hilani* of Ashurbanipal", *BASOR* 224, 1976, 49-72; 225, 1977, 29-48.

Alföldi, A. 1934. "Die Ausgestaltung des monarchischen Zeremoniells am römischen Kaiserhofe", *RM* 49, 1934, 1-118.

Alföldi, A. 1935. "Insignien und Tracht der römischen Kaiser", *RM* 50, 1935, 1-171.

Alföldi, A. 1970. *Die monarchische Repräsentation im römischen Kaiserreiche*, Darmstadt 1970.

Allara, A. 1986. "Les maisons de Doura-Europos. Questions de typologie", *Syria* 63, 1986, 39-60.

Amiet, P. 1974. "Quelques observations sur le palais de Dareius à Suse", *Syria* 51, 1974, 65-73.

Amiran, R. & Eitan, A. 1970. "Excavations in the courtyard of the Citadel, Jerusalem, 1968-1969 (Preliminary Report)", *IsrExplJ* 20, 1970, 9-17.

Amiran, R. & Eitan, A. 1972. "Herod's palace", *IsrExplJ* 22, 1972, 50-51.

Andrewes, A. 1958. *The Greek Tyrants*, London 1958 (2nd edn.).

Andronicos, M. 1984. *Vergina. The Royal Tombs and the Ancient City*, Athens 1984.

Anti, C. 1947. *Teatri Greci arcaici da Minosse a Pericle*, Padova 1947.

Arav, R. 1989. *Hellenistic Palestine. Settlement patterns and city planning, 337-31 B.C.E.* (*BAR* International Series 485), Oxford 1989.

Aspects of Hellenism 1994. *Aspects of Hellenism in Italy: Towards a Cultural Unity?*, eds. P. Guldager Bilde., I. Nielsen, M. Nielsen (Acta Hyperborea 5), Copenhagen 1994.

Auberson, P. & Schefold, K. 1972. *Führer durch Eretria*, Berlin 1972.

Aupert, P. ed. 1996, *Guide d'Amathonte*, Paris 1996.

Avigad, N. 1975. "The architecture of Jerusalem in the Second Temple Period", in: *Jerusalem Revealed*, Jerusalem 1975, 14-20.

Avigad, N. 1983. *Discovering Jerusalem*, Nashville, Camden, New York 1983.

Avigad, N. 1989. *The Herodian Quarter in Jerusalem*, Jerusalem 1989.

Bakir, T. 1992. "Daskyleion", in: *XIV Uluslararasi kazi, araştirma ve arkeometri sempozyumu. Bildiri Özetleri*, Ankara 1992, 23-24.

Barag, D. 1993: "King Herod's royal castle at Samaria-Sebaste", *Palestine Exploration Quarterly* 1993, 3-18.

Basileia 1996. *Basileia. Die Paläste der hellenistischen Könige*. Internationales Symposion in Berlin vom 16.12 1992 bis 20.12. 1992, eds. W. Hoepfner, G. Brands, Mainz 1996.

Bean, G.E. & Cook, J.M. 1957. "The Carian Coast III", *BSA* 52, 1957, 58-146.

Bergamini, G. 1977. "Levels of Babylon Rediscovered", *Mesopotamia* 12, 1977, 128-29.

Bernard, P. 1971. "La campagne des fouilles de 1970 à Aï Khanoum (Afghanistan)", *CRAI* 1971, 385-452.

Bernard, P. 1976. "Les traditions orientales dans l'architecture gréco-bactrienne", *Journal Asiatique* 264, 1976, 245-75.

Bernard, P. 1978. "Campagne des fouilles 1976-77 à Aï Khanoum (Afghanistan)", *CRAI* 1978, 421-63.

Bernard, P. 1981. "Problèmes d'histoire coloniale grecque à travers l'urbanisme d'une cité hellénistique d'Asie Centrale", in: *150 Jahre Deutsches Archäologisches Institut, 1929-1979*, Mainz 1981, 108-20.

Bernard, P. *et al*. 1973. *Fouilles d'Aï Khanoum I* (Mémoires DAFA XXI), Paris 1973.

Bichler, R. 1983. *'Hellenismus'. Geschichte und Problematik eines Epochenbegriffs*, Darmstadt 1983.

Bickerman, E.J. 1988. *The Jews in the Greek Age*, Cambridge Mass. 1988.

Bikerman, E. 1938. *Institutions des Séleucides*, Paris 1938.

Bliss, F.J. & Macalister, R.A.S. 1902. *Excavation in Palestine During the Years 1898-1900*, London 1902.

Boardman, J. 1967. *Excavations in Chios, Greek Emporio 1952-1955* (BSA Suppl. Vol. 6), London 1967.

Boehlau, J. & Schefold, K. 1940. *Die Bauten* (*Larisa am Hermos I*), Berlin 1940.

Boersma, J.S. 1970. *Athenian Building Policy from 561/0 to 405/4 BC*, Groeningen 1970.

Boëthius, A. & Ward-Perkins, J.B. 1970. *Etruscan and Roman Architecture*, Harmondsworth 1970.

Börker, C. 1983. *Festbankett und griechische Architektur*, Konstanz 1983.

Borza, E.N. 1983. "The Symposium at Alexander's Court", in: *Ancient Macedonia* 3, Thessaloniki 1983, 45-55.

Borza, E.N. 1990. *In the Shadow of Olympus: the Emergence of Macedon*, Princeton 1990.

Boucharlat, R. 1990. "Le fin des palais achémenides de Suse — Une mort naturelle", in: *Contribution à l'histoire de l'Iran. Mélanges offerts à J. Perrot*, Paris 1990, 225-33.

Boucharlat, R. & Labrousse, A. 1979. "Le palais d'Artaxerxes II sur la rive droite du Chaour à Suse", *Cahiers de la Délégation Archéologique Française en Iran* 10, 1979, 19-136.

Bouzek, J. 1996. "Palastartige Anlagen im Schwarzenmeergebiet", in: *Basileia* 1996, 213-20.

Briant, P. 1990. "The Seleucid Kingdom, the Achaemenid Empire and the history of the Near East in the first millennium BC", in: *Religion and Religious Practice in the Seleucid Kingdom*, eds. P. Bilde, T. Engberg-Pedersen, L. Hannestad, J. Zahle (Studies in Hellenistic Civilization, 1), Aarhus 1990.

Broise, H. & Jolivet, V. 1987. "Recherches sur les jardins de Lucullus", in: *L'Urbs. Espace urbain et histoire*, Rome 1987, 747-61.

Broneer, O. 1944. "The tent of Xerxes and the Greek theater", *University of California Publications in Classical Archaeology* I. 12, 1944, 305-11.

Browning, I. 1982. *Petra*, London 1982.

Budina, D. 1990. "Antigoneia. Eine Stadt der Hellenistische Periode", in: *Akten des XIII. internationalen Kongresses für klassische Archäologie Berlin 1988*, Mainz 1990, 556-59.

Calmeyer, P. 1990. "Das Persepolis der Spätzeit", in: *Achaemenid History IV*, Leiden 1990, 7-36.

Cambitoglou, A. *et al.* 1971. *Zagora 1. Excavation Season 1967; Study Season 1968-69*, Sydney 1971.

Camp, J.M. 1986. *The Athenian Agora. Excavations in the heart of Classical Athens*, London 1986.

Campbell, W.A. 1934. "The Circus", in: *Antioch-on-the-Orontes I: The Excavations of 1932*, ed. G.W. Elderkin, Princeton, 1934, 34-41.

Carettoni G. 1966-67. "I problemi della zona Augustea del Palatino alla luce dei recenti scavi", *RendPontAc* 39, 1966-67, 57-75.

Carettoni, G. 1978. "Roma. Le costruzioni di Augusto e il tempio di Apollo sul Palatino", *QuadAEI* 1, 1978, 72-74.

Carettoni, G. 1983a. "La decorazione pittorica della casa di Augusto sul Palatino", *RM* 90, 1983, 373-419.

Carettoni, G. 1983b. *Das Haus des Augustus auf dem Palatin*, Mainz 1983.

Carettoni, G. 1988. "Die Bauten des Augustus auf dem Palatin", in: *Kaiser Augustus und die verlorene Republik*, Mainz 1988, 263-67.

Carlier, P. 1984. *La Royauté en Grèce avant Alexandre*, Strasbourg 1984.

Carroll-Spillecke, M. 1989. *Kepos. Der antike griechische Garten* (Wohnen in der klassischen Polis III), München 1989.

Carroll-Spillecke, M. 1992. "Griechische Gärten", in: *Der Garten vom Antike bis zum Mittelalter* 1992, 153-75.

Caspari, F. 1916. "Das Nilschiff Ptolemaios IV", *JdI* 31, 1916, 1-74.

Castagnoli, F. 1984. "Influenze alessandrine nell'urbanistica della Roma Augustea", in: *Alessandria e il mondo ellenistico-romano. Studi in onore di A. Adriani, 3*, eds. N. Bonacasa, A. Di Vita, Roma 1984, 520-26.

Castrén, P. 1976. "Hellenismus und Romanisierung in Pompeji", in: *Hellenismus in Mittelitalien*, Kolloquium in Göttingen 1974, Göttingen 1976, 356-62.

Chrysostomou, P. 1988. "Loutra sto anaktoro tes Pellas", *AErgoMak* 2, 1988, 113-21.

Clarke, J.R. 1991. *The Houses of Roman Italy 100 B.C.-A.D. 250. Ritual, Space and Decoration*, Berkeley *et al.* 1991.

Clermont-Ganneau, C. 1921. "Le Paradeisos royal Achéménide de Sidon", *Revue Biblique* 30, 1921, 106-9.

Coarelli, F. 1975. *Guida Archeologica di Roma*, Verona 1975.

Coarelli, F. 1981. *Guida Archeologica di Roma* (Guide archeologiche Laterza), Roma-Bari 1981.

Coarelli, F. 1983a. "Il Pantheon, l'apoteosi di Augusto e l'apoteosi di Romolo", in: *Città e architettura nella Roma imperiale* (AnalRom Suppl. X), Odense 1983, 41-46.

Coarelli, F. 1983b. "Architettura sacra e architettura privata nella tarda repubblica", in: *Architecture et Société de l'archaisme grec à la fin de la République romaine*, Paris 1983, 191-217.

Coarelli, F. 1987. *I santuari del Lazio in età repubblicana*, Roma 1987.

Coarelli, F. 1988. "Rom. Die Stadtplanung von Caesar bis Augustus", in: *Kaiser Augustus und die verlorene Republik*, Berlin 1988, 68-80.

Coarelli, F. & Torelli, M. 1984. *Sicilia* (Guide archeologiche Laterza), Roma 1984.

Colledge, M. 1987. "Greek and non-Greek interaction in the art and architecture of the Hellenistic East", in: *Hellenism in the East. The interaction of Greek and non-Greek civilizations from Syria to Central Asia after Alexander*, eds. A. Kuhrt, S. Sherwin-White, London 1987, 134-62.

Cook, J.M. 1983. *The Persian Empire*, London 1983.

Cooper, F. & Morris, S. 1990. "Dining in round buildings", in: *Sympotica*, ed. O. Murray, Oxford 1990, 66-85.

Corbier, M. 1992. "De la Maison d'Hortensius à la *Curia* sur le Palatin", *MEFRA* 104,2, 1992, 871-916.

Corbo, P.V. 1963. "L'Herodion di Gebal Fureidis. Relazione preliminare delle due prime campagne di scavo 1962-1963", *StBiFranc* 13, 1963, 219-77.

Corbo, V. 1967. "L'Herodion di Gjabal Fureidis", *StBiFranc* 17, 1967, 65-121.

Dalley, S. 1994. "Niniveh, Babylon and the hanging gardens: cuneiform and classical sources reconciled", *Iraq* 56, 1994, 45-58.

De Angelis d'Ossat, G. 1971. "L'esprit architectural chez les Achéménides et les Grecs", in: *l'Architecture Classique et ses problèmes dans le Proche-Orient. IXième Congres d'Archéologie Classique, 1969)*, *AnnASyr* 21, 1971, 201-7.

D'Arms, J.H. 1970. *Romans on the Bay of Naples*, Cambridge Mass. 1970.

Degrassi, N. 1966-67. "La dimora di Augusto sul Palatino e la base di Sorrento", *RentPontAc* 39, 1966-67, 77-116.

Deller, K. 1987. "Assurbanipal in der Gartenlaube", *Bagdader Mitteilungen* 18, 1987, 229-38.

Dentzer, J.-M. 1982. *Le motif du banquet couché dans le Proche-Orient et le monde grec du VIIe au IVe siècle avant J.-C.*, Rome 1982.

Detweiler, H. & Rostovtzeff, M.I. 1952. "The palace of the *Dux Ripae* (*The Excavations at Dura Europos. Preliminary Report of the Ninth Season of Work 1935-1936. Part* III), New Haven 1952, 1-96.

Dimitrov, D.P. & Cicikova, M. 1978. *The Thracian City of Seuthopolis* (*BAR* Suppl. Series 38), Oxford 1978.

Downey, G. 1961. *A History of Antioch in Syria from Seleucus to the Arab Conquest*, Princeton N.J. 1961.

Downey, S.B. 1985. "Two buildings at Dura-Europos and the early history of the Iwan", *Mesopotamia* 20, 1985, 111-29.

Downey, S.B. 1986. "The citadel palace at Dura-Europos", *Syria* 63, 1986, 27-37.

Dreliossi-Herakleidou, A. 1996. "Späthellenistische palastartige Gebäude in der Nähe der Akropolis von Rhodos", in: *Basileia* 1996, 182-92.

Drerup, H. 1959. Die römische Villa, *MarbWPr* 1959, Marburg 1959.

Ducrey, P., Metzger, I.R., Reber, K. 1993. *Eretria. Fouilles et recherches VIII*, Lausanne 1993.

Dunbabin, K.M.D. 1998. "Ut graeco more biberetur: Greeks and Romans on the dining couch", in: *Meals in a Social Context (ASMA 1)*, eds. I. Nielsen & H. Sigismund Nielsen, Aarhus 1998.

Dura Europos report II. *Excavations at Dura Europos. Preliminary Reports* II, New Haven 1931.

Dura Europos Report III. *Excavations at Dura Europos. Preliminary Reports* III, New Haven 1932.

Dura Europos Report IV. *Excavations at Dura Europos. Preliminary Reports* IV, New Haven 1933.

Elayi, J. 1990. *Sidon, cité autonome de l'Empire Perse*, Paris 1990.

Elias, N. 1983. *The Court Society*, Oxford 1983.

Ergon 1984. "Pella", *Ergon* 1984, 38-39

Ergon 1987. "Pella", *Ergon* 1987, 65-67.

Fedak, J. 1990. *Monumental Tombs of the Hellenistic Age*, Toronto 1990.

Fehr, B. 1969. "Plattform und Blickbasis", in: *MarbWPr* 1969, Marburg 1970.

Filgis, M. N. & Radt, W. 1986. *Die Stadtgrabung*, (*Altertümer von Pergamon* XV.1), Berlin 1986.

Fischer, C.S. 1904. "The Mycenaean Palace at Nippur", *AJA* 8, 1904, 403-32.

Fittschen, K. 1976. "Zur Herkunft und Entstehung der 2. Stils. Probleme und Argumente", in: *Hellenismus in Mittelitalien* (Kolloquium in Göttingen 1974), Göttingen 1976, 539-63.

Flinder, A. 1982. "The pool of Cleopatra at Caesarea and her Cypriot sister", *BAnglo-IsrASoc* 1982, 25-27.

Foerster, G. 1995. *Masada V. The Ygael Yadin Excavations 1963-1965. Final Reports. Art and Architecture*, Jerusalem 1995.

Foerster, G. 1996. "Hellenistic and Roman trends in the Herodian architecture of Masada", in: *Judaea and the Graeco-Roman world in the time of Herod in Light of Archaeological Evidence*, eds. K. Fittdchen & G. Foerster, Göttingen 1996, 55-72.

Francis, E.D. 1980. "Greeks and Persians: The art of hazard and triumph", in: *Ancient Persia: The Art of an Empire*, ed. D. Schmandt-Besserat, Malibu 1980, 53-86.

de Francovich, G. 1966. "Problems of Achaemenid Architecture", *EastWest* 16, 1966, 201-60.

Frankfort, H. 1952. "The origin of the Bit Hilani", *Iraq* 14, 1952, 120-31.

Frankfort, H. 1970. *The art and architecture of the ancient Orient*, Harmondsworth 1970 (4th edn.).

Fraser, P.M. 1972. *Ptolemaic Alexandria* vols. 1-3, Oxford 1972.

Frederiksen, M. 1984. *Campania*, Rome 1984.

Frézouls, E. 1987. "Les Julio-Claudiens et le *Palatium*, in: *Le Système Palatial en Orient, en Grèce et à Rome*, Leiden 1987, 445-62.

Fritz, V. 1983. "Die syrische Bauform des Hilani und die Frage seiner Verbreitung", *DamasMitt* 1, 1983, 43-58.

Furtwängler, A.E. *et al.* 1995. "Gumbati. Archäologische Expedition im Kachetien 1994", *Eurasia Antiqua* 1, 1995, 177-211.

Furtwängler, A.E. *et al.* 1996. "Gumbati. Archäologische Expedition im Kachetien 1995", *Eurasia Antiqua* 2, 1996, 363-81.

Gabelmann, H. 1984. *Antike Audienz- und Tribunalszenen*, Darmstadt 1984.

von Gall, H. 1977. "Das persische Königszelt und die Hallenarchitektur in Iran und Griechenland", in: *Festschrift für F. Brommer*, eds. U. Höckmann & A. Krug, Mainz 1977, 119-32.

von Gall, H. 1979. "Das Zelt des Xerxes und seine Rolle als persischer Raumtyp in Griechenland", *Gymnasium* 86, 1979, 444-62.

Gallery, L.M. 1978. "The Garden of Ancient Egypt", in: *Immortal Egypt*. ed. D. Schwandt-Besserat, Malibou 1978, 43-49.

Ganzert, J. 1990. "Der Mars-Ultor-Tempel. Fusion von Orient und Okzident", in: *Akten des XIII. internationalen Kongresses für klassische Archäologie Berlin 1988*, Mainz 1990, 538-41.

Der Garten von der Antike bis zum Mittelalter 1992. *Der Garten von der Antike bis zum Mittelalter*, ed. M. Carroll-Spillecke, (Kulturgeschichte der antiken Welt, 57) Mainz 1992.

Genito, B. 1986. "Dahan-i Ghulaman: una città achemenide tra centro e periferia dell'impero", *Oriens Antiquus* 15, 1986, 287-317.

Gentelle, P. 1981. "Un "Paradis" hellénistique en Jordanie: étude de geo-archéologie", *Herodote* 20, 1981, 70-101.

Ghirshman, R. 1964. *Persia from the Origins to Alexander the Great*, London 1964.

Gjerstad, E. 1932. "The Palace of Vouni", in: *Corolla Archeologica* (Skrifter II), Lund 1932, 145-71.

Gjerstad, E. 1933. "Further remarks on the Palace of Vouni", *AJA* 37, 1933, 589-98.

Gjerstad, E. *et al.* 1937. *The Swedish Cyprus Expedition* III, Stockholm 1937.

Gleason, K.L. 1987-88. "Garden excavations at the Herodian Winter Palace in Jericho 1985-7", *BAngloIsrASoc* 7, 1987-88, 21-39.

Gleason, K.L. 1993. "A garden excavation in the Oasis Palace of Herod the Great at Jericho", *Landscape Journal* 12,2, 1993, 156-64.

Goodenough, E.R. 1928. "The political philosophy of Hellenistic kingship", *YaleClSt* 1, 1928, 55-102.

Greco, E & Torelli, M. 1983. *Storia dell'urbanistica. Il mondo greco*, Roma 1983.

Green, P. 1990. *Alexander to Actium. The Historical Evolution of the Hellenistic Age*, Berkeley 1990.

Gregori, B. 1982. "Considerazioni sui palazzi 'Hilani' del periodo salomonico a Megiddo", *VicOr* 5, 1982, 85-101.

Grimal, P. 1969. *Les Jardins romains*, Paris 1969 (2nd edn.).

Grimm, G. 1996a. "Riesen auf Reisen. Statuen und Architekturfragmente aus dem Meer von Alexandria geborgen", *Antike Welt* 27,3, 243-44.

Grimm, G. 1996b. "Kleopatras Palast?, Zu den jüngsten Untersuchungen im Hafenbecken von Alexandria", *Antike Welt* 27,6, 1996, 509-12.

Gros, P. 1978. *Architecture et société à Rome et en Italie centro-méridionale aux deux derniers siècles de la République* (Collection Latomus 156), Bruxelles 1978.

Haerinck, E. 1973. "Le Palais Achéménide de Babylone", *Iranica Antiqua* 10, 1973, 108-32.

Hanfmann, G.M.A. 1975. *From Croesus to Constantine*, Ann Arbor 1975.

Hanfmann, G.M.A. 1977. "On the Palace of Croesus", in: *Festschrift für F. Brommer*, eds. U. Höckmann, A. Krug, Mainz 1977, 145-54.

Heermann, V. 1986. *Studien zur makedonischen Palastarchitektur*, Diss. Erlangen-Nürnberg 1986.

Heinrich, E. 1984. *Die Paläste im alten Mesopotamien*, Berlin 1984.

Hellenism in the East 1987. *The Interaction of Greek and non-Greek civilizations from Syria to Central Asia after Alexander*, eds. A. Kuhrt, S. Sherwin-White, London, 1987.

Hellenismus in Mittelitalien 1976. *Abhandlingen der Akademie der Wissenschaften in Göttingen*, ed. P. Zanker, Göttingen 1976.

Hellström, P. 1989. "Formal banqueting at Labraunda", in: *Architecture and Society in Hecatomnid Caria* (Boreas 17), Uppsala 1989, 99-104.

Hellström, P. 1990. "Hellenistic architecture in light of late Classical Labraunda", in: *Akten des XIII. Internationalen Kongresses für klassische Archäologie Berlin 1988*, Mainz 1990, 243-52.

Hellström, P. 1991. "The architectural layout of Hecatomnid Labraunda", in: *Architecture sacrée de l'Anatolie 2, RA 2*, 1991, 297-308.

Hellström, P. 1994. "Architecture. Characteristic building-types and particularities in style and techniques. Possible implications for Hellenistic architecture", in: *Hekatomnid Caria and the Ionian Renaissance,* ed. J. Isager (Halicarnassian Studies 1), Odense 1994, 36-57.

Hermary, A. 1985. "Un nouveau chapiteau hathorique trouvé à Amathonte", *BCH* 109, 1985, 657-99.

Herzfeld, E. 1941. *Iran in the ancient East*, London 1941.

von Hesberg, H. 1988. "Die Veränderung des Erscheinungsbildes der Stadt Rom unter Augustus", in: *Kaiser Augustus und die verlorene Republik*, Berlin 1988, 93-115.

Heuzey, L. & Daumet, H. 1876. *Mission Archéologique de Macédonie*, Paris 1876.

Hoepfner, W. 1971. *Zwei Ptolemaierbauten* (AM, Beiheft I), Berlin 1971.

Hoepfner, W. 1990. "Von Alexandria über Pergamon nach Nikopolis. Städtebau und Stadtbilder hellenistischer Zeit", in: *Akten des XIII. Internationalen Kongresses für klassische Archäologie Berlin 1988*, Mainz 1990, 275-85.

Hoepfner, W. & Schwandner, E-L. 1986. *Haus und Stadt im klassischen Griechenland* (Wohnen in der klassischen Polis I), München 1986.

Hoffmann, A. 1978. "Eine Rekonstruktionsproblem der Casa del Fauno", *Bericht über die 30. Tagung für Ausgrabungswissenschaft und Bauforschung. Bericht Koldewey-Gesellschaft* 1978, 35-41.

Hoffmann, A. 1996. "Die Casa del Fauno in Pompeji. Ein Haus wie ein Palast (Kurzfassung)," in: *Basileia* 1996, 258-59.

Hölscher, T. 1990. "Römische Nobiles und Hellenistische Herrscher", in: *Akten des XIII. internationalen Kongresses für klassische Archäologie Berlin 1988*, Mainz 1990, 73-84.

Hopkins, C. (ed.) 1972. *Topography and architecture of Seleucia on the Tigris*, Ann Arbor 1972.

Hornblower, S. 1982. *Mausolus*, Oxford 1982.

Hugonot, J-C. 1989. *Le jardin dans l'Egypte ancienne* (Europäische Hochschulschriften, Reihe 38, Vol. 27); Frankfurt 1989.

Hugonot, J-C. 1992. "Ägyptische Gärten", in: *Der Garten von Antike bis zum Mittelalter* 1992, 9-44.

Invernizzi, A. 1993. "Seleucia on the Tigris: Centre and Periphery in Seleucid Asia", in: *Centre and Periphery in the Hellenistic World*, eds. P. Bilde *et al.* (SHC IV), Aarhus 1993, 230-50.

Isler, H.P. 1990. "Grabungen auf dem Monte Iato 1989", *AntKu* 33, 1990, 52-62.

Isler, H.P. 1996. "Einflüsse der makedonischen Palastarchitektur in Sizilien?", in: *Basileia* 1996, 252-57.

Jashemski, W.F. 1979. *The Gardens of Pompeii, Herculaneum and the Villas Destroyed by Vesuvius* I, New Rochelle 1979.

Jashemski, W.F. 1990. *The Gardens of Pompeii, Herculaneum, and the Villas Destroyed by Vesuvius*, II, Appendices, New Rochelle 1990.

Jashemski, W. 1992. "Antike römische Gärten in Campanien", in: *Der Garten vom Antike bis zum Mittelalter* 1992, 177-212.

Karadedos, G. 1990. "Ein spätklassisches Haus in Maroneia, Thrakien", *Egnatia* 2, 1990, 265-97.

Kawami, T.S. 1992. "Antike persische Gärten", in: *Der Garten vom Antike bis zum Mittelalter* 1992, 81-99.

Kawerau, G. & Wiegand, Th. 1930. *Die Paläste der Hochburg* (*Altertümer von Pergamon* V,1), Berlin 1930.

Kelso, J.L. & Baramki, D.C. 1955. "Excavations at New Testament Jericho and Khirbet en Nitla", *AASOR* 29-30 for 1949-51, New Haven 1955.

Kemp, B.J. 1977. "The Palace of Apries at Memphis", *MittKairo* 33, 1977, 101-8.

Kleiss, W. 1980. "Zur Entwicklung der Achaemenidische Palastarchitektur", *IranAnt* 15, 1980, 199-211.

Koldewey, R. 1931. *Die Königsburgen von Babylon. I. Die Südburg* (WVDOG 54), Leipzig 1931.

Koldewey, R. 1932. *Die Königsburgen von Babylon. II. Die Hauptburg und die Sommerpalast Nebukadnezars im Hügel Babil* (WVDOG 55), Leipzig 1932.

Krause, C. *et al.* 1985. *Domus Tiberiana. Nuove Ricerche*, Zürich 1985.

Krause, C. 1987. "La Domus Tiberiana e il suo contesto urbano", in: *L'Urbs. Espace urbane et histoire*, Rome 1987, 781-86.

Krefter, F. 1971. *Persepolis. Rekonstruktionen* (Teheraner Forschungen 3), Berlin 1971.

Lapp, P.W. 1963. "The second and third campaigns at Araq el-Emir", *BASOR* 171, 1963, 8-39.

La Rocca, E. 1986. "Il lusso come espressione di potere", in: *Le tranquille dimore degli dei*, eds. M. Cima, E. La Rocca, Venezia 1986, 3-35.

Lauter, H. 1971. "Ptolemais in Libyen. Ein Beitrag zur Baukunst Alexandrias", *JdI* 86, 1971, 149-78.

Lauter, H. 1975. "Die beiden ältere Tyrannen Paläste in Larisa am Hermos", *BonnJb* 175, 1975, 33-57.

Lauter, H. 1986. *Die Architektur des Hellenismus*, Darmstadt 1986.

Lauter, H. 1987. "Les éléments de la *REGIA* hellénistique", in: *Le Système palatial en Orient, en Grèce et à Rome*, Leiden 1987, 345-55.

Lawrence, A.W. 1967. *Greek Architecture*, Harmondsworth 1967.

Le Bohec, S. 1987. "L'entourage royal à la cour des Antigonides", in: *Le Système Palatial en Orient, en Grèce et à Rome*, Leiden 1987, 314-27.

Leroux, G. 1913. *Les origines de l'édifice Hypostyle en Grèce, en Orient et chez les Romains*, Paris 1913.

Levine, L.I. 1981. "Towards an appraisal of Herod as a builder", *The Jerusalem Cathedra* 1, 1981, 62-66.

Levine, L.I. & Netzer, E. 1986. *Excavations at Caesarea Maritima 1975-76, 79. Final Report*, Jerusalem 1986.

Lewis, D. M. 1987. "The King's dinner (Polyaenus IV.3.32)", in: *Achaemenid History* II, Leiden 1987, 79-87.

Lordkipanidse, O. 1991. *Archäologie in Georgien. Von der Altsteinzeit zum Mittelalter*, Weinheim 1991.

Loud, G. 1936-38. *Khorsabad* I-II, Chicago 1936-38.

Macurdy, G.H. 1932. *Hellenistic Queens. A study of woman-power in Macedonia, Seleucid Syria, and Ptolemaic Egypt*, Baltimore 1932.

Maier, F.G. 1989. "Palaces of Cypriot kings", in: *Cyprus and the East Mediterranean in the Iron Age*, ed. V. Tatton-Brown, London 1989, 16-19.

Makaronas, Ch. I. & E. Giouri, *Hoi oikies tis armages tes Elenes kai Dionysou tis Pellas*, 1989.

Malikhzade, F. 1973. "Daskyleion", *Anadolu* 17, 1973, 133-40.

Margueron, J-C. 1992. "Die Gärten im Vorderen Orient", in: *Der Garten vom Antike bis zum Mittelalter* 1992, 45-80.

Martin, R. 1951. *Recherches sur l'Agora Grecque. Études d'Histoire et d'Architecture urbaines*, Paris 1951.

Marzolff, P. 1976. "Zur Stadtanlage von Demetrias", and "Untersuchungen auf Höhe 33", in: *Demetrias* I, eds. V. Milojcic. D. Theocharis, Bonn 1976, 5-45.

Marzolff, P. 1979. "Bürgerliches und herrscherliches Wohnen im hellenistischen Demetrias", in: *Wohnungsbau im Altertum. Diskussionen zur archäologischen Bauforschung* 3, Berlin 1979, 129-44.

Marzolff, P. 1987. "Intervention sur les Rapports de S. Le Bohec et H. Lauter", in: *Le Système Palatial au Orient, en Grèce et à Rome*, Leiden 1987, 357-58.

Marzolff, P. 1996. "Der Palast von Demetrias — Formale und funktionale Probleme", in: *Basileia* 1996, 148-63.

Mau, A. 1909. *Pompeji in Leben und Kunst*, Leipzig 1908 (2nd edn.).

McEwan, C.W. 1934. *The Oriental Origin of Hellenistic Kingship* (The Oriental Institute of the University of Chicago. Studies in Ancient Oriental Civilization, 13), Chicago 1934.

McKay, A.G. 1975. *Houses, villas and palaces in the Roman world*, London 1975.

McKenzie, J. 1990. *The Architecture of Petra*, Oxford 1990.

Metzger, H. 1963. "L'acropole Lycienne", in: *Fouilles de Xanthos* II, Paris 1963.

Mielsch, H. 1987. *Die römische Villa. Architektur und Lebensform*, München 1987.

Millar, F. 1987. "The problem of Hellenistic Syria", in: *Hellenism in the East*, eds. A. Kuhrt, S. Sherwin-White, London 1987, 110-33.

Miller, Stella G. 1971. *Hellenistic macedonian Architecture: its style and painted ornamentation*, diss. Bryn Mawr College 1971.

Miller, Stephen G. 1978. *The Prytaneion. Its function and architectural form*, Berkeley 1978.

Milojcic, V. & Theocharis, D. 1976. *Demetrias* I. Bonn 1976.

Misaelidou-Despotidou, V. 1988. "Anaskafe sto anaktoro tes Pellas, tomeas ypostylou domatiou", *AErgoMak* 2, 1988, 101-9.

Mooren, L. 1983. "The nature of the Hellenistic Monarchy", in: *Egypt and the Hellenistic World*, eds. E. van 'T Dack, P. Van Dessel, W. Van Gucht, Levanin 1983, 205-40.

Mouton, B. "La rehabilitation du site de Doura Europos. Premier Bilan. L'example du Palais du stratège", *Syria* 69, 1992, 29ff.

Müller, V. 1932. "The Palace of Vouni in Cyprus", *AJA* 36, 408-17.

Müller, V. 1933. "A Reply" (to Gjerstad 1933), *AJA* 37, 1933, 599-601.

Murray, O. 1990. "Sympotic history", in: *Sympotica*, ed. O. Murray, Oxford 1990, 3-13.

Murray, O. 1996. "Hellenistic royal symposia", in: *Apects of Hellenistic Kingship*, eds. P. Bilde *et al.* (SHC VII), Aarhus 1996, 15-27.

Nagel, W. 1979. "Where were the 'Hanging Garden' located in Babylon?", *Sumer* 35, 1979, 241-42.

Netzer, E. 1975a. "The Hasmonaean and Herodian Winter Palaces at Jericho", *IsrExplJ* 25, 1975, 89-100.

Netzer, E. 1975b. "Cypros", *Qadmoniot* 8, 1975, 55-61.

Netzer, E. 1977a. "The winter palaces of the Judaean kings at Jericho at the end of the Second Temple Period", *BASOR* 228, 1977, 1-13.

Netzer, E. 1977b. "An Architectural and Archaeological Analysis of Building in the Herodian Period at Herodium and Jericho," unpublished thesis from 1977. Hebrew with an English abstract.

Netzer, E. 1981a. "Herod's building projects: state necessity or personal need?", *The Jerusalem Cathedra* 1, 1981, 48-61, 73-80.

Netzer, E. 1981b. Greater Herodium (Quedem 13), Jerusalem 1981.

Netzer, E. 1982. "Ancient ritual baths (miqvaot) in Jericho", *The Jerusalem Cathedra* 2, 1982, 106-19.

Netzer, E. 1986. "The swimming pools of the Hasmonaean period at Jericho", in: *Geschichtliche Wasserbauten in Ägypten, Kairo 1986*, Braunsweig 1986, 1-12.

Netzer, E. 1987a. *Herodium. An Archaeological Guide*, Jerusalem 1987.

Netzer, E. 1987b. "The Augusteum at Samaria-Sebaste — A new outlook", *Eretz-Israel* 1987, 7-105.

Netzer, E. 1989. "Jericho und Herodium: Verschwenderisches Leben in den Tagen der Hasmonäer und Herodes des Grossen", *Judaica* 45,1, 1989, 21-44.

Netzer, E. 1990. "Architecture in Palaestina prior to and during the days of Herod the Great", in: *Akten des XIII. Internationalen Kongresses für klassische Archäologie Berlin 1988*, Mainz 1990, 37-50.

Netzer, E. 1991. *Masada III. The Buildings, Stratigraphy and Architecture. The Yigael Yadin Excavations 1963-1965. Final Reports*, Jerusalem 1991.

Netzer, E. 1996. The Hasmonean palaces in Palästina", in: *Basileia* 1996, 203-8.

Netzer, 1996A. "The palaces built by Herod — A research update", in: *Judaea and the Graeco-Roman World in the Time of Herod in the Light of Archaeological Evidence*, eds. K. Fittschen & G. Foerster, Göttingen 1996, 27-35.

Netzer, E. 1997. "Il palazzo riflesso", *Archeo* 13,7, 1997, 50-54.

Netzer, E. *et al.* forthcoming. *Hasmonean and Herodian Winter Palaces at Jericho. Final Report*, Jerusalem.

Nielsen, E.O. & Philips Jr., K.M. 1985. "Poggio Civitate (Murlo)", in: *Case e palazzi d'Etruria*, ed. S. Stopponi, Milano 1985, 64-69.

Nielsen, I. 1985. "Considerazioni sulle prime fasi dell'evoluzione dell'edificio termale romano", *AnalRom* 14, 1985, 81-112.

Nielsen, I. 1990. *Thermae et Balnea. The Architecture and Cultural History of Roman Public Baths*, Aarhus 1990.

Nielsen, I. 1993. "From periphery to centre: Italic palaces", in: *Centre and Periphery in the Hellenistic World*, eds. P. Bilde, T. Engberg-Pedersen, L. Hannestad, J. Zahle, K. Randsborg (Studies in Hellenistic Civilization 4), Aarhus 1993, 210-29.

Nielsen, I. 1996. "Oriental models for Hellenistic Palaces?", in: *Basileia. Die Paläste der hellenistischen Könige*, Berlin 1996, 209-12.

Nielsen I. 1997. "Royal palaces and type of monarchy: Do the Hellenistic palaces reflect the status of the king?", *Hephaistos* 15, 1997, 137-61.

Nielsen, I. 1998. "Royal Banquets: The development of royal banquets and banqueting halls from Alexander to the Tetrarchs", in: *Meals in a Social Context* (ASMA 1), Aarhus 1998, 104-35.

Nylander, C. 1970. *Jonians in Pasargadae. Studies in old Persian architecture* (Boreas 1), Uppsala 1970.

Nylander, C. 1979. "Achaemenid Imperial art", in: *Power and Propaganda. A Symposium on Ancient Empires*, ed. M. Trolle Larsen (Mesopotamia vol. 7), Copenhagen 1979, 345-59.

Nylander, C. 1983. "Architecture Grecque et pouvoir Persian", in: *Architecture et Société de l'archaïsme grec à la fin de la République romaine*, Paris 1983, 265-70.

Nylander, C. 1993. "Darius III — The Coward King. Points and counterpoints", in: *Alexander the Great, Reality and Myth*, eds. J. Carlsen, B. Due, O.S. Due, B. Poulsen (AnalRom Suppl. XX), Rome 1993, 145-59.

Oppenheim, L. 1965. "On Royal Gardens in Mesopotamia", *Journal of Near Eastern Studies*, 24, 1965, 328-33.

Ovadiah, A. 1983. "Macedonian Elements in Israel", in: *Ancient Macedonia* III, Thessaloniki 1983, 185-93.

Pandermalis, D. 1976. "Beobachtungen zur Fassadenarchitektur und Aussichtsveranda in hellenistischen Makedonien", in: *Hellenismus in Mitttelitalien*, Göttingen 1976, 387-95.

Pandermalis, D. 1987. "E Keramose tou anaktorou ste Bergina", in: *AMETOS*, II, Thessaloniki 1987, 579-605.

Papakonstantinos-Diamantopos, D. 1971. *Pella I*, Athens 1971.

Pedersen, P. 1991. *The Maussolleion Terrace and Accessory Structures* (*The Maussolleion at Halikarnassos* vol. 3.1), Aarhus 1991.

Pedersen, P. 1994. "The Ionian Renaissance and some aspects of its origin within the field of architecture and planning", in: *Hekatomnid Caria and the Ionian Renaissance*, ed. J. Isager (Halicarnassian Studies 1), Odense 1994, 11-35.

Pelletier, A. 1962. *Le Lettre d'Aristée à Philocrate*, Paris 1962.

Perrot, J. 1981. "L'architecture militaire et palatiale Achéménides à Suse", in: *150 Jahre Deutsches Archäologisches Institut, Berlin 1979*, Mainz 1981, 79-94.

Perrot, J. & Ladiray, D. 1972. "Travaux à l'Apadana (1969-71), *Cahiers de la Délégation Archéologique Française en Iran* 2, 1972, 13-60.

Pesce, G. 1950. *"Il "Palazzo delle Colonne" in Tolemaide di Cirenaica*, Roma 1950.

Petrie, W.M. Flinders 1909. *The Palace of Apries (Memphis II)*, London 1909.

Pinkwart, D & Stemmnitz, W. 1984. *Peristylhäuser westlich der unteren Agora (Altertümer von Pergamon* XIV), Berlin 1984.

Pisani Sartorio, G. 1983. "Una *domus* sotto il giardino del Pio Istituto Rivaldi sulla Velia", in: *Città e architettura nella Roma Imperiale*, ed. K. de Fine Licht (AnalRom Suppl. X), Odense 1983, 147-68.

Pomeroy, S.B. 1984. *Women in Hellenistic Egypt*, New York 1984.

Pougatchenkova, G.A. 1990. "La culture de la Bactriane du nord", in: *Akten des XIII. internationalen Kongresses für klassische Archäologie Berlin 1988*, Mainz 1990, 62-66.

Préaux, Cl. 1947. *Les Grecs en Égypte d'après les archives de Zénon*, Bruxelles 1947.

Préaux, Cl. 1978. *Le monde hellénistique de la mort d'Alexandre à la conquête romain de la Grèce. La Grèce et l'Orient (323-146 av. J.-C)*, vols. 1-2, Paris 1978.

Pritchard, J.B. 1958. "The Excavation at Herodian Jericho 1951", *AASOR* 32-33 for 1952-54, New Haven 1958.

Radt, W. 1973. *Guide to Pergamon*, Istanbul 1973.

Radt, W. 1988. *Pergamon. Geschichte und Bauten, Funde und Erforschung einer antiken Metropole*, Köln 1988.

Raeder, J. 1988. "Vitruv, De architectura VI 7 (*aedificia Graecorum*) und die hellenistische Wohnhaus- und Palastarchitektur", *Gymnasium* 95, 1988, 316-68.

Rajak, T. 1994. "Judaea under Hasmonean Rule", in: *The Cambridge Ancient History* 9 (2nd edn.), Cambridge 1994.

Rajak, T. 1996. "Hasmonean kingship and the invention of tradition", in: *Aspects of hellenistic Kingship*, eds. P. Bilde *et al.* (SHC VII), Aarhus 1996, 99-115.

Rapin, C. 1992. *La trésorerie du palais hellénistique d'Ai Khanoum (Fouilles d'Ai Khanoum VIII)*, Paris 1992.

Rathje, A. 1993. "Il fregio di Murlo: Status sulle considerazioni", in: *Deliciae Fictiles*, eds. E. Rystedt, C. Wikander, Ö. Wikander (Skrifter Sv.Inst.Rom 50) Rome 1993, 135-38.

Ratté, C.J. 1989. *Lydian Masonry and Monumental Architecture at Sardis*, diss. Berkeley, Ann Arbor 1989.

Reber, K. 1990. "Die spätklassisch-hellenistischen Häuser von Eretria", in: *Akten des XIII. internationalen Kongresses für klassische Archäologie Berlin 1988*, Mainz 1990, 486-487.

Reuter, O. & Koldewey, R. 1926. *Die Innenstadt von Babylon (Merka)* (WVDOC 47), Leipzig 1926.

Reutti, F. 1990 (ed.). *Die römische Villa*, Darmstadt 1990.

Richard, J.C. 1970. "'Mausoleum'. D'Halicarnasse à Rome, puis à Alexandrie", *Latomus* 29, 1970, 370-88.

Rolle, R. *et al.* 1991. *Gold der Steppe. Archäologie der Ukraine*, Schleswig 1991.

Root, M.C. 1978. *The King and kingship in Achaemenid art. Essays on the creation of an iconography of empire* (Acta Iranica Ser. III, 9), Téhéran-Liège 1978.

Rostovtzeff, M.I. 1938. *Dura Europos and its art*, Oxford 1938.

Salza Prina Ricotti, E. 1988-89. "Le tende convivali e la tenda di Tolemeo Filadelfo", in: *Studia Pompeiana & Classica in honor of Wilhelmina F. Jashemski*, ed. R.I. Curtis, vol. II, 1988-89, 199-240.

Sancisi-Weerdenburg, H. 1993. "Alexander and Persepolis", in: *Alexander the Great. Reality and Myth* (eds. J. Carlsen, B. Due, O.S. Due, B. Poulsen (AnalRom Suppl. XX), Rome 1993, 177-88.

Sackville-West, V. 1953. "Persian Gardens", in: *The Legacy of Persia*, ed. A.J. Arberry, Oxford 1953, 259-91.

Scerrato, U. 1966. "Excavations at Dahan-i Ghulaman (Seistan-Iran). First preliminary report (1962-1963)", *EastWest* 16, 1966, 9-30.

Schäfer, J. 1960. "Ein 'Perserbau' in Altpaphos?", *OpAth* 3, 1960, 155-75.

Schefold, K. 1978. "Die Residenz von Larisa am Hermos im Licht neuer Forschungen", in: *The Proceedings of the Xth International Congress of Classical Archaeology, Ankara-Izmir 1973*, Ankara 1978, 549-64.

Schmidt, E.F. 1953. *Persepolis* I (Oriental Institute Publications 68), Chicago 1953.

Schmidt-Colinet, A. 1991. "Exedra duplex. Überlegungen zum Augustusforum", *HefteABern* 14, 1991, 43-60.

Schmitt, H.H. 1996. "Literarische Nachrichten zu Palästen und zur Funktion von Palästen", in: *Basileia* 1996, 250-51.

Shapiro, H.A. 1989. *Art and Cult under the Tyrants in Athens*, Mainz 1989.

Shear, T.L. Jr. 1978. "Tyrants and buildings in Archaic Athens", in: *Athens Comes of Age: From Solon to Salamis*, Princeton 1978, 1-19.

Sherwin-White S. 1987. "Seleucid Babylonia: a case-study for the installation and development of Greek rule", in: *Hellenism in the East*, London 1987, 1-31.

Sherwin-White, S. & Kuhrt, A. 1993. *From Samarkhand to Sardis. A new approach to the Seleucid empire*, London 1993.

Siganidou, M. 1984 (1988). "Anaskafes Pellas", *Praktika* 1984, 75-94.

Siganidou, M. 1987. "To anaktoriko synkrotema tes Pellas", *AErgoMak* 1, 1987, 119-24.

Siganidou, M. 1989. "To mnemeiako propylo tou anaktorou tes Pellas", *AErgoMak* 3, 1989, 59-63.

Siganidou, M. 1990. "Poleodomika problemata tes Pellas", in: *Polis kai kora sten arkaia Makedonia kai Trake*, Thessaloniki 1990, 167-72.

Siganidou, M. 1996. "Die Basileia von Pella", in: *Basileia* 1996, 144-47.

Smith, W. Stevenson 1965. *The Art and Architecture of Ancient Egypt*, Harmondsworth 1965.

Sonne, W. 1996. "Hellenistische Herrschaftsgärten", in: *Basileia* 1996, 136-43.

van der Spek, R.J. 1987. "The Babylonian city", in: *Hellenism in the East*, London 1987, 57-74.

Starkey, J.L. 1933. "Tell Duweir", *Palestine Exploration Fund. Quarterly Statement*, 1933, 190-99.

Stern, E. 1982. *Material culture of the land of the Bible in the Persian period 538-332 B.C.*, Warminster 1982.

von Steuben, H. 1989. "Die Agora des Kleisthenes — Zeugnis eines radikalen Wandels?", in: *Demokratie und Architektur*, ed. W. Schuller *et al.* (Wohnen in der klassischen Polis II), München 1989, 81-87.

Stronach, D. 1978. *Pasargadae*, Oxford 1978.

Stronach, D. 1985. "The Apadana: A signature of the line of Darius I", in: *De l'Indus aux Balkans. Recueil à la mémoire de Lean Deshayes*, Eds. J.-L. Huot, M. Yon, Y. Calvet, Paris 1985, 433-45.

Stronach, D. 1989. "The royal garden at Pasargadae. Evolution and legacy", in: *Archeologia Iranica et Orientalis. Miscellanea in Honorem Louis Vanden Berghe*, Gant 1989, 475-502.

Stucchi, S. 1975. *Architettura Cirenaica*, Roma 1975.

Studniczka, F. 1914. *Das Symposion Ptolemaios II* (AbhLeipzig 30,2), Leipzig 1914.

Swoboda, K.M. 1969. *Römische und romanische Paläste*, Wien 1969 (3rd edn.)

Le Système Palatial 1987. *Le Système Palatial en Orient, en Grèce et à Rome. Actes du Colloque de Strasbourg 1985*, ed. E. Lévy, Leiden 1987.

Tamm, B. 1963. *Auditorium and Palatium*, Stockholm 1963.

Thompson, D.J. 1988. *Memphis under the Ptolemies*, Princeton 1988.

Tilia, A.B. 1972. *Studies and reconstructions at Persepolis and other sites of Fars*, I, Rome 1972.

Tilia, A.B. 1974. "Discovery of an Achaemenian palace near Takht-I Rustam to the north of the terrace of Persepolis", *Iran* 12, 1974, 200-4.

Tilia , A.B. 1978. *Studies and Restorations at Persepolis and other sites of Fars*, II, Rome 1978.

Tölle-Kastenbein, R. 1974. *Das Kastro Tigrani*, I. "Die Hellenistische Villa" (*Samos* XIV), Berlin 1974, 13-69.

Tolstikov, V.P. 1989. "Archäologische Forschungen im Zentrum von Pantikapaion und einzige Probleme der Stadtplanung von 6. bis zum 3. Jahrh. v. Chr.", in: *Demokratie und Architektur* (Wohnen in der klassischen Polis II), München 1989, 69-79.

Tomlinson, R.A. 1970. "Ancient Macedonian symposia", in: *Ancient Macedonia* I, Thessaloniki 1970, 308-15.

Tomlinson, R.A. 1983. "Southern Greek influences on Macedonian architecture", in: *Ancient Macedonia* III, Thessaloniki 1983, 285-9.

Tomlinson, R.A. 1986. "The ceiling painting of the tomb of Lyson and Kalliklides at Lefkadia", in: *Ancient Macedonia* IV, Thessaloniki 1986, 607-10.

Tosi, G. 1959. "Il palazzo principesco dall'arcaismo greco alla Domus Flavia", *ArtAntMod* 7, 1959, 241-60.

Travlos, J. 1971. *Pictorial Dictionary of Ancient Athens*, London 1971.

Tsafrir, Y. 1981. "Symmetry at Herodion, "megalomania" in Herodian architecture, and the place of Roman technology", *The Jerusalem Cathedra* 1, 1981, 68-72.

Tsafrir, Y. 1982. "The desert fortresses of Judaea in the Second Temple Period, *The Jerusalem Cathedra* 2, 1982, 120-45.

Tufnell, O. 1953. *Lachish* III, London 1953.

Ussishkin, D. 1977. "The destruction of Lachish by Sennacherib and the dating of the royal Judaean storage jars", *Tell Aviv* 4, 1977, 28-60.

Vickers, M. forthcoming. *Images on Textiles. The weave in fifth-century Athenian art and society, Xenia*, forthcoming.

Vincent, L.H. & Steve, A.M. 1954. *Jerusalem de l'Ancien Testament I. Archéologie de la Ville*, Paris 1954.

Voisin, J.L. 1987. "Exoriente sole (Suétone *Ner.* 6). D'Alexandrie à la *Domus Aurea*", in: *L'Urbs. Espace Urbain et Histoire*, Rome 1987, 509-43.

Walbank, F.W. 1984. "Monarchies and Monarchic ideas", in: *The Cambridge Ancient History VII,1. The Hellenistic World*, Cambridge 1984, 62ff.

Walbank, F.W. 1986. *The Hellenistic World*, Glasgow 1986.

Walbank, F.W. 1987. "Könige als Götter. Überlegungen zum Herrscherkult von Alexander bis Augustus", *Chiron* 17, 1987, 365-82.

Wallace-Hadrill, A. 1982. "Civilis Princeps: between citizen and king", *JRS* 72, 1982, 32-48.

Wallace-Hadrill, A. 1988. "The social structure of the Roman house", *BSR* 56, 1988, 43-97.

Wallace-Hadrill, A. 1990. "The social spread of Roman luxury. Sampling Pompeii and Herculaneum", *BSR* 58, 1990, 145-92.

Walter-Kraydi, E. 1994. *Die Nobilitierung des Wohnhauses. Lebensform und Architektur im spätklassischen Griechenland*, (Xenia 35), 1994.

Walter-Karydi, E. 1996. "Die Nobilierung des griechischen Wohnhauses", in: *Basileia* 1996, 56-61.

Wetzel, F. *et al.* 1957. *Das Babylon der Spätzeit* (WVDOG 62), Berlin 1957.

Wheeler, M. 1974. "The transformation of Persepolis architectural motifs into sculpture under the Indian Mauryan dynasty", *Acta Iranica* 2, ser.1,II, Leiden 1974, 249-61.

Will, E. 1982. "Un monument hellénistique de Jordanie. Le Qasr el'Abd d'Iraq al Amir", in: *Studies in the History and Archaeology of Jordan* I, Amman 1982, 197-200.

Will, E. 1987. "Iraq el Amir. Le château du Tobiade Hyrcan", *DossAParis* 118, 1987, 64-69.

Will, E. 1991. *Iraq Al Amir. Le chateau du Tobiade Hyrcan* (Bibliothéque Archeologique et Historique 132) Paris 1991.

Will, E. 1996. Le Chateau du Tobiade Hyrcan à Iraq al Amir", in: *Basileia* 1996, 221-25.

Wiseman, D.J. 1983. "Mesopotamian gardens", *Anatolian Studies* 33, 1983, 136-44.

Wiseman, D.J. 1985. *Nebuchadnezzar and Babylon*, Oxford 1985.

Wiseman, T.P 1984. "Cybele, Virgil and Augustus", in: *Poetry and Politics in the Age of Augustus*, eds. T. Woodman, D. West, Cambridge 1984, 117-28.

Wiseman, T.P. 1987. "*Conspicui postes tectaque digna deo*. The public image of aristocratic and imperial houses in the Late Republic and Early Empire", in: *L'Urbs. Espace urbain et histoire*, Rome 1987, 393-413.

Yadin, Y. 1965. "The excavation of Masada 1963/64. Preliminary Report", *IsrEsplJ* 15, 1965, 1-120.

Yadin, Y. 1966. *Masada. Herod's Fortress and the Zealots' Last Stand*, London 1966.

Young, R.S. 1962. "The 1961 campaign at Gordion", *AJA* 66, 1962, 153-68.

Young, R.S. 1964. "The 1963 campaign at Gordion", *AJA* 68, 1964, 279-92.

Zanker, P. 1968. *Forum Augustum. Das Bildprogram*, Tübingen 1968.

Zanker, P. 1979. "Die Villa als Vorbild des späten pompejanischen Wohngeschmacks", *JdI* 94, 1979, 460-523.

Zanker, P. 1983. "Der Apollontempel auf dem Palatin. Ausstattung und politische Sinnbezüge nach der Schlacht von Actium", in: *Città e architettura nella Roma Imperiale* (AnalRom Suppl. X), Odense 1983, 21-40.

Zanker, P. 1987. *Pompeji. Stadtbilder als Spiegel von Gesellschaft und Herrschaftsform* (Trierer Winckelmannsprogramm 9), Mainz 1987.

INDEX OF SUBJECTS AND PERSONS

architecture, religious (in general) 9, 164, 174

architecture, Roman, 10, 20, 51, 113, 147, 150, 153, 163, 164ff, 193, 198, 203, 208, 216

architecture, Seleucid 35, 112ff, 153, 208, 213

architecture, Urartaean 45

architects 35f, 189, 206, 209

architrave and archivolt 150

archives 24, 110, 128

Argeads 15

Argonautica 133

"Aristeas", Letter of 13, 19ff, 23, 25, 131

arsenal 24, 110

Artabazus I 62

Artaxerxes II 35, 39, 41

Artemisia 138

artisans 36

artists 18, 36

ashlar, see *opus quadratum*

Ashurbanipal 34

asylum, right of 74, 76f

Athenaeus 13, 17, 133

atrium 166, 168, 174

Attalids 16, 102ff, 110, 212

Attalus I 102, 110

attire, king's 17

audience (*chrematismos*) 13, 17ff, 29, 33, 79, 96, 113, 136, 198

audience, public 19f

audience hall 19ff, 22, 29, 41f, 44, 49, 59, 70, 83, 91, 93, 97f, 106, 119, 125, 130f, 134, 143f, 147, 176, 178, 187, 193, 197, 211

Augustus 10, 15, 173ff, 206, 212

aulaiai 134

aule/aulai (= palace) 11 (term), 115, 130, 139

aule (courtyard) 20f, 134

avenue 27, 31, 123, 166, 207

axiality 91, 125, 146, 151, 156, 176, 189, 195f, 212

bakchikos oikos (Bacchic *oecus*) 23, 136

balcony 193

baldaquin 17

balsam 160

balustrade 81f, 100, 110, 152, 195

banquet 43, 50, 115, 117, 166ff, 171

banquet, royal 15, 21ff, 34, 134ff

banqueting hall (see also dining-room) 22ff, 29, 42f, 60f, 70, 76, 80, 82ff, 87, 91, 97f, 98, 106f, 119, 125ff, 130f, 136, 138, 143, 147, 156, 159f, 176, 182, 187, 193f, 197, 203

banqueting houses 65ff, 77f, 97, 99, 216

baris 139, 142, 155, 182

barracks 24, 103, 110

basileion/basileia 11 (term)

Basileios Stoa 113

basilica 20, 147, 166, 216

basilikoi paides 22, 25

basin 49, 168, 182

bath-tub 162

bathroom 24, 52, 56, 60, 122, 124f, 127, 138, 183

bathroom, Greek 77, 86, 92, 156, 159f, 162f, 173, 183, 187f, 204

bathroom Jewish, see *miqveh*

bath suite, Roman 183, 193ff, 198f, 203f, 206

battle scenes 13

bedroom 23f, 77, 86, 105, 136, 166

Belyses 51

bema, see also tribune 20, 130f

Bernard, P. 127f

Bickermann, E.J. 208

Bit-Hilani 53 (term), 67, 70, 72, 101, 120f, 130, 143

Boardman, J. 73

Börker, C. 78

Boëthius, A. 171

Borza, E.N. 97

Bosporan kingdom 99

bricks, sun-dried 63, 102, 123, 143, 150, 156, 206

"broad room" 33, 43, 45, 52f, 56f, 59f, 70, 88, 91, 93, 97f, 108, 116, 119, 123f, 143, 147, 159f

Broneer, O. 48f

Brown, F. 119f

bureaucracy 17, 18, 112, 130

GEOGRAPHICAL INDEX

INDEX LOCORUM

All numbers refer to notes, except those marked Cat., which refer to the Catalogue.

Evagrius
2.12 (p. 63, 30ff, ed. Bidez-Parmentier):
Cat. 15

Florus
Epitome
4.2.91: 315

FGrH
160 221
239: 81

Gellius, Aulus
Noctes Atticae
7.17.1: 158

Herodotus
History
9.80-82: 98, 106

Horace
Carmina
2.15: 308
2.18.5-6: Cat. 14

Isidorus
Orationes
6.5.1: Cat. 12
Origines
6.3.3: 158

Josephus
Antiquitates Judaicae
10.1.3 (11): Cat. 2
12.4.1 (228-236): 257, Cat. 21
13.2.1 (40-42): 224
13.5.3 (137): Cat. 15
13.13.4 (368): 217
15.3.3 (53-56): 356, Cat. 23
15.5.2 (121-122): Cat. 23
15.9.3 (318): 342
15.9.6 (331): 346
16.2.1 (12-14): Cat. 31
16.2.1 (22): 340
17.5.5-6.3 (115-162): Cat. 30
17.6.5 (174-179): Cat. 30
17.8.2 (193-195): Cat. 30
17.11.1 (301): Cat. 25

19.1.13-14 (84-113): 326
20.8 (189-192): 282
Bellum Judaicum
1.6.6 (138-140): Cat. 23
1.21.1 (401-402): 342, 344
1.21.4 (407): 354
1.21.5 (408): 346
1.21.9-10 (418-421): Cat. 31
1.33.9 (670-673): 360, Cat. 31
2.2.4 (25): Cat. 25
2.6.1 (81): Cat. 25
2.16 (344): 282
5.4.3-4 (161-183): 342
5.4.4 (177f): 63, 72
5.5.8 (238-247): 344
7.8.3-4 (280-300): Cat. 27
Contra Apionem
1.19 (128-141): Cat. 2

Justinus
Epitome
7.1: 176
12.7.1: 19
27.1.4-7: 221

Libanius
Orationes
11.206: Cat. 15

Livy
Ab Urbe Condita
9.18.3-4: 19
35.16.1: 43
35.31.9: Cat. 13
40.21-22: 178
42.51.1-2: 194, Cat. 12
44.46.4-8: 74, Cat. 12

Lucan
Bellum Civile
10.111-112: 50
10.111ff: 63, Cat. 20
10.127ff: 62
10.136ff: 38

Lucretius
De Rerum Natura
2.20ff: 63

Malalas
Chronographia
225.8: 79, Cat. 15
306.21: 220

Monumentum Ancyranum
19: Cat. 25
34.2: 319, Cat. 25
35: 320

New Testament
John
5.2: 344

Old Testament
Esther
1.3-8: 105. Cats. 5-6
II Kings
25.4: 284
I Maccabees
6.15: 34
11.45-47: Cat. 15
II Maccabees
4.9: 288
Nehemia
2.8-9: 113, 284

Ovid
Fasti
4.949-956: Cat. 25
4.951-954: 69, 319
Metamorphoses
15.864-865: Cat. 25
Tristia
3.1.33-34: 319

Pausanias
Periegesis
1.6.3: 81
1.20.4: 108
9.35.6-7: Cat. 14

Petronius
Satura
48: 298

Philo of Alexandria
In Flaccum
92: 75, Cat. 20

Philostratus
Imagines
2.31: 18

Plato
Epistolae
2.313a: 170
3.319a: 170
7.347a: 170
7.348e: 170
Respublica
264e: 311
Timaeus
24eff: 235

Pliny
Naturalis Historia
4.33: Cat. 10
5.62: Cat. 20
12.7: 167
12.115-118: Cat. 23
13.44-46: Cat. 23

Plutarch
Aemilius Paullus
8.2: 25
28: 61, 79, 298, Cat. 12
Alcibiades
12.1: 111
Alexander
20.7: 58, 105, 287
45: 19
Antony
54: 38
54.3-4: 35, 52, Cat. 20
58.5: Cat. 14
72-74: Cat. 20
Artaxerxes
22.4-6: 18
Demetrius
18: 37
23.3-4: 159
41-42: 29, 37
49: 35

Pl. 1. Audience scene from Persepolis (Photo: ISMEO).

Pl. 2. Babylon. The glazed tile decoration embellishing the front of the audience hall of the "Südburg" in the Vorderasiatische Museum in Berlin. (Photo: Staatliche Museen zu Berlin).

Pl. 3. Persepolis. The model of the terrace, seen from the north-west. (Krefter 1971, Tf. 1,2).

Pl. 4. Vouni. Model of the palace, seen from the north-west. (Gjerstad et al. 1937, fig. 121).

Pl. 5. Halicarnassus. General view of the harbour with the peninsula carrying the crusaders' castle and the probable place for the Palace of Mausolus. (Author's photo).

Pl. 6. Halicarnassus. One of the large terrace walls in the crusaders' castle, probably originally a terrace wall carrying the Palace of Mausolus. (Author's photo).

Pl. 7. Labraunda. A General view of the Sanctuary of Zeus Labraundus. (Author's photo).

Pl. 8. Labraunda. Andron A. (Author's photo).

Pl. 9. Labraunda. The monumental propylon and staircase leading to the androness *and the temple. (Author's photo).*

Pl. 10. Vergina/Aigai. Aerial view of the palace and the theatre. (Andronicos 1984, fig. 21).

Pl. 11. Vergina/Aigai. View of the main peristyle, from the north. (Author's photo).

Pl. 12. Vergina/Aigai. The Tholos in the east wing of the main peristyle, from the south. (Author's photo).

Pl. 13. Vergina/Aigai. The south wing of the main peristyle with the central exedra with pillar half-columns, decorated in mosaic, flanked by dining-rooms. (Author's photo).

Pl. 14. Pella. An overall view of the House of Dionysus, from the northeast. (Author's photo).

Pl. 15. Pella. The official peristyle, House of Dionysus. The north wing with two large halls for dining, both with floor mosaics with "kline bands". (Author's photo).

Pl. 16. Pella. The north wing of Peristyle I of the Royal Palace, from the west. (Author's photo).

Pl. 17. Pella. The western apsidal exedra in Peristyle I of the Royal Palace, from the north. (Author's photo).

Pl. 18. Pella. The eastern apsidal exedra in Peristyle I of the Royal Palace, from the west. (Author's photo).

Pl. 19. Pella. The stucchoed pool in the northern wing in Peristyle V of the Royal Palace, from the north. (Author's photo).

Pl. 20. Pergamon. Model of the Acropolis of Pergamon. (Photo: Staatliche Museen zu Berlin).

Pl. 21. Pergamon. The propylon of the Temenos of Athena as reconstructed in the Antikensammlung in Berlin. (Photo: Staatliche Museen zu Berlin).

Pl. 22. Petra. The Khasneh tomb. (Photo: N. Hannestad).

Pl. 23. Jerusalem. Reconstruction of the Hasmonean Palace, from M. Avi-Yonah's model of "Jerusalem in Herod's time", in the Holyland Hotel, Jerusalem. (Photo: Holyland Corporation).

Pl. 24. Jericho. An overall view of the oasis with the Hasmonean palace in the foreground; in the distance the Tell of Old Jericho. (Author's photo).

Pl. 25. Jericho. The miqveh *in the north-east corner of Hyrcanus I's palace, with stepped pool and reservoir. (Author's photo).*

Pl. 26. Jericho. The swimming-pools in the central area of the Hasmonean Palace, with stairs down to them. (Author's photo).

Pl. 27. Casa di Augusto. Coin with depiction of the portal of the palace. (Photo: British Museum).

Pl. 28. Jerusalem. Reconstruction of Herod's Main Palace from M. Avi-Yonah's model in the garden of the Holyland Hotel in Jerusalem. (Author's photo).

Pl. 29. Jerusalem. Reconstruction of the Antonia Fortress north of the Temple Mount, from M. Avi-Yonah's model in the Holyland Hotel. (Photo: Holyland Corporation).

Pl. 30. Masada. An overall view of the Western Palace, from the north. (Author's photo).

Pl. 31. Masada. The Western Palace. The exedra in the southern wing of the Core Palace, leading to the audience hall. (Author's photo).

Pl. 32. Masada. The Western Palace. The audience hall, seen from the exedra. (Author's photo).

Pl. 33. Masada. The Northern Palace, lower terrace with the oecus, from above. (Author's photo).

Pl. 34. Masada. The Northern Palace, the oecus of the lower terrace with half-columns and painted decoration. (Author's photo).

Pl. 35. Masada. The Northern Palace, middle terrace with tholos, from above. (Author's photo).

Pl. 36. Masada. The Northern Palace, middle terrace, the "library" behind the tholos.
(Author's photo).

Pl. 37. Jericho. An overall view of the oasis with the Herodian Palaces in the foreground, and in the distance the city of Jericho. The photo is taken from the fortress of Cypros to the southwest. (Author's photo).

Pl. 38. Jericho. A general view of Herod's main palace, from the south. (Author's photo).

Pl. 39. Jericho. The main building of the Third Winter Palace. The garden peristyle with apsidal exedra and audience hall at the back, from the south-west. (Author's photo).

Pl. 40. Jericho. The main building in the Third Winter Palace. Detail of the bath building (laconicum), *built in the Roman techniques of* opus reticulatum *and* opus mixtum. *(Author's photo).*

Pl. 41. Herodium. The artificial Tell of the upper palace seen from Lower Herodium to the north. (Author's photo).

Pl. 42. Herodium. An overall view of Lower Herodium, from the upper palace, towards the north. (Author's photo).

Pl. 43. Herodium. The peristyle of the upper palace with one of the apses in the background. The representative halls are to the right. (Author's photo).

Pl. 44. Herodium. Lower Herodium, the Hall of the Niches. (Photo: Institute of Archaeology, University of Aarhus).